Health and Wellness 1

Case Study

I. A personal friend has been experiencing severe stomach and intestinal problems for a few months. She is 35 years old and is employed as an advertisement salesperson for a local newspaper. During this past year, she has been pressured to create more income for her department. When you ask her if she has sought medical treatment, she responds that she "doesn't have the time to go to the doctor." In addition to her job responsibilities, she is a single parent of a grade-school-age child who enjoys a number of after-school activities.

  a. What physical and lifestyle factors are present in this situation?

  b. What initial responses/interventions may be helpful for this individual?

Independent Learning Activities

1. Investigate available health resources, such as a Women's and Infant's Center or Public Health Agency, in a community and develop a reference book of phone numbers and contacts.

2. Complete a risk factor assessment for a family member or friend, and discuss the findings with that individual.

Chapter Review

Match the description/definition in Column A with the correct term in Column B.

Column A

_____ 1. A person's definition and interpretation of symptoms and use of the health care system.

_____ 2. Clients are the experts and active participants in their health.

_____ 3. A subjective concept of physical appearance.

_____ 4. Developmental stage, intellectual background, emotional and spiritual factors.

_____ 5. Maximizing the health potential of an individual, family, or community.

Column B

a. High-level wellness model

b. Internal variables

c. Body image

d. Holistic health model

e. Illness behavior

Contents

Complete the following:

6. Describe the main themes of the following models of health and illness:
   a. health-illness continuum model

   b. health belief model

   c. health promotion model

   d. holistic health model

7. Identify and briefly describe the internal and external variables that influence health beliefs and practices.

8. Identify three specific holistic nursing interventions and their specific use for clients.

9. Describe two strategies for both active and passive health promotion.

10. What is the difference between an acute and a chronic illness?

11. Describe the possible impact that illness may have on the client and family in the following areas:
    a. behaviors and emotions

    b. body image

    c. self-concept

    d. family roles and dynamics

12. Provide a specific example for each of the following risk factors:
    a. age

    b. genetic/physiological

    c. environment

    d. lifestyle

Select the best answer for each of the following questions:

13. At the tertiary level of prevention, the nurse would prepare an educational program for a group requiring:
    1. chemotherapy
    2. cardiac rehabilitation
    3. genetic screening
    4. sex education

14. At the secondary level of prevention, the intervention that the nurse expects to assist with or instruct about is:
    1. immunization
    2. referral to outpatient therapy
    3. performance of a biopsy
    4. parent performance of the newborn's bath

15. The nurse is working with a client who is experiencing chronic joint pain. To help the client manage or reduce the pain, the nurse decides to use a holistic health model. With this model in mind, the nurse specifically elects to include:
    1. aromatherapy
    2. hygienic care measures
    3. analgesic medications
    4. application of heat

16. The nurse is completing an assessment for the client who has come to the medical clinic. Variables that influence the client's health beliefs and practices are being determined. The nurse is aware that an internal variable for this client is the:
    1. way in which the client celebrates family occasions
    2. manner in which the client deals with stress on the job and at home
    3. frequency of the family's visits to the health care agency
    4. amount of insurance coverage that is provided by the client's employer

17. The nurse recognizes that primary prevention is a critical aspect in health care. The target group for a program on hand washing that is aimed at this level of prevention is:
    1. fourth-grade children at the local elementary school
    2. clients in a cardiac rehabilitation program at the medical center
    3. parents of a child with a congenital heart defect
    4. clients with diabetes coming to the outpatient clinic

18. The nurse is leading a group of community members who are trying to quit smoking. In the precontemplation phase of health behavior change, the nurse anticipates that the group members will respond by:
    1. discussing prior attempts at quitting
    2. recognizing the benefits of not smoking
    3. expressing irritation when the topic of quitting is brought up
    4. requesting phone numbers of support people who have participated in the group

19. A young adult student has come to the university's health center for a physical examination. The nurse is conducting the initial interview and is looking for possible lifestyle risk factors. The nurse specifically is alerted to the student's:
    1. mild hypertension
    2. mountain climbing hobby
    3. family history of diabetes
    4. part-time job at the auto factory

Study Group Questions

- What are the different health models, and how can they be applied to different client situations? What are the advantages and disadvantages of each model?
- What are the different internal and external variables that are present in health practices and illness behavior? Give specific examples of the different variables and possible nursing interventions.
- What behaviors may be observed in a client during illness? What impact may the client's illness have on the family/significant others?
- How do the levels of prevention relate to nursing care of clients and different health care settings?

Study Chart

Create a study chart to compare the Levels of Prevention, *identifying both client and nursing activities associated with each level.*

2 The Health Care Delivery System

Case Studies

I. A neighbor who has just gotten a new job with a different benefit package stops by to ask if you know anything about managed care. He asks you what an HMO (health maintenance organization) is and what it means to him. The neighbor also tells you that he got a "big book" full of hospital and doctor names that is really confusing.
    a. What information can you provide to this individual?
    b. How could you go about assisting the neighbor to understand his HMO coverage?

II. A 54-year-old male visits the community health screening and is found to be hypertensive and demonstrating signs of depression. He served in the armed forces for 30 years and received an honorable discharge a few years ago. In discussion with this individual, it appears that he does not have any health insurance as a part-time employee in a small retail store.
    a. What health care benefits may this individual be eligible for because of his background?
    b. Where could this individual receive secondary or tertiary care if his condition warrants further treatment?

III. An 80-year-old female client has just been diagnosed with an inoperable cancerous growth in the brain. Having been told of the poor prognosis, she opts to refuse chemotherapy.
    a. Where could this individual be referred for terminal care?

Independent Learning Activities

1. Investigate an area of interest in the health care delivery system. Determine the education and experience that the nurse must possess to provide care within that agency.

2. Determine the type of health care coverage that you and your family possess. (If not covered, investigate the type of coverage that would be best for you to purchase). Find out what inpatient and outpatient services are covered by the plan.

Chapter Review

Match the description/definition in Column A with the correct term in Column B.

	Column A	Column B
_____	1. Nationwide health insurance program that provides benefits to individuals older than 65 years of age.	a. Medicaid
_____	2. Fixed amount of payment for services per enrollee.	b. Capitation
_____	3. Short-term relief for people providing care to ill, disabled older adults.	c. Managed care

_____ 4. Income eligibility for coverage is below the federal poverty level.

d. Medicare

_____ 5. Administrative control over primary health care services for a defined client population.

e. Respite care

Complete the following:

6. Identify five services usually provided by a home care agency.

7. A _____ is a system of family-centered care designed to allow clients to live with dignity while dealing with a terminal illness.

8. Describe three issues in health care delivery today.

9. Describe patient-centered care and the role of the nurse.

10. Discuss the process and purpose of discharge planning.

11. What is the influence of technology on health care delivery?

Select the best answer for each of the following questions:

12. The daughter of an older woman expresses her concern that her mother, recently diagnosed with Alzheimer's disease, has been found wandering around the neighborhood in a disoriented state while the daughter is at work. This family may benefit from the services of a(n):
    1. hospice
    2. subacute care unit
    3. adult day care center
    4. residential community

13. While working in the community health agency, the nurse visits an older adult client who is having difficulty taking care of her activities of daily living (ADLs) in her own home. The client recognizes that she needs some supervision with medications. In discussions with this client, the nurse refers the client to a(n):
    1. subacute care unit
    2. assisted living facility
    3. rehabilitation hospital
    4. primary care institution

14. A family has requested that the hospice become involved in the care of one of the members. The nurse explains that hospice services provide:
    1. daytime coverage for working family members
    2. residential care for clients requiring supervision
    3. rehabilitative nursing care measures
    4. palliative care for clients with terminal diseases

15. Nurses working on a surgical unit will be part of a work redesign effort. This is evidenced by the staff:
    1. determining the best workday and vacation schedules
    2. investigating personnel who should be reassigned or laid off
    3. shifting the decision making away from the unit and over to the supervisors
    4. delegating nonnursing activities and tasks to unlicensed personnel

16. The nurse's next-door neighbor recently has experienced some health problems. The neighbor has come to the nurse to ask about Medicaid coverage. The nurse informs the neighbor that this program is:
    1. catastrophic long-term care coverage for older adults
    2. a fee-for-service plan that provides preventive health care
    3. a two-part federally funded health care program for older adults
    4. a federally funded and state-regulated program for individuals of all ages with low income

17. A graduate of a nursing program is interested in the occupational health field. The graduate nurse decides to pursue a position at:
    1. the local medical center
    2. a car manufacturing plant
    3. an urgent care center
    4. a physician's office

18. A client is being discharged from the medical unit of the hospital. While working with the client, the nurse identifies that intermittent supervision will be required. The client also will need to rent durable medical equipment for use in the home. There is family support for the client on discharge. The nurse will refer this client to:
    1. a subacute care unit
    2. an extended care facility
    3. a home health agency
    4. an urgent care center

19. The family of a client has requested that the hospice agency become involved with the client's care. The nurse recognizes that the services provided by hospice for this client include:
    1. extensive rehabilitative measures
    2. daytime coverage for the working caregivers
    3. residential care with an emphasis on a return to functioning
    4. provision of symptom management and comfort measures for the terminally ill

Study Group Questions

- What types of health care financing are available, who is eligible, and what services are covered?
- What does managed care mean to clients and health care providers?
- According to the levels of prevention, what health care agencies and services are available, and what are the usual nurses' roles in each agency?
- To whom may the nurse delegate care responsibilities? What types of responsibilities may be delegated legally and safely?
- What impact has the institution of "work redesign" had on nursing?
- What are some of the key competencies required of nurses today?

Study Chart

Create a study chart to compare the Types of Health Care Delivery Agencies, *identifying the different health care services provided and the nursing roles and activities for each.*

Legal Principles in Nursing 3

Case Studies

I. In preparation for surgery, you are to have the client sign the consent form for the procedure. The client, in discussions about the postoperative care, does not appear to understand what will be done during the surgery.
   a. What are your responsibilities in this situation?

II. You are reviewing the doctor's orders for the medications to be given to the client. One of the medication orders is very difficult to read. The charge nurse tells you that she is sure it is Lasix 40 mg PO.
   a. What should you do in this circumstance?
   b. What legal implications may be involved if the order is incorrect?

III. A child is brought into the emergency room in critical condition. His parents are divorced.
   a. What issues concerning consent for treatment may be involved in this child's case?

IV. You have been observing a nursing colleague on your unit, and she appears to be taking narcotics from the medication cart. There have been occasions where her behavior has been erratic.
   a. What, if any, are your legal responsibilities regarding this colleague's behavior?

Independent Learning Activities

1. Review the Patient's Bill of Rights to see how nursing practice may be influenced.

2. Obtain detailed information on your malpractice insurance, including any limitations of coverage.

3. Research an article in a nursing journal on a legal issue that affects nursing practice today.

Chapter Review

Match the description/definition in Column A with the correct term in Column B.

	Column A	Column B
_____	1. A law concerned with the relationships among people and the protection of a person's rights.	a. Tort
_____	2. Any willful attempt or threat to harm another.	b. Negligence
_____	3. A civil wrong or injury for which remedy is in the form of money damages.	c. Living wills
_____	4. A crime of a serious nature that usually carries a penalty of imprisonment.	d. Statutory law

_____ 5. Limitation of liability for health care professionals offering assistance at the scene of an accident.

_____ 6. Conduct that falls below the standard of care.

_____ 7. Any intentional touching of another's body without consent.

_____ 8. A form of contemporary law created by elected legislative bodies.

_____ 9. Documents instructing physicians to withhold or withdraw life-sustaining procedures.

_____ 10. A form of contemporary law created by judicial decision in court when cases are decided.

e. Good Samaritan Law

f. Assault

g. Common law

h. Battery

i. Civil law

j. Felony

Complete the following:

11. Identify three ways in which a nurse may avoid being liable for negligence.

12. Identify two areas where standards of care are defined.

13. What is the liability of a student nurse in client care situations?

14. What criteria are necessary for informed consent?

15. Name two circumstances that the nurse is obligated to report to an appropriate authority.

16. Describe the role of the State Board of Nursing in determining the scope of nursing practice.

17. Identify how advance directives or living wills influence nursing care.

Select the best answer for each of the following questions:

18. A clinical experience is planned for an acute care facility. The student nurse recognizes that his/her liability for client care includes:
1. no individual responsibility for actions while being supervised
2. a shared responsibility with an instructor and staff member(s)
3. activities performed while working in another capacity, such as an aide
4. accountability for information and techniques that have been learned

19. There has been a serious flu epidemic among the staff at the medical center. On arriving to work on the medical unit, the nurse discovers that all of the other nursing staff members have called in sick and there are no other nurses available in the facility. In this situation, the nurse should:

1. not accept the assignment and leave the unit
2. accept the assignment and identify the poor staffing in each client's record
3. document the situation and provide a copy to nursing administration
4. inform the hospital administration that nursing responsibilities have been delegated to other personnel

20. When preparing to administer medications, the client refuses to take them. The nurse knows that the medications are important for the client and proceeds with the injection of the medication. This is considered:
    1. invasion of privacy
    2. negligence
    3. assault
    4. battery

21. The urgent care center in town is busy this evening. There are many walk-in clients of different ages waiting for treatment, and some have other people who have come along with them. The nurse recognizes that, in a nonemergency situation, the individual who may give consent for a treatment is:
    1. a 16-year-old student
    2. the grandparent of a minor
    3. a pregnant teenager
    4. the brother of a client

22. The nurse observes the following actions and recognizes that an invasion of client privacy is evident when the nurse:
    1. shares client data with other agency personnel not involved in the client's treatment
    2. withholds the client's diagnosis from the family members per the client's request
    3. provides details of a major scientific advancement to the public relations department
    4. reports an incidence of an infectious disease to the health department

23. The nurse enters the room of her client and observes that an incident has occurred. The situation is documented appropriately as:
    1. Client fell out of bed. Physician notified and x-rays ordered.
    2. Client found on floor. Laceration to forehead.
    3. Client given incorrect medication, became dizzy, and slid to the floor.
    4. Client got up out of bed without assistance and appeared to have fallen.

24. A student nurse is working in a physician's office as a receptionist. One day the physician offers the student the opportunity to administer an injection to a client. The liability for this individual in this situation is based on:
    1. the job description of the receptionist
    2. the level of education received at the nursing school
    3. not being able to work in any other capacity while in school
    4. the physician accepting the responsibility for the activity

25. The nurse has administered a medication to a client with a documented allergy to that medication. A standard of care is applied when:
    1. there is a determination of an injury to the client
    2. an amount of financial compensation is determined
    3. criminal statutes from the federal government are investigated
    4. the nurse's action is compared to that of another nurse in a similar circumstance

26. A young client has verbalized suicidal intentions. This individual will be admitted involuntarily to the psychiatric unit in the medical center. The nurse informs the client's family that the client may be detained, based on a judge's order, for:
    1. 2 days
    2. 72 hours
    3. 2 weeks
    4. 21 days

Study Group Questions

- What are the sources and types of law?
- What are intentional and unintentional torts?
- How may intentional torts be applied to nursing situations?
- What criteria are necessary for negligence/malpractice to occur?
- How are the standards of care defined and applied?
- What individuals may give consent for treatment?
- What is the role of the nurse in obtaining consent?
- What is the role of the nurse in situations related to death and dying, employment contracts, and organ and tissue donation?
- How can the nurse minimize his/her liability?
- What situations require reporting by the nurse?
- How is the profession and practice of nursing influenced by legal issues?
- What are some of the legal concerns for nurses working in specialty areas, such as obstetrics?

Study Chart

Create a study chart to describe how to Minimize Liability, *identifying the nursing actions to reduce possible liability for the following situations: short staffing, floating, client incidents, and reporting/recording.*

Ethics 4

Case Study

I. You are the home care nurse for a 42-year-old male client, Mr. R., who has severe multiple sclerosis. He tells you on several occasions that he is tired of living this way, not being able to do anything for himself. Mr. R. says that he has read about individuals who have been "helped to die," and he asks if you can assist him in finding out more about this procedure.
    a. Apply the steps for processing an ethical dilemma to this situation.
    b. What is the role of the nurse in this situation?

Independent Learning Activity

1. Think about the issues that you may have strong feelings about in relation to health care and nursing. Try to identify when and where you may be faced with an ethical dilemma as a result of your values or beliefs and what steps you may have to take in that situation.

Chapter Review

Match the description/definition in Column A with the correct term in Column B.

	Column A	Column B
_____	1. Supporting the client's right to informed consent.	a. Fidelity
_____	2. Considering the client's best interest.	b. Justice
_____	3. Avoiding deliberate harm.	c. Autonomy
_____	4. Keeping promises.	d. Beneficence
_____	5. Determining the order in which clients should be treated.	e. Nonmaleficence

Complete the following:

6. Identify four modes of value transmission.

7. Compare responsibility to accountability in nursing.

8. _____ proposes that actions are right or wrong based on the essence of right and wrong in the principles of fidelity, truthfulness, and justice.

9. For the following areas, provide a specific example of how ethical concerns may be involved:

a. cost containment

b. cultural sensitivity

Select the best answer for each of the following questions:

10. A professional code of ethics includes:
    1. legal standards for practice
    2. extensive details on moral principles
    3. guidelines for approaching common ethical dilemmas
    4. a collective statement of group expectations for behavior

11. By administering medication to a client on a unit in an extended care facility, the nurse is applying the ethical principle of:
    1. justice
    2. fidelity
    3. autonomy
    4. beneficence

12. The nurse has been working with a client who has had abdominal surgery. The client is experiencing discomfort and has been calling for assistance quite often. The ethical principle of fidelity is demonstrated when the nurse:
    1. changes the dressing
    2. provides a back rub using warm lotion
    3. informs the client of the actions of the medications administered
    4. returns to assist the client with breathing exercises at the agreed on times

13. The student nurse is assigned to work with a family who refuses to have essential medical treatment provided to their child. The medical center is pursuing a court order to force the family to accept the treatment plan that will assist the child. The nurse has strong feelings for the family's position and for the importance of the medical treatment. The first step for the nurse to

take in attempting to resolve this ethical dilemma is to:
    1. examine personal values
    2. evaluate the outcomes
    3. gather all of the facts
    4. verbalize the problem

14. Application of the deontological ethical theory is illustrated by the nurse's statement of:
    1. "It would never be right to stop providing feedings to a client."
    2. "I believe that the client was cured because of a divine intervention."
    3. "The loss of his leg in the accident has helped this client to become a stronger person."
    4. "The surgery did not eliminate the client's problem entirely, but it has helped to reduce the level of discomfort."

Study Group Questions

- What are ethics, and what is the purpose of a code of ethics in a profession?
- What principles are promoted in a profession?
- How can the nurse be a client advocate?
- What are the basic standards of ethics?
- What are values, and how are they developed?
- How do values relate to ethics?
- How does the professional determine that an ethical dilemma exists?
- What are the steps for processing an ethical dilemma?
- What ethical dilemmas may arise in health care and nursing practice?

Study Chart

Create a study chart to compare the Ethical Systems, *identifying the different themes in each— deontology, utilitarianism, feminist ethics, and ethics of care.*

Critical Thinking and Nursing Judgment 5

Case Study

I. You are the home care nurse and have been assigned to visit a client who requires dressing changes for a foot ulceration. When you arrive in the home, you find that the client does not have any commercially packaged dressings or saline solution. You have used the last of your supplies and the drive back to the office will take more than 1 hour. The dressing that the client has on her foot is saturated with purulent drainage.
    a. What options are available to you in this situation?
    b. What further investigation about the client and her living situation may be necessary?

Independent Learning Activities

1. Apply the critical thinking competencies to a current problem. List the steps that you need to take to complete the problem-solving process. Evaluate the outcome of your decision making.

2. Apply the critical thinking competencies to a problem that you have encountered in the past. Identify the steps you took to solve the problem. Evaluate whether the process was effective. If your approach was not successful, identify how it may have been improved through the steps of the critical thinking process.

Chapter Review

Match the description/definition in Column A with the correct term in Column B.

	Column A		Column B
_____	1.	Process of recalling an event to determine its meaning and purpose.	a. Scientific method
_____	2.	Series of clinical judgments that result in informal or formal diagnoses.	b. Decision making
_____	3.	End point of critical thinking that leads to problem resolution.	c. Inference
_____	4.	Significance or meaning of findings in relation to one another.	d. Diagnostic reasoning
_____	5.	Process that moves from observable facts from an experience to a reasonable explanation of those facts.	e. Reflection

Complete the following:

6. Identify at least five of the attitudes for critical thinking, with an example of how each attitude may be demonstrated in a clinical situation.

7. Describe how critical thinking is used throughout the steps of the nursing process.

Select the best answer for each of the following questions:

8. In critical thinking, the first step that the nurse should use is:
   1. evaluation
   2. decision making
   3. self-regulation
   4. interpretation

9. Having worked for a number of years in the acute care environment, the nurse has achieved an ability to utilize a complex level of critical thinking. The nurse:
   1. acts solely on his/her opinions
   2. trusts the experts to have the answers to problems
   3. implements creative and innovative options
   4. applies rules and principles the same way in every situation

10. Clinical care experiences recently have begun for the student nurse. When beginning to work with clients, the student nurse implements critical thinking in practice by:
    1. asking for assistance if uncertain
    2. sharing personal ideas with peers
    3. acting on independent judgments
    4. relying on standardized, textbook approaches

11. The nurse has an extremely large client assignment this evening and begins to feel overwhelmed. The priority activity, based on the following choices, is for the nurse to:
    1. share her feelings with colleagues
    2. call the supervisor and ask for assistance
    3. review the overall assignment to get his/her bearings
    4. move right into client care, starting with the room closest to the nurse's station

12. Orientation for the new nurses has begun. The instructor for the orientation is putting together information on critical thinking and nursing approaches. The instructor recognizes that critical thinkers in nursing:
    1. make quick, single-solution decisions
    2. act on intuition over experience
    3. review data in a disciplined manner
    4. alter interventions for every circumstance

13. The nurse is caring for a client who is experiencing a respiratory disorder. Intuition is a part of the critical thinking process for the nurse. While caring for the client, the nurse demonstrates intuition by:
    1. reviewing the care with the client in advance
    2. observing communication patterns
    3. establishing a nursing diagnosis
    4. sensing that the client was not doing as well this morning

14. On entering the room at 2:00 AM, the nurse notes that the client is out of bed and in the chair and states that she is having difficulty sleeping. Using critical thinking, the nurse responds by:
    1. assisting the client back into bed
    2. determining more about what the client means
    3. positioning the client and providing a warm blanket
    4. obtaining an order for a hypnotic medication

15. The nurse has a diverse client assignment this evening. When reviewing the status of the clients, the nurse determines that the first individual to be seen is the client who is:
    1. hypotensive
    2. just receiving a visit from a family member
    3. having a treatment given by the respiratory therapist
    4. waiting for the effects of an analgesic that was given 5 minutes ago

Study Group Questions

- How is critical thinking integrated into nursing practice?
- What attitudes are needed by the nurse for him/her to be a critical thinker?
- How are the competencies of critical thinking applied in clinical practice?
- Why is critical thinking important throughout the nursing process?

6 Nursing Process

Case Studies

I. Mr. B., a 47-year-old client, has come to the annual community health fair. During a routine blood pressure screening, it is determined that his blood pressure is significantly above normally expected levels.
   a. What additional assessment data should be obtained from the client and family?
   b. What limitations exist in this situation for completing an assessment?

II. Mr. B. returns for a follow-up visit at the medical center's adult health clinic. Mr. B. is diagnosed with hypertension and an antihypertensive medication is prescribed, but he appears unsure about how and when he should take the prescription. Mr. B. also identifies that his father had a heart attack and died when he was 54 years of age.
   a. Identify the relevant assessment data for this client.
   b. Based on this information, identify two nursing diagnoses.

III. When Mr. B. came for his appointment at the adult health clinic, it was found that his blood pressure had increased since his last visit although antihypertensive medication had been prescribed. Mr. B. did not have any prior knowledge of or experience with hypertension or taking this type of prescription.
   a. Based on the nursing diagnoses that were developed, identify one long-term or short-term goal for each diagnosis, and identify at least one expected outcome for each goal.

Nursing diagnoses	Long-term or short-term goals	Expected outcomes
1.		
2.		

   b. Identify two nursing interventions that may be appropriate in helping the client achieve the expected outcomes and goals.

IV. At his next visit to the adult health clinic, Mr. B. tells the nurse that, "when he remembers," he is taking the antihypertensive medication that was ordered by the physician. He says that he is trying to use the relaxation techniques he was taught during his last visit, but he does not use them regularly.
   a. What nursing implementation methods should take priority at this time?
   b. What, if any, alterations need to be made in the original plan of care designed with Mr. B.?

V. Mr. B. returns to the adult health clinic for evaluation of his status. His blood pressure is lower than before, but it remains slightly above normal limits. He exercises once or twice a week and states that this is making him feel better. Mr. B. shows the nurse a calendar where he has marked down the times for taking his medication. Mr. B. relates that he has been trying very hard to use the relaxation techniques when he starts to feel anxious or overwhelmed. He identifies that he cannot control all of his "destiny," but he is going to try to do things that may help him avoid what happened to his father.
   a. In accordance with previously identified outcomes, what nursing evaluation may be made on this client's status?

   b. What areas, if any, may require reassessment?

Independent Learning Activities

1. Practice assessment techniques with friends and family members, focusing on observation and effective communication. Try observing unknown individuals in the community to determine their appearance and behavior patterns during everyday activities.

2. Research an article in a current nursing journal on a specific area of assessment and/or use of an assessment tool.

3. Practice completion of the nursing health history for family or friends.

4. Practice assessment on classmates, family members, or friends, and write nursing diagnoses for identified needs (e.g., altered sleep patterns).

5. Take diagnostic labels/statements and see how the nursing approach may vary when the etiology is different.

6. Practice writing long-term and short-terms goals, expected outcomes, and possible nursing interventions. (Nursing diagnoses may focus on changes in sleep patterns associated with studying or other areas related to attending school.) Use an agency care plan, if available, to practice documentation.

7. Investigate the different types of consultants available in the health care system.

8. Research an article in a nursing journal on the use of critical pathways.

9. Ask nurses in different health care settings how they have altered their nursing care to meet a client's changing needs.

10. Research an article in a nursing journal that deals with a particular nursing implementation method.

11. Complete a self-evaluation of your attainment of personal or academic goals. Identify areas that you would reassess and work to improve on in the future.

12. Practice documentation of the nursing process using actual or simulated client situations. Try using different types of care plan formats.

Chapter Review

Match the description/definition in Column A with the correct term in Column B.

Column A
_____ 1. Unintended effect of a medication, diagnostic test, or intervention.
_____ 2. Observations or measurements made by the nurse.
_____ 3. Comparing data with another source to determine accuracy and relevancy.

Column B
a. Auscultation
b. Subjective data
c. Activities of daily living (ADLs)

_____	4.	Multidisciplinary, outcome-based care plan.
_____	5.	Clinical judgment about client responses to health problems or life processes.
_____	6.	Tapping of the body's surface to produce vibration.
_____	7.	Activities performed in the course of a normal day.
_____	8.	Support for why a specific nursing action is chosen.
_____	9.	Listening to sounds made by the body.
_____	10.	Information provided by the client verbally.

d. Percussion
e. Critical pathway
f. Nursing diagnosis
g. Objective data
h. Scientific rationale
i. Validation
j. Adverse reaction

Complete the following:

11. Identify five strategies for effective communication, and provide a specific example of each.

12. Identify the three phases of an interview.

13. Identify the four physical assessment techniques and the type of client data that may be obtained with each one.

14. Identify the steps of the nursing diagnostic process.

15. What are some common errors that may occur in formulating the nursing diagnosis?

16. Identify the seven guidelines for determining goals and outcomes.

17. Identify at least one goal, one expected outcome, and one nursing intervention for the following nursing diagnoses:
   a. Knowledge deficit related to the need for postoperative care at home

   b. Alteration in elimination: constipation related to lack of physical activity

18. Identify specific examples of how the nurse may use these skills in client care:
   a. cognitive

   b. interpersonal

   c. psychomotor

19. What general safety checks are necessary prior to implementing standing orders?

20. Identify three ways in which nursing care is communicated.

21. Identify two factors involved in the evaluation of nursing interventions.

Select the best answer for each of the following questions:

22. The new graduate is preparing to work with clients on the medical unit. The nursing process is applied as a:
    1. method for processing the care of many clients
    2. tool for diagnosing and treating clients' health problems
    3. guideline for determining the nurse's accountability in client care
    4. logical, problem-solving approach to providing client care

23. On admission, the nurse begins to assess the client. The client appears uncomfortable, stating that she has severe abdominal pain. The nurse should:
    1. inquire specifically about the discomfort
    2. let the client rest, returning later to complete the assessment
    3. perform a complete physical examination immediately
    4. ask the family about the client's health history

24. The following nursing diagnoses are proposed for clients on the medical unit. The diagnostic statement that contains all of the necessary components is:
    1. impaired gas exchange related to accumulation of lung secretions
    2. altered nutrition related to chemotherapy treatment
    3. ineffective grieving process
    4. pain related to abdominal surgery

25. The nurse is working with clients who come to the community center for health screenings and educational sessions. An example of a wellness nursing diagnosis label that is appropriate for this group is:
    1. risk for impaired skin integrity
    2. family coping: potential for growth
    3. altered parent/infant attachment
    4. fluid volume deficit

26. In reviewing the nursing diagnoses written by the new staff member, the supervisor identifies the correctly written nursing diagnosis as:
    1. altered respiratory function related to abnormal blood gases
    2. urinary infection related to long-term catheterization
    3. knowledge deficit related to need for cardiac monitoring
    4. pain related to severe arthritis in finger joints

27. The nurse is working with a client who has the following: dyspnea, ankle edema, weight gain, abdominal distention, and hypertension. The nursing diagnosis that is most appropriate for these signs and symptoms is:
    1. altered tissue perfusion
    2. body image disturbance
    3. impaired gas exchange
    4. fluid volume excess

28. A client is to have abdominal surgery tomorrow. The nurse determines that an outcome for this client that meets the necessary criteria is:
    1. client will be positioned every 2 hours
    2. client will express fears about surgery
    3. client will achieve normal elimination pattern before discharge
    4. client will perform active range of motion every 2 hours while in bed

29. There are a number of activities that are to be performed by the nurse during the clinical shift. In deciding to perform an independent or "nurse-initiated" intervention, the nurse:
    1. administers oral medications
    2. orders laboratory tests

3. changes a sterile dressing
4. teaches newborn hygienic care

30. The nurse is implementing a preventive nursing action when:
    1. immunizing clients
    2. assisting with hygienic care
    3. inserting a urinary catheter
    4. providing crisis-intervention counseling

31. The nurse has been working with the client in the rehabilitative facility for 2 weeks. The nurse is in the process of evaluating the client's progress. During the evaluation phase, the nurse recognizes that:
    1. nursing diagnoses always remain the same
    2. time frames for client outcomes may be adjusted
    3. evaluative skills differ greatly from those for client assessment
    4. the number of nursing diagnoses and outcomes is most important

32. An expected outcome for a client is "Pulse will remain below 120 beats/minute during exercise." If the client's pulse exceeds 120 beats/minute once out of every three exercise periods, the nurse appropriately evaluates the client's goal attainment as:
    1. client has achieved desired behavior
    2. client requires further evaluation of progress
    3. client's response indicates need for elimination of exercise
    4. client does not comply with therapeutic regimen

33. The nurse is caring for a client who has been medically stable. During the change-of-shift report, the nurse is informed that the client is experiencing a slight arrhythmia. To avoid complications during the implementation of care, the nurse plans to:
    1. evaluate the client's vital signs
    2. ask about the client's prior diagnoses
    3. contact the physician immediately
    4. tell the nurse's aide to perform the usual care for the client

34. For a client in the acute care facility, the nurse identifies several interventions. The statement that best communicates the activity of the nurse is:
    1. assist with range of motion exercises
    2. take the client's vital signs
    3. refer the client to a physical therapist
    4. provide 30 ml of water with the NG tube feedings q4h

35. The nurse is working with a client who has diabetes mellitus. The nursing diagnosis that the nurse identifies is *Fluid volume deficit related to osmotic diuresis.* An appropriate client outcome, based on this nursing diagnosis, is:
    1. client will have an increased urinary output
    2. client will decrease the amount of fluid intake over 24 hours
    3. client will demonstrate a decrease in edema in the lower extremities
    4. client will have palpable peripheral pulses and good capillary refill

36. The nurse is working with a client who is experiencing abnormal breath sounds and thick secretions. The nurse identifies a nursing diagnosis of:
    1. fluid volume deficit
    2. airway clearance, ineffective
    3. risk for altered mucous membranes
    4. dysfunctional ventilatory weaning response

Study Group Questions

- What is involved in client assessment, and what priorities does the nurse have in completing an assessment?
- How does the client assessment fit into the nursing process?
- Why does an error in the assessment phase influence the remaining implementation of the process, and how may the nurse avoid errors?
- What methods may be used to obtain client data, and what type of data are obtained with each method?

- What is involved in a client interview?
- How may the nurse optimize the environment for a client interview?
- How may the nurse use different communication strategies to obtain data during client assessment?
- What is a nursing diagnosis?
- What are the components of a nursing diagnosis?
- How are actual and potential nursing diagnoses different?
- How are medical and nursing diagnoses different?
- What errors are possible in formulating nursing diagnoses, and how may they be avoided?
- Which nursing diagnoses become priorities in planning client care?
- How are long-term and short-term goals different from one another?
- How are goals and expected outcomes different from one another?
- What are the guidelines for formulating goals and outcomes?
- In selecting nursing interventions, what are three essential nurse competencies?
- How are the three types of nursing interventions different from one another?
- What factors should be considered when selecting nursing interventions?
- What is the purpose of the care plan, and what types are available for use?

- How does the critical pathway differ from the "traditional" care plan?
- How does the consultation process begin, and who and what may be involved in the process?
- What is the focus of the implementation phase of the nursing process?
- What are standing orders and protocols, and how are they used in client care situations?
- What are the five preparatory nursing activities that are completed prior to implementing the care plan?
- What are the nursing implementation methods?
- How is nursing implementation communicated to other members of the health care team?
- How is evaluation incorporated into the nursing process?
- How is evaluation used in client situations and in nursing practice and health care delivery settings?
- What circumstances would lead to a modification of the care plan?

Study Chart

Create a study chart to compare the Steps of the Nursing Process, *identifying the different activities involved in each step.*

7 Documentation and Reporting

Case Studies

I. Mrs. Q. has just been returned to her room from the post-anesthesia care unit (PACU) following a right hip replacement. She has been brought down on a stretcher accompanied by a nurse from the PACU. Vital signs were taken on transfer and were found to be within expected limits. A dressing is in place to the client's right hip. Mrs. Q. does not appear to be having any difficulty at the moment.
   a. What information should be provided by the PACU nurse to the primary nurse on the surgical unit when Mrs. Q. is transferred to her room?
   b. What additional information may Mrs. Q.'s primary nurse want to obtain from the PACU nurse?

II. The primary nurse begins to plan and provide care for Mrs. Q. On entering the client's room, Mrs. Q. is found to be grimacing and moaning in pain. She says that she is having intense pain in her right hip area. The dressing to her hip is dry and intact. Mrs. Q. says that she does not want to move because it really hurts. The primary nurse helps Mrs. Q. get into a more comfortable position and goes to prepare the pain medication ordered by the physician. The primary nurse administers the pain medication, and, after about a half hour, the client says that the pain has been reduced.
   a. Using SOAP or DAR methods, document the nursing interaction with Mrs. Q.

Independent Learning Activities

1. Practice different types of documentation (e.g., narrative, problem-oriented) for actual and/or simulated client situations.

2. Review medical terminology to help ensure documentation and reporting will be accurate.

Chapter Review

Match the description/definition in Column A with the correct term in Column B.

	Column A	Column B
_____	1. An oral or written exchange of information between health care providers.	a. Record
_____	2. Information about clients only is provided to appropriate personnel.	b. POMR
_____	3. Permanent written communication with clients' health care management.	c. Acuity charting

_____ 4. Structured method of documentation with emphasis on the client's problems.

d. Report

_____ 5. Documentation that requires staff to identify interventions and allows clients to be compared to one another.

e. Confidentiality

Complete the following:

6. Identify three types of either oral or written exchanges of information between caregivers.

7. Identify seven purposes of the client record.

8. Describe how the Joint Commission on Accreditation of Healthcare Organizations (JCAHO) standards are applied to documentation.

9. The following are guidelines for documentation. Indicate the correct action to be taken by the nurse for each guideline.
    a. Never erase entries or use correction fluid, and never use pencil.

    b. Do not write retaliatory or critical comments about clients.

    c. Avoid using generalized, empty phrases.

    d. Do not scratch out errors.

e. Do not leave blank spaces.

f. Do not speculate or guess.

g. Do not record "physician made error."

h. Never chart for someone else.

i. Do not wait until the end of the shift to record important information.

Select the best answer for each of the following questions:

10. The nurse is working in a facility that uses computerized documentation of client information. To maintain client confidentiality with the use of computerized documentation, nurses should:
     1. delete any and all errors made in the record
     2. only give their password to other nurses working with the client
     3. log off of the file or computer when not using the terminal
     4. remove sensitive client information, such as communicable diseases, from the record

11. The nursing center is using a documentation format where client

assessment data are kept separate from the flow charts. The nurse who has just been hired will need to learn:

1. PIE format
2. SOAP format
3. SOAPIE format
4. narrative notations

12. The nurses on the medical unit in an acute care facility are meeting to select a documentation format to use. They recognize that there will be less fragmentation of client data if they implement:

1. source records
2. focus charting
3. charting by exception
4. critical pathways

13. While caring for a client on the surgical unit, the nurse notes that the client's blood pressure has dropped significantly since the last measurement. The nurse shares this information immediately with the health care team in a:

1. flow sheet record
2. incident report
3. telephone report
4. change-of-shift report

14. Documentation of client care is reviewed during the orientation to the facility. The new graduate nurse understands that the acceptable method for written documentation is:

1. using red ink to chart client entries
2. charting all of the client care at the end of the shift
3. beginning each entry with the time of the treatment or observation
4. leaving space at the end of the notations to allow for additional documentation

15. The nurse has been very busy during the shift trying to get all of the client-care activities completed. While documenting

one of the client's responses to a pain medication, the nurse mistakenly writes on the wrong client's chart. The nurse:

1. notes the error at the bottom of the page
2. erases the error and completes the entry on the correct chart
3. uses a dark color marker to completely cover the error
4. draws a straight line through the note and initials the error

16. The nurse is caring for a client who has had abdominal surgery. Accurate and complete documentation of the care provided by the nurse is evident by the notation of:

1. vital signs taken
2. Tylenol with codeine given for pain
3. provided adequate amount of fluid
4. IV fluids increased to 100 ml/hr according to protocol

Study Group Questions

- What is the purpose of documentation and reporting?
- What are the legal guidelines for documentation?
- How do the guidelines influence nursing documentation and reporting?
- What methods are available for documentation of client data?
- How do the different types of documentation (e.g., SOAP, DAR, narrative) compare to one another?
- How does written documentation compare to computerized systems, and what are the advantages and disadvantages of each method?
- What types of forms are used for client documentation?
- How does client documentation change in different health care settings?
- What information is necessary when doing change of shift, telephone, transfer, and incident reports?

Communication 8

Case Studies

I. For the following client situations, identify the communication techniques that may be most effective in establishing a nurse–client relationship:
   a. an older adult client who has a moderate hearing impairment
   b. the Russian-speaking parents of a young child who has been brought into the emergency room after being involved in a bicycle accident
   c. a young adult client who is blind and requires daily insulin injections
   d. a 60-year-old Hispanic woman who will be having her first internal pelvic examination

Independent Learning Activities

1. Using the challenging communication situations (refer to textbook, Box 8–1), think about how you should respond to the client.

2. Observe communication patterns between nurses and other health care professionals and their clients. Compare your observations to interactions between individuals in other social and business situations.

3. Practice using effective communication techniques with your peers, family members, or friends. Determine if overall communication is changed or improved.

Chapter Review

Match the description/definition in Column A with the correct term in Column B.

	Column A	Column B
_____	1. Person who initiates the interpersonal communication.	a. Therapeutic communication
_____	2. Information sent or expressed by the sender.	b. Metacommunication
_____	3. Means of conveying messages.	c. Sender
_____	4. Person to whom the message is sent.	d. Intonation
_____	5. Indicates whether the meaning of the sender's message was received.	e. Feedback
_____	6. Motivates one person to communicate with another.	f. Connotations
_____	7. Shades or interpretations of a word's meaning rather than different definitions.	g. Channels
_____	8. Tone of the speaker's voice that may affect a message's meaning.	h. Message
_____	9. A message within a message that conveys a sender's attitude toward the self and toward the listener.	i. Receiver
_____	10. Development of a working, functional relationship by the nurse with the client, fulfilling the purposes of the nursing process.	j. Referent

Complete the following:

11. Determine what level of communication the following examples are:
    a. a form of decision making

    b. "He looks uncomfortable, and I want to show him that I'm concerned about his discomfort."

    c. the ability to speak to consumers on health-related topics

12. Individuals maintain distances between themselves during interactions. Identify the four zones that may be used and an example of each.

13. For the following clients, identify at least two examples of how communication may be adapted:
    a. toddler

    b. adolescent

    c. older adult

14. The following are examples of *inappropriate* communication by the nurse. Specify which effective strategy is *not* being used and how the nurse may correct the situation.
    a. calling the client "honey"

    b. reporting to a nursing colleague about the "gallbladder in room 214"

    c. talking about the client to other nurses in the elevator

    d. running in the client's room to administer medications and leaving immediately

    e. informing the client that the physician will be performing an abdominal hysterectomy and that she should expect a midline incision of approximately 10 centimeters.

15. For the following examples, write a question that the nurse could ask that would be more appropriate and elicit better information from the client:
    a. "You're feeling okay today, right?"

    b. "You don't take any medication at home, do you?"

    c. "Are you having any lymphedema?"

    d. "The physician will be doing a paracentesis today. He said he explained it to you."

16. What communication techniques may be implemented for a client who is cognitively impaired?

17. Write examples of statements or questions that the nurse may use that demonstrate the following techniques:
   a. providing information

   b. clarifying

   c. avoiding giving personal opinions

18. How can the nurse be sensitive to the client's culture and gender in interpersonal communications?

19. Provide possible examples of appropriate responses by the nurse to the following client statements:
   a. "I don't take all of the medication that the doctor has ordered."

   b. "The staff is always too busy to help me."

   c. "This isn't the way the other nurses help me out of bed."

20. For the nursing diagnosis *Impaired verbal communication related to expressive aphasia,* identify at least two nursing interventions to promote communication with the client.

Select the best answer for each of the following questions:

21. The client tells the nurse that he feels anxious and afraid. The nurse responds by saying, "I will stay here with you." The nurse is using the principle of effective communication known as:
   1. empathy
   2. courtesy
   3. availability
   4. encouragement

22. Mr. J. States that he believes he may have cancer. The nurse tells him, "I wouldn't be concerned, Mr. J. I'm sure that the tests will be negative." The response by the nurse demonstrates the use of:
   1. assertiveness
   2. false reassurance
   3. professional opinion
   4. hope and encouragement

23. The nurse is assigned to a young adult male client. Gender sensitivity is demonstrated when the nurse:
   1. uses sexual innuendo
   2. engages in gender-oriented joking
   3. stereotypes male and female roles
   4. uses direct and indirect communication according to gender

24. The client comes regularly to the medical clinic. The nurse is establishing a helping relationship with the client. During the working phase of a helping relationship, the nurse:
   1. encourages and helps the client to set goals
   2. reminisces about the relationship with the client
   3. anticipates health concerns or issues
   4. identifies a location for the interaction

25. The nurse is interviewing a client who has come to the outpatient department. The nurse uses paraphrasing communication by saying:
   1. "This is your blood pressure medication. It will help to lower your blood pressure to the level where it should be."

2. "Do you mean that the pain comes and goes when you walk?"
3. "I would like to return to our discussion about your family."
4. "If I understand you correctly, you are primarily concerned about your dizzy spells."

26. The client tells you that there are other people in the room that are watching her from under the bed. The nurse uses therapeutic communication when he:
    1. identifies that there are no people under the bed
    2. tells the client that he will help her look for the people
    3. asks the client why other people are watching her
    4. reassures the client that he will tell the people to go away

27. While speaking with the client, the nurse notes that she is frowning. The nurse wants to find out about possible concerns by:
    1. asking why the client is unhappy
    2. telling the client that everything is okay
    3. identifying that she notices that the client is frowning
    4. asking if the client is angry about the health care problem

28. The client's condition has deteriorated, and he has been transferred to the intensive care unit. The roommate asks the nurse what is wrong with the client. The nurse should respond to the roommate by stating:
    1. "The client's condition is no concern of yours."
    2. "Everything is fine. Don't worry. He'll be OK."
    3. "I recognize your interest in the client, but I cannot share personal information with you without his permission."
    4. "Your roommate's condition worsened overnight and he had to be moved to the intensive care unit for observation."

29. The client is experiencing aphasia as a result of a CVA (cerebral vascular accident/stroke). To promote communication, the nurse plans to:
    1. speak louder
    2. use more questions
    3. use visual clues, such as pictures and gestures
    4. refer to a speech therapist to communicate with the client

30. The nurse is evaluating the communication skills used during an interaction with a newly admitted client. Of all of the statements made, the nurse responded therapeutically with:
    1. "Why aren't you able to keep taking the prescribed medications?"
    2. "We need to move quickly through the rest of the interview because it will be time for your therapy."
    3. "I can understand why you don't like that physician. I think you need to find another one."
    4. "I noticed that you didn't eat any of the lunch. Is there something that is bothering you?"

Study Group Questions

- What is therapeutic communication?
- What are the basic elements of communication?
- How do nurses and clients communicate verbally and nonverbally?
- What factors may influence communication?
- How may a client's physical, psychosocial, and developmental status influence communication with the nurse?
- How is a helping relationship established with a client?
- What are the principles/techniques of effective communication?
- How are the principles/techniques used by the nurse in a caring relationship?
- How is communication used within the steps of the nursing process?

- What are some of the barriers to effective communication, and how may they be overcome by the nurse?

identifying how each one may influence the nurse–client interaction (e.g., intonation).

Study Chart

Create a study chart to compare the Components of Verbal and Nonverbal Communication,

9 Client Education

Case Study

I. Your client is Ms. T., a 47-year-old married woman who has come to the medical clinic for evaluation. She has been diagnosed with hypertension and placed on an antihypertensive medication. Ms. T. has no prior knowledge or experience with the diagnosis or medication. There is a family history of coronary disease—her father died of a heart attack at 54 years of age.
   a. What information about Ms. T. may affect her motivation to learn?
   b. Formulate a teaching plan for Ms. T., including goals and teaching strategies.

Independent Learning Activities

1. Identify the types of teaching methods that work best in helping you to learn different information or skills.

2. Research an article in a nursing journal on specific strategies implemented for client education. Focus on a client situation that you have had experience with and/or are interested in learning more about.

3. Select a simple nursing skill (e.g., bed making, taking a pulse) and try to teach family members or friends how to perform the procedure correctly. Determine what factors may have assisted in the learning process.

Chapter Review

Match the description/definition in Column A with the correct term in Column B.

Column A

_____ 1. Expression of feelings, attitudes, opinions, and values.
_____ 2. Mental state that allows for focus and comprehension of material.
_____ 3. Acquiring skills.
_____ 4. Intellectual behaviors, including knowledge and understanding.
_____ 5. Desire to learn.

Column B

a. Cognitive learning
b. Motivation
c. Attentional set
d. Affective learning
e. Psychomotor learning

Complete the following:

6. Identify at least three teaching methods that may be implemented specifically for the following individuals:
   a. infant

   b. school-age child

   c. older adult

7. What factors should the nurse consider when selecting an environment for teaching?

8. Describe each of the following principles of learning and the nurse's role in applying each one:
   a. motivation

   b. ability to learn

   c. learning environment

9. What factors influence an individual's ability to learn psychomotor skills?

10. Provide at least four examples of resources that the nurse may use in teaching a client.

11. For the nursing diagnosis *Noncompliance with medication regime related to insufficient knowledge of purpose and actions,* identify possible learning goals and outcomes and nursing interventions.

12. Identify three types of reinforcers, and provide examples of each type.

13. For the following, identify the domain of learning and an example of a nursing technique that may be used for client teaching:
    a. self-injection of insulin

    b. coping with care of a family member

    c. complications to be aware of after a heart attack

14. Provide an example of when each of the following instructional techniques may be used:
    a. preparatory instruction

    b. demonstration

    c. role playing

15. How can teaching be integrated into the daily care of the client?

Select the best answer for each of the following questions:

16. The nurse is preparing to teach a group of new parents about infant care. The nurse recognizes that learning can be enhanced with:
    1. prior unfamiliarity with the topic area
    2. fear of health outcomes
    3. mild discomfort
    4. mild anxiety level

17. While preparing a teaching plan for a group of clients with diabetes, the nurse integrates the basic principle of education that:
    1. material should progress from complex to simpler ideas
    2. prolonged teaching sessions improve concentration and attentiveness
    3. learning is improved when more than one body sense is stimulated
    4. prior knowledge of a topic area interferes with the acquisition of new information

18. During a teaching session for a client with heart disease, the nurse uses reinforcement to stimulate learning. An example of reinforcement for this client is:
    1. allowing the clients to manage self-care needs
    2. teaching about the disease process while delivering nursing care
    3. outlining an exercise plan and providing explicit instructions
    4. complimenting the client on the ability to identify the action of prescribed medications

19. After about 20 minutes has passed in the educational session, the nurse notices that the client is slightly slumped over in the chair and is no longer maintaining eye contact. The nurse:
    1. repositions the client in the chair
    2. moves the client to a cooler, brighter room
    3. reschedules the remainder of the teaching for another time
    4. continues with the teaching session to cover the necessary content

20. When preparing to teach a self-injection technique to a client, the nurse begins with:
    1. having the client demonstrate the procedure
    2. discussing the procedure and equipment
    3. providing written materials and having the client practice the technique
    4. demonstrating to the client how to perform the procedure correctly

21. After teaching the client about the cerebral vascular accident (CVA/stroke), the nurse is going to evaluate the client's psychomotor domain of learning. This is accomplished by the nurse:
    1. observing the client use a cane to ambulate
    2. asking the client about the basic etiology of the stroke
    3. determining the client's attitudes about the treatment regime
    4. having the client complete a written schedule for daily activities at home

22. When the teaching session has been completed, the nurse evaluates the client's cognitive domain of learning to see if there are areas that require additional time. The nurse evaluates the client's ability to:
    1. perform the range-of-motion exercises independently
    2. identify the equipment necessary for the surgical wound care
    3. demonstrate the proper use of crutches to go up and down stairs
    4. discuss concerns about the difficulty in keeping track of the treatments

Study Group Questions

- What are the standards (e.g., JCAHO) for client education?
- How does client education promote, maintain, and restore health?
- What are the principles of teaching and learning?
- What factors may influence a client's ability to learn?
- How does an individual's developmental status influence the selection of teaching methodologies?
- How does the teaching process compare with the communication and nursing processes?
- How does the nurse develop a teaching plan for a client?
- What teaching approaches and instructional methods may be used by the nurse?
- How is client education documented?

10 Infection Control

Case Studies

I. Your client is an 86-year-old woman in an extended care facility. She has a urinary catheter attached to a drainage system.
   a. What precautions should be taken to prevent a urinary infection for this client?

II. The client is a 45-year-old man who had abdominal surgery yesterday. He has a large midline abdominal incision covered by a sterile dressing. He will require dressing changes bid.
   a. What precautions should be taken to prevent a wound infection for this client?

Independent Learning Activities

1. Review the processes of the body's immune system.

2. Review microbiology concepts, including the chain of infection and illness-producing microorganisms.

3. Practice the skills associated with infection control with peers and at home.

4. Research an article in a current nursing journal on Standard Precautions and/or resilient infectious agents.

Chapter Review

Match the description/definition in Column A with the correct term in Column B.

	Column A	Column B
_____	1. Arises from microorganisms outside of the client.	a. Exudate
_____	2. Results from a diagnostic or therapeutic procedure.	b. Aseptic technique
_____	3. Picked up when a person contacts another object.	c. Nosocomial infection
_____	4. Microorganisms resistant to antibiotics that cause another infection.	d. Sterilization
_____	5. Infection developed that was not present at the time of client admission.	e. Iatrogenic infection
_____	6. Methods to reduce or eliminate disease-producing microorganisms.	f. Transient flora
_____	7. Client's flora altered through an overgrowth of another microorganism.	g. Pathogen
_____	8. Process that eliminates all forms of microbial life.	h. Endogenous infection

_____ 9. Disease-producing microorganism.
_____ 10. Substance formed through the inflammatory process that may ooze from openings in the skin or mucous membranes.

i. Supra infection
j. Exogenous infection

Complete the following:

d. environmental factors

11. Identify and briefly describe the stages in the course of an infection.

e. disease history

16. Identify possible alterations in the normal body system defenses for the following:
a. skin

12. Identify the normal defenses that the body has against infection.

b. respiratory tract

13. Identify at least four possible risks for a nosocomial infection.

c. urinary tract

d. gastrointestinal tract

14. Identify health promotion activities that may be implemented for infection control.

17. What is the procedure for collecting a urine specimen?

15. Identify two examples for each of the following factors affecting susceptibility to infection:
a. age

18. What results would be expected for the following laboratory studies in the presence of an infection?
a. white blood cells

b. nutritional status

b. erythrocyte sedimentation rate

c. personal habits

c. iron level

d. neutrophils

e. basophils

19. Identify at least five strategies to prevent or control infections in the home environment.

20. What should the community health nurse take for a visit to a client who has no soap or running water?

21. Provide an example of possible nursing interventions for each of the following infection-control measures:
    a. control or eliminate the infectious agent

    b. control or eliminate the reservoir

    c. control the portals of exit

    d. control the transmission

22. Identify the personal protective equipment that may be used by the nurse in client-care

situations, and provide the rationale for the use of each one.

23. What is the procedure for transporting a client with an infectious respiratory disease?

24. Identify treatments or situations when surgical asepsis is used.

25. Indicate for the following if appropriate asepsis or contamination has occurred:
    a. handling a sterile dressing with clean gloves

    b. holding a sterile bowl above waist level using sterile gloves

    c. keeping the hands above the elbows after a surgical scrub

26. Compare the signs and symptoms of a local and systemic infection.

27. For the nursing diagnosis *Skin integrity, impaired, related to 2-inch-diameter pressure ulcer on sacrum,* identify a client goal, objectives, and nursing interventions.

28. Number the flaps on the sterile package in the photo according to which one should be opened first, second, and last.

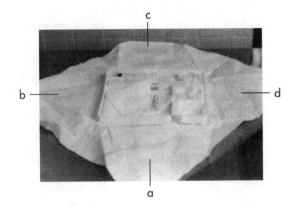

Select the best answer for each of the following questions:

29. At the community health fair, the nurse is asked by one of the residents about the influenza vaccine. The nurse responds to the resident that the influenza vaccine is recommended for individuals who are:
    1. health care workers
    2. traveling to other countries
    3. less than 6 years of age
    4. between 40 and 65 years of age

30. The nurse is preparing a room for a client with tuberculosis. The specific aspect for this tier of Standard Precautions that is different from Tier One is that the care should include:
    1. a private room with negative air flow
    2. hand washing after gloves are removed
    3. eye protection if splashing is possible
    4. disposal of sharp objects in a puncture-resistant container

31. The nurse is preparing a teaching plan for clients about the Hepatitis B virus. The nurse informs them that this virus may be transmitted by:
    1. mosquitoes
    2. droplet nuclei
    3. blood products
    4. improperly handled food

32. The nurse is working on a unit with a number of clients who have infectious diseases. One of the most important methods for reducing the spread of microorganisms is:
    1. sterilization of equipment
    2. the use of gloves and gowns
    3. maintenance of isolation precautions
    4. hand washing before and after client care

33. Today's assignment for the nurse includes a client with tuberculosis. When caring for this client, the nurse routinely should use:
    1. regular masks and eyewear
    2. regular masks, gowns, and gloves
    3. surgical hand washing and gloves
    4. particulate filtration masks and gowns

34. The nurse is caring for a client who has a large abdominal wound that requires a sterile saline soak and dressing. While performing the care, the nurse drops the saline-soaked 4×4 gauze near the wound on the client's abdomen. The nurse:
    1. discontinues the procedure at this time
    2. throws the gauze away and prepares a new 4×4
    3. picks up the 4×4 with sterile forceps and places it on the wound
    4. rinses the 4×4 with saline and places it on the wound using sterile gloves

35. The nurse is checking the laboratory results of a client admitted to the medical unit. The nurse is alerted to the presence of an infectious process based on the finding of:
    1. iron—80g/100 ml
    2. neutrophils—65%
    3. erythocyte sedimentation rate (ESR)—64%
    4. white blood cells (WBC)—16,000/mm^3

36. The nurse is working with a client who has a deep laceration to the right lower extremity. To reduce a possible reservoir of infection, the nurse:
    1. wears gloves and masks at all times
    2. isolates the client's personal articles
    3. has the client cover the mouth and nose when coughing
    4. changes the dressing on the extremity when it becomes soiled

Study Group Questions

- What is the nature of the infectious process?
- What are the components of the infection chain?
- What are the body's normal defenses against infection?
- What is a nosocomial infection, who are the clients at risk, and how may the nurse prevent this infection?
- How is the nursing process applied to infection control in the acute care, extended care, and home care environments?
- What nursing measures may be implemented to prevent or control the spread of infection?
- What is included in Standard Precautions?
- What information may be taught to the client and family for prevention or control of infectious processes?
- How does the nurse perform the procedures that are important for infection control?

Name_____ Date_____ Instructor's Name_____

Performance Checklist: Skill 10-1

Hand washing

	S	U	NP	Comments
1. Inspect surface of hands for breaks or cuts in skin or cuticles. Note condition of nails. Cover any skin lesions before providing client care.	____	____	____	_____
2. Inspect hands for heavy soiling.	____	____	____	_____
3. Assess client's risk for or extent of infection.	____	____	____	_____
4. Push wristwatch and long uniform sleeves above wrists. Avoid wearing rings. If worn, remove during washing.	____	____	____	_____
5. Be sure fingernails are short, filed, and smooth.	____	____	____	_____
6. Stand in front of sink, keeping hands and uniform away from sink surface. (If hands touch sink during hand washing, repeat.)	____	____	____	_____
7. Turn on water. Turn faucet on, push knee pedals laterally, or press pedals with foot to regulate flow and temperature.	____	____	____	_____
8. Avoid splashing water against uniform.	____	____	____	_____
9. Regulate flow of water so that temperature is warm.	____	____	____	_____
10. Wet hands and wrists thoroughly under running water. Keep hands and forearms lower than elbows during washing.	____	____	____	_____
11. Apply a small amount of soap or antiseptic, lathering thoroughly.	____	____	____	_____
12. Wash hands using plenty of lather and friction for at least 10 to 15 seconds. Interlace fingers and rub palms and back of hands with circular motion at least 5 times each. Keep fingertips down.	____	____	____	_____

	S	U	NP	Comments
13. Clean under fingernails of other hand with soap or clean orangewood stick.	___	___	___	_____
14. Rinse hands and wrists thoroughly, keeping hands down and elbows up.	___	___	___	_____
15. Dry hands thoroughly from fingers to forearms with paper towel, single-use cloth, or warm air dryer.	___	___	___	_____
16. If used, discard paper towel in proper receptacle.	___	___	___	_____
17. To turn off hand faucet, use clean, dry paper towel, avoiding touching handles with hands. Turn off water with foot or knee pedals (if applicable).	___	___	___	_____
18. Inspect surface of hands for obvious signs of dirt or other contaminants.	___	___	___	_____

Vital Signs 11

Case Studies

I. You are involved in taking blood pressures at a community health fair.
    a. What blood pressure readings will indicate a need to recommend follow-up?
    b. What other information may be obtained from the client while taking the blood pressure?

II. Your client has bilateral casts on the upper arms.
    a. How will you obtain the client's pulse and blood pressure?

III. You are working in an extended care facility and the nurse reporting off identifies that one of the clients is febrile.
    a. What signs and symptoms do you expect to find with a client who is febrile?
    b. What interventions are indicated for febrile clients?

IV. The client is being monitored with pulse oximetry. The device does not appear to be working.
    a. What "troubleshooting" can you attempt to see if the pulse oximetry will work properly?

Independent Learning Activities

1. Review the normal anatomy and physiology of the body's temperature-regulating mechanisms and circulatory and respiratory systems.

2. Practice taking vital signs with your peers, family members, or friends. Determine possible reasons for any differences in findings (e.g., age, activity).

3. Investigate strategies for adapting vital sign measurement for clients with different health problems, such as casts and contractures.

4. Research an article on new developments or guidelines for vital sign measurement.

Chapter Review

Match the description/definition in Column A with the correct term in Column B.

Column A	Column B
_____ 1. Decrease of systolic and diastolic pressure below normal.	a. Tachypnea
_____ 2. Another word for fever.	b. Diffusion
_____ 3. Rate and depth of respirations increases.	c. Bradypnea
_____ 4. Pulse rate below 60 beats per minute for an adult.	d. Pyrexia
_____ 5. 140/90 for two or more readings.	e. Apnea
_____ 6. Rate of breathing is regular but abnormally rapid.	f. Bradycardia

_____ 7. Controls body temperature like a thermostat in a home.

_____ 8. Respirations cease for several seconds.

_____ 9. Rate of breathing is regular but abnormally slow.

_____ 10. Movement of oxygen and carbon dioxide between the alveoli and red blood cells.

g. Hypotension
h. Hyperventilation
i. Hypothalamus
j. Hypertension

Complete the following:

11. Identify at least five circumstances when vital signs should be taken.

12. What errors in blood pressure measurement may result in false high or low readings?

13. Convert the following temperature readings:
    a. 97° F = _____ ° C

    b. 38.4° C = _____ ° F

    c. What readings on a Fahrenheit and Centigrade thermometer should alert the nurse to an alteration in the client's temperature regulation?

14. Indicate on the model where the following pulses should be palpated:
    a. brachial

    b. radial

c. apical

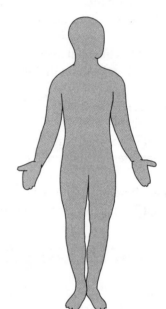

15. Indicate on the aneroid and mercury scales where the following blood pressure readings would be noted:
    a. Korotkoff sounds first heard at 164 and inaudible at 92.

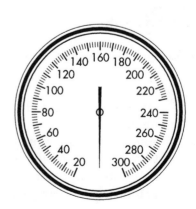

b.   Korotkoff sounds first heard at 112 and inaudible at 64.

b.   hypotension

c.   hyperthermia

d.   dyspnea

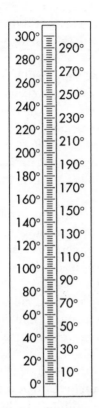

18.   Identify circumstances when a temperature should not be taken by the oral or rectal route.

Select the best answer for each of the following questions:

16.   Identify at least two considerations for each measurement in older adults:
   a.   temperature

19.   The nurse is working on a pediatric unit and assessing the vital signs of an infant admitted for gastroenteritis. The nurse expects that the vital signs are normally:
   1.   BP = 90/50, P = 122, R = 46
   2.   BP = 90/60, P = 80, R = 20
   3.   BP = 100/60, P = 140, R = 32
   4.   BP = 110/50, P = 98, R = 40

   b.   pulse

20.   While working in the extended care facility, the nurse expects the vital signs of an older adult client to be:
   1.   BP = 98/70, P = 60, R = 12
   2.   BP = 120/60, P = 110, R = 30
   3.   BP = 140/90, P = 74, R = 14
   4.   BP = 150/100, P = 90, R = 25

   c.   respirations

   d.   blood pressure

21.   The student nurse is taking vital signs for her assigned clients on the surgical unit. The student is aware that a client's body temperature may be reduced after:
   1.   exercise
   2.   emotional stress
   3.   periods of sleep
   4.   cigarette smoking

17.   Identify nursing interventions for clients having the following alterations:
   a.   tachycardia

22. While working in the emergency room, the nurse is monitoring carefully the vital signs of the clients who have been admitted. The nurse is alert to the potential for a serious decrease in a client's pulse as a result of:
    1. hemorrhage
    2. hypothyroidism
    3. respiratory difficulty
    4. epinephrine (adrenalin) administration

23. A client is being treated for hyperthermia. The nurse anticipates that the client's response to this will be:
    1. generalized pallor
    2. bradycardia
    3. reduced thirst
    4. diaphoresis

24. Several friends have gone on a ski trip and have been exposed to very cold temperatures. One of the individuals appears to be slightly hypothermic. The best initial response by the nurse in the ski lodge is to give this individual:
    1. soup
    2. coffee
    3. cocoa
    4. brandy

25. When checking the temperature of the client, the nurse notes that he is febrile. An antipyretic medication is ordered. The nurse prepares to administer:
    1. Gantrisin
    2. prednisone
    3. theophylline
    4. acetaminophen

26. The nurse has a number of different clients as an assignment today in the long-term care unit. When taking vital signs, the nurse is alert to the greater possibility of tachycardia for the client with:
    1. anemia
    2. hypothyroidism
    3. a temperature of 95° F
    4. a PCA pump with morphine drip

27. While reviewing the vital signs taken by the aide this morning, the nurse notes that one of the clients is hypotensive. The nurse will be checking to see if the client is experiencing:
    1. lightheadedness
    2. a decreased heart rate
    3. increased urinary output
    4. increased warmth to the skin

28. Vital sign measurement has been completed on all of the assigned clients. The nurse will need to report immediately a finding of:
    1. pulse pressure—40
    2. apical pulses—78, 80, 76
    3. apical pulse—82, radial pulse—70
    4. BP 140/80—left arm, 136/74—right arm

29. The nurse is preparing to take vital signs for the clients on the acute care unit. A tympanic temperature assessment is indicated for the client:
    1. after rectal surgery
    2. wearing a hearing aid
    3. experiencing otitis media
    4. following an exercise session

30. Blood pressure monitoring is being conducted on the cardiac care unit. The nurse is determining whether an automatic blood pressure device is indicated for use. This device is selected for the client with:
    1. an irregular heartbeat
    2. Parkinson's disease
    3. peripheral vascular disease
    4. systolic blood pressure above 140 mm/Hg

31. A 34-year-old client has come to the physician's office for an annual physical examination. The nurse is completing the vital signs before the client is seen by the physician. The nurse alerts the physician to a finding of:
    1. T—37.6° C
    2. P—120
    3. R—18
    4. BP—116/78

32. The nurse is assigned to the well-child center that is affiliated with the acute care facility. A 1$\frac{1}{2}$-year-old child is brought in

by his mother for his immunizations. The nurse assesses his pulse by checking the:
1.   radial artery
2.   apical artery
3.   popliteal artery
4.   femoral artery

Study Group Questions

- What are the guidelines for vital sign measurement?
- When should vital signs be taken?
- How does the nurse determine which sites and equipment to use for measurement of vital signs?
- What body processes regulate temperature?
- What factors influence body temperature?
- How is the temperature measurement converted from Centigrade to Fahrenheit and vice versa?
- What sites and equipment are used for temperature measurement?
- What nursing interventions are appropriate for increases and decreases in the client's body temperature?
- What factors influence the pulse rate?
- What sites may be used for pulse assessment?
- How should the stethoscope be used?
- What changes may occur in the pulse rate and rhythm?
- What nursing interventions are appropriate for alterations in the pulse?

- What is the blood pressure?
- What factors may increase or decrease the blood pressure?
- What are the abnormal alterations in blood pressure?
- What equipment is used for blood pressure measurement?
- What nursing interventions are appropriate for increases and decreases in the blood pressure?
- What body processes are involved in respiration?
- How are respirations assessed?
- What alterations may be noted in the client's respirations?
- How does pulse oximetry work and what is it used for?
- What are the procedures for assessment of the temperature, pulse, respirations, blood pressure, and pulse oxygen saturation?
- What should be included in client and family teaching for measurement and evaluation of vital signs?

Study Chart

Create a study chart to compare the Vital Signs Across the Life Span, *identifying expected temperature, pulse, respiration, and blood pressure for each age group.*

Name_____ Date_____ Instructor's Name_____

Performance Checklist: Skill 11-1

Measuring Body Temperature

	S	U	NP	Comments

1. Assess for signs and symptoms of temperature alterations and for factors that influence body temperature. _____ _____ _____ _____

2. Determine any previous activity that would interfere with accuracy of temperature measurement. Wait 20 to 30 minutes before measuring oral temperature if client has smoked or ingested hot or cold liquid or food. _____ _____ _____ _____

3. Determine appropriate site and measurement device to be used. _____ _____ _____ _____

4. Explain route by which temperature will be taken and importance of maintaining proper position until reading is complete. _____ _____ _____ _____

5. Wash hands. _____ _____ _____ _____

6. Assist client in assuming comfortable position that provides easy access to route through which temperature is to be measured. _____ _____ _____ _____

7. Obtain temperature reading.
   a. Oral temperature measurement with electronic thermometer
      (1) Apply disposable gloves (optional). _____ _____ _____ _____
      (2) Remove thermometer pack from charging unit. Attach oral probe (blue tip) to thermometer unit. Grasp top of probe stem, being careful not to apply pressure on the ejection button. _____ _____ _____ _____
      (3) Slide disposable plastic probe cover over thermometer probe until cover locks in place. _____ _____ _____ _____
      (4) Ask client to open mouth; then gently place thermometer probe under tongue in posterior sublingual pocket lateral to center of lower jaw. _____ _____ _____ _____
      (5) Ask client to hold thermometer probe with lips closed. _____ _____ _____ _____

	S	U	NP	Comments

(6) Leave thermometer probe in place until audible signal occurs and client's temperature appears on digital display; remove thermometer probe from under client's tongue.

(7) Push ejection button on thermometer stem to discard plastic probe cover into appropriate receptacle.

(8) Return thermometer stem to storage well of recording unit.

(9) If gloves worn, remove and dispose in appropriate receptacle. Wash hands.

(10) Return thermometer to charger.

b. Rectal temperature measurement with electronic thermometer

(1) Draw curtain around bed and/or close room door. Assist client to Sims' position with upper leg flexed. Move aside bed linen to expose only anal area. Keep client's upper body and lower extremities covered with sheet or blanket.

(2) Apply disposable gloves.

(3) Remove thermometer pack from charging unit. Attach rectal probe (red tip) to thermometer unit. Grasp top of probe stem, being careful not to apply pressure on the ejection button.

(4) Slide disposable plastic probe cover over thermometer probe until it locks in place.

(5) Squeeze liberal portion of lubricant onto tissue. Dip probe cover's end into lubricant, covering 2.5 to 3.5 cm (1 to 1 $^1/_2$ inches) for adult.

(6) With nondominant hand, separate client's buttocks to expose anus. Ask client to breathe slowly and relax.

(7) Gently insert thermometer probe into anus in direction of umbilicus 3.5 cm (1 $^1/_2$ inches) for adult. Do not force thermometer.

(8) Leave thermometer probe in place until audible signal occurs and client's temperature appears on digital display; remove thermometer probe from anus.

(9) Push ejection button on thermometer stem to discard plastic probe cover into appropriate receptacle.

(10) Return thermometer stem to storage well of recording unit.

	S	U	NP	Comments
(11) Wipe client's anal area with tissue or soft wipe to remove lubricant or feces and discard tissue. Assist client in assuming a comfortable position.	___	___	___	_____
(12) Remove and dispose of gloves in appropriate receptacle. Wash hands.	___	___	___	_____
(13) Return thermometer to charger.	___	___	___	_____

c. Axillary temperature measurement with electronic thermometer

	S	U	NP	Comments
(1) Wash hands.	___	___	___	_____
(2) Draw curtain around bed and/or close room door. Assist client to supine or sitting position. Move clothing or gown away from shoulder and arm.	___	___	___	_____
(3) Remove thermometer pack from charging unit. Be sure oral probe (blue tip) is attached to thermometer unit. Grasp top of probe stem, being careful not to apply pressure on ejection button.	___	___	___	_____
(4) Slide disposable plastic probe cover over thermometer probe until it locks in place.	___	___	___	_____
(5) Raise client's arm away from torso, and inspect for skin lesions and excessive perspiration. Insert probe into center of axilla, lower arm over probe, and place arm across chest.	___	___	___	_____
(6) Hold probe in place until audible signal occurs and temperature appears on digital display.	___	___	___	_____
(7) Push ejection button on thermometer stem to discard plastic probe cover into appropriate receptacle.	___	___	___	_____
(8) Return thermometer stem to storage well of recording unit.	___	___	___	_____
(9) Assist client in assuming a comfortable position, replacing linen or gown.	___	___	___	_____
(10) Wash hands.	___	___	___	_____
(11) Return thermometer to charger.	___	___	___	_____

d. Tympanic membrane temperature with electronic tympanic thermometer

	S	U	NP	Comments
(1) Assist client in assuming comfortable position with head turned toward side, away from you. Right-handed persons should obtain temperature from client's right ear.	___	___	___	_____

	S	U	NP	Comments

(2) Note if there is obvious earwax in the client's ear canal.

(3) Remove thermometer handheld unit from charging base, being careful not to apply pressure on the ejection button.

(4) Slide disposable speculum cover over otoscope-like tip until it locks into place. Becareful not to touch lens cover.

(5) Insert speculum into ear canal following manufacturer's instructions for tympanic probe positioning

  (a) Pull ear pinna backward, up and out for an adult.

  (b) Move thermometer in a figure-eight pattern.

  (c) Fit otoscope probe snugly into canal and do not move.

  (d) Point speculum tip toward nose.

(6) As soon as probe is in place, depress scan button on handheld unit. Leave thermometer probe in place until audible signal occurs and client's temperature appears on digital display.

(7) Carefully remove speculum from auditory meatus.

(8) Push ejection button on handheld unit to discard plastic probe cover into appropriate receptacle. If a second reading is necessary replace probe lens cover and wait 2 minutes before inserting the probe tip.

(9) Return handheld unit to charging base.

(10) Assist client in assuming a comfortable position.

(11) Wash hands.

8. Discuss findings with client as needed.

9. If temperature is assessed for the first time, establish temperature as baseline if it is within normal range.

10. Compare temperature reading with client's previous temperature and normal temperature range for client's age-group.

11. Record temperature in client's record.

12. Report abnormal findings to nurse in charge or physician.

Name_____ Date_____ Instructor's Name_____

Performance Checklist: Skill 11-2

Assessing the Radial and Apical Pulses

	S	U	NP	Comments
1. Determine need to assess radial and/or apical pulse.	___	___	___	_____
2. Assess for factors that influence pulse rate and rhythm.	___	___	___	_____
3. Determine client's previous baseline pulse rate (if available) from client's record.	___	___	___	_____
4. Explain that pulse or heart rate is to be assessed. Encourage client to relax and not speak.	___	___	___	_____
5. Wash hands.	___	___	___	_____
6. If necessary, draw curtain around bed and/or close door.	___	___	___	_____

7. Obtain pulse measurement.
   a. Radial pulse

	S	U	NP	Comments
(1) Assist client to assume a supine or sitting position.	___	___	___	_____
(2) If supine, place client's forearm straight alongside or across lower chest or upper abdomen with wrist extended straight. If sitting, bend client's elbow 90 degrees and support lower arm on chair or on your arm. Slightly flex the wrist with palm down.	___	___	___	_____
(3) Place tips of first two fingers of your hand over groove along radial or thumbside of client's inner wrist.	___	___	___	_____
(4) Lightly compress against radius, obliterate pulse initially, and then relax pressure so pulse becomes easily palpable.	___	___	___	_____
(5) Determine strength of pulse.	___	___	___	_____
(6) After pulse can be felt regularly, look at watch's second hand and begin to count rate.	___	___	___	_____
(7) If pulse is regular, count rate for 30 seconds and multiply total by 2.	___	___	___	_____

	S	U	NP	Comments

(8) If pulse is irregular, count rate for 60 seconds. Assess frequency and pattern of irregularity.

(9) When pulse is irregular, compare radial pulses bilaterally.

b. Apical pulse

(1) Wash hands.

(2) Draw curtain around bed and/or close door.

(3) Assist client to supine or sitting position. Move aside bed linen and gown to expose sternum and left side of chest.

(4) Locate anatomical landmarks to identify the point of maximal impulse (PMI), also called the apical impulse. Find angle of Louis just below suprasternal notch between sternal body and manubrium; it can be felt as a bony prominence. Slip fingers down each side of angle to find second intercostal space (ICS). Carefully move fingers down left side of sternum to fifth ICS and laterally to the left midclavicular line (MCL). A light tap felt within an area 1 to 2 cm ($^1/_2$ to 1 inch) of the PMI is reflected from the apex of the heart.

(5) Place diaphragm of stethoscope in palm of hand for 5 to 10 seconds.

(6) Place diaphragm of stethoscope over PMI at the fifth ICS, at left MCL, and auscultate for normal S_1 and S_2 heart sounds (heard as "lub dub").

(7) When S_1 and S_2 are heard with regularity, use watch's second hand and begin to count rate.

(8) If apical rate is regular, count for 30 seconds and multiply by 2.

(9) If heart rate is irregular or client is receiving cardiovascular medication, count for 1 minute (60 seconds).

(10) Note regularity of any dysrhythmia (S_1 and S_2 occurring early or later after previous sequence of sounds.)

(11) Replace client's gown and bed linen; assist client in returning to comfortable position.

	S	U	NP	Comments
(12) Wash hands.	____	____	____	_____
(13) Clean earpieces and diaphragm of stethoscope with alcohol swab routinely after each use.	____	____	____	_____
8. Discuss findings with client as needed.	____	____	____	_____
9. Wash hands.	____	____	____	_____
10. Compare readings with previous baseline and/or acceptable range of heart rate for client's age.	____	____	____	_____
11. Compare peripheral pulse rate with apical rate, and note discrepancy.	____	____	____	_____
12. Compare radial pulse equality, and note discrepancy.	____	____	____	_____
13. Correlate pulse rate with data obtained from blood pressure and related signs and symptoms.	____	____	____	_____
14. Record pulse rate with assessment site in Client's record.	____	____	____	_____
15. Report abnormal findings to nurse in charge or physician.	____	____	____	_____

Name_____ Date_____ Instructor's Name_____

Performance Checklist: Skill 11-3

Measuring Blood Pressure

	S	U	NP	Comments
1. Determine need to assess client's BP.	___	___	___	_____
2. Determine best site for BP assessment.	___	___	___	_____
3. Select appropriate cuff size.	___	___	___	_____
4. Determine previous baseline BP (if available) from client's record.	___	___	___	_____
5. Encourage client to avoid exercise and smoking for 30 minutes before assessment of BP.	___	___	___	_____
6. Have client assume sitting or lying position. Be sure room is warm, quiet, and relaxing.	___	___	___	_____
7. Explain to client that BP is to be assessed and have client rest at least 5 minutes before measurement. Ask client not to speak when BP is being measured.	___	___	___	_____
8. Wash hands. With client sitting or lying, position client's forearm or thigh, supported if needed. For arm, turn palm up; for thigh, position with knee slightly flexed.	___	___	___	_____
9. Expose extremity (arm or leg) fully by removing constricting clothing.	___	___	___	_____
10. Palpate brachial artery (arm) or popliteal artery (leg). Position cuff 2.5 cm (1 inch) above site of pulsation (antecubital or popliteal space).	___	___	___	_____
11. Apply bladder of cuff above artery by centering arrows marked on cuff over artery. If no center arrows on cuff, estimate the center of the bladder and place this center over artery. With cuff fully deflated, wrap cuff evenly and snugly around extremity.	___	___	___	_____
12. If possible, position manometer vertically at eye level.	___	___	___	_____

	S	U	NP	Comments

13. Measure blood pressure.
   a. Two-step method
      (1) Relocate brachial pulse. Palpate artery distal to the cuff with fingertips of nondominant hand while inflating cuff. Note point at which pulse disappears, and continue to inflate cuff to a pressure 30 mm Hg above that point. Note the pressure reading. Slowly deflate cuff, and note point when pulse reappears. Deflate cuff fully and wait 30 seconds.
      (2) Place stethoscope earpieces in ears and be sure sounds are clear, not muffled.
      (3) Relocate brachial artery and place diaphragm of stethoscope over it. Do not allow chestpiece to touch cuff or clothing.
      (4) Close valve of pressure bulb clockwise until tight.
      (5) Quickly inflate cuff to 30 mm Hg above client's estimated systolic pressure.
      (6) Slowly release pressure bulb valve and allow mercury or needle of aneroid manometer gauge to fall at rate of 2 to 3 mm Hg/sec.
      (7) Note point on manometer when first clear sound is heard. The sound slowly will increase in intensity.
      (8) Continue to deflate cuff gradually, noting point at which sound disappears in adults. Note pressure to nearest 2 mm Hg. Listen for 20 to 30 mm Hg after the last sound and then allow remaining air to escape quickly.

   b. One-step method
      (1) Place stethoscope earpieces in ears and be sure sounds are clear, not muffled.
      (2) Relocate brachial artery and place diaphragm of stethoscope over it. Do not allow chestpiece to touch cuff or clothing.
      (3) Close valve of pressure bulb clockwise until tight.
      (4) Quickly inflate cuff to 30 mm Hg above client's usual systolic pressure.

	S	U	NP	Comments

(5) Slowly release pressure bulb valve and allow mercury or needle of aneroid manometer gauge to fall at rate of 2 to 3 mm Hg/sec.

(6) Note point on manometer when first clear sound is heard. The sound slowly will increase in intensity.

(7) Continue to deflate cuff gradually, noting point at which sound disappears in adults. Note pressure to nearest 2 mm Hg. Listen for 20 to 30 mm Hg after the last sound and then allow remaining air to escape quickly.

14. Remove cuff from extremity unless measurement must be repeated. If this is the first assessment of client, repeat procedure on the other extremity.

15. Assist client in returning to comfortable position and cover upper arm if previously clothed.

16. Discuss findings with client as needed.

17. Wash hands.

18. Compare reading with previous baseline and/or acceptable value of blood pressure for client's age.

19. Compare blood pressure in both arms or both legs.

20. Correlate blood pressure with data obtained from pulse assessment and related cardiovascular signs and symptoms.

21. Inform client of value and need for periodic reassessment.

22. Record blood pressure in client's record.

23. Report abnormal findings to nurse in charge or physician.

Name_____ Date_____ Instructor's Name_____

Performance Checklist: Skill 11-4

Assessing Respiration

	S	U	NP	Comments
1. Determine need to assess client's respiration.	___	___	___	_____
2. Assess pertinent laboratory values.	___	___	___	_____
3. Determine previous baseline respiratory rate (if available) from client's record.	___	___	___	_____
4. Be sure client is in comfortable position, preferably sitting or lying with the head of the bed elevated 45 to 60 degrees.	___	___	___	_____
5. Draw curtain around bed and/or close door. Wash hands.	___	___	___	_____
6. Be sure client's chest is visible. If necessary, move bed linen or gown.	___	___	___	_____
7. Place client's arm in relaxed position across the abdomen or lower chest, or place your hand directly over client's upper abdomen.	___	___	___	_____
8. Observe complete respiratory cycle (one inspiration and one expiration).	___	___	___	_____
9. After cycle is observed, look at watch's second hand and begin to count rate.	___	___	___	_____
10. If rhythm is regular, count number of respirations in 30 seconds and multiply by 2. If rhythm is irregular, less than 12, or greater than 20, count for 1 full minute.	___	___	___	_____
11. Note depth of respirations.	___	___	___	_____
12. Note rhythm of ventilatory cycle.	___	___	___	_____
13. Replace bed linen and client's gown.	___	___	___	_____
14. Wash hands.	___	___	___	_____
15. Discuss findings with client as needed.	___	___	___	_____

	S	U	NP	Comments

16. If respiration is assessed for the first time, establish rate, rhythm, and depth as baseline if within normal range.   _____ _____ _____ _____

17. Compare respiration with client's previous baseline and normal rate, rhythm, and depth.   _____ _____ _____ _____

18. Record respiratory rate and character in client's record. Indicate type and amount of oxygen therapy if used by client during assessment.   _____ _____ _____ _____

19. Report abnormal findings to nurse in charge or physician.   _____ _____ _____ _____

Name_____ Date_____ Instructor's Name_____

Performance Checklist: Skill 11-5

Measuring Oxygen Saturation (Pulse Oximetry)

	S	U	NP	Comments
1. Determine need to measure client's oxygen saturation. Review client's record.	___	___	___	_____
2. Assess for factors that normally influence measurement of SpO_2.	___	___	___	_____
3. Determine previous baseline SpO_2 (if available) from client's record.	___	___	___	_____
4. Explain purpose of procedure to client and how oxygen saturation will be measured.	___	___	___	_____
5. Assess site most appropriate for sensor probe placement.	___	___	___	_____
6. Wash hands.	___	___	___	_____
7. Position client comfortably. If finger is chosen as monitoring site, support lower arm.	___	___	___	_____
8. If finger is to be used, remove any fingernail polish with acetone from digit to be assessed.	___	___	___	_____
9. Attach sensor probe to monitoring site.	___	___	___	_____
10. Turn on oximeter by activating power. Observe pulse waveform/intensity display and audible beep. Correlate oximeter pulse rate with client's radial pulse.	___	___	___	_____
11. Leave probe in place until oximeter readout reaches constant value and pulse display reaches full strength during each cardiac cycle. Read SpO_2 on digital display.	___	___	___	_____
12. Verify alarm limits and volume for continuous monitoring.	___	___	___	_____
13. Discuss findings with client as needed.	___	___	___	_____
14. Remove probe and turn oximeter power off.	___	___	___	_____

	S	U	NP	Comments
15. Assist client in returning to comfortable position.	___	___	___	_____
16. Wash hands.	___	___	___	_____
17. Compare SpO_2 readings with client baseline and acceptable values.	___	___	___	_____
18. Correlate SpO_2 with SaO_2 obtained from arterial blood gas measurements if available.	___	___	___	_____
19. Correlate SpO_2 reading with data obtained from respiratory rate, depth, and rhythm assessment.	___	___	___	_____
20. Record SpO_2 value in client's record, indicating type and amount of oxygen therapy used by client during assessment. Also record any signs and symptoms of oxygen desaturation.	___	___	___	_____
21. Report abnormal findings to nurse in charge or physician.	___	___	___	_____
22. Record client's use of continuous or intermittent pulse oximetry. Document use of equipment for third-party payers.	___	___	___	_____

12 Health Assessment and Physical Examination

Case Study

I. You are assigned to assist with physical examinations in the outpatient clinic. On the schedule for today are three clients. One of the clients is a 72-year-old Hispanic woman, another is a 16-year-old female, and the last is a 4-year-old boy.

    a. How can you help each of these clients feel more at ease before and during the physical examination?

Independent Learning Activities

1. Review anatomy and physiology in preparation for the physical examination.

2. Review medical terminology for reporting and documentation of findings.

3. Practice the physical assessment techniques and procedures (e.g. cranial nerve assessment) with peers, family, and friends. Practice using some of the equipment for examination, including a stethoscope, penlight, etc. Think about how findings should be reported and recorded.

Chapter Review

Match the description/definition in Column A with the correct term in Column B.

Column A		Column B	
_____	1. Black, tarlike stools.	a.	Ptosis
_____	2. Fluid accumulation, swelling.	b.	Alopecia
_____	3. Loss of hair.	c.	Edema
_____	4. Drooping of eyelid over the pupil.	d.	Jaundice
_____	5. Tiny, pinpoint red spots on the skin.	e.	Bruit
_____	6. Curvature of the thoracic spine.	f.	Melena
_____	7. Yellow–orange discoloration.	g.	Kyphosis
_____	8. Increased gastrointestinal motility; growling sounds.	h.	Petechiae
_____	9. Blowing, swishing sound in blood vessel.	i.	Nystagmus
_____	10. Abnormal eye movements.	j.	Borborygmi

Complete the following:

11. Identify the basic principles for a complete physical examination.

12. Describe the five purposes for performing physical examinations.

13. Identify the five skills used in physical assessment, and briefly describe each.

14. Explain the use of the following positions for physical examination:
    a. lithotomy

    b. dorsal recumbent

    c. knee-chest

    d. Sims'

    e. lateral recumbent

    f. prone

15. Specify how the environment may be prepared for the physical examination.

16. What information may be obtained during a general survey?

17. What client teaching may be done for the following assessments?
    a. skin

    b. heart

18. Identify which of the pulses is being palpated in each photo.

a.
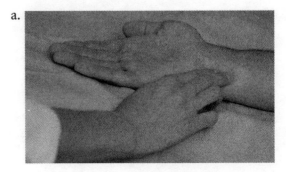

b.

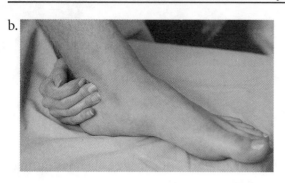

c.

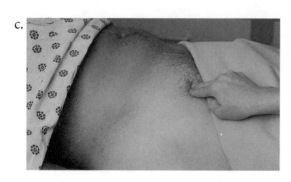

d.

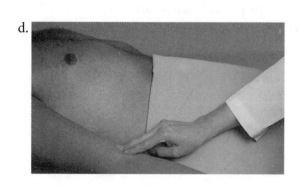

e.

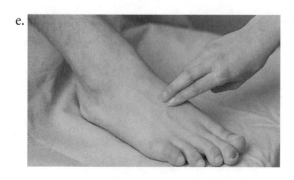

19. Correctly identify the primary skin lesion in each illustration.

a.

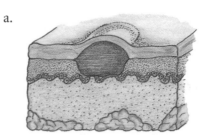

b.

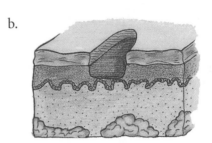

c.

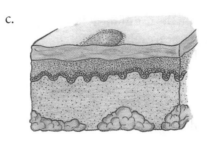

d.

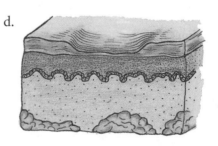

e.

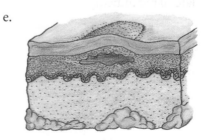

20. Identify on the illustration where the PMI is located.

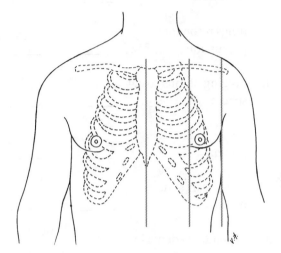

21. Describe at least three common eye and vision problems.

22. What assessment information may be obtained with olfaction?

23. Identify two physical and behavioral findings that may indicate abuse for the following:

	Physical	Behavioral
a. child sexual abuse		
b. domestic abuse		
c. older adult abuse		

24. How can you assess the client's muscle strength in the:
    a. biceps

    b. quadriceps

25. Determine the Glasgow Coma scoring for a client with the following behaviors:
    a. eyes open to pain   _____

    b. makes incomprehensible sounds   _____

    c. demonstrates abnormal flexion of muscles   _____

    SCORE   _____

26. What is the correct procedure for assessment of the patellar reflex?

27. When assessing the abdomen, the correct sequence is:

28. Check whether the following physical assessment findings would be expected or unexpected:

	Expected	Unexpected
a. skin lifts easily and snaps back	___	___
b. erythema noted over bony prominences	___	___
c. hair evenly distributed over scalp and pubic area	___	___
d. brown pigmentation of nails in longitudinal streaks (dark-skinned client)	___	___
e. clubbing of the nails	___	___
f. PEERLA	___	___
g. pupils cloudy	___	___
h. eardrum translucent, shiny, and pearly gray	___	___
i. nasal septum midline	___	___
j. nasal mucosa pale with clear, watery discharge	___	___
k. sinuses tender to touch	___	___
l. teeth chalky white with black discoloration	___	___
m. tongue medium red, moist, and slightly rough on top	___	___
n. soft palate rises when client says "ah"	___	___

	Expected	Unexpected
o. uvula reddened and edematous, tonsils with yellow exudate	___	___
p. thyroid gland small, smooth, and free of nodules	___	___
q. lungs resonant to percussion	___	___
r. bulging of intercostal spaces	___	___
s. no carotid bruit present	___	___
t. extra heart sound noted	___	___
u. dependent edema in ankles	___	___
v. female breasts smooth, symmetric, without retraction	___	___
w. soft, well-differentiated, movable breast lumps noted	___	___
x. bowel sounds active and audible over all four quadrants	___	___
y. rebound tenderness found	___	___
z. perineal skin smooth and slightly darker than surrounding skin	___	___
aa. Bartholin's glands palpable, with discharge expressed	___	___

		Expected	*Unexpected*
bb.	glans penis smooth and pink on all surfaces	_____	_____
cc.	testes smooth and ovoid	_____	_____
dd.	no crepitus found on range of motion	_____	_____
ee.	hips and shoulder aligned parallel	_____	_____
ff.	lordosis of spine noted	_____	_____
gg.	reflexes symmetrical	_____	_____
hh.	able to recall past events, unable to repeat series of five numbers	_____	_____
ii.	able to perform rapidly alternating movements	_____	_____

Select the best answer for each of the following questions:

29. The nurse is assessing the client's nail beds. An expected finding is indicated by:
    1. softening of the nail bed
    2. a concave curve to the nail
    3. brown linear streaks in the nail bed
    4. a 160-degree angle between the nail plate and nail

30. An adolescent female has come to the family planning center for a physical examination. For this client the nurse expects to find that the:
    1. breast tissue is softer than an older woman's breast tissue
    2. nipple projects and the areola has receded

3. areolae are dark and have increased in diameter
4. breasts are elongated and the nipples are smaller and flatter than an older woman's

31. The nurse has checked the medical record and found that the client is experiencing anemia. The presence of anemia is accompanied by the nurse's finding of:
    1. pallor
    2. erythema
    3. jaundice
    4. cyanosis

32. A client with asthma has come to the urgent care center for treatment. On auscultation of the lungs, the nurse hears rhonchi. These sounds are described as:
    1. dry and grating
    2. loud, low-pitched, and coarse
    3. high-pitched, fine, and short
    4. high-pitched and musical

33. The client is admitted to the medical center with a peripheral vascular problem. The nurse is performing the initial assessment of the client. While assessing the lower extremities, the nurse is alert to a venous insufficiency as indicated by:
    1. marked edema
    2. thin, shiny skin
    3. coolness to touch
    4. dusky red coloration

34. The nurse is performing a complete neurological assessment on the client following a cerebral vascular accident (CVA/stroke). To assess cranial nerve III, the nurse:
    1. uses the Snellen chart
    2. lightly touches the cornea with a wisp of cotton
    3. whispers into one ear at a time
    4. measures pupil reaction to light and accommodation

35. Student nurses are practicing the neurological assessment and the determination of cranial nerve functioning. To assess cranial nerve VII, the nurse should ask the client to:
    1. say "ah"
    2. shrug the shoulders
    3. smile and frown
    4. stick out the tongue

36. While completing the physical examination, the nurse assesses and reports that the client has petechiae. The nurse has found:
    1. light perspiration on the skin
    2. moles with regular edges
    3. thickness on the soles of the feet
    4. pinpoint-size, flat, red spot

37. The nurse reviews the chart and sees that the client who has been admitted to the unit this morning has a hyperthyroid disorder. The nurse anticipates that an examination of the eyes will reveal:
    1. diplopia
    2. strabismus
    3. exophthalmos
    4. nystagmus

38. In preparation for an examination of the internal ear, the nurse anticipates that the color of the eardrum should appear:
    1. white
    2. yellow
    3. slightly red
    4. pearly gray

39. A client with a history of smoking and alcohol abuse has come to the clinic for a physical examination. Based on this history, the nurse is particularly alert during an examination of the oral cavity to the presence of:
    1. spongy gums
    2. pink tissue
    3. thick , white patches
    4. loose teeth

40. The client in the physician's office has an increased anteroposterior diameter of the chest. The nurse should inquire specifically about the client's history of:
    1. smoking
    2. thoracic trauma
    3. spinal surgery
    4. exposure to tuberculosis

41. When auscultating the chest the nurse hears what appears to be an S_3 sound. This is an expected finding if the client is:
    1. 10 years old
    2. 35 years old
    3. 56 years old
    4. 82 years old

42. The client in the medical center has been on a prolonged period of bed rest. There is a possibility that the client may have developed phlebitis. The nurse assesses the presence of this by:
    1. palpating the ankles for pitting edema
    2. checking the popliteal pulses bilaterally
    3. inspecting the thighs for clusters of ecchymosis
    4. supporting the leg and dorsiflexing the foot

43. When teaching the 45-year-old client in the gynecologist's office about breast cancer, the nurse includes information on recommendations for screening. The client is informed that a woman at her age should have:
    1. annual mammograms
    2. biannual computerized tomography scans
    3. physician examinations every 3 years
    4. breast self-examination every 3 months

44. The client has been experiencing some lightheadedness and loss of balance over the past few weeks. The nurse wants to check the client's balance while waiting for the client to have other laboratory tests. The nurse administers the:
    1. Allen test
    2. Rinne test

3. Weber test
4. Romberg test

45. Screenings for scoliosis are being conducted at the junior high school. The nurse is observing the students for the presence of:
    1. an S-shaped curvature of the spine
    2. an exaggerated curvature of the thoracic spine
    3. an exaggerated curvature of the lumbar spine
    4. a bulging of the cervical vertebrae and disks

46. While reviewing the medical record, the nurse notes that the client has a suspected pancreatitis. The nurse assesses the client for:
    1. positive rebound tenderness
    2. midline abdominal pulsations
    3. hyperactive bowel sounds to all quadrants
    4. bulging of the flanks with dependent distention

47. An 80-year-old female client is being assessed by the nurse in the extended care facility. The nurse is assessing the genitalia of this client and suspects that there may be a malignancy present. The nurse's suspicion results from the finding of:
    1. scaly, nodular lesions
    2. yellow exudates and redness
    3. small ulcers with serous drainage
    4. extreme pallor and edema

48. A screening for osteoporosis is being conducted at the annual health fair. To determine the risk factors for osteoporosis, the nurse is assessing clients for:
    1. multiparity
    2. a heavier body frame
    3. an African-American background
    4. a history of dieting and/or alcohol abuse

49. A client in the rehabilitation facility has experienced a cerebral vascular accident (CVA/stroke) that has left the client with an expressive aphasia. The nurse anticipates that this client will:
    1. be unable to speak or write
    2. be unable to follow directions
    3. respond inappropriately to questions
    4. have difficulty interpreting words and phrases

Study Group Questions

- What are the purposes of the physical examination?
- How is physical assessment integrated into client care?
- How does the nurse incorporate cultural sensitivity and awareness of ethnic physiological differences into the physical examination?
- What are the physical assessment skills, and what information is obtained through their use?
- How does the nurse prepare the client and environment for the physical examination?
- What similarities and differences exist in the preparation and procedure for a physical examination of a child, adult, and older adult?
- What information is obtained through a general survey?
- What positions and equipment are used for completion of the physical examination?
- What is the usual sequence for performing the physical examination?
- What are the expected and unexpected findings of a complete physical examination?
- What self-screening procedures may be taught to clients?
- How does the nurse report and record the findings of a physical examination?

Study Chart

Create a study chart to compare the Expected vs. Unexpected Findings in a Physical Exam, *working in the sequential order of the examination from the integumentary system through the neurological system.*

Administering Medications 13

Case Studies

I. You are visiting a client at home who has poor eyesight and occasional forgetfulness. The client has four oral medications to take at different times of the day.
   a. What strategies may be implemented to assist this client in maintaining the medication regimen?

II. You are preparing to give medications in the medical center, but the prescriber's handwriting is difficult to read.
   a. What should you do to prevent medication errors?

III. The client in a long-term care facility is about to receive her medications, but you notice that she does not have an identification band.
   a. What is your next action?

IV. You are to administer an injection to a 6-year-old child on a pediatric acute care unit.
   a. What safety measures need to be implemented?

V. You are about to prepare a narcotic medication for administration to your client. You notice that the previous amount was 24 tablets remaining but that now there are only 23 tablets left in the box.
   a. What should you do?

Independent Learning Activities

1. Practice preparing medications in the skills laboratory. At home, practice preparing oral medications for administration using over-the-counter remedies. Maintain aseptic technique.

2. Practice drug calculations for commonly prescribed medications.

3. Review the pharmacological actions and nursing implications for the medications prescribed for your clients.

4. Investigate common food and drug interactions.

5. Apply the critical thinking process to determine the type of information that is necessary to safely administer medications to your clients.

6. Review abbreviations that are used in drug orders, such as bid and prn.

7. Investigate the costs of common brand name and generic drugs at local pharmacies.

Chapter Review

Match the description/definition in Column A with the correct term in Column B.

	Column A		Column B
_____	1. Placing medication under the tongue.	a.	Parenteral administration
_____	2. Two medications combined is greater than each given separately.	b.	Inhalation
_____	3. Unpredictable effect of medications.	c.	Instillation
_____	4. Fluid administered and retained in a body cavity.	d.	Buccal
_____	5. Injection into tissues below the dermis of the skin.	e.	Subcutaneous
_____	6. Inserting medication into the eye.	f.	Intraocular
_____	7. Administering medications through the oral, nasal, or pulmonary passages.	g.	Idiosyncratic reaction
_____	8. Client is taking many medications.	h.	Polypharmacy
_____	9. Placing solid medication against the mucous membranes of the cheek.	i.	Sublingual
_____	10. Injecting medication into body tissues.	j.	Synergistic effect

Complete the following:

11. How is the scope of the nurse's professional responsibility in administering medications defined and controlled?

12. What are the pharmacokinetic factors that are related to drug administration?

13. Specify how each one of the following factors may influence the actions of medications:
    a. genetic

    b. dietary

    c. physiological variables

    d. environmental conditions

    e. psychological variables

14. Briefly define the following:
    a. side effects

    b. toxic effects

    c. anaphylactic reactions

15. Identify the four routes for parenteral administration of medications.

16. Name the seven essential components of a medication order.

17. Identify the common types of medication orders, and briefly define each one.

18. Briefly explain the nurse's role and responsibility in administering medications to clients.

19. Identify the five guidelines or "rights" that the nurse uses for administering medications.

20. What factors must the nurse consider when selecting a needle and syringe for an injection?

21. What are the three principles for mixing medications from two vials?

22. What is the procedure for mixing regular and NPH insulin in one syringe?

23. Identify at least four ways that the nurse may minimize the discomfort of an injection.

24. How should a medication that is irritating to the tissues be injected?

25. Identify the correct angle for each of the following illustrations and the type of injection that is being administered:
a. _____ b. _____ c. _____

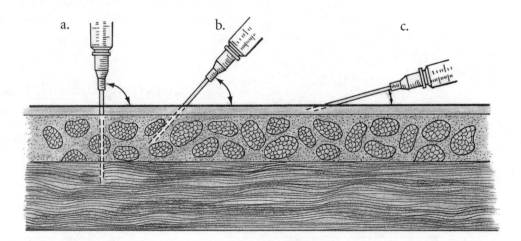

a.   b.   c.

26. Identify three ways in which medication may be administered intravenously.

27. Identify the following math formulas used for drug dosage calculation:
    a. solid or liquid adult medications

    b. pediatric dosages

28. A client is having a mild allergic reaction to a medication. What signs or symptoms most likely will be exhibited by the client?

29. Identify the meaning of the following abbreviations:
    a. ac

    b. bid

    c. prn

    d. q4h

    e. qid

    f. stat

    g. hs

30. What are four types of volume-controlled intravenous (IV) infusions?

31. Calculate the correct dosages for the following medication orders:
    a. Prescriber's order: Synthroid 0.150 mg po qd
       In stock: Scored tablets labeled 75 mcg
       How many tablets should be given?

    b. Prescriber's order: Mellaril 150 mg po bid
       In stock: Mellaril 50 mg/ml
       How much of the medication should be given?

    c. Prescriber's order: Lasix 20 mg IM stat
       In stock: Lasix 10 mg/ml
       How much medication should be given?

    d. Prescriber's order: Aldomet 250 mg po bid
       In stock: Tablets labeled 125 mg
       How many tablets should be given?

    e. Prescriber's order: Demerol 75 mg IM prn
       In stock: Demerol 25 mg/.5 ml
       How much medication should be given?

Mark the amount to be administered on the syringe

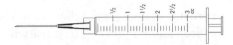

f. Prescriber's order: Regular insulin 24 U
    In stock: Regular insulin U-100
    How much medication should be administered?
    Mark the amount to be administered on the syringe

g. Child's BSA = 1.25 m^2
    Adult dosage is 25 mg
    How much medication should be given to this child?

32. What client assessments should be completed before the administration of:
     a. oral medications

     b. topical medications

     c. parenteral injections

     d. IV medications

33. Identify at least two interventions that should be considered specifically for each of the following age groups when administering medications:
     a. children

b. older adults

34. Identify areas for client teaching related to the administration of medications.

Select the best answer for each of the following questions:

35. The nurse determines the location for an injection by identifying the greater trochanter of the femur, anteriosuperior iliac spine, and iliac crest. The injection site being used by the nurse is the:
     1. rectus femoris
     2. ventrogluteal
     3. dorsogluteal
     4. vastus lateralis

36. On getting the assignment for the evening, the nurse notices that two of the clients have the same name. The best way to identify two clients on a medical unit who have the same name is to:
     1. ask the clients their names
     2. verify their names with the family members
     3. check the clients' ID bands
     4. ask another nurse about their identities

37. The nurse is to administer a subcutaneous injection to an average-size adult. The nurse selects a:
     1. 27-gauge, $^1/_2$-inch needle, and $^1/_2$-cc syringe
     2. 25-gauge, $^5/_8$-inch needle, and 1-cc syringe
     3. 22-gauge, 1-inch needle, and 3-cc syringe
     4. 20-gauge, 1-inch needle, and 3-cc syringe

38. The nurse has administered medications to all of the assigned clients on the medical unit. On assessing the response of the medications given, the nurse is alert to the

possibility of a toxic reaction. This is indicated by the client experiencing:
1. itching
2. nausea
3. dizziness
4. respiratory depression

39. The nursing staff is completing a review of the procedures used for the storage and administration of narcotics. The nurses implement the required procedure when:
1. narcotics are kept along with the client's other medications
2. small amounts of medication may be discarded without notation
3. the narcotic count is checked daily by the medication nurse
4. a separate administration record is kept in addition to the client's MAR

40. An order is written for the client to receive KCl and vitamins intravenously. The nurse goes into the medication room and selects equipment to provide the medication by a(n):
1. IV bolus administration
2. tandem administration
3. piggyback administration
4. large-volume administration

41. While completing the admission assessment, the nurse discovers that the client is allergic to shellfish. Later that morning, the nurse is preparing medications. The nurse will hold the medication for this client that contains:
1. iodine
2. alcohol
3. glucose
4. calcium carbonate

42. A client in the nurse practitioner's office is being given penicillin for the first time. The nurse asks the client to wait in the office following the administration of the medication. The nurse is observing for a possible anaphylactic response that would be demonstrated by:
1. drowsiness
2. pharyngeal edema

3. increased blood pressure
4. decreased respiratory rate

43. An order is written for the client to receive eye medication, 1 gtt OS. The nurse will administer:
1. 1 cc to the right eye
2. 1 drop to the right eye
3. 1 drop to the left eye
4. 1 drop to both eyes

Study Group Questions

- How are medications named and classified, and what forms of medications are available?
- What legislation and standards guide medication administration?
- How are medications absorbed, distributed, metabolized, and excreted from the body?
- What are the different types of medication actions?
- What are the different routes for medication administration, and what are the advantages, disadvantages, and contraindications for each route?
- What are the systems used for drug measurement, and how are amounts converted within and between the systems?
- How are dosages calculated for oral, parenteral, and pediatric medications?
- What are the roles of the health team members in the administration of medications?
- What are the five "rights"?
- What client assessment data are critical to obtain before administering medications?
- What equipment is used for the administration of medications via the different routes?
- What are the sites/landmarks for parenteral administration?
- What are the procedures for administration of medications?
- How can IV medication be administered?
- How is administration of medications adapted to clients of different ages and levels of health?

- What information is included in client/family teaching for medication administration?

Study Chart

Create a study chart to compare Parenteral Medication and Preparation, *identifying the* equipment, needle gauge, amount of medication, site to be used, and angle of injection for subcutaneous, intramuscular, and intradermal injections.

Name_____   Date_____   Instructor's Name_____

Performance Checklist: Skill 13-1

Administering Oral Medications

	S	U	NP	Comments
1. Assess for any contraindications to client receiving oral medication.	___	___	___	_____
2. Assess client's medical history, history of allergies, medication history, and diet history.	___	___	___	_____
3. Gather and review assessment and laboratory data that may influence drug administration.	___	___	___	_____
4. Assess client's knowledge regarding health and medication usage.	___	___	___	_____
5. Assess client's preferences for fluids. Maintain ordered fluid restriction (when applicable).	___	___	___	_____
6. Check accuracy and completeness of each MAR or computer printout with prescriber's written medication order.	___	___	___	_____

7. Prepare medications
    a. Wash hands.
    b. If medication cart is used, move it outside client's room.
    c. Unlock medicine drawer or cart.
    d. Prepare medications for one client at a time. Keep all pages of MARs or computer printouts for one client together.
    e. Select correct drug from stock supply or unit-dose drawer. Compare label of medication with MAR or computer printout.
    f. Check expiration date on all medications.
    g. Calculate drug dose as necessary. Double-check calculation.
    h. When preparing narcotics, check narcotic record for previous drug count and compare with supply available.
    i. To prepare tablets or capsules from a floor stock bottle, pour required number into bottle cap and transfer medication to medication cup. Do not touch

	S	U	NP	Comments

medication with fingers. Return
extra tablets or capsules to bottle.
Medications that need to be broken to
administer half the dosage can be broken,
using a gloved hand, or cut with a
pillating device. Tablets that are to be
broken in half must be prescored.

j. To prepare unit-dose tablets or capsules, _____ _____ _____ _____
place packaged tablet or capsule directly
into medicine cup. (Do not remove
wrapper)

k. All tablets or capsules to be given to client _____ _____ _____ _____
at same time may be placed in one
medicine cup. Medications requiring
preadministration assessments should
be placed in separate cups.

l. If client has difficulty swallowing and _____ _____ _____ _____
liquid medications are not an option, use
a pill-crushing device, such as a mortar
and pestle, to grind pills. If a pill-crushing
device is not available, place tablet
between two medication cups and grind
with a blunt instrument. Mix ground
tablet in small amount of soft food
(e.g., custard, applesauce).

m. To prepare liquids:

(1) Gently shake container. Remove _____ _____ _____ _____
bottle cap from container and place
cap upside down or open the
unit-dose container. If unit-dose
container has correct amount to
administer, no further preparation
is necessary.

(2) Hold bottle with label against palm _____ _____ _____ _____
of hand while pouring.

(3) Hold medication cup at eye level _____ _____ _____ _____
and fill to desired level. Scale should
be even with fluid level at its surface
or base of meniscus, not edges.
Volumes less than 10 ml should be
drawn up in syringe without needle.

(4) Discard any excess liquid into sink. _____ _____ _____ _____
Wipe lip and neck of bottle with
paper towel.

(5) Liquid medications packaged in _____ _____ _____ _____
single-dose cups need not be poured
into medicine cups. They can be
administered directly from the
single-dose cup.

(6) For small doses of liquid medications, _____ _____ _____ _____
draw liquid into a calibrated oral
syringe, with needle attached.

	S	U	NP	Comments
n. Check expiration date on all medications.	___	___	___	_____
o. When preparing narcotics, check narcotic record for previous drug count and compare with supply available.	___	___	___	_____
p. Compare MAR or computer printout with prepared drug and container.	___	___	___	_____
q. Return stock containers or unused unit-dose medications to shelf or drawer, and read label again.	___	___	___	_____
r. Do not leave drugs unattended.	___	___	___	_____

8. Administering medications

	S	U	NP	Comments
a. Take medications to client at correct time.	___	___	___	_____
b. Identify client by comparing name on MAR or computer printout with name on client's identification bracelet. Ask client to state name.	___	___	___	_____
c. Explain purpose of each medication and its action to client. Allow client to ask any questions about drugs.	___	___	___	_____
d. Assist client to sitting position. Use side-lying position if sitting is contraindicated.	___	___	___	_____
e. Administer medication.				
(1) **For tablets:** Client may wish to hold solid medications in hand or cup before placing in mouth.	___	___	___	_____
(2) Offer water or juice to help client swallow medications. Give cold carbonated water if available and not contraindicated.	___	___	___	_____
(3) **For sublingual medications:** Have client place medication under tongue and allow it to dissolve completely. Caution client against swallowing tablet whole.	___	___	___	_____
(4) **For buccal medications:** Have client place medication in mouth against mucous membranes of the cheek until it dissolves. Avoid administering liquids until buccal medication has dissolved.	___	___	___	_____
(5) Caution client against chewing or swallowing lozenges.	___	___	___	_____
(6) **For powdered medications:** Mix with liquids at bedside, and give to client to drink.	___	___	___	_____
(7) Give effervescent powders and tablets immediately after dissolving.	___	___	___	_____
f. If client is unable to hold medications, place medication cup to	___	___	___	_____

	S	U	NP	Comments

the lips and gently introduce each drug into the mouth, one at a time. Do not rush.

g. If tablet or capsule falls to the floor, discard it and repeat preparation.

h. Stay until client has completely swallowed each medication. Ask client to open mouth if uncertain whether medication has been swallowed.

i. For highly acidic medications, offer client nonfat snack if not contraindicated by client's condition.

j. Assist client in returning to comfortable position.

k. Dispose of soiled supplies, and wash hands.

l. Record administration of medication on MAR or computer printout. Return MAR or computer printout to appropriate file for next administration time.

m. Replenish stock such as cups and straws, return cart to medicine room, and clean work area.

9. Evaluate client's response to medications at times that correlate with the medication's onset, peak, and duration.

10. Notify prescriber if client exhibits a toxic effect or allergic reaction or side effects occur. Withhold further doses.

Name_____ Date_____ Instructor's Name_____

Performance Checklist: Skill 13-2

Administering Nasal Instillations

	S	U	NP	Comments
1. For nasal drops, determine which sinus is affected by referring to medical record.	___	___	___	_____
2. Assess client's history of hypertension, heart disease, diabetes mellitus, and hyperthyroidism.	___	___	___	_____
3. Inspect condition of nose and sinuses. Palpate sinuses for tenderness.	___	___	___	_____
4. Assess client's knowledge regarding use of nasal instillations and technique for instillations and willingness to learn self-administration.	___	___	___	_____
5. Check client's identification bracelet, and ask name.	___	___	___	_____
6. Explain procedure to client regarding positioning and sensations to expect.	___	___	___	_____
7. Wash hands. Arrange supplies and medications at bedside. Apply gloves if client has nasal drainage.	___	___	___	_____
8. Instruct client to clear or blow nose gently unless contraindicated.	___	___	___	_____
9. Administer nasal drops				
a. Assist client to supine position and position head properly.	___	___	___	_____
(1) For access to posterior pharynx, tilt client's head backward.	___	___	___	_____
(2) For access to ethmoid or sphenoid sinus, tilt head back over edge of bed or place small pillow under client's shoulder and tilt head back.	___	___	___	_____
(3) For access to frontal or maxillary sinus, tilt head back over edge of bed or pillow with head turned toward side to be treated.	___	___	___	_____

	S	U	NP	Comments

b. Support client's head with nondominant hand.

c. Instruct client to breathe through mouth.

d. Hold dropper 1 cm ($^1/_2$ inch) above nares, and instill prescribed number of drops toward midline of ethmoid bone.

e. Have client remain in supine position 5 minutes.

f. Offer facial tissue to blot runny nose, but caution client against blowing nose for several minutes.

10. Assist client to a comfortable position after drug is absorbed.

11. Dispose of soiled supplies in proper container, and wash hands.

12. Observe client for onset of side effects 15 to 30 minutes after administration.

13. Ask if client is able to breathe through nose after decongestant administration. May be necessary to have client occlude one nostril at a time and breathe deeply.

14. Reinspect condition of nasal passages for swelling or irritation between instillations.

15. Ask client to review risks of overuse of decongestants and methods for administration.

16. Have client demonstrate self-medication with next dose.

17. Record medication administration, and record client's response.

18. Report any unusual systemic effects to nurse in charge or physician.

Name_____ Date_____ Instructor's Name_____

Performance Checklist: Skill 13-3

Administering Ophthalmic Medication

	S	U	NP	Comments
1. Review prescriber's medication order for number of drops and eye to receive medication.	___	___	___	_____
2. Assess condition of external eye structures.	___	___	___	_____
3. Determine whether client has any known allergies to eye medications. Also ask if client has allergy to latex.	___	___	___	_____
4. Determine whether client has any symptoms of visual alterations.	___	___	___	_____
5. Assess client's level of consciousness and ability to follow directions.	___	___	___	_____
6. Assess client's knowledge regarding drug therapy and desire to self-administer medication.	___	___	___	_____
7. Assess client's ability to manipulate and hold equipment necessary for eye medication.	___	___	___	_____
8. Check client's identification bracelet, and ask name.	___	___	___	_____
9. Explain procedure to client before and during procedure.	___	___	___	_____
10. Wash hands and arrange supplies at bedside; apply clean gloves.	___	___	___	_____
11. Ask client to lie supine or sit back in chair with head slightly hyperextended.	___	___	___	_____
12. If crust or drainage is present along eyelid margins or inner canthus, gently wash away. Soak crusts that are dried and difficult to remove by applying a damp wash-cloth or cotton ball over eye for a few minutes. Always wipe clean from inner to outer canthus.	___	___	___	_____

	S	U	NP	Comments

13. Hold cotton ball or clean tissue in nondominant hand on client's cheekbone just below lower eyelid.

14. With tissue or cotton resting below lower lid, gently press downward with thumb or forefinger against bony orbit.

15. Ask client to look at ceiling.

16. Administer ophthalmic medication.
   a. To instill eye drops:
     (1) With dominant hand resting on client's forehead, hold filled medication eye dropper or ophthalmic solution approximately 1 to 2 cm ($^1/_2$ to $^3/_4$ inch) above conjunctival sac.
     (2) Drop prescribed number of medication drops into conjunctival sac.
     (3) If client blinks or closes eye or if drops land on outer lid margins, repeat procedure.
     (4) After instilling drops, ask client to close eye gently.
     (5) When administering drugs that cause systemic effects, apply gentle pressure with your finger and clean tissue on the client's nasolacrimal duct for 30 to 60 seconds.
   b. To instill eye ointment:
     (1) Ask client to look at ceiling.
     (2) Holding ointment applicator above lower lid margin, apply thin stream of ointment evenly along inner edge of lower eyelid on conjunctiva from the inner canthus to outer canthus.
     (3) Have client close eye and roll eye behind closed eyelid.
   c. To administer intraocular disk:
     (1) Application:
       (a) Open package containing the disk. Apply gloves. Gently press your fingertip against the disk so that it adheres to your finger. Position the convex side of the disk on your fingertip.
       (b) With your other hand, gently pull the client's lower eyelid away from the eye. Ask client to look up.

	S	U	NP	Comments
(c) Place the disk in the conjunctival sac so that it floats on the sclera between the iris and lower eyelid.	___	___	___	_____
(d) Pull the client's lower eyelid out and over the disk.	___	___	___	_____
(2) Removal:				
(a) Wash hands, and put on gloves.	___	___	___	_____
(b) Explain procedure to client.	___	___	___	_____
(c) Gently pull down on the client's lower eyelid.	___	___	___	_____
(d) Using your forefinger and thumb of your opposite hand, pinch the disk and lift it out of the client's eye.	___	___	___	_____
17. If excess medication is on eyelid, gently wipe it from inner to outer canthus.	___	___	___	_____
18. If client had eye patch, apply clean one by placing it over affected eye so entire eye is covered. Tape securely without applying pressure to eye.	___	___	___	_____
19. If client receives more than one eye medication to the same eye at the same time, wait at least 5 minutes before administering the next medication.	___	___	___	_____
20. If client receives eye medication to both eyes at the same time, use a different tissue or cotton ball with each eye.	___	___	___	_____
21. Remove gloves, dispose of soiled supplies in proper receptacle, and wash hands.	___	___	___	_____
22. Note client's response to instillation; ask if any discomfort was felt.	___	___	___	_____
23. Observe response to medication by assessing visual changes and noting any side effects.	___	___	___	_____
24. Ask client to discuss drug's purpose, action, side effects, and technique of administration.	___	___	___	_____
25. Have client demonstrate self-administration of next dose.	___	___	___	_____
26. Record drug, administration, and appearance of eye(s).	___	___	___	_____
27. Record and report any undesirable side effects to nurse in charge or physician.	___	___	___	_____

Name_____ Date_____ Instructor's Name_____

Performance Checklist: Skill 13-4

Using Metered-Dose Inhalers

	S	U	NP	Comments
1. Assess client's ability to hold, manipulate, and depress canister and inhaler.	____	____	____	_____
2. Assess client's readiness to learn.	____	____	____	_____
3. Assess client's ability to learn.	____	____	____	_____
4. Assess client's knowledge and understanding of disease and purpose and action of prescribed medications.	____	____	____	_____
5. Determine drug schedule and number of inhalations prescribed for each dose.	____	____	____	_____
6. If previously instructed in self-administration of inhaled medicine, assess client's technique in using an inhaler.	____	____	____	_____
7. Help client into a comfortable position, such as sitting in chair in hospital room or sitting at kitchen table in home.	____	____	____	_____
8. Check client's identification bracelet, and ask name.	____	____	____	_____
9. Explain procedure to client. Be specific if client wishes to self-administer drug. Explain where and how to set up in the home.	____	____	____	_____
10. Provide adequate time for teaching session.	____	____	____	_____
11. Wash hands, and arrange equipment needed.	____	____	____	_____
12. Have client manipulate inhaler, canister, and spacer device. Explain and demonstrate how canister fits into inhaler.	____	____	____	_____
13. Explain what metered dose is, and warn client about overuse of inhaler, including drug side effects.	____	____	____	_____

	S	U	NP	Comments

14. To administer inhaled dose of medication
    (demonstrate steps when possible):
    a. Remove mouthpiece cover from inhaler. ____ ____ ____ _____
    b. Shake inhaler well. ____ ____ ____ _____
    c. Have client take a deep breath and exhale. ____ ____ ____ _____
    d. Instruct the client to position the inhaler ____ ____ ____ _____
       in one of two ways:
       (1) Open lips and place inhaler in ____ ____ ____ _____
           mouth with opening toward back of
           throat.
       (2) Position the device 1 to 2 inches from ____ ____ ____ _____
           the mouth.
    e. With the inhaler properly positioned, ____ ____ ____ _____
       have client hold inhaler with thumb at
       the mouthpiece and the index finger and
       middle finger at the top.
    f. Instruct client to tilt head back slightly, ____ ____ ____ _____
       inhale slowly and deeply through mouth,
       and depress medication canister fully.
    g. Hold breath for approximately 10 seconds. ____ ____ ____ _____
    h. Exhale through pursed lips. ____ ____ ____ _____

15. To administer inhaled dose of medication ____ ____ ____ _____
    using a spacer such as an aerochamber
    (demonstrate when possible):
    a. Remove mouthpiece cover from MDI ____ ____ ____ _____
       and mouthpiece of aerochamber.
    b. Insert MDI into end of aerochamber. ____ ____ ____ _____
    c. Shake inhaler well. ____ ____ ____ _____
    d. Place aerochamber mouthpiece in mouth, ____ ____ ____ _____
       and close lips. Do not insert beyond
       raised lip on mouthpiece. Avoid covering
       small exhalation slots with the lips.
    e. Breathe normally through aerochamber ____ ____ ____ _____
       mouthpiece.
    f. Depress medication canister, spraying ____ ____ ____ _____
       one puff into aerochamber.
    g. Breathe in slowly and fully. ____ ____ ____ _____
    h. Hold full breath for 10 to 15 seconds. ____ ____ ____ _____

16. Instruct client to wait at least 1 minute ____ ____ ____ _____
    between inhalations or as ordered by
    prescriber.

17. Explain that client may feel gagging ____ ____ ____ _____
    sensation in throat caused by droplets of
    medication on pharynx or tongue.

18. Instruct client in removing medication ____ ____ ____ _____
    canister and cleaning inhaler in warm water.

19. Have client explain and demonstrate steps ____ ____ ____ _____
    in use of inhaler.

	S	U	NP	Comments
20. Ask client to explain medication schedule, side effects, and when to call health care provider.	____	____	____	_____
21. Teach client how to determine fullness of canisters, using displacement in water.	____	____	____	_____
22. After medication instillation, assess client's respirations and auscultate lungs.	____	____	____	_____
23. Record client education and client's ability to perform self-administration.	____	____	____	_____

Name_____ Date_____ Instructor's Name_____

Performance Checklist: Skill 13-5

Preparing Injections

	S	U	NP	Comments
1. Check client's name and drug name, dosage, route of administration, and time of administration.	___	___	___	_____
2. Review pertinent information related to medication, including action, purpose, side effects, and nursing implications.	___	___	___	_____
3. Assess client's body build, muscle size, and weight if giving SQ or IM medication.	___	___	___	_____
4. Wash hands and assemble supplies.	___	___	___	_____
5. Check medication order or MAR against label on medication.	___	___	___	_____

6. Prepare medication.
   a. Ampule preparation

	S	U	NP	Comments
(1) Tap top of ampule lightly and quickly with finger until fluid moves from neck of ampule .	___	___	___	_____
(2) Place small gauze pad around neck of ampule.	___	___	___	_____
(3) Snap neck of ampule quickly and firmly away from hands	___	___	___	_____
(4) Draw up medication quickly, using a filter needle long enough to reach bottom of ampule.	___	___	___	_____
(5) Hold ampule upside down, or set it on a flat surface. Insert filter needle into center of ampule opening. Do not allow needle tip or shaft to touch rim of ampule.	___	___	___	_____
(6) Aspirate medication into syringe by gently pulling back on plunger.	___	___	___	_____
(7) Keep needle tip under surface of liquid. Tip ampule to bring all fluid within reach of the needle.	___	___	___	_____
(8) If air bubbles are aspirated, do not expel air into ampule.	___	___	___	_____
(9) To expel excess air bubbles, remove needle from ampule.	___	___	___	_____

	S	U	NP	Comments

Hold syringe with needle pointing
up. Tap side of syringe to cause
bubbles to rise toward needle. Draw
back slightly on plunger, and then
push plunger upward to eject air.
Do not eject fluid.

(10) If syringe contains excess fluid, use
sink for disposal. Hold syringe
vertically with needle tip up and
slanted slightly toward sink. Slowly
eject excess fluid into sink. Recheck
fluid level in syringe by holding it
vertically.

(11) Cover needle with its safety sheath
or cap. Replace filter needle with
regular needle.

b. Vial containing a solution

(1) Remove cap covering top of unused
vial to expose sterile rubber seal. If a
multidose vial has been used before,
cap is removed already. Firmly and
briskly wipe surface of rubber seal
with alcohol swab and allow it to dry.

(2) Pick up syringe and remove needle
cap. Pull back on plunger to draw
amount of air into syringe equivalent
to volume of medication to be
aspirated from vial.

(3) With vial on flat surface, insert tip
of needle through center of rubber
seal. Apply pressure to tip of needle
during insertion.

(4) Inject air into the vial's air space,
holding on to plunger. Hold plunger
with firm pressure; plunger may be
forced backward by air pressure
within the vial.

(5) Invert vial while keeping firm hold
on syringe and plunger. Hold vial
between thumb and middle fingers
of nondominant hand. Grasp end of
syringe barrel and plunger with
thumb and forefinger of dominant
hand to counteract pressure in vial.

(6) Keep tip of needle below fluid level.

(7) Allow air pressure from the vial to
fill syringe gradually with medication.
If necessary, pull back slightly on
plunger to obtain correct amount
of solution.

(8) When desired volume has been
obtained, position needle into vial's

	S	U	NP	Comments

air space; tap side of syringe barrel carefully to dislodge any air bubbles. Eject any air remaining at top of syringe into vial.

    (9) Remove needle from vial by pulling back on barrel of syringe.

  (10) Hold syringe at eye level, at 90-degree angle, to ensure correct volume and absence of air bubbles. Remove any remaining air by tapping barrel to dislodge any air bubbles. Draw back slightly on plunger, then push plunger upward to eject air. Do not eject fluid.

  (11) If medication is to be injected into client's tissue, change needle to appropriate gauge and length according to route of medication.

  (12) For multidose vial, make label that includes date of opening vial and your initials.

  c. Vial containing a powder (reconstituting medications)

    (1) Remove cap covering vial of powdered medication and cap covering vial of proper diluent. Firmly swab both caps with alcohol swab, and allow to dry.

    (2) Draw up diluent into syringe following Steps 6B(2) through 6B(10).

    (3) Insert tip of needle through center of rubber seal of vial of powdered medication. Inject diluent into vial. Remove needle.

    (4) Mix medication thoroughly. Roll in palms. Do not shake.

    (5) Reconstituted medication in vial is ready to be drawn into new syringe. Read label carefully to determine dose after reconstitution.

7. Dispose of soiled supplies. Place broken ampule and/or used vials and used needle in puncture-proof and leak-proof container. Clean work area, and wash hands.

Name_____ Date_____ Instructor's Name_____

Performance Checklist: Skill 13-6

Administering Injections

	S	U	NP	Comments

For all injections:

1. Review physician's medication order for client's name, drug name, dose, time, and route of administration.

2. Assess client's history of allergies and know substances client is allergic to and normal allergic reaction.

3. Check date of expiration for medication vial or ampule.

4. Observe verbal and nonverbal responses toward receiving injection.

5. Assess for contraindications

6. Aseptically prepare correct medication dose from ampule or vial. Check carefully. Be sure all air is expelled.

7. Identify client by checking identification arm band and asking client's name. Compare with MAR.

8. Explain steps of procedure, and tell client injection will cause a slight burning or sting.

9. Close room curtain or door.

10. Wash hands thoroughly and apply clean disposable gloves.

11. Keep sheet or gown draped over body parts not requiring exposure.

12. Select appropriate injection site. Inspect skin surface over sites for bruises, inflammation, or edema.
    a. SQ: Palpate sites for masses or tenderness. Be sure needle is correct size by grasping skinfold at site with thumb and forefinger. Measure fold from top to bottom. Needle should be one-half length.

	S	U	NP	Comments

b. IM: Note integrity and size of muscle, and palpate for tenderness or hardness. Avoid these areas. If injections are given frequently, rotate sites.

c. ID: Note lesions or discolorations of forearm. Select site three or four fingerwidths below antecubital space and one handwidth above wrist. If forearm cannot be used, inspect the upper back.

13. Assist client to comfortable position
    a. SQ: Have client relax arm, leg, or abdomen, depending on site chosen for injection.
    b. IM: Position client depending on site chosen.
    c. ID: Have client extend elbow and support it and forearm on flat surface.
    d. Talk with client about subject of interest.

14. Relocate site using anatomical landmarks.

15. Cleanse site with an antiseptic swab. Apply swab at center of the site and rotate outward in a circular direction for about 5 cm (2 inches).

16. Hold swab or gauze between third and fourth fingers of nondominant hand.

17. Remove needle sheath or cap from needle by pulling it straight off.

18. Hold syringe between thumb and forefinger of dominant hand.
    a. SQ: Hold as dart, palm down.
    b. IM: Hold as dart, palm down.
    c. ID: Hold bevel of needle pointing up.

19. Administer injection.
    a. Subcutaneous
       (1) For average-size client, spread skin tightly across injection site or pinch skin with nondominant hand.
       (2) Inject needle quickly and firmly at 45- to 90-degree angle. Then release skin, if pinched.
       (3) For obese client, pinch skin at site and inject needle at 90-degree angle below tissue fold.
       (4) Inject medication slowly

	S	U	NP	Comments

b. Intramuscular
  (1) Position hand or hands at proper anatomical landmarks and pull skin down with nondominant hand to administer in a Z-track. Inject needle quickly at 90-degree angle into muscle.
  (2) If client's muscle mass is small, grasp body of muscle between thumb and fingers.
  (3) After needle pierces skin, grasp lower end of syringe barrel with nondominant hand to stabilize syringe. Continue to hold skin tightly with nondominant hand. Move dominant hand to end of plunger. Do not move syringe.
  (4) Pull back on plunger 5 to 10 seconds. If no blood appears, inject medication slowly.
  (5) Wait 10 seconds.
c. Intradermal
  (1) With nondominant hand, stretch skin over site with forefinger or thumb.
  (2) With needle almost against client's skin, insert it slowly at a 5- to 15-degree angle until resistance is felt. Then advance needle through epidermis to approximately 3 mm ($^1/_8$ inch) below skin surface. Needle tip can be seen through skin.
  (3) Inject medication slowly. Normally, resistance is felt. If not, needle is too deep; remove and begin again.
  (4) While injecting medication, note that small bleb (approximately 6 mm [$^1/_2$ inch]) resembling mosquito bite appears on skin surface.

20. Withdraw needle while applying alcohol swab or gauze gently over site.

21. Apply gentle pressure. Do not massage site. Apply bandage if needed.

22. Assist client to comfortable position.

23. Discard uncapped needle or needle enclosed in safety shield and attached syringe into puncture- and leak-proof receptacle.

24. Remove disposable gloves and wash hands.

	S	U	NP	Comments

25. Stay with client, and observe for any allergic reactions.

26. Return to room, and ask if client feels any acute pain, burning, numbness, or tingling at injection site.

27. Inspect site, noting any bruising or induration.

28. Observe client's response to medication at times that correlate with the medication's onset, peak, and duration.

29. Ask client to explain purpose and effects of medication.

30. *For ID injections*, use skin pencil and draw circle around perimeter of injection site. Read site within appropriate amount of time, designated by type of medication or skin test given.

31. Correctly record medication administration and client's response.

32. Report any undesirable effects from medication to nurse in charge or physician.

Name_____   Date_____   Instructor's Name_____

Performance Checklist: Skill 13-7

Adding Medications to Intravenous Fluid Containers

	S	U	NP	Comments
1. Check physician's order to determine type of IV solution to use and type of medication and dosage.	___	___	___	_____
2. Collect information necessary to administer drug safely, including action, purpose, side effects, normal dose, time of peak onset, and nursing implications.	___	___	___	_____
3. When more than one medication is to be added to IV solution, assess for compatibility of medications.	___	___	___	_____
4. Assess client's systemic fluid balance.	___	___	___	_____
5. Assess client's history of drug allergies.	___	___	___	_____
6. Assess IV insertion site for signs of infiltration or phlebitis.	___	___	___	_____
7. Assess client's understanding of purpose of drug therapy.	___	___	___	_____
8. Wash hands thoroughly.	___	___	___	_____
9. Assemble supplies in medication room.	___	___	___	_____
10. Prepare prescribed medication from vial or ampule.	___	___	___	_____
11. Add medication to new container (usually done in medication room or at medication cart).				
a. *Solutions in a bag*: Locate medication injection port on plastic IV solution bag.	___	___	___	_____
b. *Solutions in bottles*: Locate injection site on IV solution bottle, which often is covered by a metal or plastic cap.	___	___	___	_____
c. Wipe off port or injection site with alcohol or antiseptic swab.	___	___	___	_____
d. Remove needle cap or sheath from syringe, and insert needle of syringe through center of injection port or site; inject medication.	___	___	___	_____

	S	U	NP	Comments
e. Withdraw syringe from bag or bottle.	___	___	___	_____
f. Mix medication and IV solution by holding bag or bottle and turning it gently end to end.	___	___	___	_____
g. Complete medication label with name and dose of medication, date, time, and your initials. Stick it on bottle or bag. *Optional (check institution's policy): Apply a flow strip that identifies the time the solution was hung and intervals indicating fluid levels.*				
12. Bring assembled items to client's bedside.	___	___	___	_____
13. Identify client by reading identification band and asking name. Compare with MAR.	___	___	___	_____
14. Prepare client by explaining that medication is to be given through existing IV line or one to be started. Explain that no discomfort should be felt during drug infusion. Encourage client to report symptoms of discomfort.	___	___	___	_____
15. Regulate infusion at ordered rate.	___	___	___	_____
16. Add medication to existing container.				
a. Check volume of solution remaining in bottle or bag.	___	___	___	_____
b. Close off IV infusion clamp.	___	___	___	_____
c. Wipe off medication injection port with an alcohol or antiseptic swab.	___	___	___	_____
d. Remove needle cap or sheath from syringe, insert syringe needle through injection port, and inject medication.	___	___	___	_____
e. Withdraw syringe from bag or bottle.	___	___	___	_____
f. Lower bag or bottle from IV pole, and gently mix. Rehang bag.	___	___	___	_____
g. Complete medication label, and stick it to bag or bottle.	___	___	___	_____
h. Regulate infusion to desired rate.	___	___	___	_____
17. Properly dispose of equipment and supplies. Do not cap needle of syringe. Specially sheathed needles are discarded as a unit with needle covered.	___	___	___	_____
18. Wash hands.	___	___	___	_____
19. Observe client for signs or symptoms of drug reaction.	___	___	___	_____
20. Observe for signs and symptoms of fluid volume excess.	___	___	___	_____

	S	U	NP	Comments
21. Periodically return to client's room to assess IV insertion site and rate of infusion.	___	___	___	_____
22. Observe for signs or symptoms of IV infiltration.	___	___	___	_____
23. Record solution and medication added to parenteral fluid on appropriate form.	___	___	___	_____
24. Report any side effects to nurse in charge or physician.	___	___	___	_____

Name_____ Date_____ Instructor's Name_____

Performance Checklist: Skill 13-8

Administering Intravenous Medications by Piggyback, Intermittent Intravenous Infusion Sets, and Mini-Infusion Pumps

	S	U	NP	Comments
1. Check physician's order to determine type of IV solution to be used, type of medication, dose, route, and time of administration.	___	___	___	_____
2. Collect information necessary to administer drug safely, including action, purpose, side effects, normal dose, time of peak onset, and nursing implications.	___	___	___	_____
3. Assess compatibility of drug with existing IV solution.	___	___	___	_____
4. Assess patency of client's existing IV infusion line.	___	___	___	_____
5. Assess IV insertion site for signs of infiltration or phlebitis: redness, pallor, swelling, or tenderness on palpation.	___	___	___	_____
6. Assess client's history of drug allergies.	___	___	___	_____
7. Assess client's understanding of purpose of drug therapy.	___	___	___	_____
8. Assemble supplies at bedside. Prepare client by informing client that medication will be given through IV equipment.	___	___	___	_____
9. Wash hands.	___	___	___	_____
10. Check client's identification by looking at arm band and asking client's name.	___	___	___	_____
11. Explain purpose of medication and side effects to client, and explain that medication is to be given through existing IV line. Encourage client to report symptoms of discomfort at site.	___	___	___	_____

12. Administer infusion.
   a. Piggyback or tandem infusion

	S	U	NP	Comments

(1) Connect infusion tubing to medication bag. Allow solution to fill tubing by opening regulator flow clamp. Once tubing is full, close clamp and cap end of tubing.

(2) Hang piggyback medication bag above level of primary fluid bag. (Hook may be used to lower main bag.) Hang tandem infusion at same level as primary fluid bag.

(3) Connect tubing of piggyback or tandem infusion to appropriate connector on primary infusion line.

    (a) *Stopcock*: Wipe off stopcock port with alcohol swab, and connect tubing. Turn stopcock to open position.

    (b) *Needleless system*: Wipe off needleless port of IV tubing, and insert tip of piggyback or tandem infusion tubing.

    (c) *Needle system*: Connect sterile needle to end of piggyback or tandem infusion tubing, remove cap, cleanse injection port on main IV line, and insert needle through center of port. Secure by taping connection.

(4) Regulate flow rate of medication solution by adjusting regulator clamp.

(5) After medication has infused, check flow regulator on primary infusion.

(6) Regulate main infusion line to desired rate if necessary.

(7) Leave IV piggyback bag and tubing in place for future drug administration or discard in appropriate containers.

b. Mini-infusion administration

(1) Connect prefilled syringe to mini-infusion tubing.

(2) Carefully apply pressure to syringe plunger, allowing tubing to fill with medication.

(3) Place syringe into mini-infusion pump (follow product directions). Be sure syringe is secure.

(4) Connect mini-infusion tubing to main IV line.

    (a) *Stopcock*: Wipe off stopcock port with alcohol swab, and connect tubing. Turn stopcock to open position.

	S	U	NP	Comments

(b) *Needleless system*: Wipe off needleless port of IV tubing, and insert tip of the mini-infusion tubing.

(c) *Needle system*: Connect sterile needle to mini-infusion tubing, remove cap, cleanse injection port on main IV line or saline lock, and insert needle through center of port. Consider placing tape where IV tubing enters port to keep connection secured.

(5) Hang infusion pump with syringe on IV pole alongside main IV bag. Set pump to deliver medication within time recommended. Press button on pump to begin infusion.

(6) After medication has infused, check flow regulator on primary infusion. Regulate main infusion line to desired rate as needed.

  c. Volume-control administration set (e.g., Volutrol)

(1) Prepare medication from vial or ampule.

(2) Fill Volutrol with desired amount of fluid (50 to 100 ml) by opening clamp between Volutrol and main IV bag.

(3) Close clamp, and check to be sure clamp on air vent of Volutrol chamber is open.

(4) Clean injection port on top of Volutrol with antiseptic swab.

(5) Remove needle cap or sheath, and insert syringe needle through port, then inject medication. Gently rotate Volutrol between hands.

(6) Regulate IV infusion rate to allow medication to infuse in time recommended by institutional policy, a pharmacist, or a medication reference manual.

(7) Label Volutrol with name of drug, dosage, total volume including diluent, and time of administration.

(8) Dispose of uncapped needle or needle enclosed in safety shield and syringe in proper container.

13. Observe client for signs of adverse reactions.

	S	U	NP	Comments
14. During infusion, periodically check infusion rate and condition of IV site.	___	___	___	_____
15. Ask client to explain purpose and side effects of medication.	___	___	___	_____
16. Record drug, dose, route, and time administered.	___	___	___	_____
17. Record volume of fluid in medication bag or Volutrol.	___	___	___	_____
18. Report any adverse reactions to nurse in charge or physician.	___	___	___	_____

14 Fluid, Electrolyte, and Acid-Base Balances

Case Studies

I.   The client is taking digoxin and Lasix
    a.   What client teaching is indicated in relation to possible fluid and electrolyte imbalances?

II. You are working with two clients today. One of the clients is unconscious and is experiencing a period of prolonged immobility. The other client has a long history of alcoholism. You are alert to possible alterations in fluid and electrolyte imbalance.
    a.   What specific signs and symptoms may these clients exhibit as a result of their present conditions?

III. An adult male client has come to the outpatient clinic for an examination. During the initial interview, the client tells you that he has smoked 2 $\frac{1}{2}$ packs of cigarettes each day for the last 25 years.
    a.   What physical signs do you anticipate finding because of the client's history?
    b.   What acid-base imbalance is this client most likely to experience?

Independent Learning Activities

1.   Review the basic physiologic principles of fluid, electrolyte, and acid-base regulation in the body.

2.   Investigate the components of fluids that are used regularly for intravenous (IV) therapy.

3.   Investigate equipment that is available for home IV therapy.

4.   Review diagnostic test results for common fluid, electrolyte, and acid-base imbalances.

5.   Research an article in a current nursing journal on nursing interventions for fluid, electrolyte, and acid-base imbalances.

6.   Investigate possible food–drug or drug–drug interactions that may create imbalances.

Chapter Review

Match the description/definition in Column A with the correct term in Column B.

Column A

_____ 1. Positively charged electrolytes.

_____ 2. Having the same osmotic pressure.

_____ 3. Movement of water across a semipermeable membrane.

_____ 4. Ability of a solution to create osmotic pressure.

_____ 5. Movement of molecules from an area of higher concentration to an area of lower concentration.

_____ 6. Negatively charged electrolytes.

_____ 7. Movement of solutes out of a solution with greater hydrostatic pressure.

_____ 8. Number of molecules in a liter of solution.

_____ 9. Having a lower osmotic pressure.

_____ 10. Movement of molecules to an area of higher concentration.

Column B

a. Anions

b. Diffusion

c. Filtration

d. Active transport

e. Cations

f. Isotonic

g. Osmolality

h. Hypotonic

i. Osmosis

j. Osmolarity

Complete the following:

11. Identify the following terms:
    a. all fluids outside of the cell

    b. fluid between the cells and outside the blood vessels

    c. all fluids within the cell

12. Name two major cations and two anions, identify if they are primarily extracellular or intracellular, and indicate their major function(s) in the body.

13. The three types of acid-base regulators within the body are:

14. What two age groups are most susceptible to fluid and acid-base imbalances?

15. Identify whether the following solutions are isotonic, hypertonic, or hypotonic:
    a. dextrose 5% in water (D_5W)

    b. 0.45% sodium chloride (0.45% NS)

    c. 0.9% sodium chloride (0.9% NS)

    d. lactated Ringer's (LR)

    e. dextrose 5% in 0.45% sodium chloride ($D_5/^1/_2$ NS)

16. Identify five major risk factors for fluid, electrolyte, or acid-base imbalances that may be assessed.

17. Give examples of three types of medications that may cause fluid, electrolyte, or acid-base imbalances.

18. Specify two possible nursing diagnoses for clients experiencing fluid, electrolyte, or acid-base imbalances.

19. Describe how the nurse should institute fluid restrictions for a client.

20. Identify the most commonly used sites for an IV infusion.

21. What are some of the complications that may occur with IV therapy, and how can you manage them?

22. What information should be taught to the client and/or family for IV therapy in the home?

23. What are the advantages of the client having a peripherally inserted central catheter (PICC) line?

24. What checks and assessments need to be done before a blood transfusion?

25. The advantages of an autologous blood transfusion are:

26. Identify the electrolyte imbalance that is associated with each of the following test results:
    a. serum sodium level: 125 mEq/L

    b. serum potassium level: 5.8 mEq/L

    c. serum calcium level: 3.7 mEq/L

    d. serum magnesium level: 1.2 mEq/L

27. Calculate the following IV infusion rates:
    a. IV 500 ml D_5W to infuse in 5 hours. Administration set = 15 gtt/ml. How many gtt/min should infuse?

b. IV 1000 ml NS to infuse in 8 hours. Administration set = 10 gtt/ml. How many gtt/min should infuse?

c. IV 200 ml NS to infuse in 4 hours. Administration set = 60 gtt/ml. How many gtt/min should infuse?

d. IV 2L D_5W to infuse in 18 hours. How many ml/hour should be set on the infusion pump?

28. What is TPN, and why is it used?

29. An IV is not infusing properly. Describe how you may "troubleshoot" the problem.

30. For the nursing diagnosis *Fluid Volume, Deficit*, identify a client goal/outcome and possible nursing interventions.

Select the best answer for each of the following questions:

31. The client who is experiencing a gastrointestinal problem has had periods of prolonged vomiting. The nurse is observing the client for signs of a:
1. metabolic acidosis
2. metabolic alkalosis
3. respiratory acidosis
4. respiratory alkalosis

32. The nurse is working with a client who has had emphysema for many years. The nurse believes that the client has an uncompensated respiratory acidosis. This belief is a result of an analysis of the client's blood gas values that reveals:
1. pH = 7.35, $PaCO_2$ = 40, HCO_3^- = 22
2. pH = 7.40, $PaCO_2$ = 45, HCO_3^- = 28
3. pH=7.30, $PaCO_2$ = 50, HCO_3^- = 24
4. pH= 7.45, $PaCO_2$ = 55, HCO_3^- = 18

33. The client has been admitted to the medical center for stabilization of congestive heart failure. The physician has prescribed Lasix (diuretic) for the client. This client should be observed for:
1. diarrhea
2. edema
3. tachycardia
4. hyperactive reflexes

34. The client has a potassium level above the normal value. The nurse anticipates that treatment for this client with hyperkalemia will include:
1. fluid restrictions
2. foods high in potassium
3. administration of diuretics
4. IV infusion of calcium

35. The client has lost a large amount of body fluid. In assessment of this client with hypovolemia (fluid volume deficit), the nurse expects to find:
1. oliguria
2. hypertension
3. periorbital edema
4. neck vein distention

36. The nurse is determining the care that is to be provided to the clients on the medical unit. There are a number of clients who have the potential for a fluid and electrolyte imbalance. A nurse-initiated (independent) intervention for these clients is:
1. administration of IV fluids
2. monitoring of intake and output
3. performance of diagnostic tests
4. dietary replacement of necessary fluids/electrolytes

37. For a client who is experiencing a fluid volume excess, the nurse plans to determine the fluid status. The best way to determine the fluid balance for the client is to:
    1. obtain diagnostic test results
    2. monitor IV fluid intake
    3. weigh the client daily
    4. assess vital signs

38. The client is admitted to the trauma unit following an accident with power tools at home. The client experienced a significant blood loss and required a large infusion of citrated blood. The nurse assesses this client for the development of:
    1. urinary retention
    2. poor skin turgor
    3. increased blood pressure
    4. positive Trousseau's sign

39. The client is experiencing a severe anxiety reaction, and the respiratory rate has increased significantly. Nursing intervention for this client who may develop respiratory alkalosis is:
    1. sitting the client up
    2. providing nasal oxygen
    3. having the client breathe into a paper bag
    4. having the client cough and breathe deeply

40. A client with normal renal function is to be maintained NPO. An IV of 1000 ml D_5W is ordered to infuse over 8 hours. The nurse should:
    1. infuse the IV at a faster rate
    2. add multivitamins to the solution
    3. provide oral fluids as a supplement
    4. question the order for potassium to be added

41. A client with an IV infusion may develop phlebitis. The nurse recognizes this at the IV infusion site as:
    1. pallor
    2. swelling
    3. redness
    4. cyanosis

42. The client has had an IV line inserted. On observation of the IV site, the nurse notes that there is evidence of an infiltration. The nurse should first:
    1. slow the infusion
    2. discontinue the infusion
    3. change the IV bag and tubing
    4. contact the prescriber immediately

43. The nurse is reviewing the hospital policy for maintenance of IV infusions. The guidelines for changing IV tubing (nonblood administration sets) are based on the IV tubing remaining sterile for:
    1. 24 hours
    2. 36 hours
    3. 48 hours
    4. 72 hours

44. The client has just started to receive the blood transfusion. The nurse is performing the client assessment and notes the client has chills and flank pain. The nurse stops the infusion and then:
    1. calls the physician
    2. administers epinephrine
    3. collects a urine specimen
    4. sets up a piggyback IV infusion with 0.9% saline

45. A client who has been admitted with a renal dysfunction is demonstrating signs and symptoms of a fluid volume excess (hypervolemia). On completing the client assessment, the nurse anticipates finding:
    1. poor skin turgor
    2. decreased blood pressure
    3. neck vein distention
    4. increased urine-specific gravity

46. The nurse is assisting the client with a fluid volume deficit to select an optimum replacement fluid. The nurse suggests that the client drink:
    1. tea
    2. milk
    3. coffee
    4. fruit juice

47. A client with congestive heart failure and fluid retention is placed on a fluid restriction of 1000 ml/24 hours. Based on the guidelines for clients with restrictions, the nurse plans to provide, from 7:00 AM to 3:30 PM:
    1. 250 ml
    2. 400 ml
    3. 500 ml
    4. 750 ml

48. The client has come to the orthopedist's office for treatment of osteoporosis. The nurse is explaining to the client some of the possible complications from this disorder that may affect the fluid and electrolyte balance. The nurse informs the client to report:
    1. low back pain
    2. tingling in the fingers
    3. muscle twitching
    4. positive Trousseau's sign

Study Group Questions

- How are body fluids distributed in the body?
- What is the composition of body fluids?
- How do fluids move throughout the body?
- How is the intake of body fluids regulated?
- What are the major electrolytes, and what is their function in the body?
- How is acid-base balance maintained?
- What are the major fluid, electrolyte, and acid-base imbalances and their causes?
- What signs and symptoms will the client exhibit in the presence of a fluid, electrolyte, or acid-base imbalance?

- What diagnostic tests are used to determine the presence of imbalances?
- What information is critical to obtain in a client assessment to determine the presence of a fluid, electrolyte, or acid-base imbalance?
- What health deviations increase a client's susceptibility to an imbalance?
- What nursing interventions should be implemented for clients with various fluid, electrolyte, and acid-base imbalances?
- What information should be included in client/family teaching for prevention of imbalances or restoration of fluid, electrolyte, or acid-base balance?
- What are the nursing responsibilities associated with the initiation and maintenance of IV therapy?
- What are the responsibilities of the nurse for blood transfusions?

Study Charts

Create study charts to compare:

I. *Electrolyte Imbalances and Client Responses,* including etiology, diagnostic test results, client assessment, and nursing interventions for sodium, potassium, calcium, and magnesium.

II. *Acid-Base Imbalances and Client Responses,* including etiology, diagnostic test results, client assessment, and nursing interventions for metabolic acidosis and alkalosis and respiratory acidosis and alkalosis.

Name_____   Date_____   Instructor's Name_____

Performance Checklist: Skill 14-1

Initiating Intravenous Therapy

	S	U	NP	Comments
1. Review physician's order for type and amount of IV fluid and rate of fluid administration.	___	___	___	_____
2. Assess for clinical factors/conditions that will respond to or be affected by IV fluid administration.	___	___	___	_____
3. Assess client's previous or perceived experience with IV therapy and arm placement preference.	___	___	___	_____
4. Obtain information from drug reference books or pharmacist about composition of IV fluids, purposes of administration, potential incompatibilities, and side effects to monitor for.	___	___	___	_____
5. Determine if client is to undergo any planned surgeries or is to receive blood infusion later.	___	___	___	_____
6. Assess for risk factors.	___	___	___	_____
7. Assess laboratory data and client's history of allergies.	___	___	___	_____
8. Prepare client and family by explaining the procedure, its purpose, and what is expected of client. Also explain sensations client is to expect.	___	___	___	_____
9. Assist client to comfortable sitting or supine position with bed raised to nurse's level.	___	___	___	_____
10. Wash hands.	___	___	___	_____
11. Organize equipment on clean, clutter-free bedside stand or over-bed table.	___	___	___	_____
12. Change client's gown to the more easily removed gown with snaps at the shoulder, if available.	___	___	___	_____

	S	U	NP	Comments

13. Open sterile packages using sterile aseptic technique.   _____ _____ _____ _____

14. Prepare IV infusion tubing and solution.
   a. Check IV solution, using five rights of medication administration. Make sure prescribed additives, such as potassium and vitamins, have been added. Check solution for color, clarity, and expiration date. Check bag for leaks, which is best if done before reaching the bedside.   _____ _____ _____ _____
   b. Open infusion set, maintaining sterility of both ends of tubing. Many sets allow for priming of tubing without removal of end cap.   _____ _____ _____ _____
   c. Place roller clamp about 2 to 5 cm (1 to 2 inches) below drip chamber and move roller clamp to "off" position.   _____ _____ _____ _____
   d. Remove protective sheath over IV tubing port on plastic IV solution bag.   _____ _____ _____ _____
   e. Insert infusion set into fluid bag or bottle. Remove protector cap from tubing insertion spike, not touching spike, and insert spike into opening of IV bag. Cleanse rubber stopper on bottled solution with antiseptic, and insert spike into black rubber stopper of IV bottle.   _____ _____ _____ _____
   f. Prime infusion tubing by filling with IV solution:
     (1) Compress drip chamber and release.   _____ _____ _____ _____
     (2) Allow it to fill one-third to one-half full.   _____ _____ _____ _____
   g. Remove protector cap on end of tubing (some tubing can be primed without removal), and slowly release roller clamp to allow fluid to travel from drip chamber through tubing to needle adapter. Return roller clamp to "off" position after tubing is primed (filled with IV fluid).   _____ _____ _____ _____
   h. Be certain tubing is clear of air and air bubbles. To remove small air bubbles, firmly tap IV tubing where air bubbles are located. Check entire length of tubing to ensure that all air bubbles are removed. If multiple port tubing is used, turn ports upside down and tap to fill and remove air.   _____ _____ _____ _____
   i. Replace cap protector on end of infusion tubing.   _____ _____ _____ _____

15. Option: Prepare heparin or normal saline lock for infusion.

	S	U	NP	Comments

a. If a loop or short extension tubing is needed because of an awkward IV site placement, use sterile technique to connect the IV plug to the loop of short extension tubing. ___ ___ ___ _____

b. Inject 1 to 3 ml normal saline through the plug and through the loop or short extension tubing. ___ ___ ___ _____

c. Keep ends sterile until ready to attach to IV device. ___ ___ ___ _____

16. Apply disposable gloves. Eye protection and mask may be worn if splash or spray of blood is possible. ___ ___ ___ _____

17. Identify accessible vein for placement of IV catheter or needle. Apply flat tourniquet around arm above antecubital fossa or 4 to 6 inches (10 to 15 cm) above proposed insertion site. Do not apply tourniquet too tightly to avoid injury or bruising to skin. Check for presence of radial pulse. Try applying tourniquet on top of a thin layer of clothing such as a gown sleeve. ___ ___ ___ _____

18. Select the vein for IV insertion.

a. Use the most distal site in the nondominant arm, if possible. ___ ___ ___ _____

b. Avoid areas that are painful to palpation. ___ ___ ___ _____

c. Select a vein large enough for catheter placement. ___ ___ ___ _____

d. Choose a site that will not interfere with client's activities of daily living (ADLs) or planned procedures. ___ ___ ___ _____

e. Palpate the vein by pressing downward and noting the resilient, soft, bouncy feeling as the pressure is released. Always use the same fingers to palpate. ___ ___ ___ _____

f. If possible, place extremity in dependent position. ___ ___ ___ _____

g. Select well-dilated vein. Methods to foster venous distention include:

(1) Stroking the extremity from distal to proximal below the proposed venipuncture site. ___ ___ ___ _____

(2) Having client alternately open and close the fist. ___ ___ ___ _____

(3) Applying warmth to the extremity for several minutes, for example, with a warm washcloth. ___ ___ ___ _____

h. Avoid sites distal to previous venipuncture site, veins in antecubital fossa or inner wrist, sclerosed or hardened ___ ___ ___ _____

	S	U	NP	Comments

veins, infiltrate site or phlebotic vessels, bruised areas, and areas of venous valves.
  i. Avoid fragile dorsal veins in older adult clients and vessels in an extremity with compromised circulation.

19. Release tourniquet temporarily and carefully. Clip arm hair with scissors.

20. Place needle adapter end of infusion set nearby on sterile gauze or sterile towel.

21. Cleanse insertion site using friction and a circular motion (middle to outward) with antiseptic prep solution; refrain from touching the cleansed site; allow the site to dry for at least 2 minutes (povidone or chlorhexidine) or 60 seconds (alcohol).

22. Place tourniquet 10 to 12 cm (4 to 5 inches) above anticipated insertion site. Check presence of distal pulse.

23. Perform venipuncture. Anchor vein below site by placing thumb over vein and by stretching the skin against the direction of insertion 2 to 3 inches (5 to 7.5 cm) distal to the site. Warn client of a sharp, quick stick.
  a. *Over-the-needle catheter (ONC):* Insert with bevel up at 20- to 30-degree angle slightly distal to actual site of venipuncture in the direction of the vein.
  b. *IV catheter with safety device:* Insert using same position as for ONC.
  c. *Butterfly needle:* Hold needle at 20- to 30-degree angle with bevel up slightly distal to actual site of venipuncture.

24. Look for blood return through flashback chamber of catheter, or tubing of butterfly needle, indicating that needle has entered vein. Lower catheter until almost flush with skin. Advance catheter another $1/4$ inch into vein and then loosen stylet. Continue to hold skin taut and advance catheter into vein until hub rests at venipuncture site. *Do not reinsert the stylet once it is loosened.* (If available, advance the safety device by using push-off tab to thread the catheter.) Advance butterfly needle until hub rests at venipuncture site.

25. Stabilize catheter/needle with one hand and release tourniquet with other. Apply gentle

	S	U	NP	Comments

but firm pressure with index finger of nondominant hand 1 $^1/_4$ inches (3 cm) above the insertion site. Keep a needle stable. Remove the stylet of ONC. Do not recap the stylet. For a safety device, slide the catheter off the stylet while gliding the protective guard over the stylet. A click indicates the device is locked over the stylet. (NOTE: techniques will vary with each IV device.)

26. Quickly connect needle adapter of infusion tubing set or the heparin/saline lock adapter to hub of catheter or butterfly tubing. Do not touch point of entry of needle adapter.

27. *Intermittent infusion:* Hold the sterile heparin/saline lock firmly with nondominant hand. Insert prefilled syringe containing flush solution into injection cap. Flush slowly with flush solution. Withdraw the syringe while still flushing.

28. *Continuous infusion:* Begin infusion by slowly opening the slide clamp or adjusting the roller clamp of the IV tubing.

29. Tape or secure catheter needle (follow agency policy).
    a. Transparent dressing: Secure catheter with non-dominant hand while preparing to apply dressing.
    b. Sterile gauze dressing: Place narrow piece ($^1/_2$ inch) of sterile tape under catheter hub with sticky side up and cross tape over catheter hub. Place tape only on the catheter, never over the insertion site. Secure site to allow easy visual inspection. Avoid applying tape around the arm.

30. Apply sterile dressing over site.
    a. Transparent dressing: Carefully remove adherent backing. Apply one edge of dressing, and then gently smooth remaining dressing over IV site, leaving connection between IV tubing and catheter hub uncovered. Curl a loop of tubing alongside the arm, and place a second piece of tape directly over the tubing, securing the tubing.
    b. Sterile gauze dressing

	S	U	NP	Comments

(1) Fold a 2 × 2 gauze in half and cover with a 1-inch–wide tape extending about an inch from each side. Place under the tubing/catheter hub junction. Curl a loop of tubing alongside the arm, and place a second piece of tape directly over the tubing and padded 2 × 2, securing tubing in two places.

(2) Place 2 × 2 gauze pad over insertion site and catheter hub. Secure all edges with tape. Do not cover connection between IV tubing and catheter hub.

31. For IV fluid administration recheck flow rate to correct drops per minute.

32. Write date and time of IV placement and catheter/needle gauge size on dressing.

33. Dispose of sheathed stylet or other sharps in appropriate sharps container. Discard supplies. Remove gloves and wash hands.

34. Instruct client in how to move about in and out of bed without dislodging IV catheter.

35. Peripheral IV access should be changed every 72 hours (INS, 2000) or per physician orders or more frequently if complications occur. CDC (2001) allows for replacement every 96 hours.

36. When solution has less than 100 ml remaining, present nursing shift should have new solution at client's bedside and slow flow rate.

37. Observe client every 1 to 2 hours.
   a. Check if correct amount of IV solution has infused by looking at time tape on IV bag or by checking infusion pump record.
   b. Count drip rate (if gravity drip) or check rate on infusion pump.
   c. Check patency of IV catheter or needle: Briefly compress cannulated vein proximal to site. Observe for slowing or momentary cessation of IV rate.
   d. Observe client during compression of vessel for signs of discomfort.

	S	U	NP	Comments
e. Inspect insertion site, and note color. Inspect for presence of swelling. Palpate temperature of skin above dressing.	___	___	___	_____
38. Observe client every hour to determine response to therapy.	___	___	___	_____
39. Record IV insertion, type of fluid, insertion site by vessel, flow rate, size, and type of catheter or needle, and when infusion was begun.	___	___	___	_____
40. Record IV infusion and client's response.	___	___	___	_____
41. Report type of fluid, flow rate, status of venipuncture site, amount of fluid remaining in present solution, expected time to hang next IV bag or bottle, and any side effects.	___	___	___	_____

Name_____ Date_____ **Instructor's Name**_____

Performance Checklist: Skill 14-2

Regulating Intravenous Flow Rate

	S	U	NP	Comments
1. Check client's medical record for correct solution and additives. Follow five rights of medication administration.	____	____	____	_____
2. Observe for patency of IV line and catheter or needle.				
a. Open drip regulator, and observe for rapid flow of fluid from solution into drip chamber. Then close drip regulator to prescribed rate.	____	____	____	_____
b. Compress cannulated vein slightly proximal to end of catheter and observe drip chamber.	____	____	____	_____
3. Check client's knowledge of how positioning of IV site affects flow rate.	____	____	____	_____
4. Verify with client how venipuncture site feels; for example, determine if there is pain or burning.	____	____	____	_____
5. Have paper and pencil to calculate flow rate.	____	____	____	_____
6. Know calibration (drop factor) in drops per milliliter (gtt/ml) of infusion set.	____	____	____	_____
7. Select one of the following formulas to calculate flow rate after determining ml/hr.	____	____	____	_____
8. Read physician's orders, and follow five rights for correct solution and proper additives.	____	____	____	_____
9. Intravenous fluids usually are ordered for 24-hour period, indicating how long each liter of fluid should run.	____	____	____	_____
10. Determine hourly rate by dividing volume by hours, for example.	____	____	____	_____
11. Place marked adhesive tape or commercial fluid indicator tape on IV bottle or bag next to volume markings.	____	____	____	_____

	S	U	NP	Comments
12. After hourly rate has been determined, calculate minute rate based on drop factor of infusion set.	___	___	___	_____
13. Determine flow rate by counting drops in drip chamber for 1 minute by watch, then adjust roller clamp to increase or decrease rate of infusion.	___	___	___	_____
14. Follow this procedure for infusion controller or pump:				
a. Place electronic eye on drip chamber below origin of drop and above fluid level in chamber, or consult manufacturer's directions for setup of the infusion. If a controller is used, ensure that IV bag is 36 inches above IV site.	___	___	___	_____
b. IV infusion tubing is placed into chamber of control device in direction of flow. Consult manufacturer's directions for use of pump. Secure portion of tubing through "air in line" alarm system. Turn on pump, and select rate per hour and total volume to be infused. Close door to control chamber.	___	___	___	_____
c. Open drip regulator completely while infusion controller or pump is in use.	___	___	___	_____
d. Monitor infusion rates and IV site for infiltration according to agency policy. Rate of infusion should be checked by watch, even when infusion pump is used.	___	___	___	_____
e. Assess patency of system when alarm sounds.	___	___	___	_____
15. Follow this procedure for a volume-control device:				
a. Place volume-control device between IV bag and insertion spike of infusion set.	___	___	___	_____
b. Place 2 hours' allotment of fluid into device.	___	___	___	_____
c. Assess system at least hourly; add fluid to volume-control device. Regulate flow rate.	___	___	___	_____
16. Monitor IV infusion at least every hour, noting volume of IV fluid infused and rate.	___	___	___	_____
17. Observe client for signs of overhydration or dehydration to determine response to therapy and restoration of fluid and electrolyte balance.	___	___	___	_____

	S	U	NP	Comments
18. Evaluate for signs of infiltration: inflammation at site, clot in catheter, or kink or knot in infusion tubing.	___	___	___	_____
19. Record solution and rate of infusion every 4 hours or according to agency policy.	___	___	___	_____
20. Immediately record any new IV fluid rates.	___	___	___	_____
21. Document use of any electronic infusion device or controlling device and number on that device.	___	___	___	_____
22. Report rate of infusion to nurse in charge or next nurse assigned to care for client.	___	___	___	_____

Name_____ Date_____ Instructor's Name_____

Performance Checklist: Skill 14-3

Changing Intravenous Solution and Infusion Tubing

	S	U	NP	Comments
Changing IV Solution				
1. Check physician's orders for type of fluid and infusion rate.	____	____	____	_____
2. If order is written for keep vein open (KVO) or to keep open (TKO), note date and time when solution was last changed.	____	____	____	_____
3. Determine the compatibility of all IV fluids and additives by consulting appropriate literature or the pharmacy.	____	____	____	_____
4. Determine client's understanding of need for continued IV therapy.	____	____	____	_____
5. Assess patency of current IV access site.	____	____	____	_____
6. Have next solution prepared at least 1 hour before needed. If prepared in pharmacy, be sure it has been delivered to the client's hospital unit. Check that solution is correct and properly labeled. Check solution expiration date.	____	____	____	_____
7. Check client's identification by checking arm bracelet and asking client to state name.	____	____	____	_____
8. Prepare to change solution when about 50 ml of fluid remains in bottle or bag.	____	____	____	_____
9. Prepare client and family by explaining the procedure, its purpose, and what is expected of client.	____	____	____	_____
10. Be sure drip chamber is at least half full.	____	____	____	_____
11. Wash hands.	____	____	____	_____
12. Prepare new solution for changing. If using plastic bag, remove protective cover from IV tubing port. If using glass bottle, remove metal cap and metal and rubber disks.	____	____	____	_____

	S	U	NP	Comments
13. Move roller clamp to stop flow rate.	——	——	——	————————————
14. Remove old IV fluid container from IV pole.	——	——	——	————————————
15. Quickly remove spike from old solution bag or bottle and, without touching tip, insert spike into new bag or bottle.	——	——	——	————————————
16. Hang new bag or bottle of solution.	——	——	——	————————————
17. Check for air in tubing. If bubbles form, they can be removed by closing the roller clamp, stretching the tubing downward, and tapping the tubing with the finger. For a larger amount of air, insert syringe into a port below the air and aspirate the air into the syringe. Swab port with alcohol and allow to dry before inserting syringe into port. Reduce air in tubing by priming slowly instead of allowing a wide-open flow.	——	——	——	————————————
18. Make sure drip chamber is one-third to one-half full. If the drip chamber is too full, pinch off tubing below the drip chamber, invert the container, squeeze the drip chamber, hang up the bottle, and release the tubing.	——	——	——	————————————
19. Regulate flow to prescribed rate.	——	——	——	————————————
20. Observe client for signs of overhydration or dehydration to determine response to IV fluid therapy.	——	——	——	————————————
21. Observe IV system for patency and development of complications.	——	——	——	————————————

Changing IV Tubing

22. Determine when new infusion set is needed.	——	——	——	————————————
23. Prepare client and family by explaining the procedure, its purpose, and what is expected of client.	——	——	——	————————————
24. Wash hands.	——	——	——	————————————
25. Open new infusion set and connect filter and/or extension tubing, keeping protective coverings over infusion spike and end of tubing.	——	——	——	————————————
26. Apply nonsterile, disposable gloves.	——	——	——	————————————

	S	U	NP	Comments

27. If IV catheter hub or needle is not visible, remove IV dressing. Hold catheter or needle hub securely with nondominant hand. Do not remove tape securing catheter or needle to skin.

28. For IV infusion:
    a. Move roller clamp on new IV tubing to "off" position.
    b. Slow rate of infusion by regulating drip rate on old tubing. Be sure rate is at KVO rate.
    c. With old tubing in place, compress drip chamber and fill chamber.
    d. Remove old tubing from solution and hang or tape drip chamber on IV pole 36 inches above IV pole.
    e. Place insertion spike of new tubing into old solution bag opening and hang solution bag on IV pole.
    f. Compress and release drip chamber on new tubing; slowly fill drip chamber one-third to one-half full.
    g. Slowly open roller clamp, remove protective cap from needle adapter (if necessary), and flush tubing with solution. Replace cap.
    h. Turn roller clamp on old tubing to "off" position.

29. For saline/heparin lock:
    a. If a new loop or short extension tubing is needed because of an awkward IV site placement, use sterile technique to connect the new injection cap to the loop or tubing.
    b. Swab injection cap with alcohol. Insert syringe with 1 to 3 ml saline, and inject through the injection cap into the loop or short extension tubing.

30. Stabilize hub of catheter or needle, and apply pressure over vein just above insertion site. Gently disconnect old tubing. Maintain stability of hub and quickly insert adapter of new tubing or saline lock into hub.

31. Open roller clamp on new tubing. Allow solution to run rapidly for 30 to 60 seconds.

32. Regulate IV drip rate according to physician's orders, and monitor rate hourly.

	S	U	NP	Comments
33. If necessary, apply new dressing. Secure tubing to extremity with tape.	____	____	____	_____
34. Discard old tubing in proper container.	____	____	____	_____
35. Remove and dispose of gloves. Wash hands.	____	____	____	_____
36. Evaluate flow rate and observe connection site for leakage.	____	____	____	_____
37. Observe client for signs of overhydration or dehydration.	____	____	____	_____
38. Record changing of tubing and solution on client's record.	____	____	____	_____
39. Place a piece of tape or preprinted label with the date and time of tubing change and attach to tubing below the level of drip chamber.	____	____	____	_____

Name_____   Date_____   Instructor's Name_____

Performance Checklist: Skill 14-4

Changing a Peripheral Intravenous Dressing

	S	U	NP	Comments
1. Determine when dressing was last changed.	____	____	____	_____
2. Observe present dressing for moisture and intactness.	____	____	____	_____
3. Observe IV system for proper functioning or complications: current flow rate, presence of kinks in infusion tubing or IV catheter. Palpate the catheter site through the intact dressing for subjective complaints of pain or burning.	____	____	____	_____
4. Inspect exposed catheter site for inflammation and swelling.	____	____	____	_____
5. Monitor body temperature.	____	____	____	_____
6. Assess client's understanding of the need for continued IV infusion.	____	____	____	_____
7. Explain procedure and purpose to client and family. Explain that affected extremity must be held still and how long procedure will take.	____	____	____	_____
8. Wash hands. Apply disposable gloves.	____	____	____	_____
9. Remove tape, gauze, and/or transparent dressing from old dressing one layer at a time, leaving tape that secures IV needle or catheter in place. Be cautious if catheter tubing becomes tangled between two layers of dressing. When removing transparent dressing, hold catheter hub and tubing with nondominant hand.	____	____	____	_____
10. Observe insertion site for signs and/or symptoms of infection, namely redness, swelling, and exudate.	____	____	____	_____
11. If infiltration, phlebitis, or clot occur or if ordered by physician, discontinue infusion.	____	____	____	_____

	S	U	NP	Comments

12. If IV is infusing properly, gently remove tape securing needle or catheter. Stabilize needle or catheter with one hand. Use adhesive remover to cleanse skin and remove adhesive residue, if needed.

13. Using friction and circular motion, cleanse peripheral IV insertion site with alcohol, povidone-iodine solution, and/or chlorhexidine, starting at insertion site and working outwards, creating concentric circles. Allow each solution to dry for 2 minutes.

14. Tape or secure catheter.
   a. Applying gauze dressing: Place a narrow piece ($^1/_2$ inch) of tape under hub of catheter with adhesive side up, and cross tape over hub. Place tape only on the catheter, never over the insertion site.
   b. Applying transparent dressing: Secure catheter with nondominant hand while preparing to apply dressing.

15. Apply sterile dressing over site.
   a. Sterile gauze dressing
      (1) Fold a 2×2 gauze in half and cover with a 1-inch–wide piece of tape extending about an inch from each side. Place gauze under the tubing/catheter hub junction. Curl a loop of tubing alongside the arm and place a second piece of tape directly over the padded 2×2, securing tubing in two places.
      (2) Place another 2×2 gauze pad over the venipuncture site and catheter hub. Secure all edges with tape. Do not cover connection between IV tubing and catheter hub.
   b. Transparent dressing
      (1) Carefully remove adherent backing.
      (2) Apply one edge of dressing, and then gently smooth remaining dressing over IV site, leaving end of catheter hub uncovered.

16. Remove and discard gloves.

17. Anchor IV tubing with additional pieces of tape if necessary. When using transparent dressing, avoid placing tape over dressing.

	S	U	NP	Comments
18. Place date and time of dressing change and size and gauge of catheter directly on dressing.	———	———	———	———————————————
19. Discard equipment and wash hands.	———	———	———	———————————————
20. Observe IV flow rate, and compare with rate at time dressing change began.	———	———	———	———————————————
21. Monitor client's body temperature.	———	———	———	———————————————
22. Record and report dressing change and observation of IV system.	———	———	———	———————————————

Caring in Nursing Practice 15

Case Study

I. The daughter of a client in an extended care facility has traveled from another state to visit. When she arrives with her husband and teenage son, she finds that her mother has deteriorated dramatically from the last time she spoke with her. The client, in the terminal stages of liver disease, is now only minimally responsive, with episodes of agitation and disorientation. The family, especially the daughter, is emotionally distraught.
    a. What can be done to demonstrate caring for this client's family?

Independent Learning Activities

1. Reflect on circumstances in your life when you felt that you were cared for and see how they may apply to nurse–client interactions.

2. Research an article in a nursing journal or the writings of a nursing theorist on professional attitudes/beliefs about caring.

Chapter Review

Complete the following:

1. Describe the major concepts in the following theories of caring:
    a. caring is primary

    b. the essence of nursing and health

    c. transpersonal caring

    d. Swanson's theory of caring

2. Identify what clients perceive as caring behaviors by the nurse.

3. For the following nursing behaviors, identify an example of a clinical intervention:
    a. providing presence

    b. comforting

    c. listening

    d. knowing the client

4. Describe how the nurse's work environment may be altered to foster more caring behaviors.

Select the best answer for each of the following questions:

5. The nurse is discussing with her peers how much the client matters to her. She states that she doesn't want the client to suffer. The nurse is implementing the theory described by:
    1. Patricia Benner
    2. Jean Watson
    3. Kristen Swanson
    4. Madeleine Leininger

6. The client was admitted to the hospital to have diagnostic tests to rule out a cancerous lesion in the lungs. The nurse is sitting with the client in the room awaiting the results of the tests. The nurse is demonstrating the caring behavior of:
    1. knowing
    2. comforting
    3. providing presence
    4. maintaining belief

7. The nurse manager would like to promote more opportunities for the staff on the busy unit to demonstrate caring behaviors. The manager elects to implement:
    1. more time off for the staff
    2. a strict schedule for client treatments
    3. staff selection of client assignments
    4. staff appointment to hospital committees

8. The new graduate is looking at theories of caring. He selects Leininger's theory because it fits in the best with his belief system. Leininger defines caring as a(n):
    1. new consciousness and moral idea

2. nurturing way of relating to a valued other
3. central, unifying domain necessary for health and survival
4. improvement in the human condition, using a transcultural perspective

9. The nurse is working with a client who has been admitted to the oncology unit for treatment of a cancerous growth. This nurse is applying Swanson's theory of caring and demonstrating the concept of "maintaining belief" when:
    1. performing the client's dressing changes
    2. providing explanations about the medications
    3. keeping the client draped during the physical exam
    4. discussing how the radiation therapy will assist in decreasing the tumor's size

10. The new graduate is assigned to the surgical unit where there are a large number of procedures to be done during each shift. This nurse demonstrates a caring behavior in this situation by:
    1. avoiding situations that may be uncomfortable or difficult
    2. attempting to do all of the treatments independently and quickly
    3. seeking assistance before performing new or difficult skills
    4. telling the clients that he/she is a new graduate and unfamiliar with all of the procedures

Study Group Questions

- What is "caring" in the nursing profession?
- What are the major theories of caring and the key concepts in each one?
- How is caring perceived by clients?
- What are caring behaviors?
- How can the nurse demonstrate caring to clients and families?

Cultural Diversity 16

Case Study

I. For the following situations, identify how the nurse should approach the client and significant others to recognize cultural concerns and health care needs:
   a. The male client comes from a culture with a matriarchal organization.
   b. Large numbers of family members surround the client on the acute care unit.
   c. Dietary practices prohibit the eating of meat or meat products.
   d. A traditional healer makes calls to the client's home in between the client's visits to the physician.
   e. The client and her family speak another language.

Independent Learning Activities

1. Investigate the demographics of the population in your community and identify cultural/ethnic trends.

2. Look at your own cultural practices and health beliefs.

3. Research an article in a current nursing journal on cultural assessment and nursing intervention.

Chapter Review

Complete the following:

1. Describe the difference between culture and ethnicity.

2. What is transcultural nursing?

3. Identify three strategies that may be used to promote communication with individuals from other cultures.

4. Identify a specific cultural practice and at least two major health problems for:
   a. African Americans

   b. Hispanic Americans

   c. Asian Americans

   d. Native Americans

5. Identify examples of how a cultural health practice may be:
   a. beneficial

   b. neutral

   c. harmful

6. Identify two possible nursing diagnoses that may be related to a client's cultural needs.

7. It is predicted that by 2020 the percentage of people of European origin in North America will increase to 85%.
   True _____ False _____

Select the best answer for each of the following questions:

8. The nurse is seeing clients who are Asian American in the outpatient clinic. A client from this cultural group who demonstrates traditional health practices may use a (n):
   1. herbalist
   2. curandero
   3. root worker
   4. medicine man

9. The nurse recognizes that physiological characteristics of cultural groups may affect overall health and that there may be an increased incidence of particular disease processes within certain groups. In working with Native American Indians, the nurse is alert to the signs and symptoms that may indicate:

   1. cancer of the esophagus
   2. diabetes mellitus
   3. parasites
   4. sickle cell anemia

10. The community center where the nurse volunteers has a culturally diverse population. The nurse wants to promote communication with all of the clients from different cultures. A beneficial technique is for the nurse to:
    1. explain nursing terms that are used
    2. use direct eye contact with all clients
    3. call clients by their first names to establish rapport
    4. try to use ethnic dialects to make the client feel more comfortable

11. The client expresses to the nurse that traditional Western or American practices are used in the home for health promotion. The nurse expects that the client will use:
    1. acupuncture
    2. guided imagery
    3. aromatic therapy
    4. over-the-counter medications

12. The nurse is assessing the client for cultural practices that may influence health care. The nurse finds that the client has an beneficial cultural practice when:
    1. avoiding routine physical exams
    2. placing the child's bed in a positive energy position
    3. wrapping an infant tightly to maintain body warmth
    4. using special herbs and roots to reduce headache pain

Study Group Questions

- What is culture?
- What are the major ethnocultural groups in the country/community, their health and illness beliefs and practices, and their traditional remedies?

- How can the nurse promote communication with individuals from other cultures and/or who speak different languages?
- How can the nurse identify and respond to the client's cultural needs?
- What information may be obtained from a heritage or cultural assessment?

- What nursing approaches may be successful in assisting multicultural clients in health care settings?
- What resources are available to assist the nurse in learning about and working with clients from other cultures?

17 Spiritual Health

Case Study

I. You are working with a client in an acute care facility who practices Buddhism.
   a. What information should be obtained in relation to the client's spiritual practices?
   b. What adaptations may need to be made by the nurse, the other members of the health care team, and the acute care facility to meet the client's spiritual needs?

Independent Learning Activities

1. Explore your own spiritual beliefs and the need for recognition and acceptance of clients' beliefs in nursing practice.

2. Investigate available resources in the health care agency and community to assist clients in meeting spiritual needs.

3. Research a current article in a nursing journal on nursing assessment of and interventions to promote spirituality.

Chapter Review

Complete the following:

1. Identify the difference between spirituality and religion.

2. Describe how spirituality is said to offer a sense of "connectedness."

3. Identify two possible nursing diagnoses relating to spirituality or spiritual health.

4. Identify the health belief practices of at least two different religious sects.

5. Discuss the importance that spirituality may have to older adult clients.

Select the best answer for each of the following questions:

6. A client is admitted to the medical center for surgery to repair a fractured hip. On reviewing the client's admission history, the nurse finds that the client attends religious

services fairly routinely. The nurse supports the client's spiritual needs by stating:
1. "Do you really go to services often?"
2. "Don't worry. God will take care of you."
3. "I'll call your minister and have him stop by to see you."
4. "Is there any way that I may be able to help you with your spiritual needs?"

7. A client who is of the Jewish faith is admitted to the long-term care facility. The nurse seeks to provide support of the usual health practices that are part of this religion. The nurse discovers that the usual Jewish tradition is for:
1. no euthanasia
2. a faith healer to be used
3. refusal of modern medical treatment
4. physical exams to be done only by individuals of the same gender

8. While caring for a client in the intensive care unit, the client has a cardiac arrest. The client is resuscitated successfully. Following this near-death experience, the client is progressing physically but appears withdrawn and concerned. The nurse assists the client by stating:
1. "The experience that you had is easy to explain and understand."
2. "That was a very close call. It must be very frightening for you."
3. "Other people have had similar experiences and worked through their feelings."
4. "If you would like to talk about your experience, I will stay with you."

9. A client has been brought into the emergency department following a traumatic automobile accident. The client needs immediate surgery to repair internal damage. While beginning to prepare the client for surgery, the client whispers to the nurse that he is a Jehovah's Witness. The nurse recognizes that this will influence the care to be provided because individuals of this faith:

1. must receive Last Rites before the surgical procedure
2. must have a religious leader present to oversee the procedure
3. are opposed to the use of blood transfusions
4. bury any body parts that are lost or removed

10. For the client with a diagnosis of a chronic disease, the nurse wishes to support the feelings of hope. The nurse recognizes that hope provides:
1. a meaning and purpose for the client
2. an organized approach to dealing with the disease process
3. a connection to the cultural background of the client
4. a binding relationship with the divine being of the client's religion

11. The nurse is reviewing the plan of care for a 66-year-old home care client who is experiencing the beginning stages of Alzheimer's disease. Several nursing diagnoses have been identified from the initial home visit and assessment. The nurse believes that the client may need to be assessed for spiritual needs based on the diagnosis of:
1. impaired memory
2. altered health maintenance
3. ineffective individual coping
4. altered thought process

Study Group Questions

- What is spirituality, and how does it relate to an individual's health status?
- What are the concepts of spirituality/spiritual health?
- What spiritual or religious problems may arise?
- How can the nurse assess a client's spirituality/spiritual health?

- What is the role of the nurse in promoting spiritual health?
- How can the nurse avoid imposing his/her own beliefs on the client?

- What are the differences and similarities in spiritual practices and health beliefs between the major religious sects?
- How is hope related to spirituality?

Growth and Development 18

Case Studies

I. You have been assigned as a student nurse on an inpatient pediatric unit in a medical center. You have two clients, an infant and a 5 year old.
    a. How will you promote growth and development needs for these two clients in the acute care environment?

II. Your client in the extended care facility is an 86-year-old woman who occasionally is disoriented to time, place, and person.
    a. How will you approach this client to assist her in meeting her developmental needs?

III. You are working as a summer camp nurse with 8- to 10-year-old children. It is your turn to select diversional activities for your group.
    a. What types of games or activities are appropriate for this age group?

IV. You are teaching the parents of adolescents the signs that may indicate a potential suicidal tendency in their children.
    a. What signs/behaviors will you identify for these parents?

V. A middle-adult-aged husband and wife have come to the clinic and want information on the type of health screenings that should be done on a regular basis now that they are both beyond age 40.
    a. What health screenings are recommended for this age group?

Independent Learning Activities

1. Observe individuals of different ages in the community, and identify the differences in behavior.

2. Research an article in a current nursing journal on adaptation of nursing care to meet growth and development needs.

3. Review the theories of growth and development, and select the one that best fits your beliefs.

Chapter Review

Match the description in Column A with the correct theorist in Column B.

	Column A	**Column B**
_____	1. Development of cognition	a. Freud
_____	2. Psychosexual focus	b. Erickson
_____	3. Based on human needs	c. Maslow
_____	4. Moral development	d. Piaget
_____	5. Psychosocial development	e. Kohlberg

Complete the following:

6. Define the following terms:
   a. growth

   b. development

   c. maturation

7. Identify the external forces that influence growth and development.

8. What is the role of "play" for a hospitalized child?

9. For the following age groups, identify at least two physiologic changes, two psychosocial concerns, two health/safety issues, and two strategies for health promotion:

a. infant

b. toddler

c. preschool

d. school-age

e. adolescent

f. young adult

g. middle adult

h. older adult

10. What lifestyle behaviors may influence a client's pregnancy and the development of the fetus?

11. Provide an example of how a developmental skill may be used when teaching a client.

Select the best answer for each of the following questions:

12. You are assigned to prepare a teaching plan for a group of preschool children. For individuals of this age group, the nurse includes:
    1. appropriate use of medications
    2. cooking safety, including use of the stove
    3. information on prevention of obesity and hypertension
    4. guidelines for crossing the street or what to do in case of a fire

13. Children who are admitted to a hospital may experience a great deal of fear regarding the hospitalization. To reduce the fear of school-age children in an acute care environment, the nurse:
    1. restrains them for all assessments and procedures
    2. shows them the equipment that is to be used for procedures
    3. provides in-depth information on how procedures are done
    4. tells them that everything will be all right and that the procedures will not hurt

14. The student nurse is observing children in a day care center during a clinical rotation. The student is asked to assist with the activities for the preschool age children. Children in this age group usually are able to:
    1. make detailed drawings
    2. skip, throw, and catch balls
    3. easily hold a pencil and print letters

4. use a vocabulary of more than 8000 words

15. A parent of an infant asks the nurse what the child should be able to do at the end of the first year. You identify that the infant will be able to accomplish:
    1. participation in simple games, like peek-a-boo
    2. use of symbols to represent objects or people
    3. differentiation of strangers from family members
    4. recognition of his/her own name

16. The parents of a 6-month-old child are asking about the usual activities that can be expected of an infant of this age. The nurse informs the parents that a major milestone in gross motor development for a 6-month-old child is:
    1. banging handheld blocks together
    2. pulling self to a standing position
    3. sitting up independently
    4. crawling on the abdomen

17. The nurse is working with a group of young adults at the community center. There are many discussions about life and health issues. The nurse is aware that a health-related concern of young adults is that:
    1. attachment needs must be enhanced
    2. "labeling" may alter their self-perceptions
    3. development of attitudes about health are forming
    4. fast-paced lifestyles may place them at risk for illnesses or disabilities

18. As part of the assignment in the home health agency, the nurse visits a local senior citizen housing development on a weekly basis. During the visit, the nurse provides information on issues that affect older adults, including how:
    1. cognitive development is limited
    2. depression and stress-related illnesses are common

3. health maintenance programs are important to promote well-being
4. accidents and injuries are the major cause of death in this age group

19. The nurse is seeking to evaluate the effectiveness of teaching provided to the parents of a infant. The nurse determines that the teaching has been successful when the parents:
   1. place small pillows in the infant's crib
   2. position the infant on the stomach for sleeping
   3. purchase a crib with slats that are less than 2 inches apart
   4. prop a bottle up for the infant to suck on while falling asleep

20. When presenting a program for a group of individuals in their middle-adult years, the nurse informs the members to expect the following physical change:
   1. decrease in skin turgor
   2. increased breast size
   3. palpable lateral thyroid lobes
   4. a visual acuity that is greater than 20/50

21. Parents of a 3 $^1/_2$-year-old child are concerned when, following hospitalization, the child begins to suck his thumb again. The child had not sucked his thumb for more than a year. The nurse informs the parents that:
   1. their physician must be informed about this behavior
   2. the child was probably not ready to stop this behavior previously
   3. the child is feeling neglected by his parents and they should spend more time with him
   4. the behavior should be ignored because it is common for the child to regress when anxious

22. An adolescent female has come to the family planning center for information about birth control. The client asks the nurse what she should use to not get pregnant. The nurse responds:
   1. "Are your parents aware of your sexual activity?"
   2. "You've been using some kind of protection before, right?"
   3. "What are your friends doing to protect themselves?"
   4. "What can you tell me about your past sexual experiences?"

23. A client has come to the outpatient obstetric clinic for a routine checkup. The client asks the nurse what is happening with the baby now that she is in her second trimester. The nurse informs the client that:
   1. the heartbeat can be heard
   2. the fingers and toes are well-developed
   3. the organ systems are just beginning to develop
   4. the brain undergoes a tremendous growth spurt

Study Group Questions

- What are the principles of growth and development?
- How can growth and development be influenced both internally and externally?
- What are the differences and similarities of the major developmental theorists?
- How can the nurse apply the different developmental theories to client situations?
- What are the major physical, psychosocial, and cognitive changes that occur throughout the life span?
- What are the specific health needs for each developmental stage?
- How does the approach of the nurse differ for individuals in each stage to meet their developmental needs?

- What are the different teaching/learning needs of each developmental stage?

physical abilities, psychosocial/cognitive activities, and health promotion behaviors and strategies for each age group from infancy to older adulthood.

Study Chart

Create a study chart to compare Growth & Development Across the Life Span, *identifying the*

19 Self-Concept and Sexuality

Case Studies

I.   A 17-year-old male client is admitted to the rehabilitation facility. He was seriously injured during a school football game and now is paraplegic. Although medically stable, it appears that he is having difficulty dealing with his physical limitations. The client speaks frequently about his involvement in athletics and other school-related activities.
   a.   What self-concept and sexuality issues are involved in this situation?
   b.   Formulate a plan of care for this client.

II. A client that you suspect is the victim of sexual abuse has come to the clinic.
   a.   What behaviors may the client exhibit that would lead to this assessment?
   b.   What questions should you ask to get more information from the client about the possible abuse?

Independent Learning Activities

1.   Review the normal anatomy and physiology of the male and female reproductive systems.

2.   Look at the perceptions that you have of your self-concept and sexuality.

3.   Investigate available resources in the community that may assist in promoting self-concept or sexuality.

4.   Observe how the media presents self-concept and sexuality in society.

5.   Research an article in a current nursing journal on specific nursing measures to promote self-concept and/or sexuality.

Chapter Review

Match the description/definition in Column A with the correct term in Column B.

Column A	Column B
_____ 1. Set of conscious and unconscious feelings and beliefs about oneself.	a. Sexuality
_____ 2. Clear, persistent preference for persons of one sex.	b. Self-concept
_____ 3. Emotional evaluation of self-worth.	c. Homophobia
_____ 4. Sense of femaleness or maleness.	d. Self-esteem
_____ 5. Irrational fear of homosexuality.	e. Sexual orientation

Complete the following:

6. Briefly describe the components of self-concept.

7. Identify the general positive influences on and stressors to self-concept.

8. Identify five signs, symptoms, or behaviors that may indicate an altered self-concept.

9. For the following clients, identify the potential concerns related to self-concept and sexuality:
   a. a woman who has had a mastectomy

   b. a woman who is undergoing chemotherapy for cancer who has a young child at home

   c. a 7-year-old child who has been severely burned

   d. A middle-adult-age male who has had a heart attack

10. Specify three ways in which the nurse may promote self-concept in health promotion, acute care, and restorative care settings.

11. Identify four alterations in sexual health.

12. Specify five areas for client teaching that may promote sexual functioning.

13. For the nursing diagnosis *Low self-esteem, situational related to being unable to successfully pass a required college course,* identify a client goal/outcome and nursing interventions.

14. The capacity for sexuality diminishes significantly in older adults.
    True _____ False _____

15. Cultural background does not directly influence self-concept.
    True _____ False _____

Select the best answer for each of the following questions:

16. The nurse recognizes that the developmental stage that is particularly crucial for identity development is the period of:
    1. infancy
    2. preschool
    3. adolescence
    4. middle adulthood

17. An adolescent client has come to the nurse's office in the school to discuss some personal issues. The nurse wishes to determine the sexual health of this adolescent. The nurse begins by asking:
    1. "Do you use contraception?"
    2. "Have you already had sexual relations?"
    3. "Are your parents aware of your sexual activity?"
    4. "Do you have any concerns about sex or your body's development?"

18. During an interview and physical assessment of a female client in the clinic, the nurse finds that the individual has multiple lacerations and bruises and that she has experienced headaches and difficulty sleeping. The nurse suspects:
    1. sexual dysfunction
    2. emotional conflict
    3. sexually transmitted disease
    4. physical and/or sexual abuse

19. The client has come to the family planning center for assistance in selecting a birth control method. She asks the nurse about contraception that requires a prescription. The nurse responds by discussing:
    1. condoms
    2. abstinence
    3. spermicides
    4. birth control pills

20. The client is admitted to the coronary care unit following an acute myocardial infarction. He tells the nurse, "I won't be able to do what I used to at the hardware store." The nurse recognizes that the client is experiencing a problem with the self-concept component of:
    1. role
    2. identity
    3. self-esteem
    4. body image

21. An adolescent client has just been diagnosed with scoliosis and will need to wear a corrective brace. She tells the nurse angrily, "I don't know why I have to have this stupid problem!" The nurse responds:
    1. "Tell me what you do when you get angry and upset."
    2. "Don't be angry. You'll be getting the best care available."
    3. "You'll heal quickly and the brace can come off pretty soon."
    4. "It's okay to be angry around your friends, but try not to be upset around your parents."

22. During an initial assessment at the outpatient clinic, the nurse wants to determine the client's perception of identity. The nurse asks the client:
    1. "What is your usual day like?"
    2. "How would you describe yourself?"
    3. "What activities do you enjoy doing at home?"
    4. "What changes would you make in your personal appearance?"

23. The client has been in the rehabilitation facility for several weeks following a cerebral vascular accident (CVA/stroke). During the hospitalization, the nurse has identified that the client has become progressively more depressed about his physical condition. Although the client is able to, he will not participate in personal grooming and now is refusing any visitors. At this point, the nurse intervenes by:
    1. telling the client to think more positively about the future
    2. helping the client to get washed and dressed everyday
    3. leaving the client to complete activities of daily living independently
    4. contacting a representative of a support group and investigating a psychological consultation with the physician

24. The nurse is working with a client who has had a colostomy. The client asks about resuming a sexual relationship with a partner. The nurse begins by determining:
    1. the client's knowledge about sexual activity

2. how the client has dealt with other life changes in the past
3. the partner's feelings about the colostomy
4. how comfortable the client and the partner are in communicating with each other

Study Group Questions

- What are the components of self-concept?
- What stressors may influence an individual's self-concept?
- How may the nurse promote an individual's self-concept in different health care settings?
- What is sexuality, and how does it develop throughout the life span?
- How can sexual health be defined?
- What are some of the current issues related to sexuality and sexual health?
- How may sexual health be altered?
- What health-related factors may influence sexual function?

- How are self-concept and sexuality related?
- How can the nurse determine an individual's self-concept and sexual health?
- What adaptations may be made by the nurse in approaching different age groups for the assessment and promotion of self-concept and sexual health?
- How can the nurse apply the critical thinking and nursing processes to the areas of self-concept and sexuality?
- What resources are available to assist individuals to promote optimum self-concept and sexual health?
- How can the nurse make the client feel more at ease when completing an assessment of sexual health?

Study Chart

Create a study chart on Stressors Affecting Self-Concept, *identifying how the components of self-concept may be influenced, and listing nursing interventions that may be implemented to promote the client's self-concept.*

20 Family Context in Nursing

Case Study

I. A 65-year-old male has been admitted to the Coronary Care Unit in the medical center. The client experienced a myocardial infarction (heart attack) while working late in his store. His wife, who accompanied him to the medical center, has been both the "homemaker" for the family for more than 25 years and has assisted in the family business run by her husband. They have two children who live on their own. Their son lives with a male roommate in a homosexual relationship, and the daughter, who is younger, is married and has two children. The client and his wife speak readily about the daughter, but they avoid talking about their son.

    a.   What factors related to family roles and function are involved in this situation?
    b.   What stage of the family life cycle is this family in currently?
    c.   What strategies may the nurse use to promote communication in this family?
    d.   How may the role of the client and his wife influence the health education plan?
    e.   Identify a family-oriented nursing diagnosis for this situation.

Independent Learning Activities

1. Look at your own family dynamics, including the roles and relationships of the family members.

2. Investigate available community resources that support family functioning.

3. Practice using the family assessment tool with your peers, friends, and/or family.

Chapter Review

Match the following family stages with the key principle identified for that stage.

	Family Stages		**Key Principles**
_____	1. Single adult	a.	Increasing flexibility of family's boundaries to include children's independence.
_____	2. Newly married couple	b.	Accepting parent–offspring separation.
_____	3. Family with adolescents	c.	Accepting shifting of generational roles.
_____	4. Launching children and moving on	d.	Commitment to a new system.
_____	5. Family in later life	e.	Accepting a multitude of exits from and entries into the family system.

Complete the following:

6. Identify three issues that are facing the family of today.

7. Differentiate between the family as context and the family as client in relation to the primary focus of the nurse.

8. What effects can inadequate functioning have on a family?

9. What are the characteristics that demonstrate "family hardiness"?

10. For the nursing diagnosis *Risk for caregiver role strain related to need to provide care for elderly parent at home*, identify a client/family goal, outcomes, and nursing interventions.

Select the best answer for each of the following questions:

11. The nurse is working with a family where the parents, both previously divorced, have brought a total of three unrelated children together. This type of family structure is classified as:
    1. nuclear

    2. extended
    3. blended
    4. multi-adult

12. The community health nurse has been assigned to work with a client who is being discharged from a psychiatric facility. The nurse recognizes when dealing with families that:
    1. all family members do not need to understand and agree to the plan of care
    2. health behaviors of the family do not influence the health of individual family members
    3. the nurse needs to change the structure of the family to meet the needs of the client
    4. health promotion behaviors need to be tied to the developmental stage of the family

13. Preparation for working with families includes the understanding of the life-cycle stage that the client is experiencing. The nurse is working with a family that is in the "launching children and moving on" stage. It is expected that this family also will need to deal with:
    1. a review of life events
    2. determining career goals
    3. the death of an older parent
    4. development of intimate peer relationships

14. The nurse is working with a family that has been taking care of a parent with Alzheimer's disease for several years in their home. A nursing diagnosis of *Risk for caregiver role strain* is identified. The nurse initially plans for:
    1. respite care
    2. more medication for the parent
    3. placement in a long-term care facility
    4. consultation with a family therapist

15. Following an initial assessment, the nurse determines that this is a healthy family. This assessment is based on the finding that:

1. the family responds passively to stressors
2. change is viewed negatively and strongly resisted
3. the family structure is flexible enough to adapt to crises
4. minimum influence is exerted by the members on their environment

16. A client who has had surgery is going to be discharged tomorrow. The client has a visual deficit and will need dressing changes twice a day. The nurse:
    1. refers the client to a community agency
    2. arranges for a private-duty nurse to take care of the client 24 hours a day
    3. informs the client that the dressing changes will need to be managed independently
    4. investigates the availability of a family member or neighbor who will be able to learn and perform the dressings

17. While working in the community health center, the nurse uses principles of family-centered care. The nurse is concerned with:
    1. caring for the expectant family
    2. strengthening the family unit
    3. providing care outside of the hospital for the family members
    4. promoting the health of the family as a unit and the health of the individual members

Study Group Questions

- What are the attributes of a family?
- What are the different family forms?
- What are the current issues/trends influencing the family of today?
- How does the structure and function of the family influence family relationships?
- How does communication affect family relationships?
- How are the nursing approaches to the family as client and the family as context similar and how are they different?
- How may the critical thinking and nursing processes be applied to family-centered nursing?
- What specific assessments should the nurse make in relation to the family?
- How does the nurse plan for the educational needs of the client within a family?
- What does the nurse need to consider to meet the health needs of clients within families?
- How are psychosocial/cultural factors involved in family processes and the nursing approach to families?
- What resources are available within the health care setting and community to assist and support family functioning?

Stress and Coping 21

Case Study

I. A young-adult female client is getting ready to be married in a few months. She also has had a recent job promotion that requires many additional hours to be spent at work. She is seen in the nurse practitioner's office for vague symptoms.
   a. What possible signs and symptoms may be demonstrated if this client is experiencing a stress reaction?
   b. What relaxation techniques may be presented to this client?

Independent Learning Activities

1. Review your own experiences with and responses to stressors.

2. Practice relaxation/stress reduction techniques to determine the ones that are most beneficial for you.

3. Develop a time-management schedule that includes school, home, and work responsibilities, as appropriate.

Chapter Review

1. Describe the three stages of the general adaptation syndrome (GAS).

2. Identify the different types of stress that may affect an individual.

3. Specify at least five factors that influence an individual's response to stress.

4. Identify at least three indicators of stress for each of the following areas:
   a. cognitive

   b. gastrointestinal

   c. behavior

   d. neuroendocrine

5. Identify the difference between stress and crisis.

6. Provide examples for each of the following factors that may produce stress:
   a. situational

   b. maturational

   c. sociocultural

   d. post-traumatic stress disorder

7. Provide specific examples of work- or job-related stressors.

8. Identify at least three interventions that may be implemented to reduce stressful situations or promote greater resistance to stress.

Select the best answer for each of the following questions:

9. The client has been hospitalized with a serious systemic infection. If the client is in the resistance stage of GAS and moving toward recovery, the nurse expects that the client will demonstrate a:
   1. stabilization of hormone levels

2. greater degree of tissue damage
3. reduction in cardiac output
4. greater involvement of the sympathetic nervous system

10. While working in the psychiatric emergency room, the nurse is alert to clients who are having severe difficulty in coping. A priority for the nurse is the safety of the client and others, so the nurse asks clients:
    1. "How can we help you?"
    2. "Are you thinking of harming yourself?"
    3. "What physical symptoms are you having?"
    4. "What happened that is different in your life?"

11. As a result of the client's health problem, the family is experiencing an economic difficulty and demonstrating signs of crisis. As part of crisis intervention, the nurse:
    1. refers the client for financial assistance
    2. recommends inpatient psychiatric therapy
    3. plans to teach the family about long-term health needs
    4. has the client avoid discussions about personal feelings and emotions

12. A nurse working on the surgical unit notes that the client has been exhibiting nervous behavior the evening before the operation. To assess the degree of stress that the client is experiencing, the nurse asks:
    1. "Would you like me to call your family for you?"
    2. "How dangerous do you think the surgery will be?"
    3. "You seem anxious. Would you like to talk about the surgery?"
    4. "Would you like to speak with another client who has had the procedure already?"

13. An 80-year-old client was admitted to the hospital with a diagnosis of pneumonia. The client is lethargic and not communicating and respirations are extremely labored. The nurse assesses that the client is experiencing the general adaptation stage of:

1. alarm
2. resistance
3. exhaustion
4. reflex response

14. The client has come to the employee support center with complaints of fatigue and general uneasiness. The client believes that there may be a relationship to the increased amount of work that is expected in the job. The nurse recommends initially that the client attempt to reduce or control the stress by:
    1. leaving the job immediately
    2. enrolling in a self-awareness course
    3. seeking the assistance of a psychiatrist
    4. employing relaxation techniques, such as deep breathing

Study Group Questions

- What is stress?
- What theories are associated with stress and stress response?
- How does GAS work?
- How do nursing theorists explain stress and stress response?
- What factors influence the response to stress?
- What assessment data may indicate the presence of a stress reaction?
- How does stress relate to illness?
- What are coping/defense mechanisms, and how may they be used by individuals to deal with stress?
- What is the role of the nurse in reducing or eliminating stress for clients in health promotion, acute care, and restorative care settings?
- What is involved in crisis intervention?
- What are possible relaxation/stress reduction techniques?

22 Loss and Grief

Case Study

I. Mrs. R.'s husband committed suicide, and she is devastated by the event. In anticipation of potential difficulties, the nurse should be alert to a complicated bereavement.
   a. What assessment data may indicate that Mrs. R. is experiencing a complicated period of bereavement?
   b. Identify a possible nursing diagnosis, goal, and nursing intervention for an individual who is determined to be having a complicated bereavement.

Independent Learning Activities

1. Review the Dying Person's Bill of Rights to determine expectations that should be met.

2. Reflect on your own experiences with loss or grief, your reactions, and how you may assist others through the experience.

3. Investigate available resources in the community (e.g., hospice) for clients, families, or significant others experiencing loss and the grieving process.

4. Review the procedure for postmortem care, including cultural and/or religious practices that may influence the procedure.

Chapter Review

Complete the following:

1. Identify the five types of loss.

2. Specify particular circumstances that may affect grief resolution.

3. Provide examples of feelings, cognitions, physical sensations, and behaviors associated with normal grieving.

4. Give an example of how a client and a nurse may experience anticipatory grieving.

5. Specify a nursing intervention for each of the dimensions of hope:

a. affective

b. cognitive

c. behavioral

d. affiliative

e. temporal

f. contextual

6. Identify at least five ways in which the nurse may involve the family or significant others in the care of a dying client.

Select the best answer for each of the following questions:

7. The nurse is working with a client who has been diagnosed with a terminal disease. The client who is moving into Kübler-Ross's bargaining stage of grieving may respond:
   1. "I understand what the diagnosis means, and I know that I may die."
   2. "I would like to be able to make it to my son's wedding in June."
   3. "I think that the diagnostic tests are wrong, and they should be redone."
   4. "I don't think that I can stand to have any more treatments. I just want to feel better."

8. While working with young children in the day care center, the nurse responds to instances that occur in their lives. Toddlers at the center generally experience loss and grief associated with:
   1. anticipatory loss
   2. separation from the parents
   3. changes in physical abilities
   4. developing their identities

9. In the senior citizen center, the nurse is talking with a group of older adults. The recurrent theme associated with loss for this age group is a:
   1. confusion of fact and fantasy
   2. perceived threat to their identity
   3. change in status, role, and lifestyle
   4. determination to re-examine life goals

10. A nurse who has just recently graduated from school is employed on an oncology unit. There are a number of clients who will not improve and will need assistance with dying. The nurse prepares for this experience by:
    1. completing a detailed course on end-of-life issues
    2. controlling his/her emotions about dying clients
    3. experiencing the death of a close family member
    4. identifying his/her own feelings about death and dying

11. The client has had a long illness and now is approaching the end stages of his life. To assist this client to meet his need for self-worth and support during this time, the nurse:
    1. arranges for a grief counselor to visit
    2. leaves the client alone to deal with his life issues
    3. calls the client's family to come and take over the care
    4. plans to visit the client regularly throughout the day

12. The spouse of a client who has just died is having more frequent episodes of headaches

and generalized joint pain. The initial nursing intervention for this individual is to:

1. complete a thorough pain assessment
2. encourage the more frequent use of analgesics
3. sit with the client and encourage discussion of feelings
4. refer the client immediately to a psychologist or grief counselor

13. The client is experiencing a serious illness that may or may not be able to be cured. The nurse promotes hope for this client in the affiliative dimension when:

1. reinforcing realistic goal setting
2. encouraging the development of supportive relationships
3. offering information about the illness and its treatment
4. demonstrating an understanding of the client's strengths

14. A client in the long-term care facility is to receive palliative care measures only during the end stages of a terminal illness. The nurse anticipates that this will include:

1. pain-relief measures
2. emergency surgery
3. pulmonary resuscitation
4. transfer to intensive care if necessary

15. The client comes for outpatient chemotherapy. During this visit, the client tells the nurse that she is experiencing periods of nausea. The nurse promotes client comfort by providing:

1. milk
2. coffee
3. ginger ale
4. orange juice

Study Group Questions

- What is loss and grief?
- What are the different types of loss, and what are possible reactions to these losses?
- What are the differences and similarities between the theories of grief and loss?
- What is anticipatory grief?
- How may the grieving process be influenced by special circumstances?
- How are hope, spirituality, and self-concept related to loss and grieving?
- What behaviors are associated with loss and grieving?
- What resources are available for the client, family, and nurse to assist in the grieving process?
- What principles facilitate mourning?
- How may the nurse apply the critical thinking and nursing processes to the client or family experiencing loss and grieving?
- How are religious and cultural beliefs associated with loss, grief, death, and dying?
- How may the nurse intervene to assist the client or family with loss and the grieving process?
- What is involved in postmortem care?

Study Chart

Create a study chart on Theories of Loss and Grief, *comparing the components of the theories of Kübler-Ross, Bowlby, and Worden and identifying how the client may behave in the different stages.*

Managing Client Care

23

Case Studies

I. You are a nurse working on a busy surgical unit. This evening you have eight postoperative clients assigned to you.
   a. What types of activities could be delegated to a nurse's aide?
   b. What determination do you need to make to safely delegate to the aide?

II. As a nurse on the surgical unit, you will be involved in identifying quality improvement (QI) projects.
   a. What possible areas could be important to the nurses and clients on this unit?

III. A friend tells you that she is interested in becoming a nurse practitioner. She has just started to take general courses at a 4-year university that has a nursing program.
   a. What information can you provide to this individual about the preparation for this career role?

Independent Learning Activities

1. Research an article in a nursing journal on trends in current nursing practice or educational requirements.

2. Think about your own career interests, and investigate what educational preparation and clinical experience are necessary for that path.

3. Consider what the responsibility and accountability is for a nurse practicing in an acute care and long-term care environment.

Chapter Review

1. Identify two challenges for nursing in the future.

2. Describe the different types of nursing care delivery models.

3. Identify the key elements involved in decentralization.

4. What leadership skills are important for nursing students to develop?

5. Discuss the concept of delegation.

6. Identify the Five Rights of Delegation, and provide a clinical example for each one.

7. What should be included in a QI project?

8. Identify the role of the nurse in planning and/or implementing a QI project.

Select the best answer for each of the following questions:

9. In the course of a day, the nurse is responsible for and carries out all of the following interventions. The caring aspect of nursing is specifically evident when the nurse:
   1. documents care accurately
   2. inserts a urinary catheter using sterile technique
   3. coordinates care with other members of the health care team
   4. gets an order for the liquid version of the medication when the client has difficulty swallowing pills

10. The student nurse is working with a client who has begun to have respiratory difficulty. It is the student nurse's responsibility initially to:
    1. call the pharmacy
    2. alert the primary nurse
    3. contact the attending physician
    4. administer the prescribed medication

11. The nursing supervisor is discussing career opportunities with a nursing student. It is discovered that this individual wishes eventually to become a nurse practitioner. The supervisor explains that the nurse needs to complete a(n):
    1. master's degree program
    2. associate degree program
    3. doctoral degree program
    4. baccalaureate degree program

12. The nurses on a medical unit are discussing plans to change the focus of the unit to a primary nursing care model. In this model, the assignment for Nurse A is:
    1. Mrs. J, Mrs. R, and Mrs. T for the length of their stays
    2. to receive reports from the nursing assistant on the care of Mrs. J, Mrs. R, and Mrs. T
    3. side 1 of the unit in cooperation with Nurse B and the nursing assistant
    4. medication administration for all of the clients on the unit, while Nurse B does the physical care with the nursing assistant

13. The nurse in the long-term care facility is delegating care to the nursing assistant. It is appropriate for the nurse to delegate the care of the client who requires:
    1. catheter care
    2. an admission history
    3. oral medications administered
    4. vital sign measurement following episodes of arrhythmias

14. The student nurse is assigned to care for a client in the hospital. While taking the client's vital signs, the student experiences difficulty obtaining the blood pressure after a second attempt. The student should:
    1. keep trying to get the blood pressure
    2. use the closest measurement from the last reading
    3. ask another nurse to obtain the blood pressure measurement
    4. inform the instructor about the difficulty and request assistance

15. A nurse is working with a client who has just returned from surgery. The nurse has never worked with the type of dressing that the client has postoperatively. During an assessment, the nurse notices that the dressing has come loose and has fallen away from the surgical wound. The client tells the nurse, "Oh, you can fix it." The nurse:
    1. asks the client to help replace the dressing
    2. replaces the loosened dressing as best as possible
    3. goes to call the surgeon to come and replace the dressing
    4. covers the wound with a sterile dry dressing until assistance is obtained

16. The nurse has been assigned to work on a very busy medical unit in the hospital. It is important for the nurse to use time management skills. The nurse implements a plan to:
    1. have all of the clients' major needs met in the morning hours
    2. anticipate possible interruptions by therapists and visitors
    3. complete assessments and treatments for each client at different times each day
    4. leave each day totally unstructured to allow for changes in treatments and client assignments

17. The nurses in the medical center have been working together on QI projects. A threshold of 90% has been identified as an outcome indicator. Further review is indicated for a finding of:
    1. waiting time in the clinic decreased by 96%
    2. renal dialysis clients expressing a 95% satisfaction with care
    3. 93% of clients expressing a reduction in postoperative discomfort
    4. infections evident in 92% of clients following urinary catheter insertion

18. When designing a QI program, the indicators that evaluate the way in which nursing care is delivered to clients are identified as:
    1. team indicators
    2. client indicators
    3. process indicators
    4. structure indicators

Study Group Questions

- What are the applications of theoretical models in nursing?
- What are the standards of practice and standards of care?
- How do nurse practice acts influence nursing, including entry into practice, licensure, and role?
- What are the different types of nursing education programs and the preparation of their graduates?
- What does an advanced practice nurse require in education and experience?
- How does the nurse manager function within the health care team?
- How do the different types of nursing care delivery models differ from one another?
- What is QI, and what does it mean to nurses?
- How are the QI processes and results communicated to other members of the health care team?
- What are some of the challenges for nurses and nursing in the future?

24 Exercise and Activity

Case Study

I. You are to be working with Mrs. T., an 80-year-old woman residing in a nursing home. There is conflicting information in the chart about Mrs. T.'s ability to move around independently. You are concerned about meeting Mrs. T.'s needs for proper body mechanics, as well as her safety.
   a. What assessment information is important in meeting these needs with Mrs. T.?
   b. If Mrs. T. is found to not be able to ambulate independently, what nursing interventions should be planned?

Independent Learning Activities

1. Review the anatomy and physiology of the musculoskeletal system.

2. Practice the skills (lifting, positioning, and range of motion) associated with body mechanics with peers and at home with friends or family members.

3. Investigate available community resources where assistive devices, such as canes and crutches, may be borrowed, rented, or purchased.

Chapter Review

Match the description/definition in Column A with the correct term in Column B.

Column A

_____ 1. Awareness of the position of the body and its parts.
_____ 2. Force that occurs in a direction to oppose movement.
_____ 3. Manner or style of walking.
_____ 4. Lying face up.
_____ 5. Movement of the joint in a full circle.
_____ 6. Lying face down.
_____ 7. Movement of the foot where the toes point upward.
_____ 8. Maintenance of optimal body position.
_____ 9. Actions of walking, turning, lifting, or carrying.
_____ 10. Mobility of the joint.

Column B

a. Body mechanics
b. Prone
c. Range of motion
d. Posture
e. Circumduction
f. Dorsal flexion
g. Supine
h. Friction
i. Gait
j. Proprioception

Complete the following:

11. What physiological changes occur in the musculoskeletal system throughout the developmental stages?

12. What factors influence activity tolerance?

13. What does the nurse need to consider before and after client transfers?

14. Identify four specific pathological conditions or events that affect body alignment and mobility.

15. Describe briefly how each of the following devices are used:
    a. hand rolls

    b. hand-wrist splints

    c. trapeze bar

    d. trochanter roll

    e. footboard

16. Describe the correct method for measuring a client for crutches.

17. In the following illustrations, identify the range-of-motion exercises being performed and the primary muscle groups that are involved:

a.

b.
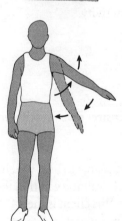

c.
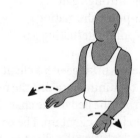

d.

e.

f.

18. Identify a nursing diagnosis associated with a change in a client's ability to maintain physical activity.

Select the best answer for each of the following questions:

19. The client is able to bear weight on one foot. The crutch walking gait that the nurse teaches to this client is the:
    1. two-point gait
    2. swing-through gait
    3. three-point alternating gait
    4. four-point alternating gait

20. The nurse is working with a client who is able only to minimally assist the nurse in moving from the bed to the chair. The nurse needs to help the client up. The correct technique for lifting the client to stand and pivot to the chair is to:
    1. keep the legs straight
    2. maintain a wide base with the feet
    3. keep the stomach muscles loose
    4. support the client away from the body

21. The nurse is assisting the client who is on extended bed rest to perform range-of-motion exercises. The nurse performs the exercises by:
    1. hyperextending the joints
    2. working from proximal to distal joints
    3. flexing the joints beyond where slight resistance is felt
    4. providing support for joints distal to the joint being exercised

22. A client has experienced an injury to his lower extremity. The orthopedist has prescribed the use of crutches and a four-point gait. The nurse instructs the client in using this gait to:
    1. move the right foot forward first
    2. move both crutches forward together
    3. move the right foot and the left crutch together
    4. move the right foot and the right crutch together

23. The client has had a CVA (cerebral vascular accident/stroke) with left hemiparesis. The nurse is instructing the client on the use of a cane for support during ambulation. The nurse instructs the client to:
    1. use the cane on the right side
    2. use the cane on the left side
    3. move the left foot forward first
    4. move the right foot forward first

24. A client is admitted to the rehabilitation facility for physical therapy following an automobile accident. In preparing to conduct an assessment of the client's body alignment, the nurse should begin by:
    1. observing the client's gait
    2. putting the client at ease
    3. determining the level of activity tolerance
    4. evaluating the full extent of joint range of motion

25. A female client with an average body size who resides in the extended care facility requires assistance to ambulate down the hall. The nurse has noticed that the client

has some weakness to her right side. The nurse helps this client ambulate by:

1. standing at her left side and holding her arm
2. standing at her right side and holding her arm
3. standing at her left side and holding one arm around her waist
4. standing at her right side and holding one arm around her waist

26. The client has a cast on the right foot and is being discharged home. Crutches will be used for ambulation, and the client must manage stairs to enter the house and get to the bedroom and bathroom. The nurse evaluates the client's correct technique in using the crutches on the stairs when the client:
    1. advances the crutches first to ascend the stairs
    2. uses one crutch for support while going up and down
    3. uses the banister or wall for support when descending the stairs
    4. advances the affected leg after moving the crutches when descending the stairs

27. The client has had a surgical procedure and is getting up to ambulate for the first time. While ambulating in the hallway, the client complains of severe dizziness. The nurse should first:
    1. call for help
    2. lower the client gently to the floor
    3. lean the client against the wall until the episode passes
    4. support the client and move quickly back to the room

Study Group Questions

- What are body mechanics?
- How is body movement regulated by the musculoskeletal and nervous systems?
- What general changes occur in the body's appearance and function throughout growth and development?
- How may body mechanics be influenced by pathological conditions?
- What client assessment data should be obtained regarding body mechanics?
- What is activity tolerance?
- How may proper body mechanics be promoted for clients in different health care settings?
- What safety measures should be implemented before client transfers and ambulation?
- What are the proper procedures for range of motion, transfers, positioning, and ambulation?
- How should the client be taught to use assistive devices, such as canes, walkers, and crutches?

Study Chart

Create a study chart to describe how to Safely Use Assistive Devices for Ambulation, *identifying the nursing actions and client instruction to reduce possible hazards for the following devices: gait belt, cane, walker, and crutches.*

Name_____   Date_____   Instructor's Name_____

Performance Checklist: Skill 24-1

Moving and Positioning Clients in Bed

	S	U	NP	Comments
1. Assess client's body alignment and comfort level while client is lying down.	____	____	____	_____
2. Assess for risk factors that may contribute to complications of immobility.	____	____	____	_____
3. Assess client's physical ability to help with moving and positioning.	____	____	____	_____
4. Assess physician's orders. Clarify whether any positions are contraindicated because of client's condition.	____	____	____	_____
5. Assess for tubes, incisions, and equipment.	____	____	____	_____
6. Assess ability and motivation of client, family members, and primary caregiver to participate in moving and positioning client in bed in anticipation of discharge to home.	____	____	____	_____
7. Raise level of bed to comfortable working height, and get extra help if needed.	____	____	____	_____
8. Explain procedure to client.	____	____	____	_____
9. Position client flat in bed if tolerated.	____	____	____	_____

10. Keep client aligned.
    a. Move immobile client up in bed (one nurse)

	S	U	NP	Comments
(1) Place client on back with head of bed flat. Stand on one side of bed.	____	____	____	_____
(2) Remove pillow from under head and shoulders, and place pillow at head of bed.	____	____	____	_____
(3) Begin at client's feet. Face foot of bed at 45-degree angle. Place feet apart with foot nearest head of bed behind other foot (forward-backward stance). Flex knees and hips as needed to bring arms level with client's legs. Shift weight from front to back leg,	____	____	____	_____

	S	U	NP	Comments

and slide client's legs diagonally toward head of bed.

(4) Move parallel to client's hips. Flex knees and hips as needed to bring arms level with client's hips.

(5) Slide client's hips diagonally toward head of bed.

(6) Move parallel to client's head and shoulders. Flex knees and hips as needed to bring arms level with client's body.

(7) Slide arm closest to head of bed under client's neck, with hand reaching under and supporting client's opposite shoulder.

(8) Place other arm under client's upper back.

(9) Slide client's trunk, shoulders, head, and neck diagonally toward head of bed.

(10) Elevate side rail. Move to other side of bed, and lower side rail.

(11) Repeat procedure, switching sides until client reaches desired position in bed.

(12) Center client in middle of bed, moving body in same three sections.

b. Assist client in moving up in bed (one or two nurses)

(1) Remove pillow from under head and shoulders, and place pillow at head of bed.

(2) Face head of bed.

   (a) Each nurse should have one arm under client's shoulders and one arm under client's thighs.

   (b) Alternative position: position one nurse at client's upper body. Nurse's arm nearest head of bed should be under client's head and opposite shoulder; other arm should be under client's closest arm and shoulder. Position other nurse at client's lower torso. The nurse's arms should be under client's lower back and torso.

(3) Place feet apart, with foot nearest head of bed behind other foot (forward-backward stance).

	S	U	NP	Comments

(4) When possible, ask client to flex knees with feet flat on bed.

(5) Instruct client to flex neck, tilting chin toward chest.

(6) Instruct client to assist moving by pushing with feet on bed surface.

(7) Flex knees and hips, bringing forearms closer to level of bed.

(8) Instruct client to push with heels and elevate trunk while breathing out, thus moving toward head of bed on count of three.

(9) On count of three, rock and shift weight from front to back leg. At the same time client pushes with heels and elevates trunk.

c. Move immobile client up in bed with drawsheet or pull sheet (two nurses)

(1) Place drawsheet or pull sheet under client, extending from shoulders to thighs; return client to supine position.

(2) Position one nurse at each side of client.

(3) Grasp drawsheet or pull sheet firmly near the client.

(4) Place feet apart with forward-backward stance. Flex knees and hips. Shift weight from front to back leg, and move client and draw-sheet or pull sheet to desired position in bed.

(5) Realign client in correct body alignment.

d. Position client in supported Fowler's position

(1) Elevate head of bed 45 to 60 degrees.

(2) Rest head against mattress or on small pillow.

(3) Use pillows to support arms and hands if client does not have voluntary control or use of hands and arms.

(4) Position pillow at lower back.

(5) Place small pillow or roll under thigh.

(6) Place small pillow or roll under ankles.

e. Position hemiplegic client in supported Fowler's position

(1) Elevate head of bed 45 to 60 degrees.

(2) Position client in sitting position as straight as possible.

	S	U	NP	Comments

(3) Position head on small pillow with chin slightly forward. If client is totally unable to control head movement, hyperextension of the neck must be avoided. Position affected hands.   _____ _____ _____ _____

(4) Flex knees and hips by using pillow or folded blanket under knees.   _____ _____ _____ _____

(5) Support feet in dorsiflexion with firm pillow or footboard.   _____ _____ _____ _____

f. Position client in supine position

   (1) Be sure client is comfortable on back with head of bed flat.   _____ _____ _____ _____

   (2) Place small rolled towel under lumbar area of back.   _____ _____ _____ _____

   (3) Place pillow under upper shoulders, neck, or head.   _____ _____ _____ _____

   (4) Place trochanter rolls or sandbags parallel to lateral surface of client's thighs.   _____ _____ _____ _____

   (5) Place small pillow or roll under ankle to elevate heels.   _____ _____ _____ _____

   (6) Place footboard or firm pillows against bottom of client's feet.   _____ _____ _____ _____

   (7) Place foot splints on client's feet.   _____ _____ _____ _____

   (8) Place pillows under pronated forearms, keeping upper arms parallel to client's body.   _____ _____ _____ _____

   (9) Place hand rolls in client's hands. Consider physical therapy referral for use of hand splints.   _____ _____ _____ _____

g. Position hemiplegic client in supine position

   (1) Place head of bed flat.   _____ _____ _____ _____

   (2) Place folded towel or small pillow under shoulder or affected side.   _____ _____ _____ _____

   (3) Keep affected arm away from body with elbow extended and palm up. (Alternative is to place arm out to side, with elbow bent and hand toward head of bed.)   _____ _____ _____ _____

   (4) Place folded towel under hip of involved side.   _____ _____ _____ _____

   (5) Flex affected knee 30 degrees by supporting it on pillow or folded blanket.   _____ _____ _____ _____

   (6) Support feet with soft pillows at right angle to leg.   _____ _____ _____ _____

	S	U	NP	Comments

h. Position client in prone position
   (1) Roll client over arm positioned close to body, with elbow straight and hand under hip. Position on abdomen in center of bed.
   (2) Turn client's head to one side and support head with small pillow.
   (3) Place small pillow under client's abdomen below level of diaphragm.
   (4) Support arms in flexed position level at shoulders.
   (5) Support lower legs with pillow to elevate toes.

i. Position hemiplegic client in prone position
   (1) Move client toward unaffected side.
   (2) Roll client onto side.
   (3) Place pillow on client's abdomen.
   (4) Roll client onto abdomen by positioning involved arm close to client's body, with elbow straight and hand under hip. Roll client carefully over arm.
   (5) Turn head toward involved side.
   (6) Position involved arm out to side, with elbow bent, hand toward head of bed, and fingers extended (if possible).
   (7) Flex knees slightly by placing pillow under legs from knees to ankles.
   (8) Keep feet at right angle to legs by using pillow high enough to keep toes off mattress.

j. Position client in lateral (side-lying) position
   (1) Lower head of bed completely or as low as client can tolerate.
   (2) Position client to side of bed.
   (3) Prepare to turn client onto side. Flex client's knee that will not be next to mattress. Place one hand on client's hip and one hand on client's shoulder.
   (4) Roll client onto side toward you.
   (5) Place pillow under client's head and neck.
   (6) Bring shoulder blade forward.
   (7) Position both arms in slightly flexed position. Upper arm is supported by pillow level with shoulder; other arm is supported by mattress.

	S	U	NP	Comments
(8) Place tuck-back pillow behind client's back. (Make by folding pillow lengthwise. Smooth area is slightly tucked under client's back.)	___	___	___	_____
(9) Place pillow under semiflexed upper leg level at hip from groin to foot.	___	___	___	_____
(10) Place sandbag parallel to plantar surface of dependent foot.	___	___	___	_____

k. Position client in Sims' (semiprone) position

	S	U	NP	Comments
(1) Lower head of bed completely.	___	___	___	_____
(2) Be sure client is comfortable in supine position.	___	___	___	_____
(3) Position client in lateral position, lying partially on abdomen.	___	___	___	_____
(4) Place small pillow under client's head.	___	___	___	_____
(5) Place pillow under flexed upper arm, supporting arm level with shoulder.	___	___	___	_____
(6) Place pillow under flexed upper legs, supporting leg level with hip.	___	___	___	_____
(7) Place sandbags parallel to plantar surface of foot.	___	___	___	_____

l. Logrolling the client (three nurses)

	S	U	NP	Comments
(1) Place pillow between client's knees.	___	___	___	_____
(2) Cross client's arms on chest.	___	___	___	_____
(3) Position two nurses on side of bed to which the client will be turned. Position third nurse on the other side of bed.	___	___	___	_____
(4) Fanfold or roll the drawsheet or pull sheet.	___	___	___	_____
(5) Move the client as one unit in a smooth, continuous motion on the count of three.	___	___	___	_____
(6) Nurse on the opposite side of the bed places pillows along the length of the client.	___	___	___	_____
(7) Gently lean the client as a unit back toward the pillows for support.	___	___	___	_____

	S	U	NP	Comments
11. Record each position change, including amount of assistance needed and client's response and tolerance.	___	___	___	_____
12. Record and report any signs of redness in areas such as over bony prominences.	___	___	___	_____

Name_____ Date_____ Instructor's Name_____

Performance Checklist: Skill 24-2

Using Safe and Effective Transfer Techniques

	S	U	NP	Comments
1. Assess client's mobility status, vital signs, and activity tolerance.	____	____	____	_____
2. Assess client's sensory status.	____	____	____	_____
3. Assess client's cognitive status.	____	____	____	_____
4. Assess client's level of motivation.	____	____	____	_____
5. Assess previous mode of transfer (if applicable).	____	____	____	_____
6. Assess client's specific risk of falling when transferred.	____	____	____	_____
7. Assess special transfer equipment needed for home setting. Assess home environment for hazards.	____	____	____	_____
8. Explain procedure to client.	____	____	____	_____
9. Transfer client.				
a. Assist client to sitting position (bed at waist level)				
(1) Place client in supine position.	____	____	____	_____
(2) Face head of bed at a 45-degree angle, and remove pillows.	____	____	____	_____
(3) Place feet apart with foot nearer bed behind other foot, continuing at a 45-degree angle to the head of the bed.	____	____	____	_____
(4) Place hand farther from client under shoulders, supporting client's head and cervical vertebrae.	____	____	____	_____
(5) Place other hand on bed surface.	____	____	____	_____
(6) Raise client to sitting position by shifting weight from front to back leg.	____	____	____	_____
(7) Push against bed using arm that is placed on bed surface.	____	____	____	_____
b. Assist client to sitting position on side of bed with bed in low position				
(1) Turn client to side, facing you on side of bed on which client will be sitting.	____	____	____	_____

	S	U	NP	Comments

(2) With client in supine position, raise head of bed 30 degrees. _____ _____ _____ _____

(3) Stand opposite client's hips. Turn diagonally so you face client and far corner of foot of bed. _____ _____ _____ _____

(4) Place feet apart with foot closer to head of bed in front of other foot. _____ _____ _____ _____

(5) Place arm nearer head of bed under client's shoulders, supporting head and neck. _____ _____ _____ _____

(6) Place other arm over client's thighs. _____ _____ _____ _____

(7) Move client's lower legs and feet over side of bed. Pivot toward rear leg, allowing client's upper legs to swing downward. _____ _____ _____ _____

(8) At same time, shift weight to rear leg and elevate client.

   (a) Remain in front until client regains balance, and continue to provide physical support to weak or cognitively impaired client. _____ _____ _____ _____

c. Transferring client from bed to chair with bed in low position

   (1) Assist client to sitting position on side of bed. Have chair in position at 45-degree angle to bed. _____ _____ _____ _____

   (2) Apply transfer belt or other transfer aids. _____ _____ _____ _____

   (3) Ensure that client has stable nonskid shoes. Weightbearing or strong leg is placed forward, with weak foot back. _____ _____ _____ _____

   (4) Spread feet apart. _____ _____ _____ _____

   (5) Flex hips and knees, aligning knees with client's knees. _____ _____ _____ _____

   (6) Grasp transfer belt from underneath. _____ _____ _____ _____

   (7) Rock client up to standing position on count of three while straightening hips and legs and keeping knees slightly flexed. Unless contraindicated, client may be instructed to use hands to push up if applicable. _____ _____ _____ _____

   (8) Maintain stability of client's weak or paralyzed leg with knee. _____ _____ _____ _____

   (9) Pivot on foot farther from chair. _____ _____ _____ _____

   (10) Instruct client to use armrests on chair for support and ease into chair. _____ _____ _____ _____

   (11) Flex hips and knees while lowering client into chair. _____ _____ _____ _____

	S	U	NP	Comments

(12) Assess client for proper alignment for sitting position. Provide support for paralyzed extremities. Lapboard or sling will support flaccid arm. Stabilize leg with bath blanket or pillow. ____ ____ ____ _____

(13) Praise client's progress, effort, or performance. ____ ____ ____ _____

d. Perform three-person carry from bed to stretcher (bed at stretcher level)

(1) Three nurses stand side by side facing side of client's bed. ____ ____ ____ _____

(2) Each person assumes responsibility for one of three areas: head and shoulders, hips and thighs, and ankles. ____ ____ ____ _____

(3) Each person assumes wide base of support with foot closer to stretcher in front and knees slightly flexed. ____ ____ ____ _____

(4) Arms of lifters are placed under client's head and shoulders, hips and thighs, and ankles, with fingers securely around other side of client's body. ____ ____ ____ _____

(5) Lifters roll client toward their chests. On count of three, client is lifted and held against nurses' chests. ____ ____ ____ _____

(6) On second count of three, nurses step back and pivot toward stretcher, moving forward if needed. ____ ____ ____ _____

(7) Gently lower client onto center of stretcher by flexing knees and hips until elbows are level with edge of stretcher. ____ ____ ____ _____

(8) Assess client's body alignment, place safety straps across body, and raise side rails. ____ ____ ____ _____

e. Use Hoyer (mechanical/hydraulic) lift to transfer client from bed to chair

(1) Bring lift to bedside. ____ ____ ____ _____

(2) Position chair near bed, and allow adequate space to maneuver lift. ____ ____ ____ _____

(3) Raise bed to high position with mattress flat. Lower side rail. ____ ____ ____ _____

(4) Keep bed side rail up on side opposite you. ____ ____ ____ _____

(5) Roll client away from you. ____ ____ ____ _____

(6) Place hammock or canvas strips under client to form sling. With two canvas pieces, lower edge fits

	S	U	NP	Comments

under client's knees (wide piece),
and upper edge fits under client's
shoulders (narrow piece).

(7) Raise bed rail. _____ _____ _____ _____

(8) Go to opposite side of bed and _____ _____ _____ _____
lower side rail.

(9) Roll client to opposite side and _____ _____ _____ _____
pull hammock (strips) through.

(10) Roll client supine onto canvas seat. _____ _____ _____ _____

(11) Remove client's glasses, if _____ _____ _____ _____
appropriate.

(12) Place lift's horseshoe bar under side _____ _____ _____ _____
of bed (on side with chair).

(13) Lower horizontal bar to sling level _____ _____ _____ _____
by releasing hydraulic valve.
Lock valve.

(14) Attach hooks on strap (chain) to _____ _____ _____ _____
holes in sling. Short chains or
straps hook to top holes of sling;
longer chains hook to bottom of
sling.

(15) Elevate head of bed. _____ _____ _____ _____

(16) Fold client's arms over chest. _____ _____ _____ _____

(17) Pump hydraulic handle using _____ _____ _____ _____
long, slow, even strokes until
client is raised off bed.

(18) Use steering handle to pull lift _____ _____ _____ _____
from bed and maneuver to chair.

(19) Roll base around chair. _____ _____ _____ _____

(20) Release check valve slowly (turn _____ _____ _____ _____
to left) and lower client into chair.

(21) Close check valve as soon as client _____ _____ _____ _____
is down and straps can be released.

(22) Remove straps and mechanical/ _____ _____ _____ _____
hydraulic lift.

(23) Check client's sitting alignment _____ _____ _____ _____
and correct if necessary.

(24) Wash hands. _____ _____ _____ _____

10. Record each transfer and position change _____ _____ _____ _____
and client's response.

25 Safety

Case Study

I. You will be accompanying the visiting nurse to the home of a family with two young children, ages 2 and 4 years old.
   a. What general assessment information should be obtained regarding home safety during the visit?
   b. What specific safety observations should be made because there are two young children residing in the home?

Independent Learning Activities

1. Investigate and correct potential or actual safety hazards that are present in your own home.

2. Investigate resources that are available in the community for promotion of client/family safety (e.g., poison control center). Compile a list of emergency phone numbers.

3. Review the health care agency's policies and procedures for safety (e.g., fire, electrical, biohazard).

Chapter Review

Complete the following:

1. Identify the basic human needs of a safe environment and the problems that may be encountered if they are not met.

2. Identify possible physical hazards that may be found in the home.

3. Identify the physiological factors that predispose older adults to accidents.

4. Identify how the nurse may prevent the following health care agency risks and promote client safety:
   a. falls

   b. client-inherent accidents

c. procedure-related risks

d. equipment-related risks

5. How are the following age groups at risk for poisoning?
   a. toddler and preschool

   b. adolescents and young adults

   c. older adults

6. What are the overall objectives for the use of client restraints?

7. Identify four alternatives to the use of restraints.

8. What are the possible hazards that a nurse is exposed to in the health care environment?

9. What safety issues are of concern for the client and family in the home environment?

Select the best answer for each of the following questions:

10. A baby-sitter calls the poison control center after a child has ingested furniture polish. The baby-sitter should be instructed to:
    1. identify the amount of substance ingested
    2. give the age-appropriate amount of syrup of ipecac
    3. position the child lying down with the head tilted back
    4. drive the child herself to the nearest emergency room

11. An older adult client is being discharged home. The client will be taking Lasix (furosemide) on a daily basis. A specific consideration for this client is:
    1. exposure to the sun
    2. taking the medication with food
    3. the location of the bathroom
    4. financial considerations for long-term care

12. While walking through the hallway in the extended care facility, the nurse notices smoke coming from the wastebasket in the client's room. On closer investigation, the nurse identifies that there is a fire starting to flare up. The nurse first should:
    1. extinguish the fire
    2. remove the client from the room
    3. contain the fire by closing the door to the room
    4. turn off all of the surrounding electrical equipment

13. The client is newly admitted to the hospital and appears to be disoriented. There is a concern for the client's immediate safety. The nurse is considering the use of restraints to prevent an injury. The nurse recognizes that the use of restraints requires:
    1. a physician's order
    2. the client's consent
    3. a family member's consent
    4. agreement among the nursing staff

14. The nurse is completing admission histories for the newly admitted clients on the unit. The nurse is alert that the client with the greatest risk of injury:
    1. is 84 years of age
    2. uses corrective lenses
    3. has a history of falls
    4. has arthritis in the lower extremities

15. A child has ingested a poisonous substance and the parent has contacted the poison control center. The parent is instructed to provide syrup of ipecac to the child to induce vomiting. For a 4-year-old child, the parent should administer:
    1. 5 ml of ipecac
    2. 10 ml of ipecac
    3. 15 ml of ipecac
    4. 30 ml of ipecac

16. While practicing blood pressure measurement in the lab, the student nurse drops the sphygmomanometer. When it hits the floor, it breaks open and the mercury is spilled. The student should:
    1. wipe the mercury up with a sponge
    2. close all of the doors and windows
    3. get the janitor to vacuum up the spill
    4. get everyone out of the room

17. A 3-year-old child is scheduled to have an intravenous (IV) line inserted. The nurse wants to maintain the integrity of the line as long as possible and prevent the child from removing the IV. The restraint to use for this child is a:
    1. wrist restraint
    2. jacket restraint
    3. elbow restraint
    4. mummy restraint

18. An older adult client in the extended care facility has been wandering around outside of the room during the late evening hours. The client has a history of falls. The nurse intervenes by:
    1. placing an abdominal restraint on the client during the night

2. keeping the light on and the television playing all night
3. reassigning the client to a room close to the nursing station
4. having the family members come and check on the client during the night

19. A parent with three children has come to the outpatient clinic. The children range in age from 2 $\frac{1}{2}$ to 15 years old. The nurse is discussing safety issues with the parent. The nurse evaluates that further teaching is required if the parent states:
    1. "I have spoken to my teenager about safe sex practices."
    2. "I make sure that my child wears a helmet when he rides his bicycle."
    3. "My 8 year old is taking swimming classes at the local community center."
    4. "Now my 2 $\frac{1}{2}$ year old can finally sit in the front seat of the car with me."

Study Group Questions

- What are the basic human needs regarding safety?
- What are some physical hazards, and how can they be reduced or eliminated?
- What developmental changes and abilities predispose individuals to accidents or injury?
- What additional risk factors may affect an individual's level of safety?
- What risks exist in the health care agency, and how may they be prevented?
- What safety measures and client teaching should be implemented in different health care settings?
- What are the procedures for the correct use of side rails and restraints?
- How can the nurse avoid the use of client restraints?
- What assessment information should be obtained regarding client/family safety?
- How can the nurse assist clients and families in reducing or eliminating safety hazards?

Name_____   Date_____   Instructor's Name_____

Performance Checklist: Skill 25-1

Use of Restraints

	S	U	NP	Comments
1. Assess if a client needs a restraint.	___	___	___	_____
2. Assess client's behavior, such as confusion, disorientation, agitation, restlessness, combativeness, or inability to follow directions.	___	___	___	_____
3. Review agency policies regarding restraints. Check physician's order for purpose and type of restraint, location, and duration of restraint. Determine if signed consent for use of restraint is needed.	___	___	___	_____
4. Review manufacturer's instructions for restraint application before entering client's room.	___	___	___	_____
5. Introduce self to client and family and assess their feelings about restraint use. Explain that restraint is temporary and designed to protect client from injury.	___	___	___	_____
6. Inspect area where restraint is to be placed. Assess condition of skin underlying area on which restraint is to be applied.	___	___	___	_____
7. Approach client in a calm, confident manner. Explain what you plan to do.	___	___	___	_____
8. Gather equipment and wash hands.	___	___	___	_____
9. Provide privacy. Position and drape client as needed.	___	___	___	_____
10. Adjust bed to proper height and lower side rail on side of client contact.	___	___	___	_____
11. Be sure client is comfortable and in correct anatomical position.	___	___	___	_____
12. Pad skin and bony prominences (if necessary) that will be under the restraint.	___	___	___	_____

	S	U	NP	Comments

13. Apply proper-size selected restraint: Always refer to manufacturer's directions.

    a. Jacket (Vest or Posey) restraint: Apply jacket or vest over gown, pajamas, or clothes. Place client's hands through armholes. Jacket restraints close in back with zippers or hook and loop. _____ _____ _____ _____

        Vest restraints should have front and back of garment labeled as such. Secure vest according to manufacturer's directions. Adjust to client's level of comfort.

    b. Belt restraint: Have client in a sitting position. Apply over clothes, gown, or pajamas. Remove wrinkles or creases from front and back of restraint while placing it around client's waist. Bring ties through slots in belt. Help client lie down if in bed. Avoid placing belt too tightly across client's chest or abdomen. _____ _____ _____ _____

    c. Extremity (ankle or wrist) restraint: This restraint designed to immobilize one or all extremities. Limb restraint is wrapped around wrist or ankle with soft part toward skin and secured snugly in place by Velcro straps. _____ _____ _____ _____

    d. Mitten restraint: This is a thumbless mitten device that restrains client's hands. Place hand in mitten, being sure end is brought all the way up over the wrist. _____ _____ _____ _____

14. Attach restraint straps to portion of bed frame that moves when head of bed is raised or lowered. Do not attach to side rails. Restraint may also be attached with client in chair or wheelchair to chair frame. _____ _____ _____ _____

15. When client is in a wheelchair, jacket restraint should be secured by placing ties under armrests and securing at back of chair. _____ _____ _____ _____

16. Secure restraints with a quick-release tie. _____ _____ _____ _____

17. Insert two fingers under secured restraint. _____ _____ _____ _____

18. Proper placement of restraint, skin integrity, pulses, temperature, color, and sensation of the restrained body part should be assessed at least every hour or according to agency policy. _____ _____ _____ _____

	S	U	NP	Comments

19. Restraints should be removed at least every 2 hours (JCAHO, 2001). If client is violent or noncompliant, remove one restraint at a time and/or have staff assistance while removing restraints.

20. Secure call light or intercom system within reach.

21. Leave bed or chair with wheels locked. Bed should be in the lowest position.

22. Wash hands.

23. Inspect client for any injury, including all hazards of immobility, while restraints are in use.

24. Observe IV catheters, urinary catheters, and drainage tubes to determine that they are positioned correctly.

25. Reassess client's need for continued use of restraint at least every 24 hours.

26. Document client's response and expected or unexpected outcomes after restraint is applied.

26 Hygiene

Case Studies

I. Your clinical experience is scheduled to be on a medical unit. It will be your responsibility to provide instruction to a client who has just been diagnosed with diabetes mellitus.
   a. What specific information on hygienic care will be included for this client's teaching session?
II. An older adult client residing in an extended care facility requires assistance with hygienic care.
   a. What developmental changes are considered when assisting this client to meet hygienic needs?

Independent Learning Activities

1. Review the anatomy and physiology of the integumentary system.

2. Investigate commercial products that are available for hygienic care, and compare the costs of popular name brands and store brands.

3. Practice the techniques for hygienic care with peers and at home with willing family members or friends.

Chapter Review

Complete the following:

1. What factors influence hygienic care practices?

2. What are the positive effects of a back rub?

3. What are the purposes for bathing a client?

4. Identify the guidelines that the nurse should implement when bathing a client.

5. Briefly describe the following common skin problems, and identify at least one intervention for treatment:
   a. acne

   b. contact dermatitis

c.   abrasion

d.   adult

6.   Briefly describe the following common hair or scalp problems:
a.   pediculosis capitis

b.   alopecia

7.   Briefly describe the following common foot or nail problems:
a.   tinea pedis

b.   paronychia

8.   What circumstances place the client at risk for impaired skin integrity?

9.   What client assessments can be completed while providing hygienic care?

10.   Identify the developmental characteristics of the skin for the following age groups:
a.   neonate

b.   toddler

c.   adolescent

11.   How does the nurse prepare a comfortable environment for the client in the health care facility?

Select the best answer for each of the following questions:

12.   The client in the hospital requires foot care. The nurse providing foot care should include:
1.   cutting away corns and calluses
2.   filing toenails in a curved or rounded shape
3.   instructing the client to wear flexible sole shoes
4.   using alcohol for dryness between the toes

13.   The nurse is caring for an older adult client in the extended care facility. The client wears dentures, and the nurse will be delegating their care to the nursing assistant. The nurse instructs the assistant that the client's dentures should be:
1.   cleaned in hot water
2.   left in place during the night
3.   brushed with a soft toothbrush
4.   wrapped in a soft towel when not worn

14.   The nurse determines, after completing the assessment, that an expected outcome for a client with impaired skin integrity will be that the skin:
1.   remains dry
2.   has increased erythema
3.   tingles in areas of pressure
4.   demonstrates increased diaphoresis

15.   A client has been hospitalized following a traumatic injury. The nurse now is able to provide hair care for the client. The nurse includes in this care:

1. using hot water to rinse the scalp
2. cutting away matted or tangled hair
3. using the nails to massage the client's scalp
4. applying peroxide to dissolve blood and rinsing with saline

16. While completing the bath, the nurse notices a red, raised skin rash on the client's chest. The next step for the nurse to take is to:
   1. moisturize the skin with lotion
   2. wash the area again with hot water and soap
   3. discuss proper hygienic care with the client
   4. assess for any other areas of inflammation

17. The nurse is working out the client assignment with the nursing assistant. In delegating the morning care for the client, the nurse expects the assistant to:
   1. cut the client's nails with scissors
   2. use soap to wash the client's eyes
   3. wash the client's legs with long strokes from the ankle to the knee
   4. place the unconscious client in high Fowler's position to provide oral hygiene

18. A client is receiving chemotherapy and is experiencing stomatitis. To promote comfort for this client, the nurse recommends that the client use:
   1. a firm toothbrush
   2. normal saline rinses
   3. a commercial mouthwash
   4. an alcohol and water mixture

19. The client requires assistance with the performance of oral hygiene. While preparing for the care, the client asks the nurse why the "lemon sticks" are not being used to clean out her mouth. The nurse responds to the client based on the knowledge that the lemon-glycerin swabs:
   1. erode the tooth enamel
   2. destroy normal mouth bacteria
   3. cause excessive bleeding in the gums and mucous membranes
   4. reduce the moisture in the mucous membranes

Study Group Questions

- What hygienic care measures are necessary for the integumentary system?
- What factors may influence a client's hygienic care practices?
- How does growth and development influence hygienic care needs?
- What are the client's teaching needs for hygienic care across the life span?
- What assessments of the integumentary system are necessary to determine integumentary alterations and hygienic care needs?
- What are the correct procedures for providing hygienic care and a comfortable environment for clients?
- How does the client's self-care ability influence the provision of hygienic care?
- How is physical assessment integrated into the provision of hygienic care?
- What should be done if the client refuses hygienic care?

Name_____ Date_____ Instructor's Name_____

Performance Checklist: Skill 26-1

Bathing a Client

	S	U	NP	Comments

1. Assess client's tolerance for activity, discomfort level, cognitive ability, musculoskeletal function, and the presence of equipment (e.g., intravenous [IV] or oxygen tubing) that may interfere with bathing hygiene.

2. Assess client's bathing preferences.

3. Ask if client has noticed any problems related to condition of skin.

4. Check physician's therapeutic bath order for type of solution, length of time for bath, and body part to be attended.

5. Review orders for specific precautions concerning client's movement or positioning.

6. Explain procedure and ask client for suggestions on how to prepare supplies. If partial bath, ask how much of bath client wishes to complete.

7. Adjust room temperature and ventilation, close room doors and windows, and draw room divider curtain.

8. Prepare equipment and supplies.

9. Complete or partial bed bath
   a. Offer client bedpan or urinal. Provide towel and washcloth.
   b. Wash hands.
   c. Lower side rail closest to you, and assist client in assuming comfortable supine position, maintaining body alignment. Bring client toward side closest to you. Place hospital bed in high position.
   d. Loosen top covers at foot of bed. Place bath blanket over top sheet. Fold and remove top sheet from under blanket. If possible, have client hold bath blanket while withdrawing sheet.

	S	U	NP	Comments

e. If top sheet is to be reused, fold it for replacement later. If not, dispose in laundry bag, taking care not to allow linen to contact uniform. ___ ___ ___ _____

f. Remove client's gown or pajamas. If an extremity is injured or has reduced mobility, begin removal from *unaffected* side. If client has IV access, remove gown from arm *without* IV first. Then remove gown from arm with IV. Remove IV from pole, and slide IV tubing and bag through the arm of client's gown. Rehang IV container and check flow rate. ___ ___ ___ _____

g. Pull side rail up. Fill washbasin two-thirds full with warm water. Check water temperature, and also have client place fingers in water to test temperature tolerance. Place plastic container of bath lotion in bathwater to warm if desired. ___ ___ ___ _____

h. Lower side rail, remove pillow, and raise head of bed 30 to 45 degrees if allowed. Place bath towel under client's head. Place second bath towel over client's chest. ___ ___ ___ _____

i. Fold washcloth around fingers of your hand to form a mitt. Immerse mitt in water and wring thoroughly. ___ ___ ___ _____

j. Inquire if client is wearing contact lenses. Wash client's eyes with plain warm water. Use different section of mitt for each eye. Move mitt from inner to outer canthus. Soak any crusts on eyelid for 2 to 3 minutes with damp cloth before attempting removal. Dry eye thoroughly but gently. ___ ___ ___ _____

k. Ask if client prefers to use soap on face. Wash, rinse, and dry well forehead, cheeks, nose, neck, and ears. (Men may wish to shave at this point or after bath.) ___ ___ ___ _____

l. Remove bath blanket from client's arm closest to you. Place bath towel lengthwise under arm. ___ ___ ___ _____

m. Bathe arm with soap and water using long, firm strokes from distal to proximal areas (fingers to axilla). Raise and support arm above head (if possible) while thoroughly washing axilla. ___ ___ ___ _____

n. Rinse and dry arm and axilla thoroughly. If client uses deodorant, apply it. ___ ___ ___ _____

	S	U	NP	Comments

o. Fold bath towel in half and lay it on bed beside client. Place basin on towel. Immerse client's hand in water. Allow hand to soak for 3 to 5 minutes before washing hand and fingernails. Remove basin and dry hand well.

p. Raise side rail and move to other side of bed. Lower side rail and repeat Steps 12 through 15 for other arm.

q. Check temperature of bathwater, and change water if necessary.

r. Cover client's chest with bath towel and fold bath blanket down to umbilicus. With one hand, lift edge of towel away from chest. With mitted hand, bathe chest using long, firm strokes. Take special care to wash skin-folds under female client's breasts. Keep client's chest covered between wash and rinse periods. Dry well.

s. Place bath towel lengthwise over chest and abdomen. (Two towels may be needed.) Fold blanket down to just above pubic region.

t. With one hand, lift bath towel. With mitted hand, bathe abdomen, giving special attention to bathing umbilicus and abdominal folds. Stroke from side to side. Keep abdomen covered between washing and rinsing. Dry well.

u. Apply clean gown or pajama top.

v. Cover chest and abdomen with top of bath blanket. Expose near leg by folding blanket toward midline. Be sure perineum is draped.

w. Bend client's leg at knee by positioning nurse's arm under leg. While grasping client's heel, elevate leg from mattress slightly and slide bath towel lengthwise under leg. Ask client to hold foot still. Place bath basin on towel on bed and secure its position next to foot to be washed.

x. With one hand supporting lower leg, raise it and slide basin under lifted foot. Make sure foot is firmly placed on bottom of basin. Allow foot to soak while washing leg. If client is unable to hold leg, do not immerse; simply wash with washcloth. (Soaking may be contraindicated).

		S	U	NP	Comments
y.	Unless contraindicated, use long, firm strokes in washing from ankle to knee and from knee to thigh. Dry well.	____	____	____	_____
z.	Cleanse foot, making sure to bathe between toes. Clean and clip nails as needed. Dry well. If skin is dry, apply lotion.	____	____	____	_____
aa.	Raise side rail and move to other side of the bed. Lower side rail and repeat Steps 22 through 26 for other leg and foot.	____	____	____	_____
bb.	Cover client with bath blanket, raise side rail for client's safety, and change bathwater.	____	____	____	_____
cc.	Lower side rail. Assist client in assuming prone or side-lying position (as applicable). Place towel lengthwise along client's side.	____	____	____	_____
dd.	Keep client draped by sliding bath blanket over shoulders and thighs. Wash, rinse, and dry back from neck to buttocks using long, firm strokes. Pay special attention to folds of buttocks and anus. Give a back rub, and change the bathwater.	____	____	____	_____
ee.	Apply disposable gloves if not done previously.	____	____	____	_____
ff.	Assist client in assuming side-lying or supine position. Cover chest and upper extremities with towel and lower extremities with bath blanket. Expose only genitalia. (If client can wash, covering entire body with bath blanket may be preferable.) Wash, rinse, and dry perineum. Pay special attention to skinfolds. Apply water-repellent ointment to area exposed to moisture.	____	____	____	_____
gg.	Dispose of gloves in receptacle.	____	____	____	_____
hh.	Apply additional body lotion or oil as desired.	____	____	____	_____
ii.	Assist client in dressing. Comb client's hair. Women may want to apply makeup.	____	____	____	_____
jj.	Make client's bed.	____	____	____	_____
kk.	Remove soiled linen and place in dirtylinen bag. Clean and replace bathing equipment. Replace call light and personal possessions. Leave room as clean and comfortable as possible.	____	____	____	_____
ll.	Wash hands.	____	____	____	_____

	S	U	NP	Comments

10. Tub bath or shower
   a. Consider client's condition, and review orders for precautions concerning client's movement or positioning.   ———— ———— ———— ————————————
   b. Schedule use of shower or tub.   ———— ———— ———— ————————————
   c. Check tub or shower for cleanliness. Use cleaning techniques outlined in agency policy. Place rubber mat on tub or shower bottom. Place disposable bath mat or towel on floor in front of tub or shower.   ———— ———— ———— ————————————
   d. Collect all hygienic aids, toiletry items, and linens requested by client. Place within easy reach of tub or shower.   ———— ———— ———— ————————————
   e. Assist client to bathroom if necessary. Have client wear robe and slippers to bathroom.   ———— ———— ———— ————————————
   f. Demonstrate how to use call signal for assistance.   ———— ———— ———— ————————————
   g. Place "occupied" sign on bathroom door.   ———— ———— ———— ————————————
   h. Fill bathtub halfway with warm water. Check temperature of bath water, then have client test water, and adjust temperature if water is too warm. Explain which faucet controls hot water. If client is taking shower, turn shower on and adjust water temperature before client enters shower stall. Use shower seat or tub chair and provide if needed.   ———— ———— ———— ————————————
   i. Instruct client to use safety bars when getting in and out of tub or shower. Caution client against use of bath oil in tub water.   ———— ———— ———— ————————————
   j. Instruct client not to remain in tub longer than 20 minutes. Check on client every 5 minutes.   ———— ———— ———— ————————————
   k. Return to bathroom when client signals, and knock before entering.   ———— ———— ———— ————————————
   l. For client who is unsteady, drain tub of water before client attempts to get out of it. Place bath towel over client's shoulders. Assist client in getting out of tub as needed and assist with drying.   ———— ———— ———— ————————————
   m. Assist client as needed in donning clean gown or pajamas, slippers, and robe. (In home setting client may put on regular clothing.)   ———— ———— ———— ————————————
   n. Assist client to room and comfortable position in bed or chair.   ———— ———— ———— ————————————
   o. Clean tub or shower according to agency policy. Remove soiled linen and place in dirty-linen bag. Discard disposable equipment in proper   ———— ———— ———— ————————————

	S	U	NP	Comments

receptacle. Place "unoccupied" sign on bathroom door. Return supplies to storage area.

   p. Wash hands. _____ _____ _____ _____

11. Observe skin, paying particular attention to areas that previously were soiled or reddened or showed early signs of breakdown. _____ _____ _____ _____

12. Observe range of motion during bath. _____ _____ _____ _____

13. Ask client to rate level of comfort. _____ _____ _____ _____

14. Record bath on flow sheet. Note level of assistance required. _____ _____ _____ _____

15. Record condition of skin and any significant findings. _____ _____ _____ _____

16. Report evidence of alterations in skin integrity to nurse in charge or physician. _____ _____ _____ _____

Name_____   Date_____   Instructor's Name_____

Performance Checklist: Skill 26-2

Providing Perineal Care

	S	U	NP	Comments
1. Identify clients at risk for developing infection of genitalia, urinary tract, or reproductive tract.	___	___	___	_____
2. Assess client's cognitive and musculoskeletal function.	___	___	___	_____
3. Apply disposable gloves and assess genitalia for signs of inflammation, skin breakdown, or infection. Discard gloves. (Option: examine genitalia as care is administered.)	___	___	___	_____
4. Assess client's knowledge of importance of perineal hygiene.	___	___	___	_____
5. Explain procedure and its purpose to client.	___	___	___	_____
6. Prepare necessary equipment and supplies.	___	___	___	_____
7. Pull curtain around client's bed, or close room door. Assemble supplies at bedside.	___	___	___	_____
8. Raise bed to comfortable working position. Lower side rail, and assist client in assuming side-lying position, placing towel lengthwise along client's side and keeping client covered with bath blanket.	___	___	___	_____
9. Apply disposable gloves.	___	___	___	_____
10. If fecal material is present, enclose in a fold of underpad or toilet tissue and remove with disposable wipes. Cleanse buttocks and anus, washing front to back. Cleanse, rinse, and dry area thoroughly. If needed, place an absorbent pad under client's buttocks. Remove and discard underpad, and replace with clean one.	___	___	___	_____
11. Change gloves if soiled.	___	___	___	_____

	S	U	NP	Comments

12. Fold top bed linen down toward foot of bed, and raise client's gown above genital area.

   a. "Diamond" drape female client by placing bath blanket with one corner between client's legs, one corner pointing toward each side of bed, and one corner over client's chest. Tuck side corners around client's legs and under hips. For male client, expose only genital area, using towels or bath blankets to cover client's chest and upper legs.

   b. Raise side rail. Fill washbasin with warm water.

   c. Place washbasin and toilet tissue on over-bed table. Place washcloths in basin.

13. Provide perineal care.

   a. Female perineal care

     (1) Assist client to dorsal recumbent position.

     (2) Lower side rail, and help client flex knees and spread legs. Note restrictions or limitations in client's positioning.

     (3) Fold lower corner of bath blanket up between client's legs onto abdomen. Wash and dry client's upper thighs.

     (4) Wash labia majora. Use nondominant hand to gently retract labia from thigh; with dominant hand, wash carefully in skinfolds. Wipe in direction from perineum to rectum (front to back). Repeat on opposite side using separate section of washcloth. Rinse and dry area thoroughly.

     (5) Separate labia with nondominant hand to expose urethral meatus and vaginal orifice. With dominant hand, wash downward from pubic area toward rectum in one smooth stroke. Use separate section of cloth for each stroke. Cleanse thoroughly around labia minora, clitoris, and vaginal orifice.

     (6) If client uses bedpan, pour warm water over perineal area. Dry perineal area thoroughly, using front-to-back method.

     (7) Fold lower corner of bath blanket back between client's legs and over perineum. Ask client to lower legs and assume comfortable position.

	S	U	NP	Comments

b. Male perineal care
  (1) Lower side rails, and assist client to supine position. Note restriction in mobility.
  (2) Fold lower corner of bath blanket up between client's legs and onto abdomen. Wash and dry client's upper thighs.
  (3) Gently raise penis, and place bath towel underneath. Gently grasp shaft of penis. If client is uncircumcised, retract foreskin. If client has an erection, defer procedure until later.
  (4) Wash tip of penis at urethral meatus first. Using circular motion, cleanse from meatus outward. Discard wash-cloth, and repeat with clean cloth until penis is clean. Rinse and dry gently.
  (5) Return foreskin to its natural position.
  (6) Wash shaft of penis with gentle but firm downward strokes. Pay special attention to underlying surface of penis. Rinse and dry penis thoroughly. Instruct client to spread legs apart slightly.
  (7) Gently cleanse scrotum. Lift it carefully, and wash underlying skinfolds. Rinse and dry.
  (8) Fold bath blanket back over client's perineum, and assist client in turning to sidelying position.

14. If client has had urinary or bowel incontinence, apply thin layer of skin barrier containing petrolatum or zinc oxide over anal and perineal skin.

15. Remove disposable gloves, and dispose in proper receptacle.

16. Assist client in assuming a comfortable position, and cover with sheet.

17. Remove bath blanket, and dispose of all soiled bed linen. Return unused equipment to storage area.

18. Inspect surface of external genitalia and surrounding skin after cleansing.

19. Ask if client feels sense of cleanliness.

	S	U	NP	Comments
20. Observe for abnormal drainage or discharge from genitalia.	____	____	____	_____
21. Record procedure and presence of any abnormal findings.	____	____	____	_____
22. Record appearance of suture line, if present.	____	____	____	_____
23. Report any break in suture line or presence of abnormalities to nurse in charge or physician.	____	____	____	_____

Name_____ Date_____ Instructor's Name_____

Performance Checklist: Skill 26-3

Performing Nail and Foot Care

	S	U	NP	Comments
1. Inspect all surfaces of fingers, toes, feet, and nails.	___	___	___	_____
2. Assess color and temperature of toes, feet, and fingers. Assess capillary refill of nails. Palpate radial and ulnar pulse of each hand and dorsalis pedis pulse of foot; note character of pulses.	___	___	___	_____
3. Observe client's walking gait. Have client walk down hall or walk straight line (if able).	___	___	___	_____
4. Ask female clients about whether they use nail polish and polish remover frequently.	___	___	___	_____
5. Assess type of footwear worn by clients.	___	___	___	_____
6. Identify client's risk for foot or nail problems.	___	___	___	_____
7. Assess type of home remedies clients use for existing foot problems.	___	___	___	_____
8. Assess client's ability to care for nails or feet: visual alterations, fatigue, musculoskeletal weakness.	___	___	___	_____
9. Assess client's knowledge of foot and nail care practices.	___	___	___	_____
10. Explain procedure to client, including fact that proper soaking requires several minutes.	___	___	___	_____
11. Obtain physician's order for cutting nails if agency policy requires it.	___	___	___	_____
12. Wash hands. Arrange equipment on over-bed table.	___	___	___	_____
13. Pull curtain around bed, or close room door (if desired).	___	___	___	_____
14. Assist ambulatory client to sit in bedside chair. Help bed-bound client to supine	___	___	___	_____

	S	U	NP	Comments

position with head of bed elevated. Place disposable bath mat on floor under client's feet or place towel on mattress.

15. Fill washbasin with warm water. Test water temperature. ⎯⎯ ⎯⎯ ⎯⎯ ⎯⎯⎯⎯⎯⎯⎯⎯

16. Place basin on bath mat or towel, and help client place feet in basin. Place call light within client's reach. ⎯⎯ ⎯⎯ ⎯⎯ ⎯⎯⎯⎯⎯⎯⎯⎯

17. Adjust over-bed table to low position, and place it over client's lap. (Client may sit in chair or lie in bed.) ⎯⎯ ⎯⎯ ⎯⎯ ⎯⎯⎯⎯⎯⎯⎯⎯

18. Fill emesis basin with warm water, and place basin on paper towels on over-bed table. ⎯⎯ ⎯⎯ ⎯⎯ ⎯⎯⎯⎯⎯⎯⎯⎯

19. Instruct client to place fingers in emesis basin and place arms in comfortable position. ⎯⎯ ⎯⎯ ⎯⎯ ⎯⎯⎯⎯⎯⎯⎯⎯

20. Allow client's feet and fingernails to soak for 10 to 20 minutes. Rewarm after 10 minutes. ⎯⎯ ⎯⎯ ⎯⎯ ⎯⎯⎯⎯⎯⎯⎯⎯

21. Clean gently under fingernails with orange stick while fingers are immersed. Remove emesis basin and dry fingers thoroughly. ⎯⎯ ⎯⎯ ⎯⎯ ⎯⎯⎯⎯⎯⎯⎯⎯

22. With nail clippers, clip fingernails straight across and even with tops of fingers. Shape nails with emery board or file. If client has circulatory problems, do not cut nail; file the nail only. ⎯⎯ ⎯⎯ ⎯⎯ ⎯⎯⎯⎯⎯⎯⎯⎯

23. Push cuticle back gently with orange stick. ⎯⎯ ⎯⎯ ⎯⎯ ⎯⎯⎯⎯⎯⎯⎯⎯

24. Move over-bed table away from client. ⎯⎯ ⎯⎯ ⎯⎯ ⎯⎯⎯⎯⎯⎯⎯⎯

25. Put on disposable gloves, and scrub callused areas of feet with washcloth. ⎯⎯ ⎯⎯ ⎯⎯ ⎯⎯⎯⎯⎯⎯⎯⎯

26. Clean gently under nails with orange stick. Remove feet from basin, and dry thoroughly. ⎯⎯ ⎯⎯ ⎯⎯ ⎯⎯⎯⎯⎯⎯⎯⎯

27. Clean and trim toenails using procedures in Steps 21 and 22. Do not file corners of toenails. ⎯⎯ ⎯⎯ ⎯⎯ ⎯⎯⎯⎯⎯⎯⎯⎯

28. Apply lotion to feet and hands, and assist client back to bed and into comfortable position. ⎯⎯ ⎯⎯ ⎯⎯ ⎯⎯⎯⎯⎯⎯⎯⎯

	S	U	NP	Comments
29. Remove disposable gloves, and place in receptacle. Clean and return equipment and supplies to proper place. Dispose of soiled linen in hamper. Wash hands.	___	___	___	_____
30. Inspect nails and surrounding skin surfaces after soaking and nail trimming.	___	___	___	_____
31. Ask client to explain or demonstrate nail care.	___	___	___	_____
32. Observe client's walk after toenail care.	___	___	___	_____
33. Record procedure and observations.	___	___	___	_____
34. Report any breaks in skin or ulcerations to nurse in charge or physician.	___	___	___	_____

Name_____ Date_____ Instructor's Name_____

Performance Checklist: Skill 26-4

Providing Oral Hygiene

	S	U	NP	Comments
1. Wash hands, and apply disposable gloves.	____	____	____	_____
2. Inspect integrity of lips, teeth, buccal mucosa, gums, palate, and tongue.	____	____	____	_____
3. Identify presence of common oral problem.	____	____	____	_____
4. Remove gloves, and wash hands.	____	____	____	_____
5. Assess risk for oral hygiene problems.	____	____	____	_____
6. Determine client's oral hygiene practices.	____	____	____	_____
7. Assess client's ability to grasp and manipulate toothbrush.	____	____	____	_____
8. Prepare equipment at bedside.	____	____	____	_____
9. Explain procedure to client and discuss preferences regarding use of hygiene aids.	____	____	____	_____
10. Place paper towels on over-bed table, and arrange other equipment within easy reach.	____	____	____	_____
11. Raise bed to comfortable working position. Raise head of bed (if allowed) and lower side rail. Move client, or help client move closer. Side-lying position can be used.	____	____		_____
12. Place towel over client's chest.	____	____	____	_____
13. Apply gloves.	____	____	____	_____
14. Apply toothpaste to brush, holding brush over emesis basin. Pour small amount of water over toothpaste.	____	____	____	_____
15. Client may assist by brushing. Hold toothbrush bristles at 45-degree angle to gum line. Be sure tips of bristles rest against and penetrate under gum line. Brush inner and outer surfaces of upper and lower teeth by brushing from gum to crown of each	____	____	____	_____

	S	U	NP	Comments

tooth. Clean biting surfaces of teeth by holding top of bristles parallel with teeth and brushing gently back and forth. Brush sides of teeth by moving bristles back and forth.

16. Have client hold brush at 45-degree angle and lightly brush over surface and sides of tongue. Avoid initiating gag reflex.

17. Allow client to rinse mouth thoroughly by taking several sips of water, swishing water across all tooth surfaces, and spitting into emesis basin.

18. Allow client to gargle to rinse mouth with mouthwash as desired.

19. Assist in wiping client's mouth.

20. Allow client to floss.

21. Allow client to rinse mouth thoroughly with cool water and spit into emesis basin. Assist in wiping client's mouth.

22. Assist client to comfortable position, remove emesis basin and bedside table, raise side rail, and lower bed to original position.

23. Wipe off over-bed table, discard soiled linen and paper towels in appropriate containers, remove soiled gloves, and return equipment to proper place.

24. Wash hands.

25. Ask client if any area of oral cavity feels uncomfortable or irritated.

26. Apply gloves, and inspect condition of oral cavity.

27. Ask client to describe proper hygiene techniques.

28. Observe client brushing.

29. Record procedure, noting condition of oral cavity.

30. Report bleeding or presence of lesions to nurse in charge or physician.

Name_____ Date_____ Instructor's Name_____

Performance Checklist: Skill 26-5

Performing Mouth Care for an Unconscious or Debilitated Client

	S	U	NP	Comments
1. Wash hands. Apply disposable gloves.	___	___	___	_____
2. Test for presence of gag reflex by placing blade on back half of tongue.	___	___	___	_____
3. Inspect condition of oral cavity.	___	___	___	_____
4. Remove gloves. Wash hands.	___	___	___	_____
5. Assess client's risk for oral hygiene problems.	___	___	___	_____
6. Position client on side (Sims' position) with head turned well toward dependent side and head of bed lowered. Raise side rail.	___	___	___	_____
7. Explain procedure to client.	___	___	___	_____
8. Wash hands, and apply disposable gloves.	___	___	___	_____
9. Place paper towels on over-bed table and arrange equipment. If needed, turn on suction machine, and connect tubing to suction catheter.	___	___	___	_____
10. Pull curtain around bed, or close room door.	___	___	___	_____
11. Raise bed to its highest horizontal level; lower side rail.	___	___	___	_____
12. Position client close to side of bed; turn client's head toward mattress.	___	___	___	_____
13. Place towel under client's head and emesis basin under chin.	___	___	___	_____
14. Carefully separate upper and lower teeth with padded tongue blade by inserting blade, quickly but gently, between back molars. Insert when client is relaxed, if possible. Do not use force.	___	___	___	_____
15. Clean mouth using brush or sponge toothettes moistened with peroxide and	___	___	___	_____

	S	U	NP	Comments

water. Clean chewing and inner tooth surfaces first. Clean outer tooth surfaces. Swab roof of mouth, gums, and inside cheeks. Gently swab or brush tongue but avoid stimulating gag reflex (if present). Moisten clean swab or toothette with water to rinse. (Bulb syringe also may be used to rinse.) Repeat rinse several times.

16. Suction secretions as they accumulate, if necessary.

17. Apply thin layer of water-soluble jelly to lips.

18. Inform client that procedure is completed.

19. Raise side rails as appropriate or ordered.

20. Remove gloves, and dispose in proper receptacle.

21. Reposition client comfortably, raise side rail, and return bed to original position.

22. Clean equipment and return to its proper place. Place soiled linen in proper receptacle.

23. Wash hands.

24. Apply gloves, and inspect oral cavity.

25. Ask debilitated client if mouth feels clean.

26. Assess client's respirations on an ongoing basis.

27. Record procedure, including pertinent observations.

28. Report any unusual findings to nurse in charge or physician.

Performance Checklist: Skill 26-6

Making an Occupied Bed

	S	U	NP	Comments
1. Assess potential for client incontinence or for excess drainage on bed linen.	____	____	____	_____
2. Check chart for orders or specific precautions concerning movement and positioning.	____	____	____	_____
3. Explain procedure to the client, noting that the client will be asked to turn on side and roll over linen.	____	____	____	_____
4. Wash hands, and apply gloves (gloves are worn only if linen is soiled or there is risk for contact with body secretions).	____	____	____	_____
5. Assemble equipment, and arrange on bedside chair or table. Remove unnecessary equipment such as a dietary tray or items used for hygiene.	____	____	____	_____
6. Draw room curtain around bed or close door.	____	____	____	_____
7. Adjust bed height to comfortable working position. Lower any raised side rail on one side of bed. Remove call light.	____	____	____	_____
8. Loosen top linen at foot of bed.	____	____	____	_____
9. Remove bedspread and blanket separately. If spread and blanket are soiled, place them in linen bag. Keep soiled linen away from uniform.	____	____	____	_____
10. If blanket and spread are to be reused, fold them by bringing the top and bottom edges together. Fold farthest side over onto nearer bottom edge. Bring top and bottom edges together again. Place folded linen over back of chair.	____	____	____	_____
11. Cover client with bath blanket in the following manner: unfold bath blanket over	____	____	____	_____

	S	U	NP	Comments

top sheet. Ask client to hold top edge of
bath blanket. If client is unable to help, tuck
top of bath blanket under shoulder. Grasp
top sheet under bath blanket at client's
shoulders and bring sheet down to foot of
bed. Remove sheet and discard in linen bag.

12. With assistance from another nurse, slide
mattress toward head of bed.

13. Position client on the far side of the bed,
turned onto side and facing away from you.
Be sure side rail in front of client is up.
Adjust pillow under client's head.

14. Loosen bottom linens, moving from head
to foot. With seam side down (facing the
mattress), fanfold bottom sheet and
drawsheet toward client—first drawsheet,
then bottom sheet. Tuck edges of linen just
under buttocks, back, and shoulders. Do
not fanfold mattress pad if it is to be reused.

15. Wipe off any moisture on exposed mattress
with towel and appropriate disinfectant.

16. Apply clean linen to exposed half of bed:
    a. Place clean mattress pad on bed by
       folding it lengthwise with center crease
       in middle of bed. Fanfold top layer over
       mattress. (If pad is reused, simply smooth
       out any wrinkles.)
    b. Unfold bottom sheet lengthwise so that
       center crease is situated lengthwise along
       center of bed. Fanfold sheet's top layer
       toward center of bed alongside the client.
       Smooth bottom layer of sheet over
       mattress, and bring edge over closest side
       of mattress. Pull fitted sheet smoothly
       over mattress ends. Allow edge of flat
       unfitted sheet to hang about 25 cm
       (10 in) over mattress edge. Lower hem of
       bottom flat sheet should lie seam down
       and even with bottom edge of mattress.

17. Miter bottom flat sheet at head of bed:
    a. Face head of bed diagonally. Place hand
       away from head of bed under top corner
       of mattress, near mattress edge, and lift.
    b. With other hand, tuck top edge of
       bottom sheet smoothly under mattress
       so that side edges of sheet above and
       below mattress would meet if brought
       together.

	S	U	NP	Comments

c. Face side of bed and pick up top edge of sheet at approximately 45 cm (18 in) from top of mattress.

d. Lift sheet, and lay it on top of mattress to form a neat triangular fold, with lower base of triangle even with mattress side edge.

e. Tuck lower edge of sheet, which is hanging free below the mattress, under mattress. Tuck with palms down, without pulling triangular fold.

f. Hold portion of sheet covering side of mattress in place with one hand. With the other hand, pick up top of triangular linen fold and bring it down over side of mattress. Tuck this portion under mattress.

18. Tuck remaining portion of sheet under mattress, moving toward foot of bed. Keep linen smooth.

19. (Optional) Open drawsheet so that it unfolds in half. Lay centerfold along middle of bed lengthwise, and position sheet so that it will be under the client's buttocks and torso. Fanfold top layer toward client, with edge along client's back. Smooth bottom layer out over mattress, and tuck excess edge under mattress (keep palms down).

20. Place waterproof pad over drawsheet, with centerfold against client's side. Fanfold top layer toward client.

21. Have client roll slowly toward you, over the layers of linen. Raise side rail on working side, and go to other side.

22. Lower side rail. Assist client in positioning on other side, over folds of linen. Loosen edges of soiled linen from under mattress.

23. Remove soiled linen by folding it into a bundle or square, with soiled side turned in. Discard in linen bag. If necessary, wipe mattress with antiseptic solution, and dry mattress surface before applying new linen.

24. Pull clean, fanfold linen smoothly over edge of mattress from head to foot of bed.

25. Assist client in rolling back into supine position. Reposition pillow.

	S	U	NP	Comments

26. Pull fitted sheet smoothly over mattress ends. Miter top corner of bottom sheet (see Step 17). When tucking corner, be sure that sheet is smooth and free of wrinkles.

27. Facing side of bed, grasp remaining edge of bottom flat sheet. Lean back, keep back straight, and pull while tucking excess linen under mattress. Proceed from head to foot of bed. (Avoid lifting mattress during tucking to ensure fit.)

28. Smooth fanfolded drawsheet out over bottom sheet. Grasp edge of sheet with palms down, lean back, and tuck sheet under mattress. Tuck from middle to top and then to bottom.

29. Place top sheet over client with centerfold lengthwise down middle of bed. Open sheet from head to foot, and unfold over client.

30. Ask client to hold clean top sheet, or tuck sheet around client's shoulders. Remove bath blanket and discard in linen bag.

31. Place blanket on bed, unfolding it so that crease runs lengthwise along middle of bed. Unfold blanket to cover client. Top edge should be parallel with edge of top sheet and 15 to 20 cm (6 to 8 in) from top sheet's edge.

32. Place spread over bed according to Step 31. Be sure that top edge of spread extends about 2.5 cm (1 in) above blanket's edge. Tuck top edge of spread over and under top edge of blanket.

33. Make cuff by turning edge of top sheet down over top edge of blanket and spread.

34. Standing on one side at foot of bed, lift mattress corner slightly with one hand and tuck linens under mattress. Top sheet and blanket are tucked under together. Be sure that linens are loose enough to allow movement of client's feet. Making a horizontal toe pleat is an option.

35. Make modified mitered corner with top sheet, blanket, and spread.
    a. Pick up side edge of top sheet, blanket, and spread approximately 45 cm (18 in)

	S	U	NP	Comments

from foot of mattress. Lift linen to form
triangular fold, and lay it on bed.
b. Tuck lower edge of sheet, which is _____ _____ _____ _____
hanging free below mattress, under
mattress. Do not pull triangular fold.
c. Pick up triangular fold, and bring it _____ _____ _____ _____
down over mattress while holding linen
in place along side of mattress. Do not
tuck tip of triangle.

36. Raise side rail. Make other side of bed; _____ _____ _____ _____
spread sheet, blanket, and bedspread out
evenly. Fold top edge of spread over blanket
and make cuff with top sheet (see Step 33);
make modified mitered corner at foot of bed
(see Step 35).

37. Change pillowcase:
a. Have client raise head. While supporting _____ _____ _____ _____
neck with one hand, remove pillow.
Allow client to lower head.
b. Remove soiled case by grasping pillow at _____ _____ _____ _____
open end with one hand and pulling case
back over pillow with the other hand.
Discard case in linen bag.
c. Grasp clean pillowcase at center of closed _____ _____ _____ _____
end. Gather case, turning it inside out
over the hand holding it. With the same
hand, pick up middle of one end of the
pillow. Pull pillowcase down over pillow
with the other hand.
d. Be sure pillow corners fit evenly into _____ _____ _____ _____
corners of pillowcase. Place pillow under
client's head.

38. Place call light within client's reach, and _____ _____ _____ _____
return bed to comfortable position.

39. Open room curtains, and rearrange _____ _____ _____ _____
furniture. Place personal items within easy
reach on over-bed table or bedside stand.
Return bed to a comfortable height.

40. Discard dirty linen in hamper or chute and _____ _____ _____ _____
wash hands.

41. Ask if client feels comfortable. _____ _____ _____ _____

42. Inspect skin for areas of irritation. _____ _____ _____ _____

43. Observe client for signs of fatigue, dyspnea, _____ _____ _____ _____
pain, or discomfort.

Oxygenation 27

Case Study

I. You are the nurse in an outpatient clinic where a 32-year-old female client has come for ongoing medical treatment. She tells you that she has had asthma since she was a young child. While speaking with the client, you notice that she is exhibiting mild wheezing and a productive cough. She appears slightly pale.
   a. What additional assessment questions should be asked of this client?
   b. Identify a possible nursing diagnosis for this client.
   c. What nurse-initiated actions may be taken at this time?
   d. Identify general information that should be included in client teaching for promoting oxygenation.

Independent Learning Activities

1. Review the anatomy and physiology of the cardiovascular and respiratory systems.

2. Practice the skills for assessment and promotion of oxygenation, including auscultation, suctioning, and chest physiotherapy, in the skill laboratory.

3. Practice the techniques for coughing, deep breathing, and pursed-lip breathing at home.

4. Investigate actual and/or potential environmental factors in the community that may influence oxygenation.

Chapter Review

Match the description/definition in Column A with the correct term in Column B.

	Column A	Column B
_____	1. Collapse of alveoli, preventing exchange of oxygen and carbon dioxide.	a. Hypoxia
_____	2. Tachypnea pattern of breathing associated with metabolic acidosis.	b. Pneumothorax
_____	3. Need to sit upright to breathe easier.	c. Atelectasis
_____	4. Blue discoloration of the skin and mucous membranes.	d. Cyanosis
_____	5. Collection of air in the pleural space.	e. Apneustic
_____	6. Periods of apnea and shallow breathing caused by a central nervous system disorder.	f. Kussmaul's respiration
_____	7. Inadequate tissue oxygenation at the cellular level.	g. Orthopnea

_____   8.   Increasing and decreasing pattern caused by alterations in acid-base status.

_____   9.   Collection of blood in the pleural space.

_____   10.   Increased inspiratory time with short grunting expiratory time.

h.   Hemothorax

i.   Cheyne-Stokes respiration

j.   Biot's respiration

Complete the following:

11.   Identify developmental factors that may affect oxygenation.

12.   What are three conditions that affect chest movement?

13.   Briefly describe the difference in signs and symptoms for left- and right-sided heart failure.

14.   What assessment findings indicate that a client is experiencing a decrease in oxygenation?

15.   What information should be provided to clients to promote cardiovascular and respiratory health?

16.   Briefly define the following abnormal chest wall movements:
   a.   retraction

   b.   paradoxical breathing

17.   How do the following physiological processes affect oxygenation?
   a.   anemia

   b.   airway obstruction

   c.   fever

18.   Which type of asepsis is used for tracheal suctioning?

19.   Continuous bubbling in the chest tube water-seal chamber indicates:

20. Identify nursing interventions that may be implemented to achieve the following:
    a. dyspnea management

    b. patent airway

    c. lung expansion

    d. mobilization of secretions

21. Identify the different types of oxygen delivery systems and the flow rate for each.

22. Identify four safety measures that should be implemented when the client is using home oxygen therapy.

23. For the nursing diagnosis, *Ineffective airway clearance related to the presence of tracheobronchial secretions,* identify a client outcome and a nursing intervention to assist the client to meet the outcome.

Select the best answer for each of the following questions:

24. Individuals have come to the health fair to receive their free influenza vaccine. The nurse briefly discusses the medical backgrounds of the clients. The influenza vaccine will be withheld from the:
    1. HIV-positive male
    2. older adult female
    3. male with chronic arthritis
    4. female with a hypersensitivity to eggs

25. The client has a chest tube in place to drain bloody secretions from the chest cavity. When caring for a client with a chest tube, the nurse should:
    1. keep the drainage device above chest level
    2. clamp the chest tube when the client is ambulating
    3. have the client cough if the tubing becomes disconnected
    4. leave trapped fluid in the tubing and estimate the amount

26. The nurse is making a home visit to a client who has emphysema. Instruction for the client with an increased residual volume of air should include:
    1. coughing
    2. deep breathing
    3. pursed-lip breathing
    4. diaphragmatic breathing

27. The client has been admitted to the medical center with a respiratory condition and dyspnea. A number of medications are prescribed for the client. For a client with this difficulty, the nurse should question the order for:
    1. steroids
    2. depressants
    3. mucolytics
    4. bronchodilators

28. Following a client assessment, the nurse suspects hypoxia. This is based on the nurse finding that the client is experiencing:
    1. restlessness
    2. bradypnea
    3. bradycardia
    4. hypotension

29. The client has experienced some respiratory difficulty and is placed on oxygen via nasal cannula. The nurse assists the client with this form of oxygen delivery by:
    1. changing the tubing every 4 hours
    2. assessing the nares for breakdown
    3. inspecting the back of the mouth q8h
    4. securing the cannula to the nose with nonallergic tape

30. The client is being seen in the outpatient medical clinic. The nurse has reviewed the client's chart and finds that there is a history of a cardiopulmonary abnormality. This is supported by the nurse's assessment of the client having:
    1. scleral jaundice
    2. reddened conjunctiva
    3. symmetrical chest movement
    4. splinter hemorrhages in the nails

31. The student nurse is assigned to care for a client who has been diagnosed with pneumonia. The student recognizes that the major problem that is experienced by the client with this disease process is:
    1. lowered oxygen-carrying capacity
    2. decreased concentration of inspired oxygen
    3. poor tissue perfusion from circulatory insufficiency
    4. decreased diffusion of oxygen from the alveoli to the blood

32. The nurse is assessing the client who has a severe central nervous system disorder. The client is observed having periods of apnea and shallow breathing. This assessment finding is documented by the nurse as:
    1. Biot's respiration
    2. Bradypnea
    3. Eupnea
    4. Cheyne-Stokes respiration

33. A 65-year-old client is seen in the physician's office for a routine annual checkup. As part of the physical examination, an electrocardiogram (ECG) is performed. The ECG reveals a normal P wave, P-R interval, and QRS complex with a rate of 60. The nurse evaluates this finding as:
    1. sinus tachycardia
    2. sinus bradycardia
    3. sinus dysrhythmia
    4. supraventricular bradycardia

34. The client is admitted to the medical center with a diagnosis of left-sided congestive heart failure. The nurse is completing the physical assessment and is anticipating finding that the client has:
    1. liver enlargement
    2. peripheral edema
    3. pulmonary congestion
    4. jugular neck vein distention

35. A client has just had abdominal surgery and is returning to the unit. The nurse is planning care for this client and is considering interventions to promote pulmonary function and prevent complications. The nurse:
    1. teaches the client to do leg exercises
    2. asks the physician to order nebulizer treatments
    3. demonstrates the use of a flow-oriented incentive spirometer
    4. informs the client that he will have to be suctioned to remove secretions

36. The nurse manager is evaluating the care that is provided by the new staff nurse during the orientation period. One of the clients requires nasotracheal suctioning, and the nurse manager determines that the appropriate technique is used when the new staff nurse:
    1. places the client in the supine position
    2. prepares for a clean or nonsterile procedure
    3. suctions the oropharyngeal area first, then moves to the nasotracheal area
    4. applies intermittent suction for 10 seconds while the suction catheter is being removed

37. Chest tubes have been inserted into the client following thoracic surgery. In working with this client, the nurse should:

1. coil and secure excess tubing next to the client
2. clamp off the chest tubes except during respiratory assessments
3. milk or strip the tubing every 15–30 minutes to maintain drainage
4. remove the tubing from the connection to check for adequate suction

38. The client is being discharged to the home with an order for oxygen PRN. In preparing to teach the client and family, a priority for the nurse is to provide information on the:
    1. use of the oxygen delivery equipment
    2. physiology of the respiratory system
    3. use of the PaO_2 levels to determine oxygen demand
    4. length of time that the oxygen is to be used by the client

Study Group Questions

- How does the anatomy and physiology of the cardiovascular and respiratory systems promote oxygenation?
- What physiologic factors affect oxygenation?
- How does growth and development influence oxygenation?
- How do behavioral and environmental factors influence oxygenation?
- What are some common alterations in cardiovascular and pulmonary functioning?
- How are the critical thinking and nursing processes applied with clients having difficulty with oxygenation?
- What assessment information should be obtained to determine the client's oxygenation status?
- What findings are usually seen in a client who has inadequate oxygenation?
- How can the nurse promote oxygenation for clients in the health promotion, acute care, and restorative care settings?
- What specific measures and procedures should be implemented by the nurse to manage dyspnea, maintain a patent airway, mobilize secretions, and expand the lungs?
- What should be included in client/family teaching for promotion and maintenance of oxygenation?
- What safety measures should be implemented for the use of oxygen in the home?

Name_____ Date_____ Instructor's Name_____

Performance Checklist: Skill 27-1

Suctioning

	S	U	NP	Comments
1. Assess signs and symptoms of upper and lower airway obstruction requiring nasotracheal or orotracheal suctioning.	____	____	____	_____
2. Determine factors that normally influence upper or lower airway functioning.	____	____	____	_____
3. Assess client's understanding of procedure.	____	____	____	_____
4. Obtain physician's order if indicated by agency policy.	____	____	____	_____
5. Explain to client how procedure will help clear airway and relieve breathing problems. Explain that temporary coughing, sneezing, gagging, or shortness of breath is normal during the procedure. Encourage client to cough out secretions. Practice coughing, if able. Splint surgical incisions, if necessary.	____	____	____	_____
6. Explain importance of and encourage coughing duirng procedure.	____	____	____	_____
7. Assist client to assume position comfortable for nurse and client (usually semi-Fowler's or sitting upright with head hyperextended, unless contraindicated).	____	____	____	_____
8. Place pulse oximeter on client's finger. Take reading and leave pulse oximeter in place.	____	____	____	_____
9. Place towel across client's chest, if needed.	____	____	____	_____
10. Perform appropriate suction technique. a. Performing nasopharyngeal and nasotracheal suctioning				
(1) Wash hands, and apply face shield if splashing is likely.	____	____	____	_____
(2) Connect one end of connecting tubing to suction machine, and place other end in convenient location near client. Turn suction device on, and set vacuum regulator to appropriate negative pressure.	____	____	____	_____

	S	U	NP	Comments

(3) If indicated, increase supplemental **oxygen therapy** to 100% or as ordered by physician. Encourage client to breathe deeply.

(4) Prepare suction catheter.

   (a) Open suction kit or catheter with use of aseptic technique. If sterile drape is available, place it across client's chest or on the overbed table. Do not allow the suction catheter to touch any nonsterile surfaces.

   (b) Unwrap or open sterile basin, and place on bedside table. Be careful not to touch inside of basin. Fill with about 100 ml sterile normal saline solution or water.

   (c) Open lubricant. Squeeze small amount onto open sterile catheter package without touching package.

(5) Apply sterile glove to each hand, or apply nonsterile glove to nondominant hand and sterile glove to dominant hand.

(6) Pick up suction catheter with dominant hand without touching nonsterile surfaces. Pick up connecting tubing with nondominant hand. Secure catheter to tubing.

(7) Check that the equipment is functioning properly by suctioning small amount of normal saline solution from basin.

(8) Lightly coat distal 6 to 8 cm (2 to 3 in) of catheter tip with water-soluble lubricant.

(9) Remove oxygen delivery device, if applicable, with nondominant hand. Without applying suction and using dominant thumb and forefinger, gently but quickly insert catheter into naris during inhalation. Following natural course of the naris, slightly slant the catheter downward or through mouth. Do not force through naris.

   (a) Pharyngeal suctioning: In adults, insert catheter about 16 cm (6 in); in older children, 8 to 12 cm (3 to 5 in); in infants and young children, 4 to 8 cm (2 to 3 in).

	S	U	NP	Comments

(b) Tracheal suctioning: In adults, insert catheter about 20 cm (8 in); in older children, 14 to 20 cm (5.5 to 8 in); and in young children and infants, 8 to 14 cm (3 to 5.5 in).

(c) Positioning option for tracheal suctioning: In some instances turning client's head to right helps nurse suction left mainstem bronchus; turning head to left helps nurse suction right mainstem bronchus. If resistance is felt after insertion of catheter for maximum recommended distance, catheter probably has hit carina. Pull catheter back 1 to 2 cm before applying suction.

(10) Apply intermittent suction for up to 10 seconds by placing and releasing nondominant thumb over vent of catheter and slowly withdrawing catheter while rotating it back and forth between dominant thumb and forefinger. Encourage client to cough. Replace oxygen device, if applicable.

(11) Rinse catheter and connecting tubing with normal saline or water until cleared.

(12) Assess for need to repeat suctioning procedure. When possible, allow adequate time (1 to 2 minutes) between suction passes for ventilation and oxygenation. Assist client to deep breathe and cough.

(13) When pharynx and trachea sufficiently are cleared of secretions, perform oral pharyngeal suctioning to clear mouth of secretions. Do not suction nose again after suctioning mouth.

(14) When suctioning is completed, roll catheter around fingers of dominant hand. Pull glove off inside out so that catheter remains coiled in glove. Pull off other glove over first glove in same way to seal in contaminants. Discard in appropriate receptacle. Turn off suction device.

	S	U	NP	Comments

(15) Remove towel, place in laundry or appropriate receptacle, and reposition client. (Nurse may need to wear clean gloves for personal care.)

(16) If indicated, readjust oxygen to original level because client's blood oxygen level should have returned to baseline.

(17) Discard remainder of normal saline into appropriate receptacle. If basin is disposable, discard into appropriate receptacle. If basin is reusable, rinse it out and place it in soiled utility room.

(18) Remove face shield, and discard into appropriate receptacle. Wash hands.

(19) Place unopened suction kit on suction machine table or at head of bed.

(20) Assist client to a comfortable position, and provide oral hygiene as needed.

b. Performing artifical airway suctioning

   (1) Wash hands, and apply face shield.

   (2) Connect one end of connecting tubing to suction machine, and place other end in convenient location. Turn suction device on, and set vacuum regulator to appropriate negative pressure (see manufacturer's directions).

   (3) Prepare proper suction catheter.

   (4) Aseptically open suction catheter package. If sterile drape is available, place it across client's chest. Do not allow suction catheter to touch any nonsterile surface.

   (5) Unwrap or open sterile basin, and place on bedside table. Be careful not to touch inside of basin. Fill with about 100 ml of sterile normal saline.

   (6) Apply one sterile glove to each hand, or apply nonsterile glove to nondominant hand and sterile glove to dominant hand.

   (7) Pick up suction catheter with dominant hand without touching nonsterile surfaces. Pick up connecting tubing with nondominant hand. Secure catheter to tubing.

	S	U	NP	Comments
(8) Check that equipment is functioning properly by suctioning small amount of saline from basin.	____	____	____	_____
(9) Hyperinflate and/or hyperoxygenate client before suctioning, using manual resuscitation Ambu-bag connected to oxygen source or sigh mechanism on mechanical ventilator.	____	____	____	_____
(10) If client is receiving mechanical ventilation, open swivel adapter or if necessary remove oxygen or humidity delivery device with nondominant hand.	____	____	____	_____
(11) Without applying suction, gently but quickly insert catheter using dominant thumb and forefinger into artificial airway until resistance is met or client coughs, then pull back 1 cm. (Best to time catheter insertion during client inspiration.)	____	____	____	_____
(12) Apply intermittent suction by placing and releasing nondominant thumb over vent of catheter; slowly withdraw catheter while rotating it back and forth between dominant thumb and forefinger. Encourage client to cough. Watch for respiratory distress.	____	____	____	_____
(13) If client is receiving mechanical ventilation, close swivel adapter or replace oxygen delivery device.	____	____	____	_____
(14) Encourage client to deep breathe, if able. Some clients respond well to several manual breaths from the mechanical ventilator or Ambu-bag.	____	____	____	_____
(15) Rinse catheter and connecting tubing with normal saline until clear. Use continuous suction.	____	____	____	_____
(16) Assess client's cardiopulmonary status (vital signs, oxygen saturation), secretion clearance, and complications. Repeat Steps (9) through (15) once or twice more to clear secretions. Allow adequate time (at last 1 full minute) between suction passes for ventilation and reoxygenation.	____	____	____	_____
(17) Perform nasopharyngeal and oropharyngeal suctioning. Do not reinsert into ET or tracheostomy tube.	____	____	____	_____

	S	U	NP	Comments

(18) Disconnect catheter from connecting tubing. Roll catheter around fingers of dominant hand. Pull glove off inside out so that catheter remains in glove. Pull off other glove over first glove in same way to contain contaminants. Discard into appropriate receptacle. Turn off suction device. _____ _____ _____ _____

(19) Remove towel and place in laundry, or remove drape and discard in appropriate receptacle. _____ _____ _____ _____

(20) Reposition client as indicated by condition. Nurse may need to reapply clean gloves for client's personal care. _____ _____ _____ _____

(21) Discard remainder of normal saline into appropriate receptacle. If basin is disposable, discard into appropriate receptacle. If basin is reusable, rinse and place in soiled utility room. _____ _____ _____ _____

(22) Remove and discard face shield, and wash hands. _____ _____ _____ _____

(23) Place unopened suction kit on suction machine or at head of bed according to institution preference. _____ _____ _____ _____

11. Compare client's vital signs and O_2 saturation before and after suctioning. _____ _____ _____ _____

12. Ask client if breathing is easier and if congestion is decreased. _____ _____ _____ _____

13. Observe airway secretions. _____ _____ _____ _____

14. Record the amount, consistency, color, and odor of secretions and client's response to procedure; document client's presuctioning and postsuctioning respiratory status. _____ _____ _____ _____

Name_____ Date_____ Instructor's Name_____

Performance Checklist: Skill 27-2

Care of Clients with Chest Tubes

	S	U	NP	Comments
1. Assess client for respiratory distress and chest pain, breath sounds over affected lung area, and stable vital signs.	____	____	____	_____
2. Observe:				
a. Chest tube dressing.	____	____	____	_____
b. Tubing for kinks, dependent loops, or clots.	____	____	____	_____
c. Chest drainage system, which should be upright and below level of tube insertion.	____	____	____	_____
3. Provide two shodded hemostats for each chest tube, attached to top of client's bed with adhesive tape. Chest tubes are only clamped under specific circumstances per physician order or nursing policy and procedure.	____	____	____	_____
4. Position the client.				
a. Semi-Fowler's position to evacuate air (pneumothorax).	____	____	____	_____
b. High Fowler's position to drain fluid (hemothorax).	____	____	____	_____
5. Maintain tube connection between chest and drainage tubes intact and taped.				
a. Water-seal vent must be without occlusion.	____	____	____	_____
b. Suction-control chamber vent must be without occlusion when suction is used.	____	____	____	_____
6. Coil excess tubing on mattress next to client. Secure with rubber band, safety pin, or plastic clamp.	____	____	____	_____
7. Adjust tubing to hang in straight line from top of mattress to drainage chamber. If chest tube is draining fluid, indicate time that drainage was begun on drainage bottle's adhesive tape or on write-on surface of disposable commercial system.	____	____	____	_____
8. Strip or milk chest tube only if indicated.	____	____	____	_____

	S	U	NP	Comments
9. Wash hands.	⎯⎯	⎯⎯	⎯⎯	⎯⎯⎯⎯⎯⎯⎯⎯⎯⎯⎯
10. Evaluate:				
a. Chest tube dressing.	⎯⎯	⎯⎯	⎯⎯	⎯⎯⎯⎯⎯⎯⎯⎯⎯⎯⎯
b. Tubing should be free of kinks and dependent loops.	⎯⎯	⎯⎯	⎯⎯	⎯⎯⎯⎯⎯⎯⎯⎯⎯⎯⎯
c. The chest drainage system should be upright and below level of tube insertion. Note presence of clots or debris in tubing.	⎯⎯	⎯⎯	⎯⎯	⎯⎯⎯⎯⎯⎯⎯⎯⎯⎯⎯
d. Water seal for fluctuations with client's inspirations and expiration.				
(1) Waterless system: diagnostic indicator for fluctuations with client's inspirations and expirations.	⎯⎯	⎯⎯	⎯⎯	⎯⎯⎯⎯⎯⎯⎯⎯⎯⎯⎯
(2) Water-seal system: bubbling in the water-seal chamber.	⎯⎯	⎯⎯	⎯⎯	⎯⎯⎯⎯⎯⎯⎯⎯⎯⎯⎯
e. Waterless system: Bubbling is diagnostic indicator.	⎯⎯	⎯⎯	⎯⎯	⎯⎯⎯⎯⎯⎯⎯⎯⎯⎯⎯
f. Type and amount of fluid drainage: Nurse should note color and amount of drainage, client's vital signs, and skin color.	⎯⎯	⎯⎯	⎯⎯	⎯⎯⎯⎯⎯⎯⎯⎯⎯⎯⎯
g. Water-seal system: bubbling in the suction control chamber (when suction is being used).	⎯⎯	⎯⎯	⎯⎯	⎯⎯⎯⎯⎯⎯⎯⎯⎯⎯⎯
h. Waterless system: The suction control (float ball) indicates the amount of suction the client's intrapleural space is receiving.	⎯⎯	⎯⎯	⎯⎯	⎯⎯⎯⎯⎯⎯⎯⎯⎯⎯⎯
i. Vital signs.	⎯⎯	⎯⎯	⎯⎯	⎯⎯⎯⎯⎯⎯⎯⎯⎯⎯⎯
11. Record patency of chest tubes, presence of drainage, presence of fluctuations, client's vital signs, chest dressing status, type of suction, and level of comfort.	⎯⎯	⎯⎯	⎯⎯	⎯⎯⎯⎯⎯⎯⎯⎯⎯⎯⎯

Name_____ Date_____ Instructor's Name_____

Performance Checklist: Skill 27-3

Cardiopulmonary Resuscitation

	S	U	NP	Comments
1. Determine if client is unconscious by shaking client and shouting, "Are you OK?"	____	____	____	_____
2. Immediately activate emergency medical services (EMS) for adult client. If alone do Cardiopulmonary resuscitation (CPR) on infant or child for 1 minute, then activate EMS.	____	____	____	_____
3. Determine breathelessness and carotid or brachial (use with infants) pulse.				
a. To determine breathlessness, open airway using head tilt–chin lift or jaw-thrust maneuver. Look, listen, and feel for exchange of air (American Heart Association, 2000).	____	____	____	_____
4. Place victim on hard surface such as floor, ground, or backboard. Victim must be flat. If necessary, logroll victim to flat, supine position using spine precautions.	____	____	____	_____
5. Assume correct and comfortable position.				
a. One-person rescue: Position to face victim, on knees, parallel to victim's sternum.	____	____	____	_____
b. Two-person rescue: One person faces victim, kneeling parallel to victim's head. Second person moves to opposite side and faces victim, kneels parallel to victim's sternum.	____	____	____	_____
6. If available, apply gloves and face shield.	____	____	____	_____
7. Open airway:				
a. If no head or neck trauma, use head tilt–chin lift method (American Heart Association, 2000).	____	____	____	_____
b. Jaw-thrust maneuver can be used by health professionals but is not taught to general public. Grasp angles of victim's lower jaw and lift with both hands, displacing mandible forward while tilting head backward.	____	____	____	_____

	S	U	NP	Comments

8. If readily available, insert oral airway. ___ ___ ___ _____

9. If victim does not resume breathing, administer artificial respiration:
   a. Mouth-to-mouth:
      (1) *Adult*: Pinch victim's nose with ___ ___ ___ _____
          thumb and index fingers, and
          occlude mouth with nurse's mouth or
          use CPR pocket mask. Maintain head
          tilt–chin lift while administering
          breaths so air enters lungs and not
          stomach. Blow two slow full breaths
          into victim's mouth (each breath
          should take $1^1/_2$ to 2 seconds); allow
          victim to exhale between breaths.
          Continue giving 12 breaths per
          minute (American Heart Association,
          2000).
      (2) *Child*: Place nurse's mouth over ___ ___ ___ _____
          child's mouth or use CPR pocket
          mask. For mouth-to-mouth
          resuscitation of child, administer
          two slow breaths lasting 1 to $1^1/_2$
          seconds with a pause between.
          Continue giving 20 breaths per
          minute (American Heart Association,
          2000).
      (3) *Infant*: Place nurse's mouth over ___ ___ ___ _____
          infant's nose and mouth. However,
          three factors should be remembered:
          (1) rescue breaths are the single most
          important maneuver in assisting
          nonbreathing child, (2) an
          appropriate volume is one that
          makes chest rise and fall, and (3) slow
          breaths provide an adequate volume
          at lowest possible pressure, thereby
          reducing risk of gastric distention.
   b. Mouth-to-nose:
      (1) Keep victim's head tilted with one ___ ___ ___ _____
          hand on forehead. Use other hand to
          lift jaw and close mouth. Seal rescuer's
          lips around victim's nose, and blow.
          Allow passive exhalation.
   c. Ambu-bag:
      (1) *Adult and child*: For Ambu-bag ___ ___ ___ _____
          resuscitation use proper-size face
          mask and apply it under chin, up
          and over victim's mouth and nose.
          Observe for rise and fall of chest wall
          with each respiration. Listen for air
          escaping during exhalation, and feel
          for flow of air. If lungs do not inflate,

	S	U	NP	Comments

reposition head and neck and check for
visible airway obstruction, such as vomitus.

10. Suction secretions if necessary, or turn
victim's head to one side, unless
contraindicated.

11. Check for presence of carotid (adults and
children) or brachial (infants) pulse after
restoring breathing. Check pulse for 5 to
10 seconds.

12. If pulse is absent, initiate chest compressions:
   a. Assume correct hand position:
      (1) *Adult*: Place hands over lower half
         of sternum, being careful to avoid
         xiphoid process on sternum. Keep
         hands parallel to chest and fingers
         above chest. Interlocking fingers is
         helpful. Keep fingers off chest wall.
         Extend arms, and lock elbows.
         Maintain arms straight and shoulders
         directly over victim's sternum.
      (2) *Child*: Place heel of one hand on
         lower half of sternum above xiphoid
         process. Maintain head tilt with other
         hand if possible.
      (3) *Infant*: Place index and middle
         fingers of one hand on lower half of
         sternum above xiphoid process.
         Fingers should be 1 cm below nipple
         line and perpendicular to sternum
         and not slanted. An alternative
         technique is to place both thumbs side
         by side over lower half of sternum
         above xiphoid process.
   b. Compress sternum to proper depth
      from shoulders and then release pressure,
      maintaining contact with skin to ensure
      ongoing proper placement of hands. Do
      not rock, but transmit weight vertically
      down.
      (1) Adult and adolescent: 4 to 5 cm
         ($1^1/_2$ to 2 inches).
      (2) Older child: 3 to 4 cm
         (1 to $1^1/_2$ inches).
      (3) Toddler and preschooler: 2 to 4 cm
         ($^3/_4$ to $1^1/_2$ inches).
      (4) Infant: 1 to 2 cm ($^1/_2$ to 1 inch).

	S	U	NP	Comments

c. Maintain proper rate of compression:
   (1) Adult and adolescent: 80 to 100 per minute (count "one one-thousand; two one-thousand...")
   (2) Child: at least 100 per minute.
   (3) Infant: at least 100 per minute.

d. Continue mouth-to-mouth or Ambu-bag ventilations:
   (1) Adult and adolescent: every 5 seconds (12 per minute).
   (2) Older child: every 4 seconds (15 per minute).
   (3) Child: every 3 seconds (20 per minute).
   (4) Infant and toddler: every 3 seconds (20 per minute).

13. Palpate for carotid or brachial pulse with each external chest compression for first full minute (two-person rescue). If carotid pulse is not palpable, compressions are not strong enough or hand position is incorrect.

14. Continue CPR until relieved, until victim regains spontaneous pulse and respirations, until rescuer is exhausted and unable to perform CPR effectively, or until physician discontinues CPR.

15. Remove and discard into appropriate receptacle: gloves, face shield, and pocket mask.

16. Palpate carotid pulse at least every 5 minutes after first minute of CPR.

17. CPR should not be not interrupted for more than 5 seconds.

18. Immediately report arrest indicating exact location of victim.

19. In hospital setting, follow hospital policy.

20. In community setting, dial 911 or other emergency number.

21. Record onset of arrest, medication and other treatments given, procedures performed, and victim's response.

28 Sleep

Case Study

I. A middle-adult-age client has come to the physician's office to obtain a prescription for a "sleeping pill" because she has been having difficulty either falling or staying asleep. You are completing the initial nursing assessment and discover that the client is recently divorced and trying to juggle extensive work and child-care responsibilities.
    a. Identify a possible nursing diagnosis and goal for this client.
    b. Indicate nursing interventions and teaching areas for this client.

Independent Learning Activities

1. Review the physiological processes that promote sleep.

2. Investigate how the environment in a health care agency may affect sleep and how it may be changed.

3. Investigate available nonprescription remedies for promoting sleep.

Chapter Review

Match the description/definition in Column A with the correct term in Column B.

Column A

_____ 1. A cessation of breathing for a time during sleep.
_____ 2. Tooth grinding.
_____ 3. A decrease in the amount, quality, and consistency of sleep.
_____ 4. Sleep walking.
_____ 5. Sudden muscle weakness during intense emotions.
_____ 6. A difficulty in falling or staying asleep.
_____ 7. 24-hour day/night cycle.
_____ 8. Bedwetting.
_____ 9. Measurement of brain waves during the stages of sleep.
_____ 10. Excessive sleepiness during the day.

Column B

a. Cataplexy
b. Sleep deprivation
c. Circadian rhythm
d. Nocturnal enuresis
e. Narcolepsy
f. Sleep apnea
g. Bruxism
h. Polysomnogram
i. Somnambulism
j. Insomnia

Complete the following:

11. What are the stages of sleep?

12. The functions of sleep are:

13. What factors may affect sleep?

14. Identify changes that occur in the older adult that may alter sleep patterns, and list possible nursing interventions to help the client achieve adequate sleep.

15. How can the nurse promote a restful environment?

16. What safety measures should be instituted for a client with nocturia?

17. Identify at least three bedtime rituals that may assist an adult to sleep.

18. What information is obtained in a sleep history?

19. Identify how the following illnesses may alter a client's sleep:
    a. respiratory disease

    b. hyperthyroidism

    c. coronary heart disease

    d. gastric reflux/hiatal hernia

20. Identify common sleep disorders and the treatment that the nurse may anticipate for each.

Select the best answer for each of the following questions:

21. Individuals experience changes in their sleep patterns as they progress through the life cycle. The nurse assesses that the client is experiencing bedtime fears, wakefulness during the night, and nightmares. These behaviors are associated with:
    1. infants
    2. toddlers
    3. preschoolers
    4. school-age children

22. The nurse is making rounds during the night to check on her clients. When she enters one of the rooms at 3:00AM, she finds

that the client is sitting up in a chair. The client tells the nurse that she is not able to sleep. The nurse first should:
1. obtain an order for a hypnotic
2. assist the client back to bed
3. provide a glass of warm milk and a back rub
4. ask about activities that have helped her sleep previously

23. The nurse is working on a pediatric unit at the local hospital. A 4-year-old boy is admitted to the unit. To assist the child to sleep, the nurse:
1. reads to him
2. teaches him relaxation activities
3. allows the child to watch TV until he is tired
4. has him get ready for bed very quickly, without advance notice

24. The client is found to be awakening frequently during the night. There are a number of medications prescribed for this client. The nurse determines that the medications that may be creating this client's particular sleep disturbance is the:
1. narcotic
2. beta blocker
3. antidepressant
4. antihistamine

25. The nurse suspects that the client may be experiencing sleep deprivation. This suspicion is validated by the nurse in finding that the client has:
1. increased reflexes
2. blurred vision
3. excess energy
4. decreased response time

26. The nurse is working in a sleep clinic that is part of the local hospital. In preparing to work with clients with different sleep needs, the nurse understands that:
1. bedtime rituals are most important for adolescents
2. regular use of sleeping medications is appropriate

3. warm milk before bedtime may help the client sleep
4. individuals most easily are aroused from sleep during stages 3 and 4

27. The parents of a 5-year-old have brought their child to the outpatient clinic for a checkup. They identify to the nurse that the child has been experiencing difficulty sleeping. The nurse recognizes that one of the possible causes may be an insomnia-producing food allergy. The nurse questions the parents about the child's intake of:
1. meat
2. eggs
3. seafood
4. string beans

28. The nurse is visiting a client in his home. While completing a client history and home assessment, the nurse finds that there are many prescription medications kept in the bathroom cabinet. In determining possible areas that may influence the client's sleep patterns, the nurse looks for a classification of medication that may suppress the client's REM sleep. The nurse looks in the cabinet for a:
1. diuretic
2. stimulant
3. beta blocker
4. nasal decongestant

29. A newborn is brought to the pediatrician's office for the first physical exam. The parents ask the nurse when they can expect the baby to sleep through the night. The nurse responds that, although there may be an individual difference, infants usually develop a nighttime pattern of sleep by the age of:
1. 6 weeks
2. 2 months
3. 4 months
4. 10 months

30. The nurse is working with older adults in the senior center. A group is discussing problems with sleep. The nurse recognizes that older adults:

1. take less time to fall asleep
2. are more difficult to arouse from sleep
3. have a significant decline in stage 4 sleep
4. require more sleep than middle-aged adults

31. A client with congestive heart failure is being discharged from the hospital to her home. The client will be taking a diuretic daily. The nurse informs the client that she may experience:
    1. nocturia
    2. nightmares
    3. reduced REM sleep
    4. increased daytime sleepiness

32. During a home visit, the nurse discovers that the client has been having difficulty sleeping. To help the client achieve sufficient sleep, an appropriate response by the nurse is:
    1. "Do you keep your bedroom completely dark at night?"
    2. "You should nap more during the daytime hours."
    3. "Why don't you eat something right before you go to bed?"
    4. "What kinds of things do you do right before bedtime?"

33. The client has come to the sleep clinic to determine what may be creating his sleeping problems. In addition, his partner is having sleep-pattern interruptions. If this client is experiencing sleep apnea, the nurse may expect the partner to identify that the client:
    1. snores excessively
    2. talks in his sleep
    3. is very restless
    4. walks in his sleep

Study Group Questions

- What is sleep?
- What are the physiological processes involved in sleep?
- How is sleep regulated by the body?
- What are the functions of sleep?
- What purpose do dreams serve?
- What are the normal requirements and patterns of sleep across the life span?
- What factors may influence sleep?
- What are some of the common sleep disorders and nursing interventions?
- What information should be included in a sleep history?
- How are the critical thinking and nursing processes applied with clients experiencing insufficient sleep or rest?
- What measures may be implemented by the nurse to promote sleep for clients/families?
- What information should be included in client/family teaching for the promotion of rest and sleep?

Study Chart

Create a study chart to describe the Sleep Patterns Across the Life Span, *identifying the sleep patterns and needs for infants, toddlers, preschoolers, school-age children, adolescents, adults, and older adults.*

29 Promoting Comfort

Case Study

I.   A client is going to be using a patient-controlled analgesia (PCA) pump after his surgery.
    a.   What assessments need to be made before the client uses the pump?
    b.   What information is needed in the teaching plan for this client?

Independent Learning Activities

1.   Review the physiological processes involved in the reception, perception, and reaction to pain.

2.   Investigate nonprescription and nontraditional measures that are available in the health care setting or community for pain relief (e.g., acupuncture).

3.   Investigate available over-the-counter medications for pain relief, including their cost and any contraindications for use. Compare the cost and similarity between trade name and generic or store brand analgesics.

4.   Research an article in a current nursing journal on creative nursing interventions for pain relief.

Chapter Review

Complete the following:

1.   Define the following terms:
    a.   pain

    b.   analgesic

    c.   local anesthesia

    d.   exacerbation

    e.   remission

2.   Compare and contrast the following:
    a.   acute and chronic pain

    b.   superficial and visceral pain

    c.   referred and radiating pain

3.   Identify at least five physiological and five behavioral responses to pain.

4. How can pain influence an individual's activities of daily living?

5. Identify how the nurse may assess the level of pain for the following clients:
   a. toddler

   b. speaker of a different language

6. What information should be obtained from the client about the characteristics of the pain experience?

7. For the following factors, identify the nursing interventions that are most appropriate:
   a. attention level

   b. anxiety

   c. fatigue

   d. coping style

8. Specify six nonpharmacologic interventions that may be implemented to relieve pain.

9. Identify at least four types of adjuvant medications that may be used in conjunction with an analgesic to manage a client's pain.

10. The use of epidural anesthesia for pain relief has the following advantages:

11. Provide at least four examples of how the nurse may individualize a client's pain management.

12. How may the environment be adapted or altered to increase a client's comfort?

13. Three types of analgesics that may be used for treatment of mild to moderate pain are:

14. What are the advantages of a PCA pump?

15. What are the indications for the use of a continuous intravenous (IV) narcotic analgesic drip?

Select the best answer for each of the following questions:

16. Nurses may allow their own misconceptions about or interpretations of the pain experience to affect their willingness to intervene for their client.
    True _____ False _____

17. Perception is the point at which a person is aware of pain.
    True _____ False _____

18. The degree and quality of pain are related to the client's definition of pain.
    True _____ False _____

19. When clients are experiencing pain, they will not hesitate to inform you.
    True _____ False _____

20. Fatigue decreases a client's perception of pain.
    True _____ False _____

21. The nurse should provide descriptive words for the client to assist in assessing the quality of the pain.
    True _____ False _____

22. The client is experiencing pain that is not being managed by analgesics given by the oral or intramuscular (IM) routes. Epidural analgesia is initiated. The nurse is alert for a complication of this treatment and observes the client for:
    1. diarrhea
    2. hypertension
    3. urinary retention
    4. an increased respiratory rate

23. The client had a laparoscopic procedure this morning and is requesting a pain medication. The nurse assesses the client's vital signs and decides to withhold the medication based on the finding of:
    1. pulse = 90/min
    2. respirations = 10/min
    3. blood pressure = 130/80
    4. temperature = 99° F, rectally

24. The nurse is working with an older adult population in the extended care facility. Many of the clients experience discomfort associated with arthritis and have analgesics prescribed. In administering an analgesic medication to an older adult client, the nurse should:
    1. give the medication when the pain increases in severity
    2. combine narcotics for a greater effect
    3. use the IM route whenever possible
    4. give the medication before activities or procedures

25. One of the clients that the nurse is working with on an outpatient basis at the local clinic has rheumatoid arthritis. The client has no known allergies to any medications, so the nurse anticipates that the physician will prescribe:
    1. Elavil
    2. Stadol
    3. Indocin
    4. morphine

26. An adolescent has been carried to the sidelines of the soccer field after experiencing a twisted ankle. The level of pain is identified as low to moderate. The nurse observes that the client has:
    1. pupil constriction
    2. pallor and diaphoresis
    3. decreased heart rate
    4. a decreased respiratory rate

27. The nurse on the pediatric unit is finding that it is sometimes difficult to determine the presence and severity of pain in very young clients. The nurse recognizes that toddlers may be experiencing pain when they have:
    1. an increased appetite
    2. a relaxed posture
    3. an increased degree of cooperation
    4. disturbances in their sleep patterns

28. A client on the oncology unit is experiencing severe pain associated with his cancer. Although analgesics have been prescribed and administered, the client is

having "breakthrough pain." The nurse anticipates that his treatment will include:
1. the use of a placebo
2. experimental medications
3. an increase in the opioid dose
4. administration of medications every hour

29. The client is experiencing pain that is being treated with a fentanyl transdermal patch. The nurse advises this client to:
1. avoid exposure to the sun
2. change the patch site every 2 hours
3. apply a heating pad over the site
4. expect immediate pain relief when the patch is applied

30. The client is experiencing very severe pain and has been placed on a morphine drip. During the client's assessment, the nurse finds that the respiratory rate is 6/min. The nurse anticipates that the client will receive:
1. Narcan
2. additional morphine
3. incentive spirometry
4. no additional treatment for this expected response

Study Group Questions

- How may the nurse use a holistic approach to assist the client in achieving comfort?

- What is pain?
- What are the physiological components of the pain experience?
- How may the client respond, physiologically and behaviorally, to the pain experience?
- What factors influence the pain experience?
- How are acute and chronic pain different?
- How should the nurse assess a client's pain?
- How may the client characterize pain?
- What nonpharmacologic measures may be used to relieve pain?
- What interventions may the nurse implement to promote comfort and relieve pain?
- What pharmacological measures are available for pain relief ?
- How is a back rub or massage performed to achieve an optimum effect?
- What should the nurse do if comfort or pain-relief measures are not effective?
- What information should be included in client/family teaching for pain control or relief ?

Study Chart

Create a study chart to describe the Factors Influencing Pain and Comfort, *identifying how the age, gender, culture, meaning of pain, and prior experience of a client alter the pain experience.*

30 Nutrition

Case Study

I. You are working with a client who is being discharged from the acute care unit after having had a heart attack (myocardial infarction). The client's primary care provider has prescribed a diet that is low in sodium and saturated fat. The client comes from a family that values some traditional cultural practices and holiday celebrations where food plays an important role.
    a.   What would you like to know about the client and the family to assist in dietary planning?
    b.   How can you help this client meet the prescribed dietary requirements?

Independent Learning Activities

1.   Review the physiological processes associated with nutritional intake, including digestion, absorption, metabolism, and elimination.

2.   Complete a self-assessment of dietary intake for a selected period, usually in intervals of 24 hours, 3 days, or weekly. Review your intake for the specified time period to evaluate your intake of essential nutrients and their distribution on the food pyramid.

3.   Investigate available resources in the community (e.g., Women, Infants, and Children program, Meals-on-Wheels) that assist clients and families with nutrition.

4.   Visit community food stores, or check advertisements, and compare the cost of similar items to determine where clients may get the "best buys." Inquire if the stores will deliver to individuals who are not able to leave their homes to do their own shopping.

5.   Review food labels to increase your familiarity with the information that is provided to the consumer.

Chapter Review

Match the description/definition in Column A with the correct term in Column B.

Column A

_____ 1. Increase in blood glucose.

_____ 2. Breakdown of food products to smaller particles.

_____ 3. Production of more complex chemical substances through the synthesis of nutrients.

_____ 4. All biochemical and physiological processes by which the body maintains itself.

_____ 5. Organic substances present in small amounts in foods that act as coenzymes in reactions.

_____ 6. Inorganic elements that act as catalysts in biochemical reactions.

_____ 7. Substances necessary for body functioning.

_____ 8. Breakdown of body substances and tissues into simpler substances.

_____ 9. Decrease in blood glucose.

_____ 10. Measurement of size and makeup of body at specific sites.

Column B

a. Anabolism

b. Hypoglycemia

c. Digestion

d. Anthropometry

e. Catabolism

f. Nutrients

g. Minerals

h. Metabolism

i. Hyperglycemia

j. Vitamins

Complete the following:

11. Identify the seven factors that influence dietary patterns.

12. What are the nutrition-related goals for the year 2010?

13. Briefly describe the purpose of the food guide pyramid.

14. What can you tell an individual at a health fair who is interested in general nutritional guidelines?

15. Provide an example of an alternative dietary pattern.

16. What laboratory studies are useful in determining nutritional deficits?

17. What factors may influence a client's nutritional intake in an acute care setting?

18. Identify the various routes for administration of enteral feedings and problems that may be encountered with the feedings.

19. The client will be receiving parenteral nutrition (PN). Identify the following:
    a. main reason for use of PN

    b. four major nursing goals for the client receiving PN

    c. three nursing interventions to assist the client in the prevention of metabolic complications related to PN therapy

    d. recommended infusion rates for the acute care and home care environments

    e. guidelines and precautions for lipid infusions

20. Identify dietary measures that may be implemented for the client without teeth or with ill-fitting dentures.

21. A dietary assessment to determine a client's nutritional status includes:

22. Identify a nursing diagnosis and expected outcome for a client who is underweight.

Select the best answer for each of the following questions:

23. The nurse is working with a client who requires an increase in complete proteins in the diet. The nurse recommends:
    1. milk
    2. cereals
    3. legumes
    4. vegetables

24. The nurse is talking with a community resident who has come to the health fair. The resident tells the nurse that he takes lots of extra vitamins every day. Because of the potential for toxicity, the resident is advised not to exceed the dietary guidelines for:
    1. vitamin A
    2. vitamin B
    3. vitamin C
    4. folic acid

25. The nurse is working with a client who is a lactovegetarian. The food that is selected as appropriate for this dietary pattern is:
    1. fish
    2. milk
    3. eggs
    4. poultry

26. The client says that he doesn't eat fish anymore. An appropriate follow-up question by the nurse is:
    1. "Why don't you eat fish anymore?"
    2. "What caused you to lose interest in fish?"
    3. "Fish makes you feel ill in some way?"
    4. "Aren't you aware that fish is a valuable source of nutrients?"

27. The nurse is preparing to insert a nasogastric tube for enteral feedings. The nurse recognizes that this intervention is used when:
    1. the client has a gag reflex
    2. the client is not able to absorb nutrients
    3. the client is slow to eliminate food
    4. the client is not able to ingest foods

28. The nurse is preparing the enteral feeding for a client who has a nasogastric tube in place. The most effective method the nurse can use to check for placement of a nasogastric tube is to:
    1. perform a pH analysis of aspirated secretions
    2. measure the visible tubing exiting from the nose
    3. inject air into the tube and auscultate over the stomach
    4. place the end of the tube into water and observe for bubbling

29. A female client who has come to the family planning center is taking an oral contraceptive. This client should have an increase in vitamin B_6 and niacin. The nurse recommends that the client have a regular intake of:
    1. tomatoes
    2. whole grains
    3. citrus fruits
    4. green leafy vegetables

30. The client has heard on television that zinc is an important element in the body's immune response. The client asks the nurse what foods contain zinc. Because of high zinc content, the nurse recommends:
    1. fish
    2. liver
    3. whole grains
    4. green leafy vegetables

31. The nurse is assigned to make home visits to a number of clients. Of all of the clients that were visited during the day, the client with the greatest risk of a nutritional deficiency is the client with:
    1. decreased metabolic requirements
    2. an alteration in his or her dietary schedule
    3. a body weight that is 5% over the ideal weight
    4. a weight loss of 3% within the past 6 months

32. Following surgery, the client is having her dietary intake advanced. After a period of NPO, the client is placed on a clear liquid diet. The nurse calls the dietary department to order:
    1. milk
    2. soup
    3. custard
    4. Popsicles

33. While completing an assessment during a home visit, the nurse discovers that the client has a history of congestive heart failure and is taking digoxin 0.25 mg daily. Being aware that medications may influence the client's dietary patterns, the nurse is alert to the client experiencing:
    1. anorexia
    2. gastric distress
    3. an alteration in taste
    4. an alteration in smell

34. The nurse is explaining the guidelines identified in the Food Guide Pyramid to a client at the clinic. According to the Food Guide Pyramid, the client should have an intake of bread and cereals of:
    1. 1 to 3 servings/day
    2. 2 to 4 servings/day
    3. 3 to 5 servings/day
    4. 6 to 11 servings/day

35. A client on the unit has an enteral tube in place for feedings. When the nurse enters the room, the client says that he is experiencing cramps and nausea. The nurse should:
    1. cool the formula
    2. remove the tube
    3. use a more concentrated formula
    4. decrease the administration rate

36. The nurse is completing a physical assessment on a client who has just been admitted to the rehabilitation facility. The nurse suspects a nutritional alteration as a result of finding:
    1. shiny hair
    2. spoon-shaped, ridged nails
    3. moist conjunctival membranes
    4. a pink tongue with papillae present

Study Group Questions

- What are the basic principles of nutrition?
- What body processes are involved in the intake, use, and elimination of foods?
- What are the six major nutrients and their purposes and food sources?
- What are the current recommendations for daily nutritional intake?
- How do nutritional needs change across the life span?
- How does culture/ethnicity influence dietary intake?
- What are some common alternative food patterns?
- How should the nurse assess the client's nutritional status?
- What clients are at a greater risk for nutritional deficiencies?
- What nursing diagnoses may be appropriate for clients with nutritional alterations?

- How does the nurse assist clients to meet nutritional needs in the health promotion, acute care, and restorative care setting?
- What special diets may be prescribed for individuals?
- What are the nursing procedures for implementation of enteral and parenteral nutrition?
- What guidelines and precautions should be considered by the nurse in assisting the client with enteral or parenteral nutrition?
- What general information should be included for clients/families for promotion or restoration of an adequate nutritional intake?

Study Chart

Create a study chart to describe the 6 Nutrients, identifying uses of each in the body and their food sources: carbohydrates, proteins, lipids, vitamins, minerals, and water.

Name_____ Date_____ Instructor's Name_____

Performance Checklist: Skill 30-1

Inserting a Small-Bore Nasoenteric Tube for Enteral Feedings

	S	U	NP	Comments
1. Assess client for the need for enteral tube feeding.	____	____	____	_____
2. Assess client for appropriate route of administration:				
a. Close each nostril alternately, and ask client to breathe.	____	____	____	_____
b. Assess for gag reflex.	____	____	____	_____
c. Inspect nares for any irritation or obstruction.	____	____	____	_____
d. Review client's medical history for nasal problems and risk of aspiration.	____	____	____	_____
3. Assess for bowel sounds. Consult physician if bowel sounds are absent.	____	____	____	_____
4. Wash hands.	____	____	____	_____
5. Explain procedure to client.	____	____	____	_____
6. Explain to client how to communicate during intubation by raising index finger to indicate gagging or discomfort.	____	____	____	_____
7. Position client in sitting or high-Fowler's position. If client is comatose, place in semi-Fowler's position.	____	____	____	_____
8. Examine feeding tube for flaws: rough or sharp edges on distal end and closed or clogged outlet holes.	____	____	____	_____
9. Determine length of tube to be inserted and mark with tape or indelible ink.	____	____	____	_____
10. Prepare NG or NI tube for intubation:				
a. Plastic tubes should *not* be iced.	____	____	____	_____
b. Wash hands.	____	____	____	_____
c. Inject 10 ml of water from 30-ml or larger Luer-Lok or catheter-tip syringe into the tube.	____	____	____	_____

	S	U	NP	Comments

d. Make certain that guide wire is securely positioned against weighted tip and that both Luer-Lok connections are snugly fitted together.

11. Cut adhesive tape 10 cm (4 inches) long, or prepare tube fixation device.

12. Put on clean gloves.

13. Dip tube with surface lubricant into glass of water.

14. Hand client a glass of water with straw or glass with crushed ice (if able to swallow).

15. Gently insert tube through nostril to back of throat (posterior nasopharynx). This may cause client to gag. Aim back and down toward ear.

16. Have client flex head toward chest after tube has passed through nasopharynx.

17. Emphasize need to mouth breathe and swallow during the procedure.

18. When tip of tube reaches the carina (about 25 cm [10 inches] in an adult), stop and listen for air exchange from the distal portion of the tube.

19. Advance tube each time client swallows until desired length has been passed.

20. Check for position of tube in back of throat with penlight and tongue blade.

21. Check placement of tube.

22. After gastric aspirates are obtained, anchor tube to nose and avoid pressure on nares. Mark exit site with indelible ink. Use one of following options for anchoring:
   a. Apply tape
      (1) Apply tincture of benzoin or other skin adhesive on tip of client's nose and allow it to become "tacky."
      (2) Remove gloves, and split one end of the adhesive tape strip lengthwise 5 cm (2 inches).
      (3) Wrap each of the 5-cm strips around tube as it exits nose.

	S	U	NP	Comments

b. Apply tube fixation device using shaped adhesive patch
   (1) Apply wide end of patch to bridge of nose.   _____ _____ _____ _____
   (2) Slip connector around feeding tube as it exits nose.   _____ _____ _____ _____

23. Fasten end of nasogastric tube to client's gown by looping rubber band around tube in slip knot. Pin rubber band to gown.   _____ _____ _____ _____

24. For intestinal placement, position client on right side when possible until radiological confirmation of correct placement has been verified. Otherwise, assist client to a comfortable position.   _____ _____ _____ _____

25. Obtain x-ray film of chest/abdomen.   _____ _____ _____ _____

26. Apply gloves, and administer oral hygiene. Cleanse tubing at nostril with washcloth dampened in soap and water.   _____ _____ _____ _____

27. Remove gloves, dispose of equipment, and wash hands.   _____ _____ _____ _____

28. Observe client to determine response to NG or NI tube intubation:
   a. Persistent gagging   _____ _____ _____ _____
   b. Paroxysms of coughing   _____ _____ _____ _____

29. Confirm x-ray results.   _____ _____ _____ _____

30. Routinely note location of external exit site marking on the tube.   _____ _____ _____ _____

31. Record and report type and size of tube placed, location of distal tip of tube, client's tolerance of procedure, pH value, and confirmation of tube position by x-ray.   _____ _____ _____ _____

Name_____ Date_____ Instructor's Name_____

Performance Checklist: Skill 30-2

Administering Enteral Feedings via Nasoenteric Tubes

	S	U	NP	Comments
1. Assess client's need for enteral tube feeding.	____	____	____	_____
2. Auscultate for bowel sounds before feeding.	____	____	____	_____
3. Obtain baseline weight and laboratory values. Assess client for fluid volume excess or deficit, electrolyte abnormalities, and metabolic abnormalities such as hyperglycemia.	____	____	____	_____
4. Verify physician's order for formula, rate, route, and frequency.	____	____	____	_____
5. Explain procedure to client.	____	____	____	_____
6. Wash hands.	____	____	____	_____
7. Prepare feeding container to administer formula continuously:				
a. Check expiration date on formula and integrity of can or bottle.	____	____	____	_____
b. Have tube feeding at room temperature.	____	____	____	_____
c. Connect tubing to container as needed or prepare ready-to-hang container.	____	____	____	_____
d. Shake formula container well, and fill container with formula. Open stopcock on tubing, and fill tubing with formula to remove air. Hang on intravenous (IV) pole.	____	____	____	_____
8. For intermittent feeding have syringe ready and be sure formula is at room temperature.	____	____	____	_____
9. Place client in high-Fowler's position or elevate head of bed at least 30 degrees.	____	____	____	_____
10. Determine tube placement. Consider together the results from pH testing and the aspirate's appearance.	____	____	____	_____

	S	U	NP	Comments

11. Check for gastric residual.
    a. Connect syringe to end of feeding tube, and pull back evenly to aspirate gastric contents. ___ ___ ___ _____
    b. Return aspirated contents to stomach unless the volume exceeds 100 ml (check agency policy). ___ ___ ___ _____

12. Flush tubing with 30 ml water. ___ ___ ___ _____

13. Initiate feeding:
    a. Syringe or intermittent feeding
       (1) Pinch proximal end of feeding tube. ___ ___ ___ _____
       (2) Remove plunger from syringe and attach barrel of syringe to end of tube. ___ ___ ___ _____
       (3) Fill syringe with measured amount of formula. Release tube, elevate syringe to no more than 18 inches (45 cm) above insertion site, and allow it to empty gradually by gravity. Refill until prescribed amount has been delivered to client. ___ ___ ___ _____
       (4) If feeding bag is used, attach gavage tubing to end of feeding tube. Set rate by adjusting roller clamp on tubing. Allow bag to empty gradually over 30 to 60 minutes. Label bag with tube-feeding type, strength, and amount. Include date, time, and initials. ___ ___ ___ _____
    b. Continuous-drip method
       (1) Hang feeding bag and tubing on IV pole. ___ ___ ___ _____
       (2) Connect distal end of tubing to proximal end of feeding tube. ___ ___ ___ _____
       (3) Connect tubing through infusion pump, and set rate (see manufacturer's directions). ___ ___ ___ _____

14. Advance rate of concentration of tube feeding gradually. ___ ___ ___ _____

15. Following intermittent infusion or at end of continuous infusion, flush nasoenteral tubing with 30 ml of water, using irrigating syringe. Repeat every 4 to 6 hours around the clock. Have registered dietitian recommend total free water requirement per day. ___ ___ ___ _____

16. When tube feedings are not being administered, cap or clamp the proximal end of the feeding tube. ___ ___ ___ _____

	S	U	NP	Comments
17. Rinse bag and tubing with warm water whenever feedings are interrupted.	___	___	___	_____
18. Change bag and tubing every 24 hours.	___	___	___	_____
19. Measure amount of aspirate (residual) every 8 to 12 hours.	___	___	___	_____
20. Monitor finger-stick blood glucose every 6 hours until maximum administration rate is reached and maintained for 24 hours.	___	___	___	_____
21. Monitor intake and output every 8 hours.	___	___	___	_____
22. Weigh client daily until maximum administration rate is reached and maintained for 24 hours, then weigh client 3 times per week.	___	___	___	_____
23. Observe return of normal laboratory values.	___	___	___	_____
24. Record amount of feeding.	___	___	___	_____
25. Record client's response to tube feeding, patency of tube, and any side effects.	___	___	___	_____
26. Record and report type of feeding, status of feeding tube, client's tolerance, and adverse effects.	___	___	___	_____

Name_____   Date_____   Instructor's Name_____

Performance Checklist: Skill 30-3

Administering Enternal Feedings via Gastrostomy or Jejunostomy Tube

	S	U	NP	Comments
1. Assess client's need for enteral tube feedings.	___	___	___	_____
2. Auscultate for bowel sounds before feeding. Consult physician if bowel sounds are absent.	___	___	___	_____
3. Obtain baseline weight and laboratory values.	___	___	___	_____
4. Verify physician's order for formula, rate, route, and frequency.	___	___	___	_____
5. Assess gastrostomy/jejunostomy site for breakdown, irritation, or drainage.	___	___	___	_____
6. Explain procedure to client.	___	___	___	_____
7. Wash hands.	___	___	___	_____
8. Prepare feeding container to administer formula continuously:				
a. Have tube feeding at room temperature.	___	___	___	_____
b. Connect tubing to container as needed or prepare ready-to-hang container.	___	___	___	_____
c. Shake formula well. Fill container and tubing with formula.	___	___	___	_____
9. For intermittent feeding have syringe ready and be sure formula is at room temperature.	___	___	___	_____
10. Elevate head of bed 30 to 45 degrees.	___	___	___	_____
11. Apply gloves, and verify tube placement:				
a. Gastrostomy tube				
(1) Attach syringe and aspirate gastric secretions, observe their appearance, and check pH.	___	___	___	_____
(2) Return aspirated contents to stomach unless the volume exceeds 100 ml. If the volume is greater than 100 ml on several consecutive occasions, hold feeding and notify physician.	___	___	___	_____

	S	U	NP	Comments
b. Jejunostomy tube				
(1) Aspirate intestinal secretions.	___	___	___	_____
(2) Observe their appearance and check pH.	___	___	___	_____
12. Flush with 30 ml water.	___	___	___	_____
13. Initiate feedings:				
a. Syringe feedings				
(1) Pinch proximal end of the gastrostomy/jejunostomy tube.	___	___	___	_____
(2) Remove plunger, attach barrel of syringe to end of tube, then fill syringe with formula.	___	___	___	_____
(3) Release tube, and elevate syringe. Allow syringe to empty gradually by gravity, refilling until prescribed amount has been delivered to the client.	___	___	___	_____
b. Continuous-drip method				
(1) Fill feeding container with enough prescribed formula for 4 hours of feeding.	___	___	___	_____
(2) Hang container on IV pole, and clear tubing of air.	___	___	___	_____
(3) Thread tubing into feeding pump according to manufacturer's directions.	___	___	___	_____
(4) Connect end of feeding tubing to proximal end of gastrostomy/ jejunostomy tube.	___	___	___	_____
(5) Begin infusion at prescribed rate.	___	___	___	_____
14. Administer water via feeding tube as ordered with or between feedings.	___	___	___	_____
15. Flush tube with 30 ml of water every 4 to 6 hours around the clock and before and after administering medications via the tube.	___	___	___	_____
16. When tube feedings are not being administered, cap or clamp the proximal end of the gastrostomy/jejunostomy tube.	___	___	___	_____
17. Rinse container and tubing with warm water after all intermittent feedings.	___	___	___	_____
18. Leave gastrostomy/jejunostomy exit site open to air. However, if a dressing is needed because of drainage, change dressing daily or as needed and report the drainage to the physician; inspect exit site every shift.	___	___	___	_____

	S	U	NP	Comments
19. Dispose of supplies, and wash hands.	___	___	___	_____
20. Evaluate client's tolerance of tube feeding. Check amount of aspirate (residual) every 8 to 12 hours.	___	___	___	_____
21. Monitor finger-stick blood glucose every 6 hours until maximum rate of administration is reached and maintained for 24 hours.	___	___	___	_____
22. Monitor intake and output every 8 hours.	___	___	___	_____
23. Weigh client daily until maximum administration rate is reached and maintained for 24 hours, then weigh client 3 times per week.	___	___	___	_____
24. Observe return of normal laboratory values.	___	___	___	_____
25. Observe stoma site for skin integrity.	___	___	___	_____
26. Record amount and type of feeding.	___	___	___	_____
27. Record client's response to tube feeding, patency of tube, and any side effects.	___	___	___	_____
28. Report to oncoming nursing staff: type of feeding, status of feeding tube, client's tolerance, and adverse effects.	___	___	___	_____

31 Urinary Elimination

Case Studies

I. The client is coming to the medical center for an intravenous pyelogram (IVP).
   a. What nursing assessments and client teaching should be done before this test?
   b. What are the nursing responsibilities after the client has the IVP done?

II. You will be working with unlicensed assistive personnel in an extended care setting.
   a. What urinary care may be delegated safely by the nurse?

III. On an acute care unit, the client is to have her catheter removed. The primary nurse tells you that all that is necessary is to "cut it, wait for the balloon to deflate, and pull it out."
   a. How will you proceed with this catheter removal?

IV. A clean-voided or midstream urine specimen is required from your male client. He is able to perform activities of daily living, including hygienic care.
   a. How will you teach this client to obtain the specimen?

Independent Learning Activities

1. Review the normal anatomy and physiology of the urinary system.

2. Practice the procedures for promotion of urination in the skill laboratory.

3. Research an article on the promotion of urination for clients in the acute, extended, or home care setting.

4. Investigate available resources for clients in local stores/pharmacies for urinary care in the home (e.g., incontinence pads, catheters, drainage bags). Compare prices to determine the most cost-effective source for these items in the community.

Chapter Review

Match the description/definition in Column A with the correct term in Column B.

Column A

_____ 1. Accumulation of urine in the bladder, with inability of bladder to empty.

_____ 2. Painful or difficult urination.

_____ 3. Difficulty in initiating urination.

_____ 4. Volume of urine remaining in the bladder after voiding.

_____ 5. Feeling of the need to void immediately.

_____ 6. Voiding large amounts of urine.

_____ 7. Urination, particularly excessive, at night.

_____ 8. Presence of blood in the urine.

_____ 9. Voiding very often.

_____ 10. Diminished urinary output in relation to fluid intake.

Column B

a. Urgency

b. Hematuria

c. Oliguria

d. Retention

e. Nocturia

f. Frequency

g. Dysuria

h. Residual urine

i. Hesitancy

j. Polyuria

Complete the following:

11. Name three noninvasive procedures that may be used to examine the urinary system.

12. Identify seven nursing implications following a renal angiogram.

13. What are the indications for the use of intermittent and indwelling urinary catheterization?

14. What positions may be used for catheterization of a female client?

15. The recommended daily fluid intake for dilution of urine, promotion of micturition, and flushing the urethra of microorganisms is _____.
The minimum urinary output for an adult is _____/hr.

16. Identify how the following factors may influence urination:
    a. sociocultural

    b. fluid intake

    c. pathological conditions

    d. medications

17. The type of urinary incontinence that results from an increased intra-abdominal pressure, with a leakage of a small amount of urine is called:

18. Identify whether the following are expected or unexpected characteristics of urine:
    a. pH 10

    b. protein 4 mg

    c. glucose

    d. specific gravity 1.2

19. What care is necessary for a condom catheter?

20. How can the nurse help to promote normal urinary function in the health care agency?

21. Identify measures that the nurse may implement to prevent infection in the catheterized client.

22. What interventions may assist to maintain skin integrity in the client with urinary incontinence?

Select the best answer for each of the following questions:

23. The client on the medical unit is scheduled to have a 24-hour urine collection to diagnose a urinary disorder. The nurse should:
    1. keep the collection jar in ice
    2. have the client void while defecating
    3. start with the first voiding sample from the client
    4. continue with the test if a specimen is flushed away

24. One of the nurse's assigned clients is experiencing urinary retention. The nurse anticipates a medication that may be ordered for this difficulty is:
    1. propantheline
    2. oxybutynin
    3. urecholine
    4. phenylpropanolamine

25. Several clients on the long-term care unit have indwelling urinary catheters in place. The nurse is going to delegate the catheter care to the assistant. The nurse includes instruction in:
    1. using lotion on the perineal area
    2. disinfecting the first 2–3 inches of the catheter every 2 hours
    3. ensuring that the drainage bag is secured to the side rail
    4. cleansing the length of the catheter in a circular motion, proximal to distal

26. The client with recurrent urinary tract infections asks the nurse how such infections may be avoided. In addition to hygienic care, the nurse discusses with the client that selected foods may help to prevent infections, whereas other foods may

not. The nurse recommends that the client promote urinary acidity by avoiding:
1. eggs
2. prunes
3. orange juice
4. whole-grain breads

27. An outcome that is identified for a client with a urinary alteration and an indwelling catheter is prevention of infection. The nurse assists the client to attain this outcome by:
    1. emptying the drainage bag daily
    2. draining all urine after the client ambulates
    3. performing perineal care q8h and prn
    4. opening the drainage system only at the connector points to obtain specimens

28. A client has come to the urologist's office with urge incontinence. The nurse anticipates that treatment for this difficulty will include:
    1. biofeedback
    2. catheterization
    3. cholinergic drug therapy
    4. electrical stimulation

29. The nurse notes that there is an order on the client's record for a sterile urine specimen. The client has an indwelling urinary catheter. The nurse will proceed to obtain this specimen by:
    1. withdrawing the urine from a urinometer
    2. opening the drainage bag and removing urine
    3. disconnecting the catheter from the drainage tubing
    4. using a needle to withdraw urine from the catheter port

30. The client has had a laparoscopic procedure earlier in the day and is having difficulty voiding this afternoon. Before initiating invasive measures, the nurse intervenes by:
    1. administering a cholinergic agent
    2. applying firm pressure over the perineal area

3. increasing the client's fluid intake to 3000 ml
4. rinsing the perineal area with warm water

31. To determine the possibility of a renal problem, the client is scheduled to have an IVP. Immediately following the procedure, the nurse will need to evaluate the client's response and will be alert to:
    1. an infection in the urinary bladder
    2. an allergic reaction to the contrast material
    3. urinary suppression from injury to kidney tissues
    4. incontinence from paralysis of the urinary sphincter

32. The unit manager is evaluating the care that has been given to the client by the new nursing staff member. The manager determines that the staff member has implemented an appropriate technique for a clean-voided urine specimen collection if:
    1. fluids were restricted before the collection
    2. sterile gloves were applied for the procedure
    3. the specimen was collected after the initial stream of urine had passed
    4. the specimen was placed in a clean container and placed in the utility room

33. A client who has come to the urology clinic is found to have reflex incontinence. This problem was identified by the client's statement of experiencing:
    1. a constant dribbling of urine
    2. an urge to void and not enough time to reach the bathroom
    3. an uncontrollable loss of urine when coughing or sneezing
    4. no urge to void and an unawareness of the bladder being full

34. A female client has an order for urinary catheterization. The nursing student will be evaluated by the instructor on the insertion technique. The student is identified as implementing appropriate technique when:

1. advancing the catheter 7 to 8 inches
2. inflating the balloon to test it before insertion
3. reinserting the catheter if it accidentally is placed in the vagina
4. keeping both hands sterile throughout the procedure

Study Group Questions

- What is the normal anatomy and physiology of the urinary system?
- What factors may influence urination?
- What are some common urinary elimination problems, their etiologies, and client signs and symptoms?
- How does growth and development influence urinary function and patterns?
- How can urinary drainage be surgically altered, and why would an alteration be necessary?
- What measures may be implemented to prevent infection in the urinary tract?
- How does the nurse assess the client's urinary function/elimination?
- What noninvasive and invasive procedures may be used to determine urinary function?
- What diagnostic tests are used to determine the characteristics of the urine?
- What are the expected characteristics of urine?
- What nursing interventions are appropriate for promoting urination in the health care and home care setting?
- What information should be included in teaching clients/families about promotion of urination and prevention of infection?

Name_____ Date_____ Instructor's Name_____

Performance Checklist: Skill 31-1

Inserting a Straight or Indwelling Catheter

	S	U	NP	Comments
1. Assess status of client and allergy history.	____	____	____	_____
2. Review client's medical record, including physician's order and nurses' notes.	____	____	____	_____
3. Assess client's knowledge of the purpose for catheterization.	____	____	____	_____
4. Explain procedure to client.	____	____	____	_____
5. Arrange for extra nursing personnel to assist as necessary.	____	____	____	_____
6. Wash hands.	____	____	____	_____
7. Close curtain or door.	____	____	____	_____
8. Raise bed to appropriate working height.	____	____	____	_____
9. Facing client, stand on left side of bed if right-handed (on right side if left-handed). Clear bedside table and arrange equipment.	____	____	____	_____
10. Raise side rail on opposite side of bed, and put side rail down on working side.	____	____	____	_____
11. Place waterproof pad under client.	____	____	____	_____
12. Position client: a. Female client 　(1) Assist to dorsal recumbent position (supine with knees flexed). Ask client to relax thighs so the hip joints can be externally rotated.	____	____	____	_____
(2) Position female client in side-lying (Sims') position with upper leg flexed at knee and hip if unable to be supine. Take extra precautions to cover rectal area with drape during procedure to reduce change of cross contamination.	____	____	____	_____
b. Male client 　(1) Assist to supine position.	____	____	____	_____
(2) Ensure thighs are slightly abducted.	____	____	____	_____

	S	U	NP	Comments

13. Drape client:
    a. Female client
       (1) Drape with bath blanket.
       (2) Place blanket diamond fashion over client, with one corner at client's neck, side corners over each arm and side, and last corner over perineum.
    b. Male client
       (1) Drape upper trunk with bath blanket.
       (2) Cover lower extremities with bed sheets, exposing only genitalia.

14. Wearing disposable gloves, wash perineal area with soap and water as needed; dry and dispose of gloves.

15. Position lamp to illuminate perineal area. (When using flashlight, have assistant hold it.)

16. Open package containing drainage system; place drainage bag over edge of bottom bed frame and bring drainage tube up between side rail and mattress.

17. Open catheterization kit according to directions, keeping bottom of container sterile.

18. Place plastic bag that contains kit within reach of work area to use as waterproof bag to dispose of used supplies.

19. Apply sterile gloves.

20. Organize supplies on sterile field. Open inner sterile package containing catheter. Pour sterile antiseptic solution into correct compartment containing sterile cotton balls. Open packet containing lubricant. Remove specimen container (lid should be placed loosely on top) and prefilled syringe from collection compartment of tray and set them aside on sterile field if needed.

21. Before inserting indwelling catheter, a common practice is to test balloon by injecting fluid from prefilled syringe into balloon port.

22. Lubricate catheter 2.5 to 5 cm (1 to 2 inches) for women and 12.5 to 17.5 cm (5 to 7 inches) for men. NOTE: Some catheter kits will have a plastic sheath over the catheter

	S	U	NP	Comments

that must be removed before lubrication.
(Optional: Physician may order use of
lubricant containing local anesthetic.)

23. Apply sterile drape, keeping gloves sterile:
    a. Female client
       (1) Allow top edge of drape to form cuff
            over both hands. Place drape down
            on bed between client's thighs. Slip
            cuffed edge just under buttocks,
            taking care not to touch
            contaminated surface with gloves.
       (2) Pick up fenestrated sterile drape and
            allow it to unfold without touching an
            unsterile object. Apply drape over
            perineum, exposing labia and being
            sure not to touch contaminated
            surface.
    b. Male client: two methods are used for
        draping, depending on preference
       (1) First method: Apply drape over
            thighs and under penis without
            completely opening fenestrated
            drape.
       (2) Second method: Apply drape over
            thighs just below penis. Pick up
            fenestrated sterile drape, allow it to
            unfold, and drape it over penis with
            fenestrated slit resting over penis.

24. Place sterile tray and contents on sterile
    drape between legs. Open specimen
    container. NOTE: Client's size and
    positioning will dictate exact placement.

25. Cleanse urethral meatus.
    a. Female client
       (1) With nondominant hand, carefully
            retract labia to fully expose urethral
            meatus. Maintain position of
            nondominant hand throughout
            procedure.
       (2) Using forceps in sterile dominant
            hand, pick up cotton ball saturated
            with antiseptic solution and clean
            perineal area, wiping front to back
            from clitoris toward anus. Using a
            new cotton ball for each area, wipe
            along the far labial fold, near labial
            fold, and directly over center of
            urethral meatus.

	S	U	NP	Comments

b. Male client

(1) If client is not circumcised retract foreskin with nondominant hand. Grasp penis at shaft just below glans. Retract urethral meatus between thumb and forefinger. Maintain non-dominant hand in this position throughout procedure.   ____ ____ ____ _____

(2) With dominant hand, pick up cotton ball with forceps and clean penis. Move it in circular motion from urethral meatus down to base of glans. Repeat cleansing three more times, using clean cotton ball each time.   ____ ____ ____ _____

26. Pick up catheter with gloved dominant hand 7.5 to 10 cm (3 to 4 inches) from catheter tip. Hold end of catheter loosely coiled in palm of dominant hand (Optional: May grasp catheter with forceps). Place distal end of catheter in urine tray receptacle if straight catheterization is being done.   ____ ____ ____ _____

27. Insert catheter:

a. Female client

(1) Ask client to bear down gently as if to void and slowly insert catheter through urethral meatus.   ____ ____ ____ _____

(2) Advance catheter a total of 5 to 7.5 cm (2 to 3 inches) in adult or until urine flows out catheter's end. When urine appears, advance catheter another 2.5 to 5 cm (1 to 2 inches). Do not force against resistance. Place end of catheter in urine tray receptacle.   ____ ____ ____ _____

(3) Release labia and hold catheter securely with nondominant hand.   ____ ____ ____ _____

b. Male client

(1) Lift penis to position perpendicular to client's body and apply light traction.   ____ ____ ____ _____

(2) Ask client to bear down as if to void and slowly insert catheter through urethral meatus.   ____ ____ ____ _____

(3) Advance catheter 17.5 to 22.5 cm (7 to 9 inches) in adult or until urine flows out catheter's end. If resistance is felt, withdraw catheter; do not force it through urethra. When urine appears, advance catheter another 2.5 to 5 cm (1 to 2 inches). Do not use force to insert a catheter.   ____ ____ ____ _____

	S	U	NP	Comments

(4) Lower penis and hold catheter securely in nondominant hand. Place end of catheter in urine tray receptacle.

(5) Reduce (or reposition) the foreskin.

28. Collect urine specimen as needed. Fill specimen cup or jar to desired level (20 to 30 ml) by holding end of catheter in dominant hand over cup.

29. Allow bladder to empty fully unless institution policy restricts maximal volume of urine drained with each catheterization (about 800 to 1000 ml).

30. Inflate balloon fully per manufacturer's recommendations, and then release catheter with nondominant hand and pull gently to feel resistance.

31. Attach end of catheter to collecting tube of drainage system. Drainage bag must be below level of bladder; do not place bag on side rails of bed.

32. Anchor catheter:
    a. Female client
       (1) Secure catheter tubing to inner thigh with strip of nonallergenic tape (commercial multipurpose tube holders with a Velcro strap are available).
       (2) Allow for slack so movement of thigh does not create tension on catheter.
    b. Male client
       (1) Secure catheter tubing to top of thigh or lower abdomen (with penis directed toward chest).
       (2) Allow slack in catheter so movement does not create tension on catheter.

33. Assist client to comfortable position. Wash and dry perineal area as needed.

34. Remove gloves and dispose of equipment, drapes, and urine in proper receptacles.

35. Wash hands.

36. Palpate bladder.

	S	U	NP	Comments
37. Ask about client's comfort.	___	___	___	_____
38. Observe character and amount of urine in drainage system.	___	___	___	_____
39. Determine that there is no urine leaking from catheter or tubing connections.	___	___	___	_____
40. Report and record type and size of catheter inserted, amount of fluid used to inflate balloon, characteristics of urine, amount of urine, reasons for catheterization, specimen collection if appropriate, and client's response to procedure and teaching concepts.	___	___	___	_____
41. Initiate I&O records.	___	___	___	_____
42. If catheter is definitely in bladder and no urine is produced within an hour, absence of urine should be reported to physician immediately.	___	___	___	_____

Bowel Elimination 32

Case Studies

I. You have arranged with the instructor and agency to make a home visit to a 76-year-old female client. In completing your initial assessment, the client tells you that she has been having difficulty over the past 2 years in "moving her bowels." She takes you to the bathroom where she shows you a collection of over-the-counter laxatives and enemas. The client also tells you that, since the death of her husband, she doesn't do a lot of cooking, instead relying on sandwiches and prepared foods.
   a. Based on this information, identify a nursing diagnosis, client goal(s)/outcomes, and nursing interventions related to bowel elimination.

II. A client is scheduled to have a colonoscopy performed.
   a. Identify the client teaching that is provided prior to the procedure.

Independent Learning Activities

1. Review the normal anatomy and physiology of the gastrointestinal system.

2. Practice the skills for promotion of bowel elimination in the skill laboratory.

3. Investigate the different over-the-counter products that are available to promote or inhibit bowel elimination, including their costs, uses, and hazards.

Chapter Review

Match the description/definition in Column A with the correct term in Column B.

Column A

_____ 1. Propulsion of food through the gastrointestinal (GI) tract
_____ 2. Loss of appetite.
_____ 3. Artificial opening in the abdominal wall.
_____ 4. Dilated rectal veins.
_____ 5. Blood in the stool.

Column B

a. Stoma
b. Hemorrhoids
c. Melena
d. Peristalsis
e. Anorexia

Complete the following:

6. What are the dietary recommendations for a client who is experiencing constipation?

7. What are the dietary recommendations for a client experiencing diarrhea?

8. How do the following factors influence bowel elimination?
   a. diet

   b. positioning

   c. pregnancy

   d. diagnostic tests

   e. activity

   f. psychological status

9. How can the nurse promote comfort for a client with hemorrhoids?

10. Identify one possible cause for an increased total bilirubin level.

11. What clients should be cautioned against straining during defecation?

12. What are some possible risk factors for colon cancer that may be included in client teaching?

13. What is the correct position for an adult client to receive an enema?

14. An enema that is used to treat clients with hyperkalemia is:

15. For a hypertonic enema:
   a. How does it work?

   b. What are indications/contraindications for its use?

   c. What is a commonly used over-the-counter hypertonic enema?

16. How do the following factors lead to diarrhea?
    a. emotional stress

    b. medications

    c. tube feedings

17. Identify what should be included in a focused assessment of a client's bowel function.

18. What general measures are included in a bowel retraining plan?

19. What surgical procedures are anticipated for clients with:
    a. colorectal cancer

    b. diverticulitis

20. For a client with an ostomy, identify what should be included in the teaching plan in regards to:
    a. skin care

    b. irrigation

    c. pouching

21. For the following fecal characteristics, identify whether they are expected or unexpected findings:
    a. yellow stool in infant_____

    b. a frequency of greater than 3 times/day for an adult_____

    c. white color stool_____

    d. tarry stool_____

    e. soft, formed stool_____

Select the best answer for each of the following questions:

22. The client expresses a feeling of mild cramping during the administration of a saline enema. The nurse first should:
    1. discontinue the procedure
    2. change the salinity of the solution
    3. lower the bag to slow the infusion
    4. allow the solution to become cool

23. A client in a senior day care center is experiencing some constipation. A commonly prescribed medication is a wetting agent or stool softener, such as:
    1. bisacodyl (Dulcolax)
    2. phenolphthalein (Ex-Lax)
    3. magnesium hydroxide (Milk of Magnesia)
    4. dioctyl sodium sulfosuccinate (Colace)

24. A client on the surgical unit had surgery for rectal cancer. A colostomy was created. The nurse is going to begin teaching about colostomy care and will instruct the client that:
    1. an enema set may be used for irrigations
    2. an external pouch is not needed after irrigations
    3. the irrigation solution should be instilled within 10 minutes
    4. 500–1000 ml of saline or water may be used for irrigations

25. In preparing a client for an upper GI series/barium swallow, the nurse instructs the client that:
    1. light sedation will be used
    2. all jewelry and metallic objects must be removed
    3. the client will be NPO starting the morning of the test
    4. the client will need to lie absolutely still during the procedure

26. For clients on extended bed rest, the prolonged immobility may result in reduced peristalsis and fecal impaction. The nurse is alert to one of the first signs of an impaction when the client experiences:
    1. headaches
    2. abdominal distention
    3. overflow diarrhea
    4. abdominal pain with guarding

27. A client has been admitted to an acute care unit with a diagnosis of biliary disease. When assessing the client's feces, the nurse expects that they will be:
    1. bloody
    2. pus filled
    3. black and tarry
    4. white or clay colored

28. On review of the client's laboratory results, the nurse notes that the client is experiencing hypocalcemia. The nurse will plan to implement measures to prevent:
    1. gastric upset
    2. malabsorption

3. constipation
4. fluid secretion

29. The nurse is preparing to administer an enema to a 7-year-old child. When assembling the equipment, the nurse will prepare an enema of:
    1. 150–250 ml of fluid
    2. 250–350 ml of fluid
    3. 400–500 ml of fluid
    4. 500–750 ml of fluid

Study Group Questions

- What is the normal anatomy and physiology of the GI system?
- How is bowel elimination influenced by the process of growth and development?
- What are some common bowel elimination problems?
- How are continent and incontinent bowel diversions/ostomies different?
- What is included in the nursing assessment of a client to determine bowel elimination status?
- What diagnostic tests may be used to determine the presence of bowel elimination disorders?
- How are the critical thinking and nursing processes applied to situations where clients are experiencing alterations in bowel elimination?
- What nursing interventions may be implemented to promote bowel elimination and comfort for clients in the health promotion, acute care, and restorative care settings?
- What information should be included in teaching for clients/families for promotion and/or restoration of bowel elimination?

Study Chart

Create a study chart to describe Bowel Elimination Problems, *identifying possible causes, signs and symptoms, and nursing interventions for:* constipation, diarrhea, incontinence, flatulence, hemorrhoids, and bowel obstruction.

Name_____   Date_____   Instructor's Name_____

Performance Checklist: Skill 32-1

Administering a Cleansing Enema

	S	U	NP	Comments
1. Assess status of client: last bowel movement, normal bowel patterns, hemorrhoids, mobility, external sphincter control, abdominal pain.	___	___	___	_____
2. Assess for presence of increased intracranial pressure, glaucoma, or recent rectal or prostate surgery.	___	___	___	_____
3. Determine client's level of understanding of purpose of enema.	___	___	___	_____
4. Check client's medical record to clarify the rationale for the enema.	___	___	___	_____
5. Review physician's order for enema.	___	___	___	_____
6. Collect appropriate equipment.	___	___	___	_____
7. Correctly identify client and explain procedure.	___	___	___	_____
8. Assemble enema bag with appropriate solution and rectal tube.	___	___	___	_____
9. Wash hands, and apply gloves.	___	___	___	_____
10. Provide privacy by closing curtains around bed or closing door.	___	___	___	_____
11. Raise bed to appropriate working height for nurse, raise side rail on opposite side.	___	___	___	_____
12. Assist client into left side-lying (Sims') position with right knee flexed. Children may be placed in dorsal recumbent position.	___	___	___	_____
13. Place waterproof pad under hips and buttocks.	___	___	___	_____
14. Cover client with bath blanket, exposing only rectal area, with anus clearly visible.	___	___	___	_____

	S	U	NP	Comments

15. Place bedpan or commode in easily accessible position. If client will be expelling contents in toilet, ensure that toilet is free. (If client will be getting up to bathroom to expel enema, place client's slippers and bathrobe in easily accessible position.)

16. Administer enema:
   a. Enema bag
   (1) Add warmed solution to enema bag: warm tap water as it flows from faucet, place saline container in basin of hot water before adding saline to enema bag, and check temperature of solution by pouring small amount of solution over inner wrist.
   (2) Raise container, release clamp, and allow solution to flow long enough to fill tubing.
   (3) Reclamp tubing.
   (4) Lubricate 6 to 8 cm (3 to 4 inches) of tip of rectal tube with lubricating jelly.
   (5) Gently separate buttocks and locate anus. Instruct client to relax by breathing out slowly through mouth.
   (6) Insert tip of rectal tube slowly by pointing tip in direction of client's umbilicus. Length of insertion varies:
      Adult: 7.5 to 10 cm (3 to 4 inches)
      Child: 5 to 7.5 cm (2 to 3 inches)
      Infant: 2.5 to 3.75 cm (1 to $1^1/_2$ inches)
   (7) Hold tubing in rectum constantly until end of fluid instillation.
   (8) Open regulating clamp, and allow solution to enter slowly with container at client's hip level.
   (9) Raise height of enema container slowly to appropriate level above anus: 30 to 45 cm (12 to 18 inches) for high enema, 30 cm (12 inches) for regular enema, 7.5 cm (3 inches) for low enema. Instillation time varies with volume of solution administered.
   (10) Lower container or clamp tubing if client complains of cramping or if fluid escapes around rectal tube.
   (11) Clamp tubing after all solution is instilled.

	S	U	NP	Comments

b. Prepackaged disposable container

   (1) Remove plastic cap from rectal tip. Tip already is lubricated, but more jelly can be applied as needed.

   (2) Gently separate buttocks and locate rectum. Instruct client to relax by breathing out slowly through mouth.

   (3) Insert tip of bottle gently into rectum toward the umbilicus.
     Adult: 7.5 to 10 cm (3 to 4 inches)
     Child: 5 to 7.5 cm (2 to 3 inches)
     Infant: 2.5 to 3.75 cm (1 to $1^{1}/_{2}$ inches)

   (4) Squeeze bottle until all of solution has entered rectum and colon. Instruct client to retain solution until the urge to defecate occurs, usually 2 to 5 minutes.

17. Place layers of toilet tissue around tube at anus and gently withdraw rectal tube.

18. Explain to client that feeling of distention is normal, as is some abdominal cramping. Ask client to retain solution as long as possible while lying quietly in bed. (For infant or young child, gently hold buttocks together for a few minutes.)

19. Discard enema container and tubing in proper receptacle, or rinse out thoroughly with warm soap and water if container is to be reused.

20. Assist client to bathroom or help position client on bedpan.

21. Observe character of feces and solution (caution client against flushing toilet before inspection).

22. Assist client as needed in washing anal area with warm soap and water (if you administer perineal care, use gloves).

23. Remove and discard gloves, and wash hands.

24. Inspect color, consistency, and amount of stool and fluid passed.

25. Assess condition of abdomen; cramping, rigidity, or distention can indicate a serious problem.

	S	U	NP	Comments
26. Record type and volume of enema given and characteristics of results.	___	___	___	_____
27. Record and report client's tolerance of and response to procedure.	___	___	___	_____

Name_____   Date_____   Instructor's Name_____

Performance Checklist: Skill 32-2

Pouching an Ostomy

	S	U	NP	Comments
1. Auscultate for bowel sounds.	____	____	____	_____
2. Observe skin barrier and pouch for leakage and length of time in place.	____	____	____	_____
3. Observe stoma for color, swelling, trauma, and healing. Assess type of stoma.	____	____	____	_____
4. Measure the stoma with each pouching change. Follow pouch manufacturer's directions and measuring guide as to which pouch to use based on client's stoma size.	____	____	____	_____
5. Observe abdominal incision (if present).	____	____	____	_____
6. Observe effluent from stoma, and keep a record of intake and output. Ask client about skin tenderness.	____	____	____	_____
7. Assess abdomen for best type of pouching system to use.	____	____	____	_____
8. Assess the client's self-care ability to determine the best type of pouching system to use.	____	____	____	_____
9. After skin barrier and pouch removal, assess skin around stoma, noting scars, folds, skin breakdown, and peristomal suture line if present.	____	____	____	_____
10. Determine client's emotional response and knowledge and understanding of an ostomy and its care.	____	____	____	_____
11. Explain procedure to client; encourage client's interaction and questions.	____	____	____	_____
12. Assemble equipment, and close room curtains or door.	____	____	____	_____
13. Position client either standing or supine, and drape. If seated, position client either on or in front of toilet.	____	____	____	_____

	S	U	NP	Comments
14. Wash hands, and apply disposable gloves.	___	___	___	_____
15. Place towel or disposable waterproof barrier under client.	___	___	___	_____
16. Remove used pouch and skin barrier gently by pushing skin away from barrier. An adhesive remover may be used to facilitate removal of skin barrier.	___	___	___	_____
17. Cleanse peristomal skin gently with warm tap water using gauze pads or clean washcloth; do not scrub skin. Dry completely by patting skin with gauze or towel.	___	___	___	_____
18. Measure stoma for correct size of pouching system needed using the manufacturer's measuring guide.	___	___	___	_____
19. Select appropriate pouch for client based on client assessment. With a custom cut-to-fit pouch, use an ostomy guide to cut opening on the pouch $\frac{1}{16}$ to $\frac{1}{8}$ inch larger than stoma before removing backing. Prepare pouch by removing backing from barrier and adhesive. With ileostomy, apply thin circle of barrier paste around opening in pouch; allow to dry.	___	___	___	_____

20. Apply skin barrier and pouch. If creases next to stoma occur, use barrier paste to fill in; let dry 1 to 2 minutes.
   a. For one-piece pouching system

	S	U	NP	Comments
(1) Use skin sealant wipes on skin directly under adhesive skin barrier or pouch; allow to dry. Press adhesive backing of pouch and/or skin barrier smoothly against skin, starting from the bottom and working up and around sides.	___	___	___	_____
(2) Hold pouch by barrier, center over stoma, and press down gently on barrier; bottom of pouch should point toward client's knees.	___	___	___	_____
(3) Maintain gentle finger pressure around barrier for 1 to 2 minutes.	___	___	___	_____

   b. If using two-piece pouching system

	S	U	NP	Comments
(1) Apply barrier-paste flange (barrier with adhesive) as in steps above for one-piece system.	___	___	___	_____
(2) Snap on pouch and maintain finger pressure.	___	___	___	_____

	S	U	NP	Comments

c. For both pouching systems gently tug on pouch in a downward direction.

21. Apply nonallergenic paper tape around pectin skin barrier in a "picture frame" method. Half of the tape should be on skin barrier and half on client's skin. Rather than tape, some clients may prefer a belt attached to the pouch for extra security.

22. Although many ostomy pouches are odorproof, some nurses and clients like to add a small amount of ostomy deodorant into pouch. Do not use "home remedies," which can harm stoma, to control ostomy odor. Do not make a hole in pouch to release flatus.

23. Fold bottom of drainable open-ended pouches up once, and close using a closure device such as a clamp (or follow manufacturer's instructions for closure).

24. Properly dispose of old pouch and soiled equipment. Client also may request spraying of room air freshener in room if needed.

25. Remove gloves, and wash hands.

26. Change one- or two-piece pouch every 3 to 7 days unless leaking. Pouch can remain in place for tub bath or shower; after bath, pat adhesive dry.

27. Ask if client feels discomfort around stoma.

28. Note appearance of stoma around skin and existing incision (if present) while pouch is removed and skin is cleansed. Reinspect condition of skin barrier and adhesive.

29. Auscultate bowel sounds, and observe characteristics of stool.

30. Observe client's nonverbal behaviors as pouch is applied. Ask if client has any questions about pouching.

31. Document type of pouch and skin barrier applied.

32. Record amount and appearance of stool, texture, condition of peristomal skin, and sutures.

	S	U	NP	Comments
33. Record and report any of the following to the charge nurse and/or physician:				
a. Abnormal appearance of stoma, suture line, peristomal skin, character of output, abdominal tenderness or distention, and absence of bowel sounds.	____	____	____	_____
b. No flatus in 24 to 36 hours and no stool by third day.	____	____	____	_____
34. Record client's level of participation and need for teaching.	____	____	____	_____

Immobility 33

Case Study

I.   Your client, Mrs. B., has just come to the rehabilitation facility. She has been immobilized since her automobile accident that resulted in a spinal injury. You are aware of the physical hazards of immobility, but right now Mrs. B. appears withdrawn.
   a.   What can you do to prevent the possible psychological and emotional effects of Mrs. B.'s period of immobility?

Independent Learning Activities

1.   Review the normal anatomy and physiology of the body systems, as you feel necessary.

2.   While you are progressing through an average day, think about or take note of all of the different types of activities that you perform. To try to empathize with an immobile client, think about how it would be to not be able to perform those activities independently or to interact with all of the people that you see daily.

3.   Practice turning, positioning, deep breathing, coughing, and range-of-motion exercises at home.

4.   Investigate creative diversional activities that may be used for long-term immobilized clients.

5.   Research an article in a current nursing journal on new devices that may be available to prevent or treat the hazards of immobility.

Chapter Review

Complete the following:

1.   What three systems of the body need to be intact to maintain normal physical mobility?

2.   The objectives of bed rest are:

3.   What physical conditions may require bed rest?

4.   Fluid and electrolyte imbalances that may occur with prolonged immobility include:

5. What common behavioral changes may be observed in the immobilized client?

6. What is the purpose of anthropometric measurement for the immobilized client?

7. Identify three major changes that may occur in the cardiovascular system as a result of immobility, and include nursing interventions to prevent or treat each change.

8. Identify two potential respiratory complications of immobility, and include the nursing interventions to prevent or treat each complication.

9. What type of exercise program is appropriate for a hospitalized client?

10. How can the nurse assess a client for deep venous thrombosis (DVT)?

11. What general information should be included in a teaching plan for clients with limited mobility?

12. Identify the five factors that influence the dietary needs of the immobilized client.

13. Identify at least two changes that may occur in the following systems as a result of immobility, and include the nursing interventions to prevent or treat them:
    a. integumentary

    b. gastrointestinal

    c. urinary

    d. musculoskeletal

Select the best answer for each of the following questions:

14. The client has been on prolonged bed rest following a cerebral vascular accident (stroke). During assessment, the nurse is alert to the presence of:
    1. an unchanged blood pressure
    2. warmth to the calf area
    3. increased muscle mass
    4. an increased hemoglobin level

15. The older adult client had a fractured hip repaired 2 days ago. The client is having more difficulty than expected in moving around, and the nurse is concerned about possible respiratory complications. In assessing the client for possible atelectasis, the nurse expects to find:
    1. a decreased respiratory rate
    2. wheezing on inspiration

3.   asymmetrical breath sounds
4.   rubbing sounds during inspiration and expiration

16.   For a client who has been placed in a spica (full-body) cast, the nurse remains alert to possible changes in the cardiovascular system as a result of immobility. The nurse may find that the client has:
1.   hypertension
2.   tachycardia
3.   hypervolemia
4.   an increased cardiac output

17.   A possible complication for the client on prolonged bed rest is thrombus formation. For the nurse to assess the presence of this serious problem, the nurse should:
1.   attempt to elicit Chvostek's sign
2.   palpate the temperature of the feet
3.   measure the client's calf and thigh diameters
4.   observe for hair loss and skin turgor in the lower legs

18.   The client has been on extended bed rest following abdominal surgery. The client now has an order to be out of bed. The nurse first should:
1.   assess respiratory function
2.   obtain the client's blood pressure
3.   ask if the client feels lightheaded
4.   assist the client to the edge of the bed

19.   The client has been placed in skeletal traction and will be immobilized for an extended period. The nurse recognizes that there is a need to prevent respiratory complications and intervenes by:
1.   suctioning the airway every hour
2.   changing the client's position every 4–8 hours
3.   using oxygen and nebulizer treatments regularly
4.   encouraging deep breathing and coughing every hour

20.   Clients who are immobilized in health care facilities require that their psychosocial needs be met along with their physiological needs. The nurse recognizes the client's psychosocial needs when telling the client that:
1.   "The staff will limit your visitors so that you will not be bothered."
2.   "We will help you get dressed so you look more like yourself."
3.   "We can discuss the routine to see if there are any changes that we can make with you."
4.   "A roommate can sometimes be a real bother and very distracting. We can move you to a private room."

21.   A client is transferred to the rehabilitation facility from the medical center following a CVA (cerebral vascular accident/stroke). The CVA resulted in severe right-sided paralysis, and the client is very limited in mobility. To prevent the complication of external hip rotation for this client with an extended period of immobility, the nurse uses a:
1.   footboard
2.   bedboard
3.   trapeze bar
4.   trochanter roll

Study Group Questions

- What are the basic concepts of mobility?
- What is immobility?
- How is bed rest used therapeutically?
- What physiological changes may occur throughout the body as a result of immobility?
- What psychosocial and developmental changes may occur as a result of immobility?
- What assessments should be made by the nurse to determine the effect of immobility on the client?
- What nursing interventions should be implemented to prevent or treat the effects of immobility?

Name_____ Date_____ Instructor's Name_____

Performance Checklist: Skill 33-1

Applying Elastic Stockings

	S	U	NP	Comments
1. Assess client for risk factors in Virchow's triad.	____	____	____	_____
2. Observe for signs, symptoms, and conditions that might contraindicate use of elastic stockings.	____	____	____	_____
3. Obtain physician's order.	____	____	____	_____
4. Assess client's or caregiver's understanding of application of elastic stockings.	____	____	____	_____
5. Assess and document the condition of client's skin and circulation to the legs.	____	____	____	_____
6. Assess client's or caregiver's understanding of proper care of elastic stockings.	____	____	____	_____
7. Explain procedure and reasons for applying stockings.	____	____	____	_____
8. Use tape measure to measure client's legs to determine proper stocking size.	____	____	____	_____
9. Wash hands.	____	____	____	_____
10. Position client in supine position. Elevate head of bed to comfortable level.	____	____	____	_____
11. After legs are cleansed, apply small amount of talcum powder to legs and feet, provided client does not have sensitivity to talcum powder.	____	____	____	_____
12. Apply stockings:				
a. Turn elastic stocking inside out up to the heel. Place one hand into sock, holding heel. Pull top of sock with other hand inside out over foot of sock.	____	____	____	_____
b. Place client's toes into foot of elastic stocking, making sure that sock is smooth.	____	____	____	_____

	S	U	NP	Comments

c. Slide remaining portion of sock over client's foot, being sure that the toes are covered. Make sure the foot fits into the toe and heel position of the sock. Sock will now be right side out. _____ _____ _____ _____

d. Slide top of sock up over client's calf until sock is completely extended. Be sure sock is smooth and no ridges or wrinkles are present, particularly behind the knee. _____ _____ _____ _____

e. Instruct client not to roll socks partially down. _____ _____ _____ _____

13. Reposition client to position of comfort, and wash hands. _____ _____ _____ _____

14. Remove stockings at least once per shift. _____ _____ _____ _____

15. Inspect stocking to make sure there are no wrinkles or binding at top of stocking. _____ _____ _____ _____

16. Observe circulatory status of lower extremities. Observe color, temperature, and condition of skin. _____ _____ _____ _____

17. Observe client's reaction to stockings. _____ _____ _____ _____

18. Observe client or caregiver apply stockings. _____ _____ _____ _____

19. Remove stockings at least once a shift, and assess skin and circulatory status. _____ _____ _____ _____

20. Record date and time of stocking application and stocking length and size. _____ _____ _____ _____

21. Record condition of skin and circulatory assessment. _____ _____ _____ _____

22. Report changes indicating a decline in circulation. _____ _____ _____ _____

34 Skin Integrity and Wound Care

Case Study

I. You are a student nurse assigned to provide care to a client in an extended care facility. While assisting the client from the bed to the shower chair, you notice reddened areas to her sacral region and to both elbows and heels. The skin to these areas is intact, but the redness does not go away.

   a. Identify a nursing diagnosis, client goal/outcomes, and nursing interventions related to this client's assessment data.

Independent Learning Activities

1. Review the normal anatomy and physiology of the integumentary system, the inflammatory process, and wound healing.

2. Practice the procedures that are implemented to maintain skin integrity and promote wound healing in the skill laboratory.

3. Investigate resources that are available in the health care agency and community for prevention and treatment of pressure ulcers.

4. Research an article in a nursing journal on recent techniques used for wound healing.

Chapter Review

Match the description/definition in Column A with the correct term in Column B.

	Column A		Column B
_____	1. Localized collection of blood under the tissues.	a.	Cachexia
_____	2. Separation of wound layers with protrusion of visceral organs.	b.	Blanching
_____	3. Absence of normal red tones in lightly pigmented skin.	c.	Abrasion
_____	4. Superficial loss of dermis.	d.	Laceration
_____	5. Pressure exerted against the skin when the client is moved.	e.	Dehiscence
_____	6. General ill health and malnutrition, with weakness and emaciation.	f.	Fistula
_____	7. Removal of devitalized tissue.	g.	Hematoma
_____	8. Torn, jagged damage to dermis and epidermis.	h.	Evisceration
_____	9. Separation of skin and tissue layers.	i.	Debridement
_____	10. Abnormal passage between two body organs or an organ and the outside of the body.	j.	Shearing force

Complete the following:

11. Mark the areas on the body that are common sites for pressure ulcer development.

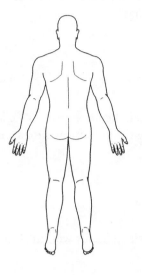

c.

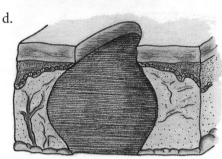

d.

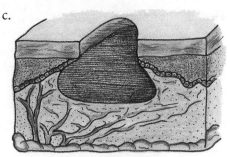

13. What clients have a greater risk for pressure ulcer development?

12. Identify and describe the following stages of pressure ulcer development:

14. Identify three ways in which the skin of an older adult is more prone to breakdown.

a.

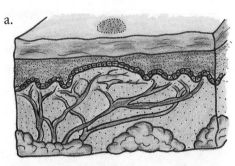

15. What nursing interventions may be implemented for the prevention of pressure ulcers?

b.

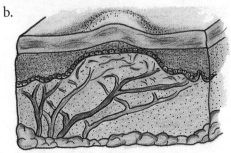

16. What is included in the documentation of the client assessment for tissue pressure indicators?

17. How do the following factors influence wound healing?
    a. age

    b. obesity

    c. diabetes

    d. immunosuppression

18. Possible complications of wound healing include:

19. Describe the following types of wound drainage:
    a. serous

    b. sanguineous

    c. serosanguineous

    d. purulent

20. Describe the procedure for obtaining an aerobic wound culture.

21. Identify the steps to care for a traumatic wound.

22. Identify at least three different types of dressings.

23. How can the nurse promote client comfort during wound care and dressing changes?

24. The principles for wound cleansing are:

25. Specify the major difference in the technique for dressing changes in the home.

26. Identify basic safety measures, indications for use, and contraindications for heat and cold therapy.
    a. heat

    b. cold

27. Identify the basic principles for applying bandages and binders.

28. Using the Braden Scale, what is this client's risk for pressure ulcer development?

		Score
Sensory	Very limited	_____
Moisture	Occasionally	_____
Activity	Chairfast	_____
Mobility	Very limited	_____
Nutrition	Probably inadequate	_____
Friction/shear	Potential problem	_____
	Total score	_____
	Client risk	_____

Select the best answer for each of the following questions:

29. To avoid pressure ulcer development for an immobilized client at home, the nurse recommends a surface to use on the bed. A surface type that is low cost and easy to use in the home is a(n):
   1. foam overlay
   2. air overlay surface
   3. air fluidized surface
   4. low air loss surface

30. For the client in the extended care facility who has a nursing diagnosis of *Impaired mobility*, the nurse will implement:
   1. massage of reddened skin areas
   2. movement of the client in the chair every 2 hours
   3. maintenance of low Fowler's position while in bed (30° or lower)
   4. placement of plastic absorptive pads directly beneath the client

31. The client has experienced a traumatic injury that will require applications of heat The nurse implements the treatment based on the principle that:
   1. long exposures help the client develop tolerance to the procedure
   2. the foot and palm of the hand are the most sensitive to temperature
   3. client response is best to minor temperature adjustments

4. clients are more tolerant to temperature changes over a large body surface area

32. An obese client has returned to the unit after having major abdominal surgery. When the nurse enters the room, it is evident that the client has moved or coughed and the wound has eviscerated. The nurse immediately should:
   1. assess vital signs
   2. contact the physician
   3. apply light pressure on the exposed organs
   4. place sterile towels soaked in saline over the area

33. A client with a knife protruding from his upper leg is brought into the emergency room. The nurse is waiting for the physician to arrive when a newly hired nurse comes to assist. The nurse delegates the new staff member to do all of the following as soon as possible except:
   1. assess vital signs
   2. remove the knife to cleanse the wound
   3. wrap a bandage around the knife and site
   4. apply pressure to the surrounding area to stop bleeding

34. The nurse is assessing the client's wound and notices that it has very minimal tissue loss and drainage. There are a number of dressings that may be used according to the protocol on the unit. The nurse selects:
   1. gauze
   2. alginate
   3. wound VAC
   4. transparent film

35. The nurse is completing an assessment of the client's skin integrity and identifies that an area is a full-thickness wound with damage to the subcutaneous tissue. The nurse identifies this stage of ulcer formation as:
   1. stage I
   2. stage II
   3. stage III
   4. stage IV

36. The client has a large wound to the sacral area that requires irrigation. The nurse explains to the client that irrigation will be done to:
    1. decrease scar formation
    2. decrease wound drainage
    3. remove debris from the wound
    4. improve circulation from the wound

37. The nurse is working with an older adult client in the extended care facility. While turning the client, the nurse notices that there is a reddened area on the client's coccyx. The nurse implements skin care that includes:
    1. soaking the area with normal saline
    2. cleaning the area with mild soap, drying, and applying a protective moisturizer
    3. washing the area with an astringent and painting it with povidone-iodine solution
    4. applying a dilute solution of hydrogen peroxide and water and using a heat lamp to dry the area

38. A client has a wound to the left lower extremity that has minimal exudates and collagen formation. The nurse identifies the healing phase of this wound as:
    1. primary intention
    2. proliferative phase
    3. secondary intention
    4. inflammatory phase

39. Following neurosurgery, the nurse assesses the client's bandage and finds that there is thin, clear drainage coming from the operative site. The nurse describes this drainage to the surgeon as:
    1. serous
    2. purulent
    3. sanguineous
    4. serosanguineous

40. The client has a surgical wound on the right upper aspect of the chest that requires cleansing. The nurse implements aseptic technique by:

1. going over the wound twice and discarding the swab
2. moving from the outer region of the wound toward the center
3. using an antiseptic solution followed by a normal saline rinse
4. starting at the drainage site and moving outward with circular motions

41 The nurse is working in a physician's office and is asked by one of the clients when heat or cold should be applied. In providing an example, the nurse identifies that cold therapy should be applied for the client with:
    1. a newly fractured ankle
    2. menstrual cramping
    3. an infected wound
    4. degenerative joint disease

42. The client will require the application of a binder to provide support to the abdomen. When applying the binder, the nurse uses the principle that:
    1. the binder should be kept loose for client comfort
    2. the client should be sitting or standing when it is applied
    3. the client must maintain adequate ventilatory capacity
    4. the binder replaces the need for underlying bandages or dressings

Study Group Questions

- What are pressure ulcers, and what contributes to their development?
- Where are pressure ulcers most likely to develop?
- What are the stages of pressure ulcer development?
- What are the classifications of wounds?
- How do wounds heal?
- What are the possible complications of wound healing?
- How do pressure ulcers affect health care costs?
- What tools may be used to predict clients' risks for pressure ulcer development?

- What should be included in the nursing assessment of clients to determine their risk for pressure ulcer development?
- How are wounds managed in emergency and stable health care settings?
- What types of drainage may be seen in wounds?
- How are wound cultures obtained?
- How can the nurse prevent pressure ulcer development?
- What nursing interventions may be implemented to treat pressure ulcers and wounds?

- What are the procedures for dressing changes and wound care?
- What criteria are used in the selection of dressings and sutures or staples?
- What are the principles involved in heat and cold therapy, including client safety?
- What information should be included in client/family teaching for prevention and treatment of pressure ulcers, wound care, and use of heat and cold therapy?

Name_____ Date_____ Instructor's Name_____

Performance Checklist: Skill 34-1

Assessment of Client for Pressure Ulcer Development: Risk Assessment and Skin Assessment

	S	U	NP	Comments
1. Identify client's risk for pressure ulcer formation using the Braden Scale; assign a score for each of the subscales.	____	____	____	_____
2. Use the risk score and evaluate based on client's overall condition.	____	____	____	_____
3. If any of the risk factors are found to receive low scores on the risk assessment tool, consider one or more interventions.	____	____	____	_____
4. Perform a systematic skin assessment of bony prominences. If open areas are noted, wear examination gloves. Look for areas of skin breakdown:				
a. Back of head	____	____	____	_____
b. Shoulders	____	____	____	_____
c. Ribs	____	____	____	_____
d. Hips	____	____	____	_____
e. Sacral area	____	____	____	_____
f. Ischiums	____	____	____	_____
g. Inner and outer knees	____	____	____	_____
h. Inner and outer ankles	____	____	____	_____
i. Heels	____	____	____	_____
j. Feet	____	____	____	_____
5. Assess the following potential areas of skin breakdown:				
a. Ears and nares	____	____	____	_____
b. Lips	____	____	____	_____
c. Tube sites	____	____	____	_____
6. When a reddened area is noted, check for the following:				
a. Blanching erythema	____	____	____	_____
b. Nonblanching erythema	____	____	____	_____
7. Assess all skin surfaces for the following:				
a. Absence of superficial skin layers	____	____	____	_____
b. Blisters	____	____	____	_____
c. Any loss of epidermis and dermis	____	____	____	_____

	S	U	NP	Comments
8. Record client's risk score.	——	——	——	_____
9. Record appearance of skin under pressure.	——	——	——	_____
10. Describe positions, turning intervals, pressure-relieving support devices, and other prevention measures.	——	——	——	_____
11. Report any need for additional consultations for the high-risk client.	——	——	——	_____

Name_____ Date_____ Instructor's Name_____

Performance Checklist: Skill 34-2

Treating Pressure Ulcers

	S	U	NP	Comments
1. Assess client's level of comfort and need for pain medication.	___	___	___	_____
2. Determine if client has allergies to latex and/or topical agents.	___	___	___	_____
3. Review order for topical agent and/or dressing.	___	___	___	_____
4. Assemble all supplies.	___	___	___	_____
5. Provide privacy for client. Wash hands, and apply clean gloves.	___	___	___	_____
6. Position client to allow dressing removal.	___	___	___	_____
7. Remove dressings; discard.	___	___	___	_____
8. Remove gloves, and replace with clean gloves.	___	___	___	_____
9. Cleanse ulcer per treatment order.	___	___	___	_____
10. Assess pressure ulcer:				
a. Measure two dimensions: length and width (per facility's protocol).	___	___	___	_____
b. Measure depth using a cotton-tipped applicator.	___	___	___	_____
c. Determine tissue type in wound bed: estimate the percentage of viable tissue (red, moist) and nonviable tissue.	___	___	___	_____
d. Determine presence of exudate, volume, color, consistency, and odor.	___	___	___	_____
e. Evaluate condition of surrounding skin; note integrity and presence of redness or moisture.	___	___	___	_____
11. Apply topical agents per treatment order. Options include:				
a. Moist saline gauze	___	___	___	_____
b. Hydrogel	___	___	___	_____
c. Hydrocolloid	___	___	___	_____

	S	U	NP	Comments
d. Alginate dressings	___	___	___	_____
e. Enzymes	___	___	___	_____
f. Topical antimicrobials	___	___	___	_____
12. Reposition client.	___	___	___	_____
13. Remove gloves, dispose of soiled supplies, and wash hands.	___	___	___	_____
14. Compare wound measurements.	___	___	___	_____
15. Determine the amount of red granular tissue versus slough or necrotic tissue, and compare this percentage of tissue with previous assessments.	___	___	___	_____
16. Record wound assessments.	___	___	___	_____
17. Describe type of topical agent used, dressing applied, and client's response.	___	___	___	_____
18. Report any deterioration in ulcer appearance and pain assessment to nurse in charge or physician.	___	___	___	_____

Name_____ Date_____ Instructor's Name_____

Performance Checklist: Skill 34-3

Applying Dressings: Wet-to-Dry, Hydrocolloid, and Transparent

	S	U	NP	Comments
1. Assess size and location of wound to be dressed.	___	___	___	_____
2. Assess client's level of comfort. Offer analgesic 30 minutes before, if appropriate.	___	___	___	_____
3. Review medical orders for frequency and type of dressing change. Obtain all equipment.	___	___	___	_____
4. Explain procedure to client, and instruct client not to touch wound area or sterile supplies.	___	___	___	_____
5. Close room or cubicle curtains and windows.	___	___	___	_____
6. Position client comfortably, and drape with bath blanket to expose only wound site. Place waterproof pad under client where dressing is to be changed.	___	___	___	_____
7. Place disposable waterproof bag within reach of work area. Fold top of bag to make cuff.	___	___	___	_____
8. Wash hands and apply clean disposable gloves. Face mask, protective eyewear, and waterproof gown are worn when risk of spray exists.	___	___	___	_____
9. Remove old dressing including tape, bandage, or ties. For easier removal of tape use adhesive remover. Pull dressing back slowly across direction of hair growth, parallel to skin.	___	___	___	_____
10. Change dressing.				
a. Wet to dry—With gloved hand or forceps, lift outer secondary layer of dressing. Then remove inner dressing. Take care not to dislodge drains or tubes.	___	___	___	_____
b. Hydrocolloid—Hydrocolloid interacts with wound fluids and forms a soft	___	___	___	_____

	S	U	NP	Comments

whitish-yellow gel that may have a
faint odor.

   c. Transparent—Ease off with cotton
swabs soaked in mineral oil. _____ _____ _____ _____

11. Observe character and amount of drainage _____ _____ _____ _____
on dressing and appearance of wound.

12. Dispose of soiled dressings in disposable _____ _____ _____ _____
bag. Avoid having client see drainage.

13. Remove gloves by pulling them inside out. _____ _____ _____ _____
Discard in bag.

14. Open sterile dressing tray or individually _____ _____ _____ _____
wrapped sterile supplies. Place on bedside
table.

15. Apply new dressing
   a. Wet to dry
     (1) Apply sterile gloves. _____ _____ _____ _____
     (2) Inspect wound for tissue appearance, _____ _____ _____ _____
        presence of drainage, and size. Note
        condition of periwound skin.
     (3) Cleanse wound with prescribed _____ _____ _____ _____
        solution. Clean from least to most
        contaminated area.
     (4) Remove excess moisture from gauze. _____ _____ _____ _____
        Unfold and apply moist fluffed mesh
        gauze or packing strip directly into
        wound surface. Continue with
        additional gauze until wound is filled.
     (5) Make sure any dead space from sinus _____ _____ _____ _____
        tracts are filled.
     (6) Apply dry, sterile 4 × 4 gauze over _____ _____ _____ _____
        moist gauze.
     (7) Cover with ABD pad, Surgipad, or _____ _____ _____ _____
        gauze.
     (8) Apply tape over dressing, Kling roll
        (for circumferential dressings), or
        Montgomery ties.
        a. Expose adhesive surface of tape on _____ _____ _____ _____
           end of each tie.
        b. Apply adhesive surface to skin _____ _____ _____ _____
           perpendicular to the wound.
        c. Position gauze over wound and _____ _____ _____ _____
           secure ties to hold dressing in place.
   b. Hydrocolloid
     (1) Pour saline or prescribed solution _____ _____ _____ _____
        over 4 × 4s.
     (2) Apply gloves (sterile or clean—check _____ _____ _____ _____
        agency policy).

	S	U	NP	Comments
(3) Cleanse area gently with moist 4 × 4s, swabbing exudate away from wound.	___	___	___	_____
(4) Thoroughly pat area dry with 4 × 4 gauze.	___	___	___	_____
(5) Inspect wound for tissue type, color, odor, and drainage. Measure wound size and depth.	___	___	___	_____
(6) Apply hydrocolloid dressings according to manufacturer's directions. Apply granules or paste before wafer dressing in deeper wounds.	___	___	___	_____
c. Transparent				
(1) Pour saline or prescribed solution over 4 × 4s.	___	___	___	_____
(2) Apply gloves (sterile or clean—check agency policy).	___	___	___	_____
(3) Cleanse gently with moist 4 × 4s, swabbing exudate away from wound.	___	___	___	_____
(4) Thoroughly pat dry skin around wound.	___	___	___	_____
(5) Inspect wound for tissue type, color, odor, and drainage. Measure if indicated.	___	___	___	_____
(6) Apply transparent dressing according to manufacturer. Film should not be stretched during application. Avoid wrinkles in film.	___	___	___	_____
16. Remove gloves and discard in bag. Remove mask, gown, and eyewear.	___	___	___	_____
17. Assist client to comfortable position.	___	___	___	_____
18. Dispose of supplies, and wash hands.	___	___	___	_____
19. Report brisk, bright-red bleeding or evidence of wound dehiscence or evisceration to physician immediately.	___	___	___	_____
20. Report wound appearance and characteristics of drainage at shift change.	___	___	___	_____
21. Record wound appearance, color, presence and characteristics of exudate, type and amount of dressings used, and tolerance of client to procedure.	___	___	___	_____
22. Write date and time dressing applied on tape in ink (not marker).	___	___	___	_____

Name_____   Date_____   Instructor's Name_____

Performance Checklist: Skill 34-4

Performing Wound Irrigation

	S	U	NP	Comments
1. Review physician's order for irrigation of open wound and type of solution to be used.	___	___	___	_____
2. Review recent recorded assessments related to client's open wound:				
a. Extent of impairment of skin integrity, including size of wound.	___	___	___	_____
b. Elevation of body temperature.	___	___	___	_____
c. Drainage from wound (amount, color, and consistency). Amount can be measured by part of dressing saturated or in terms of quantity.	___	___	___	_____
d. Odor.	___	___	___	_____
e. Wound color.	___	___	___	_____
f. Culture reports.	___	___	___	_____
g. Stage of healing of the client's wound.	___	___	___	_____
h. Dressing: dry and clean; evidence of bleeding, profuse drainage.	___	___	___	_____
3. Assess comfort level or pain, and identify symptoms of anxiety. Administer prescribed analgesic 30 to 45 minutes before starting wound irrigation.	___	___	___	_____
4. Assess client for history of allergies to antiseptics, tapes, or dressing material.	___	___	___	_____
5. Explain procedure of wound irrigation and cleansing.	___	___	___	_____
6. Position client.				
a. Position client comfortably to permit gravitational flow of irrigating solution through wound and into collection receptable.	___	___	___	_____
b. Position client so that wound is vertical to collection basin.	___	___	___	_____
c. Place padding or extra towels.	___	___	___	_____
d. Expose wound only.	___	___	___	_____
7. Warm irrigation solution to approximate body temperature. Place container in basin of hot water.	___	___	___	_____

	S	U	NP	Comments

8. Form cuff on waterproof bag, and place it near bed.

9. Wash hands.

10. Close room door or bed curtains.

11. Apply gown and goggles if needed.

12. Put on clean gloves, remove soiled dressing, and discard in waterproof bag. Discard gloves.

13. Prepare equipment; open sterile supplies.

14. Put on sterile gloves.

15. To irrigate wound with moderate pressure:
   a. Fill 35-ml syringe with irrigation solution.
   b. Attach 19-gauge needle or angiocath.
   c. Hold syringe tip 2.5 cm (1 inch) above upper end of wound and over area being cleansed.
   d. Using continuous pressure, flush wound; repeat Steps 15a, b, and c until solution draining into basin is clear.

16. To irrigate deep wound with minimal pressure:
   a. Attach soft angiocatheter to piston syringe filled with irrigation solution.
   b. Using slow, continuous pressure, flush wound.
   c. Refill syringe, and repeat until solution draining into basin is clear.

17. To cleanse would with hand-held shower:
   a. With client seated comfortably in shower chair, adjust spray in gentle flow; water temperature should be warm.
   b. Cover shower head with clean washcloth if needed.
   c. Shower for 5 to 10 minutes with shower head 12 inches (30 cm) from wound.

18. To cleanse wound with whirlpool:
   a. Adjust water level and temperature; add prescribed cleansing agent.
   b. Assist client into whirlpool, or place extremity into whirlpool.
   c. Allow client to remain in whirlpool for prescribed interval.

	S	U	NP	Comments
19. When indicated, obtain cultures after cleansing with nonbacteriostatic saline.	___	___	___	_____
20. Dry wound edges with gauze; dry client if shower or whirlpool is used.	___	___	___	_____
21. Observe type of tissue in wound bed and wound diameter.	___	___	___	_____
22. Apply appropriate dressing.	___	___	___	_____
23. Remove gloves, mask, goggles, and gown.	___	___	___	_____
24. Assist client to comfortable position.	___	___	___	_____
25. Dispose of equipment and soiled supplies, and wash hands.	___	___	___	_____
26. Inspect dressing periodically.	___	___	___	_____
27. Evaluate skin integrity.	___	___	___	_____
28. Observe client for signs of discomfort.	___	___	___	_____
29. Observe for presence of retained irrigant.	___	___	___	_____
30. Record wound irrigation and client response on progress notes.	___	___	___	_____
31. Immediately report any evidence of fresh bleeding, sharp increase in pain, retention of irrigant, or signs of shock to attending physician.	___	___	___	_____

35 Sensory Alterations

Case Studies

I. You are making a home visit to a client with diabetes mellitus who is losing his eyesight (diabetic retinopathy).
    a. What interventions may be implemented with the client to assist in maintaining adequate sensory stimulation and personal safety?

II. You have been assigned to care for a client in the intensive care unit (ICU).
    a. What sensory alterations may this client experience, and how can you prevent their occurrence?

Independent Learning Activities

1. Review the normal anatomy and physiology of the sensory systems.

2. Investigate available community agencies and organizations that are designed specifically to assist clients with sensory deficits.

3. Think about how you would need to adapt if you experienced a sensory deficit. Note areas that clients with sensory deficits will have to manage in their homes.

Chapter Review

Complete the following:

1. Identify the other terms for the following:
    a. sight

    b. hearing

    c. taste

    d. smell

    e. touch

    f. position sense

2. Describe sensory deprivation and sensory overload.

3. Identify clients who are risk for development of sensory alterations.

4. Provide the correct term for the following:
   a. a build up of earwax in the external auditory canal

   b. hearing loss associated with aging

   c. opacity of the lens resulting in blurred vision

   d. decreased salivary production/dry mouth

5. Identify how the following factors may influence sensory function.
   a. age: older adulthood

   b. medications

   c. smoking

6. Specify three methods that may be used by the nurse to assess a client's vision, hearing, and touch.

7. What effects may sensory deprivation have on an individual?

8. In teaching parents about child eyesight safety for infants and toddlers, what general information should be included?

9. Identify at least three ways to modify sensory stimulation in the health care environment.

10. Identify ways in which a nurse may communicate with a hearing-impaired client.

11. Name four specific drugs that may cause ototoxicity in clients.

12. Identify how the nurse may assist clients with the following to adapt their home environments:
    a. hearing deficit

    b. diminished sense of smell

    c. diminished sense of touch

13. Identify a nursing diagnosis that may be formulated for a client with a sensory deficit.

14. What general screenings may be conducted to determine visual and/or auditory deficits?

Select the best answer for each of the following questions:

15. An expected outcome for a client with an auditory deficit should include:
    1. minimizing use of affected sense(s)
    2. preventing additional sensory losses
    3. promoting the clients acceptance of dependency
    4. controlling the environment to reduce sensory stimuli

16. The nurse is working with clients at the senior day care center and recognizes that changes in sensory status may influence the older adult's eating patterns. For clients who are experiencing changes in their dietary intake, the nurse will assess for:
    1. presbycusis
    2. xerostomia
    3. vestibular ataxia
    4. peripheral neuropathy

17. Parents have brought in their 1 $\frac{1}{2}$-year-old child to the pediatric clinic. The parents ask the nurse if there are signs that may indicate that the child is not able to hear well. The nurse explains to the parents that they should be alert to the child:
    1. awakening to loud noises
    2. responding reflexively to sounds
    3. having delayed speech development
    4. remaining calm when unfamiliar people approach

18. The nurse is assessing the client for a potential gustatory impairment. This may be indicated if the client has a:
    1. weight loss
    2. blank look or stare
    3. increased sensitivity to odors

4. period of excessive clumsiness or dizziness

19. A client has come to the local walk-in emergency center with flulike symptoms. After visiting with the physician, the client shows the nurse the prescriptions. The client may be informed that ototoxicity may occur with the administration of:
    1. vitamin C
    2. acetaminophen
    3. erythromycin
    4. cough suppressant with codeine

20. A responsive client has had eye surgery, and patches temporarily have been placed on both eyes for protection. The evening meal has arrived, and the nurse will be assisting the client. In this circumstance, the nurse should:
    1. feed the client the entire meal
    2. encourage family members to feed the client
    3. allow the client to be totally independent and feed himself
    4. orient the client to the locations of the foods on the plate and provide the utensils

21. Following a CVA (cerebral vascular accident/stroke, the client is found to have a receptive aphasia. The nurse may assist this client with communication by:
    1. obtaining a referral for a speech therapist
    2. using a system of simple gestures and repeated behaviors
    3. providing the client with a letter chart to use to answer questions
    4. offering the client a notepad and pen to write down questions and concerns

22. A mother is bringing in her newborn for his first physical exam. She expresses concern because she may have been exposed during her pregnancy to an infectious disease and she heard that the baby's hearing could be affected. The nurse inquires if the client was exposed to:
    1. rubella

2. pneumonia
3. excessive oxygen
4. urinary tract infection

Study Group Questions

- What are the human senses and their functions?
- What factors influence sensory function?
- What are some common sensory alterations?
- What clients are at risk for developing sensory alterations?
- How should the nurse assess a client's sensory function?

- What behaviors or changes in lifestyle patterns or socialization may indicate a sensory alteration?
- How can the nurse promote sensory function, and prevent injury and isolation in the health promotion, acute, and restorative care settings?
- What screening processes are used to determine the presence of sensory alterations?
- How may the family/significant others be involved in the care of the client with a sensory alteration?
- What information should be included in client/family teaching for promotion of sensory function and prevention of injury?

36 Surgical Client

Case Studies

I. Your client is going to have extensive abdominal surgery with a large, midline incision.
   a. How can you assist this client to promote respiratory function postoperatively?

II. A client is having outpatient surgery.
   a. How may preoperative teaching be conducted?

III. While completing the preoperative checklist, the nurse discovers that the client's temperature is 101° F.
   a. What should the nurse do?

IV. Your client insists that his good-luck medallion must go with him everywhere, even to surgery.
   a. What should you do?

Independent Learning Activities

1. Investigate the types of anesthesia that commonly are used for surgical procedures, and determine potential adverse reactions for each type.

2. Investigate the types of surgery that usually are performed in an outpatient/ambulatory surgery center. Compare those procedures, and the time spent by the outpatient client, to surgeries usually performed in an acute care facility.

3. Research an article in a current nursing journal on legal implications and potential situations in the perioperative environment.

4. Inquire about family members' or friends' prior surgical experiences to get the client's perspective.

Chapter Review

Complete the following:

1. Identify the following classifications for surgical procedures:
   a. Performed on the basis of the client's choice; not essential for health

   b. Involves extensive reconstruction or alteration in body parts; poses risks to well-being

   c. Surgical exploration that allows physician to confirm medical status; may involve removal of body tissue for analysis

d.   Must be done immediately to save life or preserve function of body part

e.   Relieves or reduces intensity of disease symptoms; will not produce cure

f.   Performed to replace malfunctioning organs or structures

2.   Identify at least four medical conditions that may increase the client's surgical risk.

3.   Identify how the following factors place the older adult client at risk for surgery:
a.   cardiovascular

b.   pulmonary

c.   renal

d.   neurological

4.   What are the implications for surgical clients who are taking the following medications?
a.   heparin

b.   insulin

5.   What general information usually is included in preoperative teaching?

6.   What differences exist in client care between an acute care and ambulatory surgery postanesthesia care unit (PACU)?

7.   Identify the usual nursing interventions that are implemented in an acute care setting on the day of a client's surgery.

8.   What are the routine screening tests that are ordered for a client preoperatively?

9.   Identify the commonly used types and purposes of preoperative medications.

10.   What are the roles of the circulating nurse and scrub nurse in the operating room?

11.   Identify the uses and side effects for the following anesthetics:
a.   general anesthesia

b. regional anesthesia

c. local anesthesia

d. conscious sedation

12. How can the nurse prevent injury to the client during the operation?

13. Typical postoperative orders for clients include:

14. Identify two possible postoperative complications for each of the following systems:
a. respiratory

b. circulatory

c. gastrointestinal

d. integumentary

15. Identify the postoperative exercises that the nurse should explain and demonstrate to the client to prevent postoperative complications.

Select the best answer for each of the following questions:

16. The nurse is starting the preparations for the client who is having surgery tomorrow morning. The nurse is going to have the consent form completed. The nurse recognizes that informed consent:
1. is invalid if the client is disoriented
2. is signed by the client after the administration of preoperative medications
3. indicates that the client is aware of the procedure and its possible complications
4. requires that the nurse provide information about the surgery before the consent can by signed

17. The client is brought into the PACU after the surgery. The nurse is assessing the client and is alert to the indication of a postoperative hemorrhage if the client exhibits:
1. restlessness
2. warm, dry skin
3. a slow, steady pulse
4. a decreased respiratory rate

18. The nurse is checking the vital signs of the client who had major surgery yesterday. The nurse discovers that the client's temperature is slightly elevated. This finding is usually indicative of:
1. a postoperative wound infection
2. an allergic response to latex
3. a response to the anesthesia
4. extensive neural damage

19. The nurse is completing the preoperative checklist for a female client who is going to have a surgical procedure. While reviewing the lab results, the nurse finds that the surgeon and anesthesiologist should be informed of the client's:
1. Hgb 10 g/dl
2. potassium 4.2 mEq/L
3. platelets 210,000/mm^3
4. prothrombin time (PT) 11 seconds

20. The client has received a spinal anesthetic during the surgical procedure. The nurse is alert to possible complications of the anesthetic and is assessing the client for a:
    1. rash
    2. headache
    3. nephrotoxicity
    4. hyperthermic response

21. The client is being evaluated for transfer from the PACU back to the client's unit. The nurse determines that the client will be approved for a transfer if the client exhibits:
    1. increased wound drainage
    2. pulse oximetry at 95%
    3. respirations 30/min
    4. nonpalpable peripheral pulses

22. The client is scheduled to have abdominal surgery later this morning. At 9:00 A.M., while completing the preoperative checklist, the nurse recognizes the need to contact the surgeon right away. The nurse has identified that the client:
    1. received an enema at 6:00 A.M.
    2. admitted to recent substance abuse
    3. ate a hamburger last evening at 6:00 P.M.
    4. has bowel sounds in all four quadrants of the abdomen

23. The client is being positioned in the PACU after surgery. Unless contraindicated, the nurse should place the client:
    1. prone
    2. in high Fowler's position
    3. supine with arms across the chest
    4. on the side with the face turned downward

24. When the client first comes to the PACU, there are general nursing measures that are implemented. The nurse will:
    1. provide oral fluids
    2. allow the client to sleep
    3. provide a warm blanket
    4. remove the urinary catheter

25. The nurse is visiting the client who had surgery 9 hours ago. The nurse asks if the client has voided and the client responds negatively. At this time, the nurse:
    1. provides more oral fluid
    2. inserts an intravenous (IV) line and administers fluids
    3. obtains an order for urinary catheterization
    4. recognizes that this is a normal outcome

26. During a client assessment in the PACU, the nurse finds that the client's operative site is swollen and appears tight. The nurse suspects:
    1. infection
    2. hemorrhage
    3. lymphedema
    4. subcutaneous emphysema

27. An immediate postoperative priority in providing nursing care for the client is:
    1. airway patency
    2. relief of pain
    3. sufficient circulation to the extremities
    4. prevention of wound infection

28. A 54-year-old client is scheduled to have a gastric resection. The nurse informs the surgeon preoperatively of the client's history of:
    1. a tonsillectomy at age 10
    2. employment as a telephone repair person
    3. smoking two packs of cigarettes per day
    4. taking acetaminophen for minor body aches

29. During the intraoperative phase, the nurse's responsibility is reflected in the statement:
    1. "I think that the client requires more information about the procedure and its consequences."
    2. "There seems to be a missing sponge, so a recount must be done to see that all of the sponges were removed."
    3. "The client has signed the request. I will prepare the medications and then get the record completed."

4. "The client appears reactive and stable. Dressing to wound is dry and intact. Analgesic administered per order."

30. The nurse is assisting the client with postoperative exercises. The client tells the nurse, "Blowing into this thing [incentive spirometer] is a waste of time." The nurse explains to the client that the specific purpose of this therapy is to:
    1. stimulate the cough reflex
    2. promote lung expansion
    3. increase pulmonary circulation
    4. directly remove excess secretions from the respiratory tract

31. The client is scheduled for surgery and the nurse is completing the final areas of the preoperative checklist. After administering the preoperative medications, the nurse should:
    1. assist the client to void
    2. obtain the consent
    3. prepare the skin at the surgical site
    4. place the side rails up on the bed or stretcher

32. A client is having surgery with general anesthesia at the ambulatory surgery center. This client will be expected by the nurse to:
    1. ambulate right after being admitted to the recovery area
    2. meet all of the identified criteria to be discharged home
    3. remain in the phase I recovery area longer than a hospitalized client
    4. receive large amounts of oral fluid immediately on entering the recovery area

Study Group Questions

- How are surgeries classified?
- What are some surgical risk factors, and why do they increase the client's risk?

- How does the incision site influence a client's recovery?
- How may prior surgical experiences influence the client's expectations of surgery?
- What general information should be included in preoperative teaching?
- What is the purpose of the preoperative exercises that are explained and demonstrated to clients?
- What preoperative assessments should be made by the nurse?
- What are some of the common preoperative diagnostic tests that may be ordered for the client?
- What nursing interventions are implemented in the preoperative care of clients?
- How does the nurse prepare and assist the client in the acute care setting on the day of surgery?
- What are the roles of the nurses in the operating room and recovery setting?
- What interventions are implemented to maintain client safety and well-being in the operating room and postanesthesia care area?
- What nursing care is critical in the immediate postoperative stage?
- What are the similarities and differences between the preparation and postanesthesia care for clients in the acute care and ambulatory surgery setting?
- What general information should be included in postoperative teaching for clients/families in the acute care and ambulatory surgery setting?
- How may the family/significant others be involved in the client's perioperative experience?

Study Chart

Create a study chart on the Surgical Risk Factors, *identifying how age, nutritional status, obesity, immunocompetence, fluid/electrolyte balance, and pregnancy may affect the client's perioperative experience.*

Name_____ Date_____ Instructor's Name_____

Performance Checklist: Skill 36-1

Teaching Postoperative Exercises

	S	U	NP	Comments
1. Assess client's risk for postoperative respiratory complications.	____	____	____	_____
2. Assess client's ability to cough and deep breathe by having client take a deep breath and observing movement of shoulders, chest wall, and abdomen. Measure chest excursion during a deep breath. Ask client to cough after taking a deep breath.	____	____	____	_____
3. Assess client's risk for postoperative thrombus formation. Observe for a positive Homans sign by monitoring calf pain when dorsiflexing the client's foot with the knee flexed. Observe for calf pain, redness, swelling, or vein distention, usually unilaterally.	____	____	____	_____
4. Assess client's ability to move independently while in bed.	____	____	____	_____
5. Assess client's willingness and capability to learn exercises.	____	____	____	_____
6. Assess family members' or significant others' willingness to learn and to support client postoperatively.	____	____	____	_____
7. Assess client's medical orders preoperatively and postoperatively.	____	____	____	_____
8. Teach importance of postoperative exercises to recovery and physiological benefits. a. Diaphragmatic breathing (1) Assist client to a comfortable sitting or standing position with knees flexed. If client chooses to sit, assist to side of bed or to upright position in chair.	____	____	____	_____
(2) Stand or sit facing client.	____	____	____	_____
(3) Instruct client to place palms of hands across from each other, down, and along lower borders of anterior rib cage; place tips of third fingers lightly together. Demonstrate for client.	____	____	____	_____

	S	U	NP	Comments
(4) Have client take slow, deep breaths, inhaling through nose and pushing abdomen against hands. Tell client to feel middle fingers separate as client inhales. Explain that client will feel normal downward movement of diaphragm during inspiration.	___	___	___	_____
(5) Explain that abdominal organs descend and chest wall expands. Demonstrate for client.	___	___	___	_____
(6) Avoid using chest and shoulders while inhaling, and instruct client in same manner.	___	___	___	_____
(7) Have client hold a slow, deep breath; hold for count of three; and then slowly exhale through mouth as if blowing out a candle (pursed lips). Tell client middle fingertips will touch as chest wall contracts.	___	___	___	_____
(8) Repeat breathing exercise 3 to 5 times.	___	___	___	_____
(9) Have client practice exercise. Instruct client to take 10 slow, deep breaths every hour while awake.	___	___	___	_____
b. Incentive spirometry				
(1) Wash hands.	___	___	___	_____
(2) Instruct client to assume semi-Fowler's or high Fowler's position.	___	___	___	_____
(3) Indicate on the device the volume level to be obtained with each inhalation.	___	___	___	_____
(4) Demonstrate to client how to place mouthpiece so that lips completely cover mouthpiece.	___	___	___	_____
(5) Instruct client to inhale slowly and maintain constant flow through unit. When maximal inspiration is reached, client should hold breath for 2 to 3 seconds and then exhale slowly. Number of breaths should not exceed 10 to 12 per minute.	___	___	___	_____
(6) Instruct client to breathe normally for short period.	___	___	___	_____
(7) Have client repeat maneuver until goals are achieved.	___	___	___	_____
(8) Wash hands.	___	___	___	_____
c. Positive expiratory pressure therapy and "huff" coughing				
(1) Wash hands.	___	___	___	_____
(2) Set positive expiratory pressure (PEP) device for setting ordered.	___	___	___	_____
(3) Instruct client to assume semi-Fowler's or high Fowler's position, and place nose clip on client's nose.	___	___	___	_____

	S	U	NP	Comments

(4) Have client place lips around mouthpiece. Client should take a full breath and then exhale 2 or 3 times longer than inhalation. Pattern should be repeated for 10 to 20 breaths.

(5) Remove device from mouth, and have client take a slow, deep breath and hold for 3 seconds.

(6) Instruct client to exhale in quick, short, forced "huffs."

d. Controlled coughing

(1) Explain importance of maintaining an upright position.

(2) Demonstrate coughing. Take two slow, deep breaths, inhaling through nose and exhaling through mouth.

(3) Inhale deeply a third time, and hold breath to count of three. Cough fully for two or three consecutive coughs without inhaling between coughs. (Tell client to push all air out of lungs.)

(4) Caution client against just clearing throat instead of coughing. Explain that coughing will not cause injury to incision.

(5) If surgical incision is to be either abdominal or thoracic, teach client to place pillow or bath blanket over incisional area and place hands over pillow to splint incision. During breathing and coughing exercises, press gently against incisional area for splitting or support.

(6) Instruct client to continue to practice coughing exercises, splinting imaginary incision. Instruct the client to cough 2 or 3 times while awake.

(7) Instruct client to examine sputum for consistency, odor, amount, and color changes.

e. Turning

(1) Instruct client to assume supine position and move toward left side of bed by bending knees and pressing heels against the mattress to raise and move buttocks.

(2) Instruct client to place the right hand over incisional area to splint it.

(3) Instruct client to keep right leg straight and flex left knee up.

	S	U	NP	Comments

(4) Have client grab right side rail with left hand, pull toward right, and roll onto right side. ____ ____ ____ _____

(5) Instruct client to turn every 2 hours while awake. ____ ____ ____ _____

  f. Leg exercises

(1) Have client assume supine position in bed. Demonstrate leg exercises by performing passive range-of-motion exercises and simultaneously explaining exercise. ____ ____ ____ _____

(2) Rotate each ankle in complete circle. Instruct client to draw imaginary circles with big toe. Repeat 5 times. ____ ____ ____ _____

(3) Alternate dorsiflexion and plantar flexion of both feet. Direct client to feel calf muscles contract and relax alternately. ____ ____ ____ _____

(4) Perform quadriceps setting by tightening thigh muscle and bringing knee down toward mattress, then relaxing. Repeat 5 times. ____ ____ ____ _____

(5) Have client alternately raise each leg up from bed surface, keeping legs straight, and then have client bend leg at hip and knee. Repeat 5 times. ____ ____ ____ _____

9. Have client continue to practice exercises at least every 2 hours while awake. Instruct client to coordinate turning and leg exercises with diaphragmatic breathing, incentive spirometry, and coughing exercises. ____ ____ ____ _____

10. Observe client performing exercises independently. ____ ____ ____ _____

11. Observe family members' or significant others' ability to coach client. ____ ____ ____ _____

12. Record which exercises have been demonstrated to client and whether client can perform exercises independently. ____ ____ ____ _____

13. Record physical assessment findings. ____ ____ ____ _____

14. Report any problems client has in practicing exercises to nurse assigned to client on next shift. ____ ____ ____ _____

Name_____ Date_____ Instructor's Name_____

Performance Checklist: Skill 36-2

Inserting and Maintaining a Nasogastric Tube

	S	U	NP	Comments
Inserting and Maintaining a Nasogastric Tube				
1. Inspect client's nasal and oral cavities.	____	____	____	_____
2. Ask if client has history of nasal surgery and note if deviated nasal septum is present.	____	____	____	_____
3. Palpate client's abdomen for distention, pain, and rigidity. Auscultate for bowel sounds.	____	____	____	_____
4. Assess client's level of consciousness and ability to follow instructions.	____	____	____	_____
5. Check medical record for prescriber's order, type of nasogastric (NG) tube to be placed, and whether tube is to be attached to suction or drainage bag.	____	____	____	_____
6. Prepare equipment. Prepare a 2×3 in piece of tape with one end split in half.	____	____	____	_____
7. Explain procedure to client.	____	____	____	_____
8. Wash hands and apply disposable gloves.	____	____	____	_____
9. Position client in high Fowler's position with pillow behind client's head and shoulders. Raise bed to a comfortable working level.	____	____	____	_____
10. Provide privacy.	____	____	____	_____
11. Stand on client's right side if you are right-handed and on left side if left-handed.	____	____	____	_____
12. Place bath towel over client's chest. Give facial tissues to client.	____	____	____	_____
13. Instruct client to relax and breathe normally while occluding one naris. Repeat this action for other naris. Select nostril with greater air flow.	____	____	____	_____

	S	U	NP	Comments

14. Measure distance to insert tube: use traditional or Hanson method.

15. Mark length of tube to be inserted with small piece of tape placed so it can easily be removed.

16. Cut a 10-cm piece of tape. Split one end down the middle lengthwise 5 cm. Place on bed rail or bedside table.

17. Curve 10 to 15 cm of end of tube tightly around index finger, then release.

18. Lubricate 7.5 to 10 cm of end of tube with water-soluble lubricating jelly.

19. Alert client that procedure is to begin.

20. Instruct client to extend neck back against pillow. Insert tube slowly through naris, with curved end pointing downward.

21. Continue to pass tube along floor of nasal passage, aiming down toward ear. When resistance is felt, apply gentle downward pressure to advance tube (do not force past resistance).

22. If resistance is met, try to rotate the tube and see if it advances. If there is still resistance, withdraw tube, allow client to rest, relubricate tube, and insert into client's other naris.

23. Continue insertion of tube until just past client's nasopharynx by gently rotating tube toward client's opposite naris.
   A. Stop tube advancement, allow client to relax, and provide tissues.
   B. Explain that next step requires client to swallow. Give glass of water, unless contraindicated.

24. With tube just above oropharynx, instruct client to flex head forward, take a small sip of water, and swallow. Advance tube 2.5 to 5 cm with each swallow. If not allowed fluids, instruct client to dry swallow or suck air through straw.

25. If client begins to cough, gag, or choke, withdraw tube slightly and

	S	U	NP	Comments

stop advancement. Instruct client to breathe easily and sip water.

26. Pull tube back slightly if client continues to cough. ____ ____ ____ _____

27. If client continues to gag, check back of pharynx using flashlight and tongue blade. ____ ____ ____ _____

28. After client relaxes, continue to advance tube desired distance. ____ ____ ____ _____

29. Once tube is correctly advanced, remove tape used to mark length of tube and place the prepared split tape with nonsplit side on client's nose. Anchor tape with one of split ends while checking tube placement. ____ ____ ____ _____

30. Check tube placement: ____ ____ ____ _____
    A. Ask client to talk. ____ ____ ____ _____
    B. Inspect posterior pharynx for presence of coiled tube. ____ ____ ____ _____
    C. Aspirate gently back on syringe to obtain gastric contents. Observe color. ____ ____ ____ _____
    D. Measure pH of aspirate with color-coded pH paper with numbers from 1 to 11. ____ ____ ____ _____
    E. If tube is not in client's stomach, advance it another 2.5 to 5 cm and repeat steps 29C through 31E. ____ ____ ____ _____

31. Anchor the tube: ____ ____ ____ _____
    A. Clamp end of tube or connect it to drainage bag or suction machine after insertion.
    B. Tape tube to client's nose; avoid putting pressure on nares: ____ ____ ____ _____
        (1) Apply small amount of tincture of benzoin to lower end of client's nose and allow to dry. Secure tape over client's nose. ____ ____ ____ _____
        (2) Carefully wrap two split ends of tape around tube. ____ ____ ____ _____

	S	U	NP	Comments
(3) Alternatively, apply tube fixation device using shaped adhesive patch.	___	___	___	_____
C. Fasten end of NG tube to client's gown by looping rubber band around tube in slip knot. Pin rubber band to gown.	___	___	___	_____
D. Elevate head of bed 30 degrees, unless contraindicated.	___	___	___	_____
E. Explain to client that sensation of tube should decrease somewhat with time.	___	___	___	_____
F. Remove and dispose of gloves and wash hands.	___	___	___	_____
32. Safety:	___	___	___	_____
A. Once placement is confirmed, place a mark, either a red mark or tape, on tube to indicate where tube exits nose.	___	___	___	_____
B. Option: measure tube length from nares to connector. Document in client record.	___	___	___	_____
33. Irrigate tube:	___	___	___	_____
A. Wash hands and apply disposable gloves.	___	___	___	_____
B. Check for tube placement (see step 31). Reconnect NG tube to connecting tube.	___	___	___	_____
C. Draw up 30 ml of normal saline into regular or catheter-tipped syringe.	___	___	___	_____
D. Clamp NG tube. Disconnect it from connection tubing and lay end of connection tubing on towel.	___	___	___	_____
E. Insert tip of irrigating syringe into end of NG tube. Remove clamp. Hold syringe with tip pointed at floor and inject saline slowly and evenly. Do not force solution.	___	___	___	_____
F. If resistance occurs, check for kinks in tubing. Turn client onto left side.	___	___	___	_____
G. After instilling saline, immediately aspirate or pull back slowly on syringe to withdraw fluid. Record I & O.	___	___	___	_____

	S	U	NP	Comments

H. Reconnect NG tube to drainage or suction. (If solution does not return, repeat irrigation). ____ ____ ____ _____

I. Remove and dispose of gloves and wash hands. ____ ____ ____ _____

34. Discontinue NG tube: ____ ____ ____ _____

A. Verify order to discontinue NG tube. ____ ____ ____ _____

B. Explain procedure and reassure client that removal is less distressing than insertion. ____ ____ ____ _____

C. Wash hands and apply disposable gloves. ____ ____ ____ _____

D. Turn off suction and disconnect NG tube from drainage bag or suction. Remove tape from bridge of client's nose and unpin tube from client's gown. ____ ____ ____ _____

E. Stand on client's right side if you are right-handed and left side if you are left-handed. ____ ____ ____ _____

F. Hand the client facial tissue. Place clean towel across client's chest. Instruct client to take and hold a deep breath. ____ ____ ____ _____

G. Clamp or kink tubing securely and then pull tube out steadily and smoothly into towel held in other hand while client holds breath. ____ ____ ____ _____

H. Measure amount of drainage and note character of content. Dispose of tube and drainage equipment. ____ ____ ____ _____

I. Clean client's nares and provide month care. ____ ____ ____ _____

J. Assist client to a comfortable position and explain procedure for drinking fluids, if not contraindicated. ____ ____ ____ _____

35. Clean equipment and return to proper place. Place soiled linen in proper receptacle. ____ ____ ____ _____

36. Remove and dispose of gloves and wash hands. ____ ____ ____ _____

	S	U	NP	Comments
37. Observe amount and character of contents draining from NG tube. Ask if client feels nauseated.	___	___	___	_____
38. Palpate client's abdomen periodically for distention, pain, and rigidity, and auscultate for the presence of bowel sounds. Turn off suction while auscultating.	___	___	___	_____
39. Inspect condition of client's nares and nose.	___	___	___	_____
40. Observe position of tubing.	___	___	___	_____
41. Ask if client's throat feels sore of if there is irritation in the pharynx.	___	___	___	_____
42. Record time and type of NG tube inserted, client's tolerance of procedure, confirmation of placement, character of client's gastric contents, pH value of contents, and whether tube is clamped or connected to drainage device.	___	___	___	_____

Answers to Case Study Questions and Chapter Reviews

CHAPTER 1—Health and Wellness

CASE STUDY

a. This is an individual entering her middle adult years who is experiencing stress in her personal and professional life. She is being called on by her employer and her child to meet their expectations, and she believes that this does not allow her the time to meet her health needs. The symptoms of gastrointestinal distress may be a response to the pressures in her life.

Initially, the nurse may spend time with this client to discuss her personal feelings and needs. She may benefit from being taught stress reduction and relaxation techniques, along with a review of time management. The nurse may investigate with her if there are support people at work and in the neighborhood to assist her in keeping up with her busy schedule. This individual also may be assisted in making an appointment for medical follow-up to determine her current health status.

CHAPTER REVIEW

1. e

2. d

3. c

4. b

5. a

6. a. Health-Illness Continuum Model: This model looks at health as a dynamic state that fluctuates as a person adapts to changes in the environment. Illness is a process where the person's functioning is diminished or impaired when compared with prior levels of functioning. Risk factors are central to the model.

   b. Health Belief Model: Health beliefs are a person's ideas, convictions, and attitudes about health and illness. Health beliefs can influence health behavior and positively or negatively affect a client's level of health.

   c. Health Promotion Model: Health is defined as a positive, dynamic state. Health promotion is directed at increasing the client's level of well-being. Multidimensional individuals interact within their environment to pursue health.

   d. Holistic Health Model: A comprehensive view of the person as a biopsychosocial and spiritual being. Clients are empowered to engage in their own healing process.

7. Internal variables:
   - Developmental stage—level of growth and development
   - Intellectual background—knowledge, cognitive abilities
   - Emotional factors—reactions, ability to cope with stress
   - Spiritual factors—values and beliefs, hope and meaning in life

External variables:
- Family practices—family perceptions and health behaviors
- Socioeconomic factors—financial status, how health care is obtained
- Cultural background—beliefs, values, customs

8. Holistic nursing interventions include music therapy, reminiscence, relaxation therapy, therapeutic touch, and massage therapy. These interventions may be used to provide distraction, reduce pain, relieve anxiety or tension, and promote sleep. Therapeutic touch requires advanced training and is used to decrease pain, increase circulating hemoglobin, decrease headaches, and relieve anxiety and stress.

9. Active strategies for health promotion may include attending programs for weight reduction, smoking cessation, nutritional guidance, and exercise. Passive strategies for health promotion include fluoridation of drinking water and fortification of foods, such as milk, with vitamins.

10. An acute illness is usually shorter in duration and more severe than a chronic illness. Chronic illnesses usually last longer than 6 months.

11. The impact of illness on the client and family:
    a. Behaviors and emotions—There may be slight or extensive responses dependent on the severity and duration of the illness. Clients and families may experience shock, anger, denial, anxiety, and withdrawal.
    b. Body image—Some illnesses may directly result in physical changes. The client may experience the stages of grief/loss while adapting to the change.
    c. Self-concept—Clients and families may experience tension and conflict when expectations are not met.
    d. Family roles and dynamics—Illness may influence the roles played by and

the interactions of the client and family members. Changes in the client's ability to assume certain responsibilities may alter the structure and functioning of the family unit.

12. a. Age: risks of birth defects and complications in pregnancies of women older than age 35, some kinds of cancer (e.g., prostate) in individuals older than age 45, greater susceptibility to infection in very young and older age.
    b. Genetic/physiological factors: pregnancy, excess weight, family history of a condition (e.g., diabetes, cancer, or heart disease).
    c. Environment: where the individual works or lives (e.g., unclean, poorly heated, overcrowded), exposure to infectious diseases or toxic substances.
    d. Lifestyle: poor health practices (e.g., overeating, insufficient rest/sleep), substance abuse, high-risk activities (e.g., sunbathing, skydiving).

13. 2

14. 3

15. 1

16. 2

17. 1

18. 3

19. 2

CHAPTER 2—The Health Care Delivery System

CASE STUDIES

I. a. You may tell the neighbor that managed care is a type of program where the health needs of the client are funneled through to one party—the case manager. The design of this program is to control the cost of health care services while maintaining quality. Specific guidelines are in place for the type of services covered, length of hospital stay, and access to specialty care. An HMO (health maintenance organization) is a type of managed care program where the focus is on primary care. A comprehensive number of services usually are provided, in one location or by different facilities that are specified by the organization.

    b. You could review the HMO book with your neighbor to clarify some of the terms and conditions of the coverage, which may be confusing for someone without any experience with the health care delivery system. If there are specific questions, the neighbor could be referred to an information telephone number for the program.

II. a. This client should be eligible for benefits as a veteran and may be referred to the Department of Veterans Affairs to receive further information.

    b. He could be admitted to a military or Veterans Administration hospital for ongoing treatment.

III. a. This client could benefit from the services of a hospice organization for either home care and/or inpatient care, depending on the program.

CHAPTER REVIEW

1. d

2. b

3. e

4. a

5. c

6. Services usually provided by a home care agency include wound care, respiratory care, vital signs monitoring, promotion of nutrition and elimination, rehabilitative care, medication administration and intravenous therapy, and laboratory study collection and monitoring.

7. Hospice

8. Issues in health care delivery include:

- Cost control—resulting in staff reduction and limited resources, providing a challenge for the health care professional to continue to offer quality care.
- Access to health care—consumers desiring appropriate, cost-effective, quality care within their community.
- Accountability—consumers demanding quality and results of interactions.
- Professional topics—increased need for diversified nursing competencies, work redesign, and delegation to unlicensed assistive personnel.

9. Patient-centered care involves bringing all care providers and services to the client, with the goal of improving the effectiveness of care and client satisfaction. The nurse plays a major part in coordinating client care. Cross-trained personnel can provide multiple services and reduce the number of staff that the client will interact with in the agency. More emphasis is placed on professional nursing activities (e.g., teaching, client assessment) than on ancillary functions, such as bed making.

10. Discharge planning is a centralized, coordinated, multidisciplinary process for providing continuity of care after the client leaves the health care agency. It should begin the moment the client enters the health care agency and assists in the transition of the client's care from one environment to the other (such as from the hospital to the home). The client's ongoing needs are anticipated and identified, and necessary services/resources are coordinated before the client's discharge.

11. Developments in technology influence many aspects of health care delivery. New types of equipment for client monitoring, computerization, and electronic communication and record-keeping systems create a need for further education on the part of the health care provider.

12. 3

13. 2

14. 4

15. 4

16. 4

17. 2

18. 3

19. 4

CHAPTER 3—Legal Principles in Nursing

CASE STUDIES

I. A client who does not appear to understand a procedure should not sign a consent form. The physician will need to be contacted to provide the information to the client. The nurse's role in this situation is to witness the signing of the consent form only if the client demonstrates an understanding of the procedure. Because the nurse will not be performing the procedure, it is not his/her responsibility to describe what will or will not be done during the surgery.

II. a. Any question of a written order should be clarified with the prescriber. You should not depend on the "guess" of another colleague, even if it is a supervisor.
   b. If the medication is administered according to the charge nurse's belief, and the order is not correct, then you are accountable for the result.

III. In an emergency situation, treatment may be provided to an individual without obtaining consent. If there is sufficient opportunity to obtain consent, then the divorced parent who has legal custody of the child will need to be contacted.

IV. You will need to investigate the statutes to determine what information is required to be reported for a colleague in a suspected substance abuse situation. In many places, the nurse is held accountable if he/she is knowledgeable about an impaired practitioner but does not report the situation to the Board of Nursing. For most instances, the situation is not acted on immediately; it is investigated further by the appropriate authorities.

CHAPTER REVIEW

1. i

2. f

3. a

4. j

5. e

6. b

7. h

8. d

9. c

10. g

11. The nurse may avoid being liable by following the standards of care, providing competent care, communicating with other health care providers, documenting fully, and developing an empathetic rapport with clients.

12. Standards of care are defined in Nurse Practice Acts by Boards of Nursing, state and federal hospital licensing laws, professional and specialty organizations, and agency policies and procedures.

13. Student nurses are responsible for all of their actions that cause harm to clients. Liability may be shared with the instructor, staff, and health care facility. Student nurses

should perform activities that they are prepared to implement. Faculty members are responsible for instruction and supervision.

14. Informed consent requires the following:
    - A competent adult individual
    - Consent given voluntarily
    - Options for care are understood
    - Opportunity was provided for questions
    - A physician/client relationship exists where risks and alternatives are explained
    - Nurse witnessing of the client's signature

15. The nurse is obligated to report in the following circumstances: abuse, rape, gunshot wounds, attempted suicide, certain communicable diseases, and unsafe or impaired professionals.

16. Each State Board of Nursing defines the scope and practice of nursing and expanded nursing roles. Educational requirements for nurses are set, and nursing is distinguished from medical practice. Rules and regulations enacted by the Boards provide more specific guidelines for practice.

17. Advance directives or living wills influence nursing by determining whether nurses will be involved in the provision of life-sustaining procedures. Clients may decide to have such measures withheld when death is imminent. Nurses also need to be aware of policies and procedures within the institution for providing information to clients about these documents.

18. 4

19. 3

20. 4

21. 3

22. 1

23. 2

24. 1

25. 4

26. 4

CHAPTER 4—Ethics

CASE STUDY

a. **Step 1.** Is this an ethical dilemma?
Review of scientific data does not resolve Mr. R.'s situation, his question is perplexing, and your response and his action will have a profound relevance for human concern.

Step 2. Gather all the information relevant to the case.
Mr. R. is a 42-year-old man with severe multiple sclerosis who is unable to perform the simplest activities of daily living. He appears to be aware of his situation and is seeking an alternative to his present lifestyle. You are his home care nurse and are aware of the client's situation.

Step 3. Examine and determine one's own values on the issues.
Use of the values clarification process may assist you in determining your beliefs about assisted suicide and the quality and sanctity of life.

Step 4. Articulate the problem.
Mr. R. has an interest in being "helped to die," and he has involved you in a possible dilemma by asking you to assist him in getting more information about this method.

Step 5. Consider possible courses of action.
You may or may not be able to assist the client in his actual pursuit of an assisted suicide because of your beliefs. In addition, the legal view on assisted suicide varies from state to state and will need to be investigated before any action is taken by you or the home care agency. A discussion with your supervisor and colleagues may assist in determining a course of action. (You will want to inform the client that you will be sharing this information with other members of the health team.) If Mr. R. is intent on finding out about, and possibly

pursuing an assisted suicide, his family members (if available) may become involved.

Step 6. Negotiate the outcome.
Communication with the client may determine if there are other alternatives to his plan. Work with the client to consider all of the possibilities, but respect his wish if he continues to request information and an end to his current existence.

Step 7. Evaluate the action.
The actions taken by the nurse and other members of the home care agency should be documented. Recognize that satisfaction with the outcome by both the client and the nurse may not be possible. There are no right or wrong answers to ethical questions. Evaluation is based on the effectiveness of working through the problem to a reasonable solution.

b. The nurse in this situation should be the client's advocate. The first step is to determine if the client is truly intent on pursuing this alternative measure. If he really is interested, then the nurse may assist him in a number of ways. Information on assisted suicide may be obtained directly or indirectly for the client, or the nurse may not be able to become involved but can be supportive of the client's decision to investigate the procedure. There are legal and ethical considerations that may inhibit the nurse from having *any* involvement, in which case Mr. R. should be referred to others who may assist him in his actions.

CHAPTER REVIEW

1. c

2. d

3. e

4. a

5. b

6. The four modes of values transmission are modeling, moralizing, laissez-faire, and responsible choice.

7. Responsibility refers to the performance of duties associated with the nurse's role, such as giving a medication safely to a client. Accountability refers to the ability to answer for your actions.

8. Deontology

9. a. Cost containment: Not having enough staff or equipment with monetary cutbacks, having limitations on coverage and benefits, providing restricted hours and services.
   b. Cultural sensitivity: Accepting a client's refusal of treatment (e.g., Christian Scientist's beliefs), recognizing the need for special diets or concern for the body of the deceased.

10. 4

11. 4

12. 4

13. 3

14. 1

CHAPTER 5—Critical Thinking and Nursing Judgment

CASE STUDY

a. The nurse may choose to return to the office to obtain supplies and make a later visit to this client if there are other visits to make or if there is work to be done at the office. This option will, however, take time away from the nurse and extend her visiting hours. The nurse may choose to purchase necessary items from a local pharmacy, but the nurse may not have the necessary funds or be able to be reimbursed for this purchase. It may be most appropriate for the nurse to investigate what alternative resources are available in the client's home, such as clean cloths, boiled water, salt, and tongs (all used with client permission).

b. The nurse should determine what resources the client has in the home, including running water, waste disposal, and methods for heating and refrigerating. In addition, a financial screening may be needed if indicated for the determination of available funds and/or insurance coverage for supplies and equipment.

CHAPTER REVIEW

1. e

2. d

3. b

4. c

5. a

6. Attitudes for critical thinking:
   - Confidence—ability to accomplish a task or goal, awareness of what you know and don't know. Example: performing a skill safely and effectively.
   - Thinking independently—consideration of ideas and options before forming judgments. Example: questioning an order that appears incorrect.
   - Fairness—acting without bias or prejudice, regardless of personal feelings. Example: providing quality care to a teenage mother or substance abuser.
   - Responsibility and accountability—providing care within the standards of practice. Example: not taking shortcuts.
   - Risk taking—willingness to try different approaches. Example: trying different types of wound care.
   - Discipline—following an orderly approach. Example: thorough skin or pain assessment for a client.
   - Perseverance—determination to find solutions to client care problems. Example: using different resources to get the right ostomy equipment.
   - Creativity—original thinking and innovative problem solving. Example: coming up with unique ways to do complex dressing changes in the client's home.
   - Curiosity—asking why and analyzing client information. Example: trying to find out if a client's symptoms are related to the prescribed medication.
   - Integrity—testing of personal beliefs and knowledge, honesty. Example: admitting to the nurse manager that a medication was given in error.
   - Humility—admission of limitations in knowledge and skill. Example: asking for assistance to perform unfamiliar procedures.

7. Critical thinking is implemented throughout all of the steps of the nursing process. Knowledge and experience are applied to clinical situations, previous experiences are reflected on, and the appropriate attitudes and standards are applied to deliver safe and effective nursing care.

8. 4

9. 3

10. 1

11. 3

12. 3

13. 4

14. 2

15. 1

CHAPTER 6—Nursing Process

CASE STUDIES

I. a. The nurse should obtain additional data about Mr. B.'s medical history and current health status. Mr. B. may be seeing a physician or other primary care provider and have medication prescribed for hypertension.

    b. A community health fair allows for general screening of large numbers of people, but it usually does not offer opportunity or space for privacy to complete health histories or physical assessments. Individuals demonstrating alterations from expected norms, such as Mr. B., are referred to clinics, personal physicians, or other health care delivery agencies, as appropriate.

II. a. The relevant assessment data obtained from Mr. B. includes:

- Being newly diagnosed with hypertension
- Having a new prescription of an antihypertensive medication
- Demonstrating insecurity about the medication regimen
- Relating his father's death at age 54 from a heart attack

    b. Nursing diagnoses for Mr. B. may include:

- Knowledge deficit related to unfamiliarity with the diagnosis and treatment of hypertension.
- Knowledge deficit related to newly prescribed medication (as manifested by his verbalization of uncertainty as to how and when to take his medications).
- Fear related to possible repeat of father's medical history and early death.

III. a. Sample diagnoses, goals, and outcomes for Mr. B.

    b. Nursing interventions may include for:

Knowledge deficit

- Assessment of Mr. B.'s willingness and readiness to learn about his diagnosis and medication regimen.
- Identification and presentation of appropriate information about hypertension and the medication regimen.

Nursing Diagnoses	Goals	Expected Outcome
Knowledge deficit related to newly prescribed medication (as manifested by his verbalization of uncertainty as to how and when to take his medications).	Mr. B. will recognize the purpose of the hypertensive medication and prepare an administration schedule by the end of the clinic visit.	Mr. B. will restate the use of the antihypertensive medication and scheduling of administration during the visit.
Fear related to possible repeat of father's medical history and early death (as manifested by verbalization of concern over similar family history).	Mr. B. will demonstrate effective coping mechanisms within the next month. Mr. B. will identify a reduction or elimination of feelings of fear.	Mr. B. will discuss his concerns about his father's medical history and early death during this visit. Mr. B. will acknowledge his fear of repeating this history during his visits.
Knowledge deficit related to unfamiliarity with diagnosis of hypertension.	Mr. B. will make specific lifestyle alterations and participate in the treatment regimen.	Mr. B. will identify the etiology and therapeutic regimen for hypertension after the next two clinic visits.

- Establishment of an environment and strategy for teaching Mr. B. that is conducive to learning.
- Provision of effective learning materials, including pamphlets, videos, photos, charts, etc.

Fear

- Assess the degree of Mr. B.'s fear.
- Observe nonverbal and verbal responses.
- Listen to Mr. B.'s concerns and feelings.
- Provide information on coping mechanisms to assist in reducing his level of fear.
- Offer referral to a support program/counseling, as indicated.

IV. a. For his hypertension to be controlled, Mr. B. will need to take his medication on a regular basis. The nurse should focus on the implementation method of teaching. Counseling also may be involved, especially if Mr. B. is experiencing other difficulties at work or home that are interfering with his ability to manage his therapeutic regimen. Emphasis may be placed on Mr. B. taking his medication along with a daily routine, such as with meals or after bathing.

b. The nurse will need to look at the original goals, outcomes, and nursing interventions to determine what alterations may be necessary. The strategies for providing the information on Mr. B.'s diagnosis and medication may not have been appropriate. In addition, the client's fear about his father's history may have been blocking his ability to focus and/or influencing his degree of motivation to participate in the therapeutic plan.

V. a. Mr. B. appears to be achieving most of his goals. He states that he is exercising regularly and trying to use the relaxation techniques when he feels stressed. Mr. B. also is expressing his method of coping with his father's medical history.

b. Areas for reassessment may include Mr. B.'s actual medication schedule (because his blood pressure is still slightly elevated) to determine that it is within the prescribed regimen. Determination also may be made to see if Mr. B. may benefit from additional exercise (per review with the physician) and review of relaxation techniques.

CHAPTER REVIEW

1. j
2. g
3. i
4. e
5. f
6. d
7. c
8. h
9. a
10. b
11. Strategies for effective communication include:
    - Use of silence—sitting with the client who is crying or dealing with feelings and concerns.
    - Attentive listening—showing interest in the client who is discussing concerns or sharing family information.
    - Conveying acceptance—letting the client know that he/she may continue on a subject, saying "Go on." or "Tell me more."
    - Related questions—asking in language that is understandable to the client how certain events or feelings are associated with his/her current status.
    - Paraphrasing—taking what the client has stated and putting it in other words for the nurse and the client to hear again.

- Clarifying—asking the client to verify that the meaning of statements is clear.
- Focusing—directing the attention of the client to a particular idea in the discussion.
- Stating observations—letting the client know what the nurse has observed during the discussion, such as anxiety-related movements or expressions of pain.
- Offering information—giving the client information about the health care system, prescribed therapies, available community resources, etc.
- Summarizing—bringing together all of the data obtained, highlighting the key points, and allowing the client to validate the information.

12. The three phases of the interview are the orientation phase, working phase, and termination phase.

13. The four physical assessment techniques and the type of client data that may be obtained with each one include:
    - Inspection—visual observation of the body's external structure and function, such as the condition of the skin and mucous membranes, and the ability to move the muscles and joints.
    - Palpation—use of the hands to determine temperature, texture, pulsations, and the presence of tenderness or masses.
    - Percussion—tapping on specific surface areas of the body to produce vibration and sound that indicate the presence of air, fluid, or solid matter.
    - Auscultation—listening with a stethoscope to sounds produced by the heart, lungs, and gastrointestinal system.

14. The steps of the nursing diagnostic process are analysis and interpretation of data, identification of client needs, and formulation of nursing diagnoses.

15. Some of the common errors that may occur in the determination of the nursing diagnosis are collecting insufficient or too much data, having unreliable or invalid data, incorrectly interpreting findings or clustering data, and misstating the diagnosis itself (using the medical diagnosis, targeting the equipment or treatments, etc.).

16. The seven guidelines for determining goals and outcomes are that they should be client centered, single focused, observable, measurable, time limited, mutually determined, and realistic.

17. a. Knowledge deficit related to the need for postoperative care at home.
    Goal: Perform, or obtain assistance in performing, postoperative care at home.
    Expected outcome:
    - State the purpose and procedure for postoperative care.
    - Demonstrate postoperative care before discharge.

    Nursing interventions:
    - Provide appropriate materials for client review of postoperative care before surgery.
    - Review and demonstrate the postoperative care to client after surgery.
    - Observe the client's independent performance of postoperative care before discharge.

    b. Alteration in elimination: constipation related to lack of physical activity.
    Goals:
    - Re-establish normal pattern of elimination.
    - Participate in specified daily physical activity, to tolerance.

    Expected outcomes:
    - Ambulate up and down the hallway three times each day.
    - Perform active range of motion twice each day.

    Nursing interventions:
    - Instruct and assist client in performance of physical activity.

- Observe tolerance to physical activity.
- Assess elimination pattern daily.
- Promote additional measures to improve elimination, such as the intake of fluids and fiber.

18. Examples of how the nurse may use the following skills:
   a. Cognitive—knowledge of the rationale for therapeutic interventions, normal and abnormal physiological and psychological responses, and the needs of the client for health promotion and illness prevention.
   b. Interpersonal—ability to establish a trusting relationship and communicate clearly with, provide instruction and counseling to, and demonstrate sensitivity of the needs of the client, family, and significant others.
   c. Psychomotor—ability to understand the rationale for and demonstrate the physical ability to perform therapeutic skills (e.g., injections, catheter insertion).

19. The nurse must use sound judgment in determining the accuracy and appropriateness of the standing orders for the client. In addition, the nurse should have the knowledge and competency necessary to carry out each order safely.

20. Nursing care may be communicated through written or computerized documentation on the agency care plan or pathway. In addition, end-of-shift reports and nursing rounds provide an opportunity to verbally share nursing interventions with colleagues. Computerization and wireless telecommunication have increased the ability of nurses to communicate interventions quickly and over long distances, if necessary.

21. Factors involved in the evaluation of nursing interventions include the appropriateness of the interventions selected (per the standards of care) and the correct application of the implementation process (level of care provided, frequency of interventions, etc.).

22. 4

23. 1

24. 1

25. 2

26. 3

27. 4

28. 4

29. 4

30. 1

31. 2

32. 2

33. 1

34. 4

35. 4

36. 2

CHAPTER 7—Documentation and Reporting

CASE STUDY

a. A transfer report should include the following information:
   - Client's name, age, primary physician, and medical diagnosis
   - Summary of medical progress up to the time of transfer
   - Current physiological and psychological status
   - Current nursing diagnoses/plan of care
   - Critical assessments to be completed shortly after transfer
   - Any special equipment needed

b. More specifically, the primary nurse may want to know about the surgical procedure, how it was tolerated by the client, how the client responded to the anesthesia, and observations made and treatments completed in the PACU.

Sample SOAP documentation for Mrs. Q:
S—States she is having intense pain in her right hip area and doesn't want to move because it really hurts.
O—Grimacing and moaning in pain.
A—Alteration in comfort related to new surgical incision to right hip.
P—Reduce or eliminate discomfort by administering analgesic medication as ordered and assisting client to more comfortable position.

Sample DAR documentation for Mrs. Q:
D—Client grimacing and moaning in pain. States that she is having intense pain to right hip and does not want to move because it "really hurts." Dressing dry and intact.
A—Client assisted to more comfortable position, with leg supported. Analgesic administered per order.
R—Client expressed reduction in discomfort to tolerable level.

CHAPTER REVIEW

1. d

2. e

3. a

4. b

5. c

6. Oral or written exchanges of information between caregivers include change-of-shift and transfer reports, nursing conferences and client rounds, documentation, and consultation.

7. The following are purposes of the client record: communication, legal documentation, financial billing, education, assessment, research, auditing, and monitoring.

8. The Joint Commission on Accreditation of Hospital Organization (JCAHO) requires that all clients who are admitted to a health care facility have an assessment of physical, psychosocial, environmental, self-care, knowledge level, and discharge planning needs. Documentation is to be within the context of the nursing process, including evidence of client and family teaching. The JCAHO also recently has required documentation of pain management, including client assessment and pharmacological and non-pharmacological strategies that have been implemented. The client's progress toward the expected outcomes of care is part of the evaluation.

9. a. Draw a single line through the error, write the word *error* above the line, initial or sign the error, and complete the correct notation.
   b. Use only objective descriptions of the client and use quotes for client comments.
   c. Use complete, concise descriptions of client interactions.
   d. Draw a single line through the error, write the word *error* above the line, initial or sign the error, and complete the correct notation.
   e. Use consecutive lines for charting and do not leave margins. Draw lines through unused space and sign your name at the end of the notation.
   f. Only include factual information in the notation.
   g. Identify that the physician was called to clarify an order for the client.
   h. Have the other caregiver document the information, unless the individual calls with additional information. Document that the information was provided by another individual.
   i. Record pertinent information throughout the shift, signing each entry.

10. 3

11. 1

12. 4

13. 3

14. 3

15. 4

16. 4

CHAPTER 8—Communication

CASE STUDIES

a. The following techniques may be effective for an older individual with a moderate hearing impairment:
   - Reducing background noise
   - Checking and cleaning a hearing aid
   - Speaking slowly and clearly
   - Using a low-pitched rather than high-pitched voice
   - Avoiding shouting at the client
   - Using short, simple sentences
   - Facing the client to allow for lip reading
   - Not covering the mouth while talking
   - Talking toward the unaffected ear
   - Using facial expressions and gestures

b. The following techniques may be effective for individuals who do not speak English:
   - Speaking in a normal tone of voice
   - Establishing signals or methods of non-verbal communication
   - Obtaining an interpreter familiar with the language and culture
   - Allowing time for communication to take place
   - Developing a communication board, pictures, or cards for common requests
   - Having a dictionary available for reference

c. The following techniques may be effective for an individual who is blind:
   - Announcing yourself when entering the room
   - Communicating verbally before touching the client
   - Orienting the client to the environment
   - Explaining the procedure in advance
   - Having the client handle the equipment, as appropriate
   - Informing the client when you are done and leaving the room

d. The following techniques may be effective for an individual of another culture who is experiencing an invasive procedure for the first time:
   - Explaining the procedure in advance, using an interpreter if necessary
   - Recognizing possible discomfort with exposure and maintaining privacy
   - Staying with the client to provide emotional support

CHAPTER REVIEW

1. c

2. h

3. g

4. i

5. e

6. j

7. f

8. d

9. b

10. a

11. a. Intrapersonal level
    b. Interpersonal level
    c. Public level

12. a. Intimate zone (0–18 inches): holding a baby, performing a physical

examination, providing hygienic care for a client, changing a dressing.

b. Personal zone (18 inches–4 feet): sitting at the bedside, taking a client's history, teaching an individual client, exchanging information with colleagues at change-of-shift.

c. Social zone (4–12 feet): making rounds with a physician, sitting at the head of a conference table, teaching a class or conducting a support session for a small group.

d. Public zone (12 feet or more): speaking at a community forum, testifying at a hearing, lecturing to a class of students.

13. a. Communication may be adapted for a toddler as follows:
   - Allowing the child to touch and examine objects
   - Focusing communication on the child
   - Avoiding analogies, and using direct language the child can understand
   - Keeping unfamiliar equipment out of sight until necessary
   - Keeping facial expressions congruent with activities
   - Using dolls, puppets, or stuffed animals to communicate through

b. Communication may be adapted for an adolescent as follows:
   - Provide undivided attention and listen closely
   - Be courteous, calm, and open-minded
   - Avoid judging or criticizing
   - Avoid continuous questioning
   - Make expectations clear
   - Respect privacy and views
   - Praise positive behaviors
   - Encourage expression of ideas and feelings

c. Communication may be adapted for an older adult as follows:
   - Maintain a quiet environment, free of background noise
   - Allow time for conversation
   - Listen attentively

- Use short, simple sentences
- Avoid changing the subject frequently
- Obtain assistance, if necessary, to promote understanding (hearing aid, etc.)
- Face the individual directly
- Speak slowly and clearly—don't shout

14. a. Courtesy is not being used. The client should be called by his or her name, such as Mrs. Jones or Mr. Brown.

b. Courtesy is not being used. The client should be identified by name, not by room number or diagnosis.

c. Confidentiality is not being applied. The client should not be discussed outside of the immediate client area where anyone not involved in the client's care may overhear the conversation.

d. Availability is not being applied. The nurse should spend time with the client or identify to the client when he/she will return to be with the client.

e. Avoidance of medical jargon is not being considered. The nurse should explain to the client, in understandable terms, what to expect of the procedure.

15. The nurse could ask the client as follows to elicit more appropriate information:
   a. "How do you feel today?"
   b. "Do you take any medications at home?" or "What types of medication do you take at home?"
   c. "Have you noticed any areas of swelling around your arms or legs?"
   d. "Do you have any questions about the procedure that will be done today?" or "Has the physician explained the procedure to you?"

16. For the client who is cognitively impaired, the nurse should:
   - Reduce environmental distractions
   - Get the client's attention before speaking
   - Use simple sentences and avoid long explanations
   - Avoid shifting from one subject to another

- Allow time for the client to respond
- Include family and friends in conversations

17. The following are examples that the nurse may use:
    a. Providing information—"Mr. Green, this medication is called Lasix. It is used to help remove excess fluid from your body."
    b. Clarifying—"A thoracentesis is the removal of fluid from your chest cavity."
    c. Avoiding giving personal opinions—"Deciding on nursing home placement can be a difficult decision. Let's sit down and talk about your options."

18. The nurse can be sensitive to the client's culture by making an effort to not interpret communication through one's own perspective and considering the individual's background. Gender sensitivity means recognizing the differences that exist in male and female communication patterns.

19. Possible responses include:
    a. "You aren't taking the medication? Tell me more." or "Are you having any problems with the medications?" or "Do you have any questions or concerns about the medications?"
    b. "Do you feel that the staff doesn't have time for you?" or "Let me know more about what you mean."
    c. "How do the other nurses help you to get out of bed?" or "There are several ways to help you transfer. Would you like to try this way?"

20. To assist the client who has an aphasia, the nurse may:
    - Use simple gestures and statements
    - Provide visual cues, such as pictures or flash cards
    - Listen and observe attentively
    - Allow time for responses, either verbal or nonverbal
    - Have call bells within easy reach
    - Encourage the client to interact as much as possible

21. 3

22. 2

23. 4

24. 1

25. 4

26. 1

27. 3

28. 3

29. 3

30. 4

CHAPTER 9—Client Education

CASE STUDY

a. Ms. T. has no prior knowledge about her diagnosis or prescribed medication. She also has a prior family history of coronary disease, with her father dying of a heart attack at 54 years of age.
b. Sample teaching plan for Ms. T.:

Learning Need	Resources	Objectives	Teaching Strategies
Knowledge deficit related to newly diagnosed hypertension and antihypertensive medication therapy.	Educational media: Video and audio programs on hypertension, written materials on the diagnosis and the medication, information from the physician and other health care providers (dietician, etc.), nurse's knowledge of diagnosis and treatment regimen	Ms. T, will be able to: Describe the diagnosis, etiology, treatment, and complications; describe the actions, side effects, and time of administration for the antihypertensive; identify when to contact the physician if complications or problems occur; independently monitor and record her blood pressure daily and as necessary; develop a meal plan for a week that incorporates the therapeutic diet	Provide Ms. T. with available educational media and written information on hypertension and antihypertensive medications; use illustrations to explain the function of the heart and circulatory system and the effects of hypertension; demonstrate the technique for monitoring blood pressure, and have the client and/or significant other return to demonstrate the procedure; involve significant others in the educational program

CHAPTER REVIEW

1. d

2. c

3. e

4. a

5. b

6. a. Specific teaching methods that may be implemented for an infant include maintaining consistency in routines (bathing, feeding), holding the child firmly while smiling and speaking softly, and having the infant touch different textures.
   b. Specific teaching methods that may be implemented for a school-age child include teaching psychomotor skills needed to maintain health (e.g., using a syringe, changing a dressing), and offering opportunities to discuss health problems and answer questions.
   c. Specific teaching methods that may be implemented for an older adult include teaching when the client is alert and rested, involving the individual in discussion or activity, focusing on wellness and strengths, using approaches to enhance sensory input, and keeping sessions short. Family or significant others should be involved in the teaching process whenever possible, especially when working with children.

7. The nurse should consider the following factors when selecting an environment for teaching: privacy, room temperature, lighting, noise, ventilation, furniture, and space.

8. a. Motivation is an internal impulse that causes a person to take action and addresses a person's desire to learn. The nurse relates learning to the client's other desires, such as success. The client also should be included in the decision making during the teaching sessions.
   b. The ability to learn is influenced by the client's developmental level and physical capabilities. A client's knowledge and skill level must be considered by the nurse before developing a teaching plan.

c. The learning environment plays a part in the client's ability to focus his/her attention on the learning task. The nurse needs to determine that there is sufficient lighting and ventilation, space, privacy, temperature regulation, and comfortable furniture.

9. The ability to learn a psychomotor skill is influenced by the individual's mental and physical skills. An individual who has a cognitive or neuromuscular impairment or severe fatigue or pain will not be able to participate in the learning and demonstration of a psychomotor skill.

10. Resources for learning include brochures, books, visuals, posters, audiocassettes, computer programs, demonstration equipment, organizations, and other health care professionals.

11. For the diagnosis, *Noncompliance with medication regime related to insufficient knowledge of purpose and actions*, possible goals/outcomes and nursing interventions include:
Goals/outcomes:
- Verbalize purpose and actions of medication regimen
- Take medications as prescribed
Nursing interventions:
- Provide information about prescribed medications, including purpose and actions—give client written information about medications and their use, use visual aids as necessary to reinforce the material
- Allow opportunity for client to express concerns and ask questions

12. Three types of reinforcers are:
- Social—smiles, compliments, words of encouragement, physical contact
- Material—food, toys, music
- Activity—participation in desired activity after completion of the necessary task

13. The primary domains of learning that are involved are:
a. Psychomotor—The nurse explains and demonstrates the injection technique, then has the client handle the equipment, practice, and demonstrate the procedure.
b. Affective—The nurse provides time for discussion and problem solving with the client.
c. Cognitive—The nurse provides information about the possible complications, followed by feedback from the client demonstrating an understanding.

14. The techniques may be used as follows:
a. Preparatory instruction—Providing information to the client on sensations that are likely to be experienced during a procedure.
b. Demonstration—Teaching psychomotor skills, such as injection technique, wound/ostomy care, etc.
c. Role playing—Teaching ideas and attitudes, such as how to communicate with an older adult parent.

15. Teaching may be incorporated into the daily care of the client during any and all nursing activities. For example, while assisting the client with hygienic care, the nurse may discuss ways in which to keep the skin moist and intact. While performing colostomy care, the nurse may begin to acclimate the client to the procedure by reciting all of the necessary steps to follow. During meals, information may be provided about nutritional needs.

16. 4

17. 3

18. 4

19. 3

20. 2

21. 1

22. 2

CHAPTER 10—Infection Control

CASE STUDIES

I. The nurse should implement the following measures to prevent a urinary tract infection:
    - Provide personal hygiene, perineal care
    - Use aseptic technique when manipulating the catheter and drainage equipment
    - Keep the drainage bag unobstructed and below the level of the bladder
    - Provide ample fluids, within client's limitations

II. To prevent a wound infection, the nurse should:
    - Maintain sterile technique during dressing changes
    - Use medical asepsis in all interactions with the client
    - Instruct the client in hand washing/asepsis
    - Dispose of contaminated materials appropriately and promptly
    - Assist in keeping the client and environment clean and dry
    - Limit the number of caregivers working with the client
    - Provide optimum nutrition and fluids, within client's limitations
    - Administer antibiotics, if prescribed

CHAPTER REVIEW

1. j

2. e

3. f

4. i

5. c

6. b

7. h

8. d

9. g

10. a

11. The stages of an infection include:
    - Incubation period—interval between entrance of pathogen into the body and the appearance of symptoms.
    - Prodromal stage of illness—interval from the onset of nonspecific signs and symptoms to more specific signs and symptoms; client more capable of spreading disease to others.
    - Full stage of illness—client manifests specific signs and symptoms of the infection.
    - Convalescence—acute symptoms disappear; client begins recovery.

12. Normal flora, body system defenses, inflammation, and the immune response.

13. The following are risks for nosocomial infection: multiple illnesses, compromised immune system, numerous invasive procedures or devices, use of broad-spectrum antibiotics, use of poor aseptic technique, multiple caregivers, and extended hospitalization.

14. Health promotion activities that may be implemented for infection control include adequate nutritional intake, hygienic care, immunizations, adequate rest, and regular exercise.

15. Factors affecting susceptibility to infection:
    a. Age—immaturity of the immune system in infants, greater susceptibility in children, refined defenses in adults, decline of immune system and change in organ function in older adults

b. Nutritional status—increased susceptibility with inadequate dietary intake or reduction of protein, carbohydrates, and fats because of illness.

c. Personal habits—decreased resistance to respiratory infections from smoking, impairment of antibiotic effectiveness with alcohol ingestion, increased chance of sexually transmitted disease with risky sexual behavior (multiple partners, etc.).

d. Environmental factors—increased exposure to pathogens through crowded and unsanitary living conditions.

e. Disease history—increased susceptibility for clients with other medical conditions or recent exposure to a communicable disease.

16. Alterations in normal body system defenses:
   a. Skin—cuts, abrasions, puncture wounds, insufficient or excessive bathing
   b. Respiratory tract—smoking, high concentrations of oxygen/carbon dioxide, decreased humidity, cold air
   c. Urinary tract—catheterization, obstruction
   d. Gastrointestinal tract—use of antacids, antibiotics, or birth control pills; impaction; obstruction

17. The proper procedure for collection of a urine sample is to:
   a. Apply gloves
   b. Gather equipment—syringe (for catheter specimen), sterile container
   c. Instruct the client on how to obtain a clean voided specimen

   OR

   Aspirate urine from indwelling catheter and transfer urine from syringe to sterile container
   d. Secure the top of the container, and label and package the container per agency policy
   e. Remove gloves and wash hands

18. a. White blood cells—elevated in an acute infection, decreased in viral/overwhelming infections
   b. Erythrocyte sedimentation rate—elevated with infectious processes
   c. Iron level—decreased in chronic infections
   d. Neutrophils—elevated with acute, supportive infections; decreased with overwhelming bacterial infections
   e. Basophils—remain normal during infections

19. Infections in the home environment may be prevented by:
   • cleaning frequently in the kitchen with disinfectants (especially before and after using surfaces where raw meats have been cut)
   • discarding mops and sponges frequently
   • air drying, rather than towel drying, dishes
   • using disposable cups, utensils, and towels
   • keeping food properly refrigerated
   • washing all meats and vegetables before eating, and washing the hands and sink after handling
   • thawing meats in the refrigerator
   • using pasteurized and processed milks and juices
   • cooking foods thoroughly

20. The nurse should bring an alcohol-based hand rub and/or detergent-containing towels or wipes.

21. Nursing interventions for the following infection control measures include:
   a. Control or eliminate the infectious agent—clean, disinfect, and sterilize contaminated objects
   b. Control or eliminate the reservoir—remove sources of body fluids, drainage, or solutions that harbor microorganisms, and discard disposable articles contaminated with infectious material.
   c. Control the portals of exit—avoid talking, sneezing, or coughing directly over

a wound or sterile dressing field, teach client to protect others, and handle all body fluids carefully (hand washing and use of gloves).

   d.   Control the transmission—disinfect equipment, provide a personal set of equipment for clients, do not shake linens or allow them to come in contact with the uniform, and wash hands.

22.   Personal protective equipment includes the use of:
   • Gowns or cover-ups: to prevent contact with infected body fluids or materials
   • Mask or respirator: to prevent getting splashed with blood or body fluids; to prevent inhaling or exhaling micro-organisms.
   • Gloves: to prevent contact with blood, body fluids, or potentially infectious material
   • Eyewear and face shields: to prevent being splashed or sprayed with body fluids

23.   Clients requiring respiratory precautions are transported or ambulated while wearing masks.

24.   Surgical asepsis is used to prevent microbial contamination of an open wound or sterile item. It is used during invasive procedures (surgery, injections, catheterizations, etc.).

25.   a.   Contaminated
   b.   Appropriate asepsis
   c.   Appropriate asepsis

26.   A local infection usually is indicated by redness, heat, swelling, and pain to the area. A systemic infection usually is accompanied by a fever, lethargy, malaise, and impairment of overall functioning.

27.   For the nursing diagnosis, *Skin integrity, impaired related to 2 inch diameter pressure ulcer on sacrum,* possible client outcomes and nursing interventions include:

Client goals/outcomes:
   • Sacral ulcer will reduce in size by 1 inch (within time frame)
   • Skin will remain intact over rest of body surfaces
   • Sacral ulcer will remain free of infection
Nursing interventions:
   • Provide wound care as prescribed using aseptic technique
   • Assess condition of ulcer
   • Provide skin care—keep clean and dry, and apply moisturizers as needed
   • Turn and position client q 1 hour
   • Assess wound for presence of infection, and obtain culture if indicated
   • Provide for client's nutritional and fluid needs

28.   c first; b or d second; a last

29.   1

30.   1

31.   3

32.   4

33.   4

34.   2

35.   4

36.   4

CHAPTER 11—Vital Signs

CASE STUDIES

I.   a.   Generally, an individual who has a blood pressure reading of above 140/90 should be referred for medical follow-up. An average of two or more systolic readings above 140 mmHg and diastolic readings above 90 mmHg are usually indicative of hypertension.

b. Additional information should be noted as to the arm used and the position (e.g., sitting, standing, lying down) of the client during the measurement, previous blood pressure readings, known medical problems, and any medical care being received and medications being taken by the client.

II. The client's pulse and blood pressure may be obtained in the lower extremities. The pulses available include the femoral, popliteal, posterior tibial, and dorsalis pedis. The blood pressure is assessed by placing the thigh-sized cuff over the posterior aspect of the middle thigh region while the client is in the prone position. The popliteal artery is used for palpation and auscultation of the blood pressure. Measurement in the lower extremities may be 10–40 mmHg higher in the systolic reading than that of the upper extremities.

III. a. A febrile client may exhibit the following signs and symptoms:
- Increased body temperature
- Flushed, dry, warm skin
- Chills
- Feeling of malaise
- Tachycardia

b. Nursing interventions for febrile clients may include:
- Assessment of vital signs, especially temperature
- Observation of client response, including skin color and temperature, and chills
- Promotion of client comfort, responding to chills, thirst
- Collection of appropriate specimens, such as blood cultures
- Promotion of rest and reduction of activities that increase heat production
- Promotion of heat loss by removing coverings and keeping the client dry
- Provision of care to meet increased metabolic demands, including oxygen, nutrition, and fluid requirements
- Monitoring of ongoing status

IV. If the pulse oximeter does not appear to be working, there may be problems with light transmission or a reduction of the client's arterial pulsations. The site for measurement should be checked to determine that it is clean, warm, and dry; not directly near another light source; and receiving adequate circulation. The client also may need to be reminded to limit excessive motion of the extremity that is being used for measurement.

CHAPTER REVIEW

1. g

2. d

3. h

4. f

5. j

6. a

7. i

8. e

9. c

10. b

11. Vital signs should be taken:
- When the client is admitted to the health care agency
- On a routine schedule according to agency policy
- Before and after procedures, such as surgery and invasive diagnostic tests
- Before and after blood transfusions
- Before and after the administration of medications that may alter temperature regulation or cardiovascular or respiratory functioning
- When there are alterations in the client's status, such as change in the level of consciousness or indications of distress
- Before and after activities, including ambulation and exercises

12. False low readings may be obtained if the bladder or cuff is too wide, the arm is positioned above the heart level, the cuff is deflated too quickly (low systolic), the stethoscope is not working or is placed incorrectly, the assessment is repeated too quickly (low systolic), or different Korotkoff sounds are being used (low diastolic). False high readings may be obtained if the bladder or cuff is too narrow, the cuff is wrapped too loosely or unevenly around the arm, the cuff is deflated too slowly (high diastolic), the arm is not supported, or different Korotkoff sounds are being used (high systolic).

13. a. $(97°F - 32) \times 5/9 = 36°C$
    b. $9/5 \times 38.4° C + 32 = 101.1° F$
    c. The nurse is alerted to temperature alterations of above 100.4° F or below 96.8° F on an oral Fahrenheit thermometer, and measurements above 38° C or below 36° C on an oral Centigrade scale. Rectal temperature readings may be 0.9° F or 0.5° C higher than oral measurements, with axillary readings ranging this same number of degrees lower than oral temperatures.

14. The pulses should be palpated as follows:

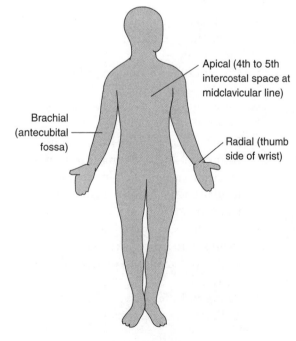

Brachial (antecubital fossa)

Apical (4th to 5th intercostal space at midclavicular line)

Radial (thumb side of wrist)

15. a. Aneroid scale:

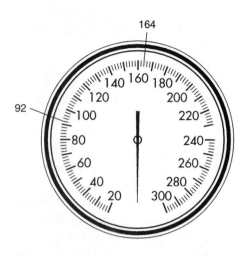

b. Mercury scale:

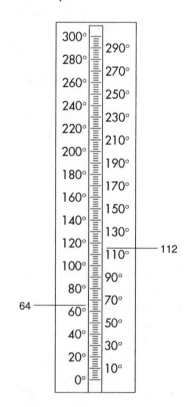

16. For older adults, the following should be considered:
    a. Temperature—usually lower, more sensitive to slight changes in self and environment, may have difficulty holding oral thermometer (with loss of teeth, muscle tone), decreased sweat gland function (prone to hyperthermia), diminished sensation to cold and

decreased insulation of subcutaneous fat (prone to hypothermia).

b. Pulse—may be difficult to palpate, arteries may feel stiff, decreased heart rate at rest, rate takes longer to return to normal after elevations, PMI may be difficult to palpate, sounds may be muffled. Pedal pulses may be difficult to palpate.

c. Respirations—more rigidity of the rib cage, possible spinal alterations (kyphosis/lordosis), decreased depth of respirations, increased use of accessory muscles, decreased efficiency of respiratory muscles, reduced response to increases in carbon dioxide and decreases in oxygen levels.

d. Blood pressure—loss of upper arm mass, increase in BP range (particularly systolic), decreased BP after eating, sensitive to position changes (orthostatic hypotension).

17. Nursing interventions for the following clients include:

a. Tachycardia:
- Assess the apical and radial pulses often, being alert for dysrhythmias
- Observe for other changes in vital signs, such as hypotension
- Assess the client's level of consciousness and mental state
- Check for possible causative factors, such as recent activity or anxiety
- Report the condition to the physician

b. Hypotension:
- Monitor the client's blood pressure before position changes
- Have the client sit up before trying to ambulate—implement safety precautions for possible lightheadedness and dizziness. Maintain bed rest for the client, if indicated.
- Observe for other changes in vital signs, such as tachycardia
- Investigate possible causative factors, such as prolonged immobility or rapid position changes
- Report the client's condition

c. Hyperthermia:
- Monitor the client's temperature
- Observe for other changes in vital signs
- Prevent chilling and shivering
- Implement temperature reduction measures, as ordered—tepid bath, hypothermia blanket
- Be alert to changes in the level of consciousness
- Allow for rest to reduce metabolic demands
- Report the client's condition

d. Dyspnea:
- Position the client upright
- Carefully monitor the respiratory status
- Provide oxygen
- Limit activity
- Stay with the client to provide support
- Monitor changes in other vital signs and level of consciousness
- Report the client's condition immediately

18. A temperature should not be taken orally if the client is experiencing dyspnea, just had something hot or cold to eat or drink, was smoking, or had oral surgery or treatments. A rectal temperature should not be taken on a client who has had rectal surgery or is experiencing diarrhea, hemorrhoids or irritation.

19. 1

20. 3

21. 3

22. 1

23. 4

24. 1

25. 4

26. 1

27. 1

28. 3

29. 1

30. 4

31. 2

32. 2

CHAPTER 12—Health Assessment and Physical Examination

CASE STUDY

For the 4-year-old boy, you are aware that the experience may be new and frightening. You can show the child the assessment procedures on a doll or model, while giving simple, understandable information, and he may handle equipment that will be used (as appropriate). The exam should be conducted in a comfortable environment, with time allowed for the child to play. The child may be called by his first name, and he may be asked assessment questions that he will understand.

For the 16-year-old female, the nurse may begin the health assessment with the parent(s) in the room with the client. There should be time, however, when the client is by herself with the nurse to discuss concerns. The adolescent female should be asked if she wants a parent present during the physical assessment, but the option is provided for the client to not be accompanied. Procedures and findings should be explained to both the parent(s) and the client.

The older, Hispanic woman may have responses to the exam that are influenced by her culture. She will need to be informed and prepared for the breast and pelvic assessments, with consideration given to her privacy. This client may desire another female to be present during the examination or to conduct the physical. Care should be taken to determine that this client understands the information and instruction provided by an examiner who may speak only English. An interpreter may be obtained if the client is conversant

in Spanish. The environment should be warm and comfortable. Ample time should be allowed for the client to answer questions and assume necessary positions for the exam.

For each of the clients, opportunity should be provided to use the bathroom before, during, and following the examination.

CHAPTER REVIEW

1. f

2. c

3. b

4. a

5. h

6. g

7. d

8. j

9. e

10. i

11. The examination should be systematic and well organized, using a head-to-toe approach of all body systems. Both sides of the body are inspected for symmetry of appearance and function. If the client is experiencing difficulty, the area of abnormality is examined first. Adequate rest periods should be provided throughout the examination. Uncomfortable procedures should be performed near the end of the exam. Consideration should be given to the client's age and developmental status.

12. The purposes for performing a physical examination are to:
   - Gather baseline information about the client's health status
   - Verify information obtained in the nursing history

- Verify nursing diagnoses
- Make clinical judgments about the client's health status and management
- Evaluate the physiological outcomes of care

13. The five skills used in physical assessment include:
- Inspection—use of vision and hearing to detect characteristics of body parts and functions
- Palpation—use of the hands to touch body parts to determine temperature, texture, position, and movement
- Percussion—striking the body surface with the finger to produce a vibration and elicit sounds
- Auscultation—listening to sounds created in the body organs (use of stethoscope)
- Olfaction—use of smell to determine the presence of characteristic odors

14. a. Lithotomy—examination of the external and internal female genitalia
  b. Dorsal recumbent—examination of the head and neck, anterior thorax and lungs, breasts, axillae, heart, and abdomen
  c. Knee-chest—examination of the rectum
  d. Sims'—examination of the rectum and vagina
  e. Lateral recumbent—examination of the heart
  f. Prone—examination of the musculoskeletal system

15. Preparation of the environment for a physical examination includes providing privacy, adequate lighting, comfortable surroundings and warmth. Explanations should be provided in advance with time allowed for questions, the client should be approached in a calm and professional manner, and another individual may be requested to remain with the client during the examination.

16. In a general survey, information may be obtained on the client's general appearance and behavior (body type, posture, gait, hygiene, grooming, mood, speech, etc.), vital signs, height, and weight.

17. Client teaching for the following areas may include:
  a. Skin—instruction on monthly self-examination, cancer warning signals (ABCD), reporting changes, prevention of overexposure to the sun, and treatment of dry skin
  b. Heart—instruction on risk factors for heart disease, nutritional information (fat and cholesterol reduction), and importance of medical follow-up

18. a. Ulnar
  b. Posterior tibial
  c. Femoral
  d. Brachial
  e. Dorsalis pedis

19. a. Papule
  b. Ulcer
  c. Macule
  d. Atrophy
  e. Wheal

20. The PMI is located in the left anterior chest wall, at approximately the fourth to fifth intercostal space, at the midclavicular line.

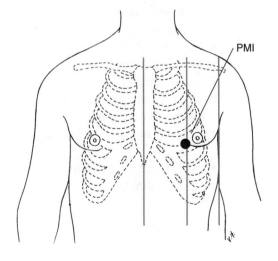

21. Common eye and visual problems include hyperopia, myopia, presbyopia, astigmatism, retinopathy, strabismus, cataracts, glaucoma, and macular degeneration. Descriptions may be found in Chapter 12 of the textbook.

22. With the use of olfaction (smell), the nurse may determine the presence of an infection, poor hygiene, gastrointestinal difficulties, acidosis, and the ingestion of alcohol.

23. The following are findings that may indicate abuse:
    a. Child sexual abuse
       Physical findings:
       - Genital discharge, bleeding, pain, itching
       - Difficulty sitting or walking
       - Foreign bodies in genital tract or rectum
       Behavioral findings:
       - Problems eating or sleeping
       - Fear of certain people or places
       - Regressive or acting out behavior
       - Preoccupation with own genitals
    b. Domestic abuse
       Physical findings:
       - Injuries and trauma inconsistent with reported cause
       - Multiple injuries, burns, bites
       - Old and new fractures
       Behavioral findings:
       - Eating or sleeping disorders
       - Anxiety, panic attacks
       - Low self-esteem
       - Depression, sense of helplessness
       - Attempted suicide
    c. Older adult abuse
       Physical findings:
       - Injuries and trauma inconsistent with reported cause
       - Bruises, hematomas, burns, fractures
       - Prolonged interval between injury and treatment

Behavioral findings:
- Dependent on caregiver
- Physically and/or cognitively impaired
- Combative, belligerent

24. a. Biceps muscle strength—determined by pulling down on the forearm as the client attempts to flex the arm
    b. Quadriceps muscle strength—determined while the client is sitting down, by applying downward pressure to the thigh while the client attempts to raise up the leg

25. The Glasgow Coma score for this client is 7.
    a. Eyes open to pain = 2
    b. Makes incomprehensible sounds = 2
    c. Demonstrates abnormal flexion of muscles = 3
    d. Total = 7

26. The patellar reflex is assessed with the client sitting and the legs hanging down freely, or with the client lying down and supporting the knee in a flexed 90-degree position. The patellar tendon is tapped briskly just below the patella. The normal response is an extension of the lower leg.

27. Inspection, auscultation, palpation, percussion

28. a. expected
    b. unexpected
    c. expected
    d. expected
    e. unexpected
    f. expected
    g. unexpected
    h. expected
    i. expected
    j. unexpected
    k. unexpected
    l. unexpected
    m. expected
    n. expected
    o. unexpected

p. expected

q. expected

r. unexpected

s. expected

t. unexpected

u. unexpected

v. expected

w. unexpected

x. expected

y. unexpected

z. expected

aa. unexpected

bb. expected

cc. expected

dd. expected

ee. expected

ff. unexpected

gg. expected

hh. unexpected

ii. expected

29. 4

30. 2

31. 1

32. 2

33. 1

34. 4

35. 3

36. 4

37. 3

38. 4

39. 3

40. 1

41. 1

42. 4

43. 1

44. 4

45. 1

46. 1

47. 1

48. 4

49. 1

CHAPTER 13—Administering Medications

CASE STUDIES

I. To assist this client to maintain the medication regimen at home, you may create a large, colorful, easy-to-read schedule, chart, or calendar that the client can use to check when medications have been taken. The client's medications also may be arranged, by time of administration, in a commercially available or homemade container so that the client also may be able to determine if the medications were taken as prescribed. (Some commercial devices will "beep" when it is time for medications to be taken).

II. If the prescriber's handwriting is illegible, it is unsafe to make assumptions about the medication order. To avoid errors, you should contact the prescriber as soon as possible and clarify the medication orders.

III. A client without an identification band should not receive medications. To verify the identity of the client, find another nurse or health care worker who is familiar with the client. On verifying the name of the client, obtain and provide the identification band for the client. Asking the client his or her name assists in verification but may be inaccurate if the client is not aware or oriented to the surroundings.

IV. When administering an injection to a child, you need to be very careful to avoid injuring or severely agitating the child. An appropriate, well-developed muscle site should be selected. You also may need to have someone else assist in holding or distracting the child by talking with him/her. The injection should be given quickly and accurately. An anesthetic ointment may be applied to the site before the injection to decrease the amount of discomfort. Children should not be told that they are receiving a "shot" or that it will not hurt. A sleeping child should be awakened before given an injection.

V. This discrepancy in the narcotic count should be reported immediately to the nurse in charge. Usually, an attempt is made to determine if the missing dose can be accounted for by checking with all of the other staff members. If the missing medication cannot be tracked down, the discrepancy will need to be documented on the computerized or written record. The agency's protocol for this situation then should be followed in relation to where and how the documentation is forwarded.

CHAPTER REVIEW

1. i

2. j

3. g

4. c

5. e

6. f

7. b

8. h

9. d

10. a

11. Federal and state legislation, state nurse practice acts, and agency policies and procedures

12. The pharmacokinetic factors are:
    - Absorption of the drug into the blood
    - Distribution of the drug to the tissues, organs, and site of action
    - Circulation through the bloodstream
    - Membrane permeability
    - Protein binding
    - Metabolism—biotransformation of the medication
    - Excretion of the medication out of the body

13. Factors influencing the actions of medications:
    a. Genetic—person's genetic makeup can influence drug metabolism
    b. Dietary—drug and nutrient interactions can alter a drug's action or the effect of the nutrient; proper drug metabolism relies on good nutrition
    c. Physiological variables—age, sex, weight, nutritional status, disease states
    d. Environmental conditions—stress, exposure to heat/cold, comfort of the setting
    e. Psychological variables—client's attitude, nurse's behavior

14. a. Side effects—secondary effects of the medication, such as nausea
    b. Toxic effects—accumulation of the drug because of impaired metabolism or excretion, usually severe (e.g., myocardial depression)
    c. Anaphylactic reaction—severe allergic response, characterized by bronchiospasm, laryngeal edema, and dyspnea.

15. The routes for parenteral administration include intramuscular, intradermal, subcutaneous, and intravenous.

16. A drug order must include the:
    1. Client's full name
    2. Date the order is written
    3. Drug name
    4. Dosage
    5. Route of administration
    6. Time and frequency of administration
    7. Signature of prescriber

17. The four common types of medication orders are:
     1. Standing order—carried out until prescriber cancels it
     2. prn order—when the client requires it
     3. Single/one-time order—drug given only once at a specific time
     4. Stat order—dose of medication to be given immediately and only once

18. The nurse is knowledgeable about the medications, administers them correctly, monitors their effects, determines whether the client should receive them at a particular time, and assesses the client's ability to take the medications.

19. Right drug, right dose, right client, right route, and right time.

20. The needle length is selected according to the client's size and weight and the type of injection to be given (e.g., subcutaneous or intramuscular). A larger needle gauge may be needed for more viscous solutions. The size of the syringe is determined by the amount of medication that is to be given at one time. The usual size syringe for IM injections is 2 or 3 cc.

21. The three principles are to:
     • Not contaminate one medication with the other
     • Ensure that the final dosage is accurate
     • Maintain aseptic technique

22. To mix insulin, the procedure is to use an insulin syringe and:
     1. Inject air, equal to the dose of the cloudy insulin, into the cloudy vial. Do not let the tip of the needle touch the insulin.
     2. Remove the syringe from the vial of cloudy insulin.
     3. With the same syringe, inject air, equal to the dose of the clear insulin, into the clear vial and withdraw the correct dose into the syringe.
     4. Remove the syringe from the clear insulin vial and dispel air bubbles.

5. Place the needle of the syringe back into the cloudy insulin vial and withdraw the correct dose.

23. The discomfort of an injection may be minimized by:
     • Using a sharp-beveled needle of the smallest possible size
     • Positioning the client comfortably
     • Selecting the proper site
     • Diverting the client's attention away from the procedure
     • Inserting the needle quickly and smoothly
     • Holding the syringe steady while injecting the solution
     • Injecting the medication slowly and steadily
     • Using the Z-track technique
     • Massaging the site, unless contraindicated

24. The Z-track technique should be used for medications that are irritating to the tissues.

25. a. Intramuscular—90° angle
     b. Subcutaneous—45° angle
     c. Intradermal—5–15° angle

26. Medication may be administered intravenously via mixtures with large volumes of IV fluids, by injection (bolus) or intermittent access devices, or piggyback through an existing IV line.

27. a. $\dfrac{\text{Dose ordered}}{\text{Dose on hand}} \times \text{Amount on hand}$
         = Dose to be administered

     b. $\dfrac{\text{Child's surface area}}{1.7 \text{ m}^2} \times \text{Adult dose}$
         = Dose to be administered

28. A client having a mild allergic reaction may have urticaria (hives), a rash (eczema), itching (pruritis), and/or rhinitis (nasal discharge).

29. a. ac = before meals
     b. bid = twice a day

c.   prn = as necessary

d.   q4h = every 4 hours

e.   qid. = four times a day

f.   stat = immediately

g.   hs = hour of sleep, bedtime

30. Volume-controlled administration set, mini-infuser pump, tandem set, and piggy-back set.

31. a. $\dfrac{150 \text{ mcg}}{75 \text{ mcg}} \times 1 \text{ tablet}$

= 2 tablets should be given

Conversion of 0.150 mg to mcg: multiply 0.150 by 1000

b. $\dfrac{150 \text{ mg}}{50 \text{ mg}} \times 1 \text{ ml} = 3 \text{ ml}$ should be given

c. $\dfrac{20 \text{ mg}}{10 \text{ mg}} \times 1 \text{ ml} = 2 \text{ ml}$ should be given

d. $\dfrac{250 \text{ mg}}{125 \text{ mg}} \times 1 \text{ tablet} = 2$ tablets should be given

e. $\dfrac{75 \text{ mg}}{25 \text{ mg}} \times 0.5 \text{ ml} = 1.5 \text{ ml}$ should be given

f.   100 U = 1cc
     24 U/100 U = 0.24 cc

g. $\dfrac{1.25 \text{ m}^2}{1.7 \text{ m}^2} \times 25 \text{ mg} = 18.4$ mg should be given

32. Client assessments that should be completed before medication administration include:

a.   Oral medications—the presence of GI alterations, ability of the client to swallow food or fluids, use of gastric suction

b.   Topical medications—the condition of the skin area where the medication will be applied

c.   Parenteral injections—the size of the client, condition of the injection site (integument and muscle condition), circulatory status

d.   IV medications—condition of the IV site, circulatory/fluid status

For all clients, the type of medication and its effect on the client are to be evaluated by the nurse.

33. Administration of medications to the following clients includes:

a.   Children—carefully calculate and prepare small dosages, closely monitor the effect of the drug, implement thoughtful administration techniques to prevent injury and agitation, provide simple explanations

b.   Older adults—limit the number of medications that need to be taken at one time, provide adequate fluid for swallowing, use liquid medications or crush tablets (if indicated), allow ample time for the client to take the medications, offer information on the use and actions of the medications

34. Areas for client teaching include proper labeling and storage of medications, disposal of outdated medications, use of the drug by the client only, information about the medication and its effects, and when to notify the physician or prescriber of side effects/problems.

35. 2

36. 3

37. 2

38. 4

39. 4

40. 4

41. 1

42. 2

43. 3

CHAPTER 14—Fluid, Electrolyte, and Acid-Base Balances

CASE STUDIES

I. A client taking both digoxin and Lasix is more susceptible to fluid volume deficit (FVD) and hypokalemia. Digoxin strengthens the contraction of the heart muscle, improving the cardiac output and circulatory volume. Lasix is a potent diuretic that does not have a potassium-sparing effect. The client should be instructed to be alert to the signs of both decreased fluid and potassium as follows:
- Hypokalemia—weakness, fatigue, decreased muscle tone, intestinal distention, change in pulse rate or rhythm
- FVD—poor skin turgor, thirst, sunken eyeballs, dryness, weakness, change in pulse rate or rhythm

The client also should be instructed in the technique for taking her own pulse and on the importance of dietary replacement of potassium (e.g., bananas, oranges, potatoes) or administration of prescribed supplements.

II. The client on prolonged immobility is prone to hypercalcemia as a result of calcium being released from the bones into the bloodstream. The nurse is alert to changes in the cardiac rate and rhythm (e.g., tachycardia) and increases in the BUN and serum calcium levels. If the client is conscious, there may be anorexia, nausea, vomiting, low back pain, and a reduction in the level of consciousness.

Alcoholic clients are more susceptible to malnutrition and hypomagnesemia. The nurse is alert to muscle tremors, hyperactive reflexes, confusion, disorientation, dysrhythmias, positive Trousseau's/Chvostek's signs, and a serum magnesium level below 1.5 mEq/L.

III. a. The nurse may anticipate that this client will have signs and symptoms of diminished oxygenation, including dyspnea, wheezing, coughing, activity intolerance, restlessness, pallor/cyanosis, and possible lack of concentration.

b. This client most likely will experience respiratory acidosis.

CHAPTER REVIEW

1. e

2. f

3. i

4. g

5. b

6. a

7. c

8. j

9. h

10. d

11. a. Extracellular fluid
    b. Interstitial fluid
    c. Intracellular fluid

12. Cations:
- Sodium (extracellular)—maintenance of water balance, nerve impulse transmission, regulation of acid-base balance, and participation in cellular chemical reactions
- Potassium (intracellular)—necessary for glycogen deposits in the liver and skeletal muscle, transmission and conduction of nerve impulses, cardiac rhythm, and skeletal and smooth muscle contraction
- Calcium (intracellular)—bone and teeth formation, blood clotting, hormone secretion, cell membrane integrity, cardiac conduction, transmission of nerve impulses, and muscle contraction

- Magnesium (intracellular)—enzyme activities, neurochemical activities, and cardiac and skeletal muscle excitability

Anions:

- Chloride (extracellular)—follows sodium
- Bicarbonate (both)—major chemical base buffer
- Phosphate (intracellular)—acid-base regulation, maintenance of bones and teeth

13. The three types of acid-base regulators within the body are chemical, biological, and physiological.

14. Infants, young children, and older adults are most susceptible to fluid and acid-base disturbances.

15. a. Isotonic
    b. Hypotonic
    c. Isotonic
    d. Isotonic
    e. Hypertonic

16. Major risk factors for fluid, electrolyte, or acid-base imbalances include age, chronic disease, trauma, certain therapies and medications, and gastrointestinal losses.

17. The types of medications that may cause fluid, electrolyte, or acid-base disturbances include diuretics, steroids, potassium supplements, depressants, antibiotics, and antacids.

18. Nursing diagnoses for imbalances include:
    - Breathing pattern, ineffective
    - Cardiac output, decreased
    - Fluid volume deficit
    - Fluid volume excess
    - Gas exchange, impaired
    - Skin integrity, impaired
    - Tissue integrity, impaired
    - Tissue perfusion, altered

19. The nurse should implement the following for a client with a fluid restriction:

- Explain the rationale for the restriction
- Identify the amount of fluid allowed and what is considered "fluid"
- Work with the client to determine the amount of fluid at meals, in between meals, at bedtime, and with medications
- Use a standard as a starting point—
  - $\frac{1}{2}$ the total fluids during the active part of the day
  - $\frac{2}{5}$ of the fluid during the evening hours
  - Remainder for the night and prn
- Determine the type of fluids that are preferred by the client, unless contraindicated
- Provide/assist with frequent mouth care
- Avoid leaving extra fluids in the room, such as a full water pitcher.

20. The most commonly used sites for IV infusions are the:
    - Inner arm—cephalic vein, basilic vein, median cubital vein, median vein, and radial vein
    - Dorsal surface of the hand—superficial dorsal veins, cephalic vein, basilic vein
    - Dorsal surface of the foot—great saphenous vein, dorsal plexus, dorsal arch

21. Possible complications of IV therapy and their management are:
    - Infiltration—The needle or catheter becomes dislodged from the vein and is in the subcutaneous space. The insertion site is cool, clammy, swollen, and sometimes painful. The IV is discontinued and the extremity is raised and wrapped in a warm towel for 20 minutes to increase circulation and reduce swelling.
    - Phlebitis—An inflammation of the vein. There is an increase in temperature over the vein, discomfort, and sometimes redness traveling along the path of the vein. The IV is discontinued, and warm, moist heat is applied to the site to provide relief.
    - Volume overload—A sudden increase in infusion volume occurs. The client may develop signs of respiratory distress and tachycardia. The infusion is discontinued or slowed, the head of the bed is

raised, vital signs are taken, and the physician is notified.

22. Teaching for clients and families with IV therapy in the home includes:
    - The purpose of the therapy
    - Aseptic technique
    - Manipulation of the equipment
    - Maintenance of the IV solution, tubing, and dressing
    - Signs and symptoms of complications and trouble-shooting
    - Indications for notification of the home health nurse
    - Managing activities of daily living with the IV

23. The advantages of a PICC line are:
    - The line may remain in place longer than a peripheral line
    - There is less risk of infiltration and phlebitis because of dilution of fluids and medications into a greater blood flow area
    - Lines may be used to infuse fluids TPN, blood and blood products, and medications

24. Prior to a blood transfusion, the nurse checks the blood/blood product with another nurse to determine that the identification and blood type is correct. The nurse also assesses the:
    - IV site, needle size, patency of infusion, and presence of 0.9% NS solution
    - Client's understanding about the procedure
    - Client's vital signs to establish a baseline before the infusion begins.

    The nurse will stay with the client for at least the first 15 minutes of the transfusion to be alert to a possible reaction.

25. Autologous transfusions reduce the risk of mismatched blood and exposure to blood-borne infectious organisms. Perioperative blood salvage also contains more red blood cells than stored blood.

26. a. Hyponatremia
    b. Hyperkalemia
    c. Hypocalcemia
    d. Hypomagnesemia

27. a. $$\frac{500\ ml}{5\ hours} = \frac{500\ ml \times 15\ gtt/ml}{5\ hours \times 60\ min/hour}$$
       $$= 25\ gtt/min$$

    b. $$\frac{1000\ ml}{8\ hours} = \frac{1000\ ml \times 10\ gtt/ml}{8\ hours \times 60\ min/hour}$$
       $$= 21\ gtt/min$$

    c. $$\frac{200\ ml}{4\ hours} = \frac{200\ ml \times 60\ gtt/ml}{4\ hours \times 60\ min/hour}$$
       $$= 50\ gtt/ml$$

    d. $$\frac{2000\ ml}{18\ hour} = 111\ ml/hour$$

28. TPN (total parenteral nutrition) is a nutritionally adequate hypertonic solution that contains glucose, other nutrients, and electrolytes.

29. For an IV that is not infusing properly, the nurse should check the patency of the system. The IV bag can be lowered below the level of the insertion site to check for blood return. The site can be assessed to determine if there are complications present, such as infiltration or phlebitis. The tubing may be kinked or obstructed by the client's positioning. Also, the height of the bag may be too low and the bag may need to be raised.

30. For the nursing diagnosis, *Fluid Volume, Deficit,* possible goals/outcomes and nursing interventions include:
    Goal: Client achievement of proper fluid volume
    Outcomes:
    - Moist mucous membranes and good skin turgor
    - Maintenance of normal blood pressure during position changes
    - Urinary output approximately equal to input

- Hematocrit and electrolytes within expected limits

Nursing interventions:
- Monitor intake and output (I&O)
- Weigh client daily
- Assess skin and mucous membranes for hydration
- Provide 2500 ml of fluids daily, unless contraindicated
- Observe urine for color/concentration
- Monitor vital signs, especially blood pressure
- Monitor laboratory results
- Instruct client on the importance of fluid intake

31. 2

32. 3

33. 3

34. 3

35. 1

36. 2

37. 3

38. 4

39. 3

40. 4

41. 3

42. 2

43. 4

44. 4

45. 3

46. 4

47. 3

48. 1

CHAPTER 15—Caring in Nursing Practice

CASE STUDY

One of the most important things that the nurse can do for the client's daughter and her family is to sit with them and allow them to verbalize their feelings about the situation. Listening to the family and acknowledging their emotions lets them know that their feelings and concerns are important. It also demonstrates that the nurse is responsive to their needs and is involved in the holistic care of the client. The nurse should explain how the client's condition has progressed and the treatments that currently are being provided for comfort and support. The nurse may provide the daughter with the opportunity to assist with or observe the physical care that is being given to the client. Providing information on available resources, such as hospice, is also important in demonstrating caring and concern for the well-being of the client and her family.

CHAPTER REVIEW

1. The major concepts of the theories of caring are:
   a. Caring is primary—Patricia Benner suggests that caring is the essence of excellent nursing practice. It means that persons, events, projects, and things matter to people. It is a word for being connected.
   b. The essence of nursing and health—Madeleine Leininger approaches caring from a transcultural perspective. Care is an essential human need, necessary for health and survival. It is assisting an individual or group in improving a human condition. Caring is seen as the dominant domain that distinguishes nursing from other health disciplines.
   c. Transpersonal caring—Jean Watson views caring as preservation of human dignity, placing care before cure. An interconnectedness forms between the one cared for and the one who is caring.
   d. Swanson's theory of caring—The processes of caring are identified as knowing, being with, doing for, enabling, and maintaining belief. Caring is defined

as a nurturing way of relating to a valued other, toward whom one feels a personal sense of commitment and responsibility.

2. Clients perceive caring behaviors of nurses as being physically present; responding and being supportive of concerns; using a soft, gentle voice; invoking feelings of security; making one feel comfortable; coming without being called; being treated with respect and dignity; assisting with pain; promoting autonomy; and providing information (refer to Chapter 15).

3. Examples of clinical interventions for the following are:
   a. Providing presence—staying with the client while waiting for a procedure or test results
   b. Comforting—holding the client's hand, giving a massage, skillfully and gently performing a procedure
   c. Listening—opening the lines of communication, attentively listening to what the client is saying, and responding appropriately
   d. Knowing the client—centering on the client and providing information that is relevant to the client's circumstances

4. The nurse's work environment may be altered to foster caring by:
   - Increasing the flexibility of the work environment and structure
   - Rewarding experienced nurses, especially those who assume mentoring responsibilities
   - Improving staffing
   - Providing sufficient autonomy

5. 1

6. 3

7. 3

8. 4

9. 4

10. 3

CHAPTER 16—Cultural Diversity

CASE STUDY

a. For a client from a culture that has a matriarchal organization, the nurse may involve the wife, mother, or sister in the plan of care and decision-making process.

b. Involvement of the family is important in assisting the client to achieve an optimal level of well-being, but there may need to be limits placed on the number of family members who may stay in the room, a reasonable time frame for visiting to allow the client to rest and receive treatment, and the determination of where the family may gather to conduct discussions.

c. The therapeutic diet may need to be adapted to avoid meat and meat products but still provide necessary nutrients (protein) or avoid unwanted ingredients (sodium). In an acute or restorative care setting, the dietician should be involved in providing a menu that meets the client's cultural preferences but is also tasteful, satisfying, and within therapeutic guidelines.

d. A healer may provide emotional as well as health care support for the client. The nurse should work with the health care team to integrate, as much as possible, the actions of the healer. Traditional remedies or treatments should be investigated, however, to determine if there may be any interaction with the prescribed medications or therapies.

e. To promote communication with individuals and families who speak another language, the nurse should obtain an interpreter who is proficient in that language, use word signs or charts, not speak louder, use appropriate titles and greetings, be attentive to nonverbal communication, and clarify uncertain areas.

CHAPTER REVIEW

1. Culture is a patterned behavioral response that develops over time as a result of patterning. It is shaped by values, beliefs, norms, and practices that are shared by members of the same group. Ethnicity includes more than biological identification. It also refers to groups whose members share a common

social and cultural heritage that is passed on to successive generations.

2. Transcultural nursing is client centered and provides culturally competent care to clients from various ethnic and cultural backgrounds.

3. Communication with individuals from other cultures may be promoted by:
   - Respecting people as individuals
   - Not treating people differently or in a patronizing manner
   - Not assuming emotional or intellectual status
   - Addressing people appropriately
   - Not trying to impress people by using dialects or saying you have friends from their culture
   - Explaining medical and nursing terms in understandable language
   - Including family members and recognizing cultural preferences in health care
   - Clarifying areas that are uncertain
   - Knowing when to initiate or avoid physical contact

4. Examples of cultural practices and major health problems are:
   a. African Americans—Use of folk medicine. Major health problems include sickle cell anemia and hypertension.
   b. Hispanic Americans—Use of folk medicine, balance of the four body humors. Major health problems include diabetes mellitus.
   c. Asian Americans—Use of herbal remedies/natural elements. Major health problems include liver and stomach cancer.
   d. Native Americans—Use of healers, natural herbs. Major health problems include heart disease and cirrhosis of the liver
   Additional examples may be found in Chapter 16

5. Examples of the effects of cultural health practices are:

   a. Beneficial—Use of a natural herb reduces the discomfort of a stomach upset
   b. Neutral—Positioning of a piece of furniture to be in line with the energy of the environment
   c. Harmful—Taking an herbal remedy that interacts with a prescribed medication or increases the blood pressure

6. Nursing diagnoses related to cultural needs may include:
   - Communication, impaired verbal
   - Coping, ineffective family
   - Health maintenance, altered
   - Social interaction, impaired
   - Noncompliance

7. False

8. 1

9. 2

10. 1

11. 4

12. 4

CHAPTER 17—Spiritual Health

CASE STUDY

a. The nurse should obtain information about the extent to which the client practices Buddhism, including whether he/she is a vegetarian, fasts and refuses treatment on holy days, avoids alcohol, and hesitates to use medications. In addition, the client's advance directives should be obtained because life support may be removed, if indicated.

b. Dependent on the degree to which the client practices his/her faith, adaptations may need to be made as follows:
   - Special dietary request for a vegetarian diet

- Scheduling of treatments, tests, etc. on days that are not considered holy
- Determination of medications that may be acceptable
- Use of medications, mouthwash that contains alcohol
- Provide contact with a Buddhist priest

CHAPTER REVIEW

1. Religion is seen as an organized way, through rules and rituals, that the individual demonstrates his/her spirituality and belief in or worship of God(s)/Supreme Being(s). Spirituality is the totality of the individual's beliefs, including faith, hope, spiritual health, and religion. The individual does not have to be religious to have spiritual well-being.

2. Intrapersonal connectedness—being connected/in touch with oneself
Interpersonal connectedness—being connected/in touch with others and the environment
Transpersonal connectedness—being connected/in touch with the unseen, God, or a higher power.

3. Possible nursing diagnoses include:
   - Spiritual well-being, potential for enhanced
   - Spiritual distress
   - Coping, ineffective individual
   - Coping, family: potential for growth
   - Family processes, altered
   - Grieving, dysfunctional
   - Anxiety
   - Hopelessness
   - Self-esteem disturbance

4. Clients who practice Hinduism, Sikhism, and Buddhism usually accept modern medical science. Members of the Islamic faith practice the Five Pillars of Islam and may have a fatalistic view of health. Jewish clients usually believe in the sanctity of life, observe the Sabbath, and also accept modern medical treatment. Refer to Chapter 17 for additional examples. Also, clients who are Christian Scientists and Jehovah's Witnesses may refuse health care interventions.

5. Older adults may find that religion helps them cope with difficult times or life events. They may be more involved in less organized spiritual activities, and there may be an increased interest in the afterlife. Spirituality is usually a source of support for clients as they age and approach the end of their lives.

6. 4

7. 1

8. 4

9. 3

10. 1

11. 3

CHAPTER 18—Growth and Development

CASE STUDIES

I. Promotion of growth and development for the hospitalized infant may include the following:
   - Having the parents/guardians provide most of the care to avoid interfering with the attachment process.
   - Limiting the number of caregivers and following the parents' directions for care to promote trust.
   - Limiting negative experiences and providing pleasurable sensations.

Promotion of growth and development for the hospitalized 5-year-old child may include the following:
   - Creating a comfortable environment for the child and parents
   - Providing consistent and appropriate care, if the parents are not available
   - Limiting the number of caregivers
   - Providing an environment of acceptance for regressive behavior and reassuring parents that the behavior is normal for children in this situation

- Allowing children to examine equipment that may be used and participate in procedures, as appropriate
- Providing comfort items, such as a tape with the parents' voice, pictures of family members, and favorite toys.
- Providing opportunities for play and social interaction with other children
- Explaining routines in understandable language
- Incorporating activities of daily living into the hospital routine

II. This client may benefit from reality orientation, which includes the following:
- Using time, date, place, and name in conversation
- Reinforcing reality and providing meaningful things to do
- Encouraging participation in activities
- Making sure that hearing aids, glasses, etc. are working or fitted correctly
- Providing bowel and bladder training
- Reinforcing positive behaviors
- Being patient and allowing sufficient time for completion of activities
- Speaking slowly and clearly, repeating as necessary
- Providing clear, simple directions
- Maintaining a caring and stimulating environment

III. Children in this age group usually are interested in games and sports. For indoor recreation, board games, electronic games, or word games may be suggested. Hobbies and crafts are also appropriate if they stimulate and maintain the children's interest. If the children will be outdoors, supervised games such as volleyball, softball/baseball, kickball, tennis, or relay races may be organized. Some sports may need to be modified to meet the physical abilities of the age group. Swimming, bicycling, rowing/canoeing, walking, and hiking are activities that do not have to involve competition but promote exercise.

IV. Suicide is one of the main causes of death in adolescents and young adults. Parents should be aware of the following warning signs:
- Diminished performance in school
- Withdrawal from social activities with family and friends
- Substance abuse
- Changes in personality
- Disturbances in sleep, appetite, and usual activity levels
- Talking about death or suicide
- Giving away personal items

V. Individuals older than age 40 should be instructed about the following recommendations for health screenings:
- Mammograms for women every 1–2 years, annually after age 50 (A baseline mammogram is usually done before age 40.)
- Proctosigmoidoscopic exams every 3–5 years and more frequently if necessary
- Rectal exam annually after age 40

CHAPTER REVIEW

1. d

2. a

3. c

4. e

5. b

6. a. Growth—the measurable (quantitative) aspect of an individual's increase in physical dimensions as a result of an increase in the number of body cells.
   b. Development—the behavior (qualitative) aspect of an individual's adaptation to the environment.
   c. Maturation—the genetically determined biological plan/sequence for an individual's growth and development.

7. The external forces that influence growth and development are the family, peer group, life experiences, health environment, and living environment.

8. Play allows the child to develop motor, cognitive, and social skills. It also provides an avenue for dealing with fears and frustrations and provides stimulation. In the strange environment of the acute care center, play is an enjoyable and anxiety-reducing activity.

9. The following table provides examples of physiologic changes, psychosocial concerns, health issues, and health promotion strategies throughout the life span. Additional information on characteristics associated with the life stages may be found in the tables and boxes that are located throughout the chapter.

10. A client's pregnancy and the development of the fetus may be influenced by substance abuse (drugs, alcohol), smoking, and hazardous behaviors (skiing, climbing, etc.).

	Physiological Changes	Psychosocial Concerns	Health/Safety Issues	Health Promotion
Infant	Rapid growth, development of motor skills, growth of teeth	Response to sensory stimuli, need for comfort, love, security	Positioning during sleep, nutritional needs, accidents	Meeting basic needs—feeding, sleeping, comforting, eliminating; immunizations
Toddler	Rapid development of motor skills, walk upright with broad gait, protuberant abdomen	Egocentricity, speaking in short sentences, parallel play, separation anxiety	Accidents as a result of greater mobility	Nutritional needs, safety precautions—supervision
Preschool	Physical development slows, better mastery of physical skills	Cognitive and psychosocial growth, associative play, imagination, problem solving	Accidents	Hygiene, safety measures, stimulation of cognitive growth, role modeling
School age	Run faster and farther, greater control over their bodies, strength increases, fine motor coordination increases	Formal education, greater socialization skills, same sex peer groups, self-esteem needs	Accidents and injuries, blood pressure elevation	Daily exercise, maintenance of body weight, safety measures, hygiene
Adolescent	Growth spurt—primary (hormones) and secondary sexual characteristics (pubic hair, breast development), increase in height and weight	Language development fairly complete—diverse communication skills, peer relationships and socialization, sexual identity development, self-esteem needs	Injuries, homicide, suicide, eating disorders—emotional distress, motor-vehicle accidents, pregnancy, sexually transmitted diseases, substance abuse	Confidential health services, risk assessment for injuries or accidents, sex education, recognize need to move into adult role
Young adult	Attain physical maturity, completion of physical growth	Education to move toward occupation, become employed, live on their own, select a significant other, highest level of cognitive ability attained	Stress, risky behaviors, violence, occupational hazards, poor adherence to screening schedules	Assist to improve health habits, community health programs for screening, family planning, parenting skills

Middle adult	Physical decline—sensory status, physical endurance, reproductive capability	"Sandwich" generation—grown children and older parents, need to adapt to physiological changes, slower performance, involvement in community activities, career changes	Stress of job changes, care of children and parents, pathologies—heart disease, diabetes, cancer	Health screening, encourage positive health behaviors, referrals for specific concerns
Older adult	Decline in muscle mass and strength, bone demineralization, visual and auditory impairment, reduced metabolism, decreased hormones, thinning hair, decreased elasticity of the skin	Retirement, vary in level of cognitive functioning, adjustment to: loss of significant others, change in role/environment	Dementia, Alzheimer's disease, chronic diseases, physiological changes, accidents, impending death	Promotion of all positive functions; referral for sensory support—glasses, hearing aids; exercise; cognitive stimulation; physiological support; promotion of dignity

11. When preparing a child for a procedure the nurse may provide the equipment (as appropriate) for the child to manipulate; or the child may be asked to draw pictures of the their concerns, or role-play with dolls or puppets their participation in the procedure. For older children fine motor skills are called upon if there is a need to know how to do procedures, such as injections or dressings. Use of specific skills is dependent upon age and developmental status of the client.

12. 4

13. 2

14. 2

15. 2

16. 4

17. 4

18. 3

19. 3

20. 1

21. 4

22. 4

23. 1

CHAPTER 19—Self-Concept and Sexuality

CASE STUDIES

I. a. This adolescent client most likely will experience alterations in his self-concept, especially the perception of his body image and identity. Adolescents may be very sensitive about their physical appearance and social status, and now the client will have to cope with an alter-

Nursing Diagnosis	Expected Outcomes	Nursing Interventions
Potential body image disturbance related to accidental injury and resultant lack of mobility and sensation to lower extremities (as manifested by his frequent verbalization of prior involvement in athletics and other school activities).	Client will adapt to change in body image by: • Discussing feelings about his injury and change in activity status • Participating in care as much as possible • Reflecting on personal strengths	Provide time for talking with the client and discussing feelings; explore coping skills that the client has used before, and encourage and support those skills; involve the client in health care activities.

| Sexuality patterns, altered related to accidental injury and resultant lack of mobility and sensation to lower extremities. | Client will learn/utilize measures to attain sexual satisfaction within limitations by:
• Discussing feelings about sexual function and adaptation
• Participating in educational program on alternate measures to promote sexual response.
• Sharing response to measures utilized and suggesting possible alternatives. | Provide time to talk with the client and discuss feelings and concerns; provide information on sexual response and stimulation for clients with paraplegia; obtain a referral/consultation, if indicated, for additional support and information; have another young male paraplegic individual speak with the client; provide for client privacy. |

ation in his social and athletic activity in school. In addition, the paraplegia will significantly influence his sexual functioning, an area where he may have been exploring and now will have to adapt.

b. Sample care plan:

II. a. The client who you suspect may be a victim of sexual abuse may be found to have:
   - Physical signs—bruises, laceration, abrasions, burns, headaches, GI problems, eating disorders, abdominal or vaginal pain
   - Behavioral signs—sleep-pattern disturbances, nightmares, insomnia, depression, anxiety, fear, decreased self-esteem, substance abuse, frequent visits to health care providers

   b. Examples of questions that should be asked include:
   - "Are you in a relationship where someone is hurting you?"
   - "Have you ever been forced to have sex when you didn't want to?"
   - "Are you afraid of the situation that you are in?"

CHAPTER REVIEW

1. b

2. e

3. d

4. a

5. c

6. The components of self-concept are developed from birth onward and will reflect the changes that occur throughout life:
   - Body image—involves experiences and attitudes related to the body, including appearance, perceptions regarding masculinity and femininity, and physical abilities
   - Self-esteem—emotional evaluation of self-worth, influenced by both our own evaluation and the evaluation of others
   - Role—set of behaviors that have been approved by the family, community, and culture as appropriate in particular situations
   - Identity—persistent individuality and sameness of a person over time and in various circumstances

7. General positive influences on self-concept include words and actions of approval, interest, and acceptance; recognition and inclusion in decision-making; trust; and support. Stressors that may influence self-concept include those that threaten body image, self-esteem, role, or identity such as the effects of traumatic accidents, surgery, and acute or chronic diseases.

8. Behaviors that may indicate an altered self-concept include avoidance of eye contact, overly apologetic, hesitant speech, overly critical, excessive anger, frequent or inappropriate crying, puts self down, excessively dependent, hesitant to express views or opinions, lack of interest in what is happening, passive attitude, difficulty in making choices, slumped posture, and unkempt appearance.

9. Potential concerns related to self-concept include:

   a. Alteration in body image—removal of breast can lead to question of feminine image and sexual desirability
   b. Alteration in body image and role—loss of hair from chemotherapy, possible hospitalizations and diminished strength may interfere with role as mother
   c. Alteration in body image and identity—physical changes in appearance and function (ability to play with others)
   d. Alteration in role and self-esteem—possible inability to maintain current occupation, dependence on others

10. Ways in which the nurse may promote self-concept include the following:
    a. Health promotion setting:
       - Supporting the development of health lifestyle measures with sound nutrition, regular exercise, adequate rest and sleep, stress reduction practices
       - Providing client education
       - Assessing alterations and making appropriate referrals
    b. Acute care setting:
       - Arranging visits with someone who has experienced similar/problems changes
       - Being sensitive to and supporting the client's needs
    c. Restorative care setting:
       - Expanding the client's self-awareness
       - Encouraging self-exploration
       - Assisting the client in self-evaluation
       - Assisting the client in forming realistic goals, becoming committed to their achievement, evaluating their achievement, and re-forming the plan as necessary.

11. Alterations in sexual health include infertility, sexual abuse, sexual dysfunction, and personal and emotional conflicts.

12. Client teaching for the promotion of sexual health may include instruction about:
    - Refraining from drinking alcohol 1–2 hours before sexual activity
    - Discussing behavior that provides the most sexual stimulation and satisfaction
    - Options available for contraception
    - Side effects of medications that alter sexual function and response
    - Use of usual positions and selection of times when client feels rested (for individuals with cardiac dysfunction)
    - Safe sex practices

13. For the nursing diagnosis, *Low self-esteem, situational, related to being unable to pass a required college course*, examples are as follows:
    - Client goal; Increased self-esteem
    - Outcome: Discusses positive aspects of self and future plans
    - Nursing interventions: Spend time with the client to allow for discussion of feelings and concerns, establish sense of trust

14. False

15. False

16. 3

17. 4

18. 4

19. 4

20. 1

21. 1

22. 2

23. 4

24. 4

CHAPTER 20—Family Context in Nursing

CASE STUDY

a. The client, who provides the major financial support to the family, has been hospitalized with a serious health problem. His wife has maintained a traditional role as "homemaker" while her husband has worked. The younger daughter has assumed a family life that appears to be more acceptable to her parents, whereas the older son is involved in an alternative family form. The younger daughter may be more involved in her parents' life because of her family pattern.

b. The family is apparently progressing from "Launching children and moving on" to the "Family in later life" stage. There are elements of both stages within this situation.

c. The nurse may begin discussions with the father and mother initially, moving toward a total family meeting at a later date. Providing opportunities for family members to express their feelings about both the health care and the family situation may facilitate open communication about family structure and relationships. The family may need to be referred for ongoing counseling if there is a negative impact on the health/recovery of the client.

d. The client may have feelings about his business and family roles and his ability to resume them when he is discharged. His wife will need to be involved in the educational process to follow through with the plan of care. The client's wife may need to assume a greater decision-making role with the client to maintain the economic and emotional status of the family.

e. Possible family-oriented nursing diagnoses include:
- Family processes, altered
- Role performance, altered
- Coping, ineffective family

CHAPTER REVIEW

1. b

2. d

3. a

4. e

5. c

6. The family of today is facing the following issues: decrease in family size, marriage in later life, delay of childbirth, increase in divorce, increase in the need for child and older adult care, alternate lifestyles and family forms, increase in working women, increase in teenage pregnancy, and increase in the older population. In addition, major concerns of the family include a change in economic status, family violence, and AIDS.

7. Family as context—the primary focus is the health and well-being of the individual family members.

   Family as client—the focus is on the health and well-being of the family as a whole unit.

8. Inadequate functioning can have many effects on the family, including stress, impaired cardiovascular and neuroendocrine functioning, and interference with decision making and problem solving.

9. "Family hardiness" is demonstrated by internal strength and durability of the family unit, having a sense of control over outcomes of life events, viewing change as beneficial and growth producing, and responding actively to stressors.

10. For the nursing diagnosis, *Risk for care giver role strain related to need to provide care for elderly parent at home,* examples of goals, outcomes, and interventions are Client/ family goal: Maintain a healthy level of family functioning while caring for older parent.

Outcomes:
- Verbalize concerns about providing care for the older parent
- Identify available support systems
- Discuss plan for respite care/assistance with care

Nursing interventions:
- Sit with family and discuss plans for providing care
- Listen to client/family feelings and concerns
- Identify and refer the family to available community resources

11. 3

12. 4

13. 3

14. 1

15. 3

16. 4

17. 4

CHAPTER 21—Stress and Coping

CASE STUDY

a. This client may demonstrate the following:
- Physical signs—increased heart rate, respirations, and blood pressure; headaches; fatigue; sleep disturbances; restlessness; gastrointestinal distress; weight gain or loss; backaches; amenorrhea; frequent or prolonged colds or flu
- Psychological signs—forgetfulness, preoccupation, increased fantasizing, decreased creativity, slower reactions and thinking, confusion, decreased attention span
- Emotional signs—crying tendencies, lack of interest, irritability, negative thinking, worrying
- Behavioral signs—diminished activity or hyperactivity, withdrawal, suspiciousness,

substance abuse, change in communication or interaction with others

b. A number of alternatives may be presented to this client so that she may select those that are most beneficial to her. The nurse may use guided imagery, biofeedback, progressive muscle relaxation, hypnosis, music/art therapy, humor, assertiveness training, or journal/diary entry.

CHAPTER REVIEW

1. The three stages of the general adaptation syndrome (GAS) are:
   a. Alarm reaction—hormone levels rise resulting in increases in blood volume, blood sugar, epinephrine and norepinephrine amounts, heart rate, blood flow to the muscles, oxygen intake, and mental alertness. The pupils dilate for a greater visual field. This is identified as the "fight-or-flight" stage.
   b. Resistance stage—the body stabilizes, with hormone levels, heart rate, blood pressure, and cardiac output returning to normal. The body repairs any damage that may have occurred.
   c. Exhaustion stage—the body is no longer able to resist the effects of the stressor and the energy is depleted. Death may occur in severe instances.

2. The different types of stress that may influence an individual are situational stress, maturational stress, sociocultural stress, and posttraumatic disorders.

3. An individual's response to stress may be influenced by the intensity, scope, duration, and number and nature of the stressors present. In addition, the individual's level of personal control, feelings of competence, cognitive appraisal of the event, and availability of support systems may influence the response.

4. a. Cognitive—forgetfulness, denial, increased fantasy life, poor concentration, inattention to detail, orientation to the past, decreased creativity, slower thinking and reactions, learning difficul-

ties, apathy, confusion, lower attention span, calculation difficulties

  b. Gastrointestinal—nausea, diarrhea, vomiting, weight gain or loss, change in appetite, bleeding
  c. Behavior—change in activity level, withdrawal, suspiciousness, change in communication and interaction with others, substance abuse, excessive humor or silence, no exercise, hyperactivity
  d. Neuroendocrine—headaches/migraines, fatigue, insomnia/sleep disturbances, feeling of being uncoordinated, restlessness, tremors, profuse sweating, dry mouth

5. Crisis differs from stress in the severity of the circumstance. The stress is so severe that the client is unable to cope in any of the ways that worked before. Stress ends when the stressor is gone, but crisis can last much longer.

6. Examples for the factors that may produce stress are:
  a. Situational—associated with work, relationships, chronic illness
  b. Maturational—associated with life stages, such as adolescent identity discovery
  c. Sociocultural—associated with financial status, living conditions, abuse
  d. Post-traumatic stress disorder—associated with accidents, rape, disasters, war

7. Job-related stressors include promotions, transfers, downsizing, restructuring, increased work responsibilities, and change of personnel/supervisor.

8. Nursing interventions that may be implemented to reduce stress or promote resistance include client teaching on:
  • Improvement of working conditions for greater flexibility and less hazards
  • Analysis of new job possibilities
  • Avoidance of excessive lifestyle changes
  • Scheduling of personal time
  • Exercise and relaxation

  • Development of alternative goals
  • Building coping resources—financial, educational, personal

9. 1

10. 2

11. 1

12. 3

13. 3

14. 4

CHAPTER 22—Loss and Grief

CASE STUDY

a. Mrs. R. may demonstrate the following behaviors indicative of complicated bereavement:
  • Overactivity without a sense of loss
  • Alteration in relationships with friends and family
  • Anger against particular people
  • Agitated depression—tension, guilt, feelings of worthlessness
  • Decreased participation in religious or cultural activities
  • Inability to discuss the loss without crying (even after a year or more after)
  • False euphoria
  • Eliminating all signs of the deceased (e.g., pictures) or creating a "shrine"
  • Alterations in eating and sleeping patterns
  • Regressive behavior

b. Possible nursing diagnoses for Mrs. R. may be:
  • Grieving, dysfunctional related to sudden loss/suicide of husband
  • Coping, ineffective individual related to inability to deal with husband's loss/suicide

c. Possible goals may be:
- Mrs. R. will accept the reality of her husband's death
- Mrs. R. will renew activities of daily living and complete a normal grieving process

d. Nursing interventions may include:
- Using therapeutic communication to promote Mrs. R.'s verbalization of feelings concerning her husband's suicide
- Demonstrating support of the client by staying with her and using comfort measures, such as touch
- Referring the client to support groups, clergy, and/or counseling as appropriate for her needs

CHAPTER REVIEW

1. The five types of loss are loss of external objects, known environment, significant other, aspect of self, or own life.

2. Special circumstances that may influence grief resolution include suicide, sudden death, miscarriage/child's death, and AIDS.

3. Examples of feelings, cognitions, physical sensations, and behaviors associated with normal grieving:
- Feelings—sadness, anger, guilt, anxiety, loneliness, fatigue, helplessness, shock, relief
- Cognitions—disbelief, confusion, preoccupation with or sense of presence of the deceased, hallucinations
- Physical sensations—hollowness in stomach, tightness in chest or throat, oversensitivity to noise, feeling short of breath, muscle weakness, lack of energy, dry mouth
- Behaviors—sleep and appetite disturbances, absentmindedness, dreams of the deceased, sighing, crying

4. A client who is to have surgery to remove a breast or other body part may experience anticipatory grief over the impending loss. A nurse who is working with clients who have terminal cancer or AIDS also may experience anticipatory grieving over their impending deaths.

5. a. Affective—showing an empathetic understanding of the client's and family members' strengths
   b. Cognitive—offering information about an illness or treatment and correcting misinformation
   c. Behavioral—assisting the client to use personal resources
   d. Affiliative—strengthening or fostering relationships with others
   e. Temporal—promoting the client's experience of time and development of short-term goals
   f. Contextual—encouraging development of achievable goals, reminiscing

6. The family/significant others of a dying client may be involved by:
- Assisting them to schedule visits to avoid client fatigue
- Allowing young children to visit dying parents/grandparents
- Being willing to listen to complaints, feelings about care
- Helping family members to interact with the client
- Assisting them to get rest and "time off"
- Supporting grieving and providing privacy as needed
- Providing information about the client's condition
- Communicating about impending death
- Providing a caring environment for the family
- Assisting in decision making after death

7. 2

8. 2

9. 3

10. 4

11. 4

12. 3

13. 2

14. 1

15. 3

CHAPTER 23—Managing Client Care

CASE STUDIES

I.
  a. After determining what needs to be done and prioritizing your interventions, you can delegate to the nurse's aide activities such as vital sign measurement, evening hygienic care, basic procedures (catheter care), and assistance with meals. The aide may also be asked to obtain necessary supplies and equipment for client care. You also may have the aide check on the general status of the clients and report back any immediate problems.

  b. To safely delegate activities, you need to determine the level of acuity of the clients and the knowledge and ability of the aide. If some of the clients are having abnormal vital signs, such as dysrhythmias, then it would not be appropriate to delegate pulse measurement to the aide.

II. Possible areas for QI projects on the surgical unit may include client satisfaction, postoperative infection rates, the success of preoperative teaching and postoperative exercises, and frequency of respiratory or circulatory complications.

III. To become a nurse practitioner, this individual will need to complete the bachelor's degree in nursing and progress on to a graduate program in nursing to obtain a master's degree. Advanced practice nurses, such as nurse practitioners, require additional education in advanced physical assessment, pharmacology, and clinical care, as well as expertise in their field. The individual also will need to be licensed in the state where she will practice.

CHAPTER REVIEW

1. Challenges for nursing in the future include:

- Ever-expanding need for new skills with new technology
- Cross-training
- Use of unlicensed assistive personnel, delegation
- Increasing need for clinical research
- Increasing generalization of practice
- Increasing responsibility for coordination of care

2. The different types of nursing care delivery models include:
- Functional nursing—task focused, not client focused. Tasks are divided, with one nurse assuming responsibility for specific tasks, such as medication administration.
- Team nursing—the RN leads a team composed of other RNs, LPNs/LVNs, and nurse assistants or technicians. The team members provide direct care to groups of clients, under the direction of the RN team leader. Nurse assistants are given client assignments, not just tasks.
- Total patient care—the RN is responsible for all aspects of care for one or more clients. The nurse works directly with the client, family, physician, and health care team members. The model typically has a shift-based focus.
- Primary nursing—the RN assumes responsibility for a caseload of clients over time, caring for the same clients during their stay in the health care setting.
- Case management—coordinates and links health care services to clients and their families. A professional nurse maintains responsibility for client care from admission to discharge.

3. Decentralization includes the movement of decision making down to the level of the staff. The nurse manager becomes a critical member of an effective nursing unit/group.

4. Nursing students need to learn how to become responsible and productive team members by taking responsibility and accountability for the care provided to

clients. Making good clinical decisions, learning from mistakes and seeking guidance, collaborating closely with professional nurses, and striving to improve performance during client interactions are critical aspects of learning to become a leader.

5. Delegation is the process of assigning responsibility to another qualified person. The individual delegating the tasks is responsible for determining the qualifications of the individual and is still accountable for their completion.

6. The Five Rights of Delegation are:
   1. Right task—repetitive, relatively noninvasive, such as catheter care or temperature measurement
   2. Right circumstances—appropriate setting and resources, such as the client is stable and the equipment is familiar
   3. Right person—the person who delegated the task and the person who is to do the task, such as the aide who has worked on the unit before with the nurse
   4. Right direction/communication—clear, concise description of the task, such as explaining what type of specimen is to be collected, when, and with what equipment
   5. Right supervision—appropriate monitoring, evaluation, and feedback, such as making sure that the vital signs are recorded correctly and match the client assessment

7. A quality improvement (QI) project should include the study and improvement of processes involved in the provision of health care. Desirable outcomes for the client and professionals need to be determined. A systematic approach should be taken for the collection, analysis, and reporting of data.

8. The role of the nurse in planning or implementing a QI project includes identifying the process to improve, organizing the project and/or team, clarifying knowledge of the process involved, collecting and analyzing data, and communicating plans and results.

9. 4

10. 2

11. 1

12. 1

13. 1

14. 4

15. 4

16. 2

17. 4

18. 3

CHAPTER 24—Exercise and Activity

CASE STUDY

a. Mrs. T. should be assessed for her ability to move independently, including her posture, muscle strength, range of motion, gait (if able), balance, activity tolerance, and cognitive status. If Mrs. T. is able to bear weight on both legs and maintain an erect position, the nurse must determine if she is capable of ambulating safely. Initial assessment of Mrs. T.'s transfer out of bed should be accomplished with assistance in the event that the client is unable to maintain a standing position.

b. If Mrs. T. is not able to ambulate independently, she may be able to use an assistive device, such as a cane or walker. If possible, one or more nurses may use a gait belt to assist Mrs. T. in ambulating. Should Mrs. T. not be able to ambulate safely, even with assistance, a wheelchair may be necessary. To assist Mrs. T. in gaining muscle strength, a program of exercise may be implemented.

CHAPTER REVIEW

1. j

2. h

3. i

4. g

5. e

6. b

7. f

8. d

9. a

10. c

11. The physiological changes that occur in the musculoskeletal system throughout the life span include:
    - Newborn—spine is flexed and lacks anteroposterior curves of the adult
    - Infant to toddler—thoracic spine straightens, lumbar spinal curve appears, allowing for sitting and standing
    - Toddler—awkward posture with slight swayback and protruding abdomen
    - Toddler to preschooler—posture less awkward, cervical and lumbar vertebrae curves are accentuated, foot eversion disappears
    - Preschooler to adolescent—musculoskeletal system growth, greater coordination that allows for tasks with fine motor skills
    - Adolescent—tremendous growth spurt, usually uneven; appears awkward and uncoordinated; muscular development increases in chest, arms, shoulders, and upper legs
    - Adult—has the musculoskeletal development necessary to carry out ADLs
    - Older adult—progressive loss of total bone mass, slower gait, less coordination, smaller steps with feet closer together, unstable balance

12. Physiological (e.g., musculoskeletal abnormalities, diminished cardiovascular function), emotional (e.g., anxiety, depression), and developmental (e.g., age, sex) factors and pregnancy influence activity tolerance.

13. Before and after client transfers the nurse should:
    - Review the steps of transfer
    - Assess the client's mobility, strength, and cognitive status
    - Determine the amount and type of assistance needed to transfer
    - Explain the procedure to the client
    - Raise the side rail on the other side of the bed
    - Position the bed at a safe and comfortable level
    - Assess the client for proper alignment and positioning after transfer

14. Pathological conditions or events that may influence body mechanics include congenital disorders, neuromuscular diseases, musculoskeletal or neurological trauma, and prolonged immobility.

15. a. Hand rolls—maintain the hand, thumb, and fingers in functional position
    b. Hand-wrist splints—molded for the client to maintain alignment of the thumb and wrist
    c. Trapeze bar—allows the client to use the upper extremities to assist in moving around in bed, transfers, and exercises
    d. Trochanter roll—prevents external rotation of the hips
    e. Footboard—prevents foot drop by maintaining dorsiflexion of the foot

16. The length of the crutch should be 3 to 4 finger widths from the axilla to a point 6 inches lateral to the client's heel.

17. a. Rotation of the neck—Sternocleidomastoid, trapezius

b. Abduction of the arm—Deltoid, supraspinatus
   Adduction of the arm—Pectoralis major
c. Supination of the forearm—Supinator, biceps brachii
   Pronation of the forearm—Pronator teres, pronator quadratus
d. Circumduction of the arm—Deltoid, coracobrachialis, latissimus dorsi, teres major
e. Hyperextension of the hip—Gluteus maximus, semitendinosus, semimembranosus
f. Flexion of the knee—Biceps femoris, semitendinosus, semimembranosus, sartorius
g. Extension of the knee—Rectus femoris, vastus lateralis, vastus medialis, vastus intermedius

18. Possible nursing diagnoses associated with a change in a client's ability to maintain physical activity include:
    - Activity intolerance
    - Disturbed body image
    - Risk for injury
    - Impaired physical mobility
    - Impaired skin integrity
    - Pain

19. 3

20. 2

21. 4

22. 1

23. 1

24. 2

25. 4

26. 4

27. 2

CHAPTER 25—Safety

CASE STUDY

a. You should assess some of the following areas regarding home safety:
   - Location of the home in the community
   - Security measures within the home
   - Environmental conditions—lighting, temperature, sanitation, stairways, floors/carpeting
   - Fire and electrical safety measures/hazards
   - Exposure to pollutants/pathogens

b. With a toddler and preschool child in the home, safety measures are extremely important. Accidents are one of the major problems for children, including falls and poisoning. If there are stairs in the home, gates should be in use or doors to the outside should be locked. For upper-level apartments or rooms, child-safety devices should be in place on the windows. Any household chemicals or medications should be out of reach and/or locked. There also may be locks on other kitchen cabinets, drawers, and the refrigerator to prevent access. Electrical outlets should have covers, and plugs should be out of sight of the children. The family should have a fire safety plan, fire extinguishers, and smoke/fire alarms. Items that may be swallowed or broken should be out of reach. Additional safety measures may be in place in the kitchen and bathroom, such as faucet covers.

CHAPTER REVIEW

1. Basic human needs in a safe environment and examples of what may affect them are:
   - Oxygen—carbon monoxide, improper ventilation, pollutants
   - Degree of humidity—excessive dryness
   - Nutrition—improper storage/refrigeration, inadequate cleaning of cooking surfaces
   - Optimal temperature—excessive heat or cold

2. Inadequate lighting, clutter, lack of security, fire/electrical hazards

3. Diminished vision, hearing, mobility, reflexes, and circulation

4. The following are examples of how the nurse may prevent health care agency risks:
   a. Falls—complete a risk assessment, provide supervision, place the client close to the nurse's station, orient the client to the surroundings, use physical restraints if absolutely necessary
   b. Client-inherent accidents—institute seizure precautions, remove foreign substances or hazardous items (sharps), provide supervision of the client's activities
   c. Procedure-related risks—follow policies and procedures carefully, use appropriate technique for performing procedures
   d. Equipment-related risks—learn how to operate the equipment, have it checked regularly for proper functioning

5. Risks for poisoning for the following age groups:
   a. Toddler and preschool—hazardous substances, such as household chemicals or medicines, within reach of the curious youngster
   b. Adolescents and young adults—experimental ingestion of drugs or alcohol, suicide attempts, insect or snake bites
   c. Older adults—accidental ingestion of toxic substances because of poor vision, overmedication due to forgetfulness

6. The objectives in the use of restraints are to reduce the risk of falls, prevent interruption of the treatment regimen, prevent the removal of life-support equipment (confused/combative client), and reduce the risk of injury to others by the client.

7. The following alternative measures may be implemented:
   - Orienting clients/families to the surroundings
   - Explaining routines and procedures
   - Encouraging family and friends to stay with the client
   - Providing adequate stimulation, diversional activity

- Using relaxation techniques
- Instituting exercise and activity plans
- Eliminating bothersome therapies as soon as possible
- Maintaining toileting routines
- Evaluating the effect of medications
- Performing regular assessments of the client's status

8. Hazards that the nurse may be exposed to in the health care environment are communicable diseases, blood and body fluids, chemical splashes, needle sticks, equipment malfunctions, muscular injuries, and intentional or unintentional client-induced injuries.

9. Safety issues that are a concern for the client and family in the home environment are:
   - Adequate lighting
   - Properly working appliances
   - Safe setting of hot water thermostat
   - Nonskid bathroom surfaces
   - Smoke and carbon monoxide detectors, fire extinguisher
   - Secure floor coverings and clutter-free walk spaces
   - Properly stored and labeled medications
   - Accessible phone and emergency numbers

10. 1

11. 3

12. 2

13. 1

14. 3

15. 3

16. 4

17. 3

18. 3

19. 4

CHAPTER 26—Hygiene

CASE STUDIES

I.   For the client with diabetes mellitus, you
     should include the following in the teaching:
     - Carefully inspect the skin surfaces, par-
       ticularly the extremities
     - Perform daily foot care using lukewarm
       water, no soaking—dry the feet well,
       especially between the toes
     - Do not cut corns or calluses
     - Apply bland powder if the feet perspire
     - File the toenails straight across, no
       cutting
     - Wear clean, dry socks daily
     - Do not walk barefoot
     - Wear properly fitting, flexible shoes
     - Exercise regularly
     - Avoid hot water bottles or heating pads
       to the extremities
     - Clean minor cuts immediately and apply
       only mild antiseptics, if necessary
     - Avoid wearing elastic stockings, tight
       hose, or noncotton socks
     - Avoid crossing the legs
     - Avoid the use of commercial prepara-
       tions for corn/callus removal, athlete's
       foot, or ingrown toenails
     - Consult a podiatrist as needed for foot
       problems

II. The older adult client may be experiencing
     changes in their skin integrity. The skin is
     more fragile, so hot water and strong cleans-
     ing agents should be avoided. Older adults
     usually perspire less, so bathing need not be
     as frequent (unless personally desired).
     There may be an increased sensitivity or
     itching that may be relieved with the use of
     hydrocortisone cream, moisturizing soaps,
     or petrolatum jelly. Humidity should be
     higher in the environment to alleviate skin
     dryness. Care should be taken to avoid
     injury to the skin as wound healing is slower
     in this population.

CHAPTER REVIEW

1.   The factors that influence hygienic care prac-
     tices include body image, economic status,
     knowledge, sociocultural variables, personal
     preferences, and physical condition.

2.   A back rub promotes relaxation, relieves
     muscular tension, stimulates circulation, and
     can promote a feeling of well-being.

3.   Bathing allows for cleansing of the skin, stimu-
     lation of circulation, improved self-image,
     reduction of body odors, promotion of range
     of motion, and assessment of the client's
     integument, mobility, and state of mind.

4.   The guidelines for bathing a client are:
     - Maintain privacy and dignity
     - Promote safety
     - Maintain warmth and comfort
     - Promote independence
     - Anticipate client needs

5.   Common skin problems:
     a. Acne—inflammatory, papulopustular
         skin eruption, usually involving bacterial
         breakdown of sebum; appears on face,
         neck, shoulders, and back. Wash the hair
         and skin with hot water and soap.
         Minimize the use of cosmetics and
         creams. Provide proper nutrition. Apply
         topical antibiotics or medications as
         ordered.
     b. Contact dermatitis—inflammation of
         skin characterized by abrupt onset with
         erythema, pruritus, pain, and scaly ooz-
         ing lesions; seen on face, neck, hands,
         forearms, and genitalia. Avoid exposure
         to causative agents. Apply medication if
         ordered.
     c. Abrasion—scraping or rubbing away of
         epidermis; may result in localized bleed-
         ing and weeping of serous fluid. Wash
         with mild soap and water. Leave open, if
         possible.

6.   Common hair or scalp problems:
     a. Pediculosis captitis—tiny, grayish-white
         parasitic insects that attach to hair
         strands; eggs look like oval particles,
         resembling dandruff; bites or pustules
         may be observed behind ears and at
         hairline

b. Alopecia—balding patches in periphery of hair line; hair becomes brittle and broken; caused by improper use of hair care products/techniques

7. Common foot or nail problems:
   a. Tinea pedis—(athlete's foot) fungal infection of foot; scaliness and cracking of skin between toes and on soles of feet; small blisters containing fluid may appear
   b. Paronychia—inflammation of tissue surrounding nail after hangnail or other injury; occurs in people who frequently have their hands in water; common in diabetic clients

8. The client may be at risk for impaired skin integrity if he/she is immobile, has reduced sensation, vascular insufficiency, altered skin integrity, alterations in nutrition or hydration, reduction in skin moisture, or application of external devices.

9. While providing hygienic care, the nurse may assess the:
   - Skin—especially in the skin folds (axillae, groin, under the breasts)
   - Oral cavity—teeth, gums, mucous membranes
   - Range of motion
   - Level of consciousness
   - Communication patterns
   - Emotional status
   - Circulatory and respiratory status
   - General hygienic practices

10. The developmental characteristics of the skin are:
    a. Neonate—relatively immature and thin, epidermis and dermis loosely bound together
    b. Toddler—skin layers more tightly bound together, greater resistance to infection and skin irritation
    c. Adolescent—sebaceous glands more active, acne possible, eccrine and apocrine sweat glands fully functional
    d. Adult—elastic, well-hydrated, firm, smooth

With aging, the skin loses its resiliency and moisture, the epithelium thins, and elastic collagen fibers shrink, making the skin more fragile.

11. The nurse prepares a comfortable environment for the client by controlling the room temperature, providing for adequate ventilation and lighting, limiting noise, reducing odors, and keeping the room neat.

12. 3

13. 3

14. 1

15. 4

16. 4

17. 3

18. 2

19. 1

CHAPTER 27—Oxygenation

CASE STUDY

a. To gather further information from the client about her current respiratory status, the nurse should ask the following questions:
   - "When do you experience shortness of breath/difficulty breathing?"
   - "What activities bring on the shortness of breath?"
   - "Does the shortness of breath interfere with your activities of daily living?"
   - "Do you find that it is hard to inhale or exhale?"
   - "Do you sleep with extra pillows at night?"
   - "Are you more tired than usual?"
   - "Do you smoke?" or "Are you exposed to smokers or other environmental hazards at home or at work?"
   - "When does the cough start?"

- "Are there times when your breathing/coughing is better or worse?"
- "What are you bringing up when you cough?"
- "Have you been exposed to anyone with a respiratory infection?"
- "Have you recently had an upper respiratory infection?"
- "Have you had pain in your chest when you breathe?"
- "Are you currently taking any medications?"

b. Based on additional information from the client, possible nursing diagnoses for this client may be:
- Activity intolerance
- Airway clearance, ineffective
- Gas exchange, impaired
- Infection, risk for

c. Nurse-initiated actions may include measurement of vital signs, auscultation of lung sounds, inspection of sputum, positioning for optimum respiratory function and comfort, and preparation of oxygen and suctioning equipment in case severe respiratory distress develops.

d. General teaching for health promotion should include the importance of:
- Having the pneumococcal and influenza vaccines (if she has not had them)
- Limiting exposure to crowds and environmental pollutants
- Avoiding smoking or secondhand smoke
- Covering the mouth and nose if out in cold air
- Determining and improving activity and exercise tolerance
- Taking medications regularly
- Performing breathing/coughing exercises

CHAPTER REVIEW

1. c

2. f

3. g

4. d

5. b

6. j

7. a

8. i

9. h

10. e

11. Behavioral factors that may affect oxygenation include exercise, smoking, substance abuse, anxiety, and nutritional intake.

12. Conditions that may affect chest wall movement include pregnancy, obesity, musculoskeletal abnormalities, abnormal structural configuration, trauma, muscle diseases, and nervous system diseases.

13. Left-sided heart failure is related to inadequate functioning of the left ventricle as a result of increased pressures and pulmonary congestion. Assessment findings may include decreased activity tolerance, breathlessness/dyspnea, dizziness, and confusion. Physical findings may include crackles on auscultation, hypoxia, shortness of breath on exertion, cough, and paroxysmal nocturnal dyspnea. Right-sided heart failure is related to inadequate functioning of the right ventricle, usually as a result of pulmonary disease or left-sided failure. Findings include weight gain, distended neck veins, hepatomegaly and splenomegaly, and dependent peripheral edema—all signs of systemic venous congestion.

14. Assessment findings associated with a decrease in oxygenation include changes in breathing patterns, arrhythmias, altered heart and/or lung sounds, fatigue, weakness, dizziness, apprehension, restlessness, disorientation, headache, cyanosis, pallor, nonproductive/productive coughing, clubbing,

alterations in chest movement, petechiae, and edema.

15. Information provided to promote cardiopulmonary health includes:
    - Maintaining ideal body weight
    - Eating a low-fat, low-salt diet
    - Exercising regularly
    - Avoiding smoking, secondhand smoke, and environmental pollutants
    - Having regular checkups
    - Having pneumococcal and influenza vaccines
    - Avoiding large crowds
    - Covering the mouth and nose when sneezing and when out in cold weather

16. a. Retraction is the visible sinking in of the soft tissues of the chest between and around firmer tissue and ribs; seen often in the intercostal spaces.
    b. Paradoxical breathing is asymmetrical or asynchronous breathing where the chest contracts during inspiration and expands during expiration.

17. a. Anemia affects oxygenation by decreasing the oxygen-carrying capacity of the blood.
    b. An airway obstruction limits the amount of inspired air that reaches the alveoli in the lungs.
    c. A fever increases the body's metabolic rate, which increases the oxygen demand of the tissues.

18. Surgical asepsis or sterile technique is used to suction the trachea.

19. Continuous bubbling in the chest tube water-seal chamber indicates an air leak.

20. Nursing interventions to achieve the following include:
    a. Dyspnea management— administration of medications (e.g., bronchodilators), supervision of oxygen therapy, and instruction in breathing and coughing techniques and relaxation measures

    b. Patent airway—instruction in coughing techniques, suctioning, and airway placement
    c. Lung expansion—positioning, administering chest physiotherapy, instruction in the use of incentive spirometry, and management of chest tubes
    d. Mobilization of secretions—hydration of the client, humidification/nebulization of oxygen therapy, and administration of chest physiotherapy

21. The different types of oxygen delivery systems and usual flow rates are:
    - Nasal cannula—24% (1 L/min)–44% (6 L/min)
    - Nasal catheter—Approximately 30% (6 L/min)
    - Transtracheal—60%–80%
    - Simple face mask—30%–60% (6–8 L/min) (Plastic face mask—80%–90% (10 L/min)
    - Venturi mask—24% (2 L/min)–55% (14 L/min)
    Refer to Chapter 27 for additional information on oxygen delivery systems.

22. The nurse instructs the client/family and/or implements the following safety measures for home oxygen therapy:
    - Placement of "no smoking" signs around the client area, with visitors informed that smoking is prohibited where the oxygen is being used
    - Check of the electrical equipment to determine that it is functioning properly and will not create sparks.
    - Review of fire procedures and location of extinguishers.
    - Check of the oxygen level to ensure a sufficient amount is present (an additional source may be obtained as a backup).
    - Have an alternate source of oxygen in case of a power failure.

23. For the nursing diagnosis, *Ineffective airway clearance related to the presence of tracheobronchial secretions*, possible client outcomes and nursing interventions are:

Client outcomes:
- Sputum will be clear within 24–36 hours
- No adventitious lung sounds auscultated
- Respiratory rate of 16–24/min
- Coughing and clearing airway within 24 hours

Nursing interventions:
- Instruct client on coughing and deep breathing
- Assist with position changes and ambulation
- Provide 2000–2500 ml fluid, if not contraindicated
- Monitor vital signs
- Suction prn
- Provide chest physiotherapy, if indicated

24. 4

25. 3

26. 3

27. 2

28. 1

29. 2

30. 4

31. 4

32. 1

33. 2

34. 3

35. 3

36. 4

37. 1

38. 1

CHAPTER 28—Sleep

CASE STUDY

a. A possible nursing diagnosis for this client is *Sleep pattern disturbance related to current life situation: stress at home and work.* Goals include:
- Client will achieve an adequate amount of nightly sleep within 1 month
- Client will identify and verbalize about current life stressors
- Client will practice stress reduction/relaxation techniques as needed

b. The nurse may implement the following:
- Sit with the client and offer an opportunity for her to ventilate about her feelings and concerns
- Instruct the client on stress reduction/relaxation techniques
- Advise about the value of exercise and activity before sleep
- Discuss manipulation of the environment to provide maximum comfort and minimum distraction
- Instruct the client on the avoidance of heavy meals before bedtime and excessive caffeine or alcohol intake
- Have the client maintain a log of sleep/rest patterns

CHAPTER REVIEW

1. f

2. g

3. b

4. i

5. a

6. j

7. c

8. d

9. h

10. e

11. Stages 1 and 2 (NREM) are periods of lighter sleep, where the client is aroused more easily. Stages 3 and 4 (NREM) are periods of deeper, slow wave sleep, where the individual is more difficult to awaken. The individual also has phases of REM sleep where vivid dreaming occurs, the eyes move rapidly, and the vital signs fluctuate up and down.

12. Sleep allows for the restoration and repair of physiological and cognitive processes. It preserves cardiovascular function, conserves energy, and prepares the individual for the next period of wakefulness.

13. Sleep may be affected by physical illness, medications/substances, lifestyle changes, sleep pattern alterations, emotional stress, environmental variations, exercise, fatigue, and food and caloric intake.

14. Older adults have less stage 3 and stage 4, NREM sleep. REM sleep periods are shorter. Older adults tend to awaken more frequently during the night, and it may take longer to fall asleep. Naps during the day may increase. Sleep also may be influenced by the presence of chronic illnesses and discomfort. Older adult clients may be assisted to sleep by:
    - Maintaining regular sleep and wake times
    - Eliminating naps, unless they are part of the routine
    - Going to bed when sleepy, and getting up if not sleepy
    - Sleeping where they sleep best
    - Minimizing noise, distractions
    - Regulating the environmental temperature
    - Limiting alcohol, caffeine, and nicotine in late afternoon/evening
    - Drinking warm milk before bedtime
    - Decreasing fluid intake 2–4 hours before sleep
    - Elevating the head of the bed
    - Using prescribed analgesics

    - Avoiding sedatives and hypnotics, unless needed
    - Using relaxation techniques

15. The nurse may promote a restful environment by checking that the:
    - Client's bed is clean and dry
    - Lights are lowered and out of the client's eyes
    - Temperature and ventilation in the room are at comfortable levels
    - Amount of noise is decreased
    - Number of distractions are decreased

16. Safety measures for a client with nocturia include keeping a night light on, removing clutter from the path to the bathroom, keeping a hospital bed at a level close to the floor, and placing a call bell within reach.

17. Bedtime rituals for adults include avoiding physical and mental stimulation right before bedtime, exercising 2 hours before bedtime, engaging in relaxing activities, using the bedroom only as a bedroom, and maintaining a consistent bedtime.

18. The components of a sleep history are:
    - Description of a client's sleep problem
    - Prior usual sleep pattern
    - Recent changes in sleep pattern
    - Bedtime routines and sleeping environment
    - Use of sleep and other medications
    - Dietary and substance (e.g., alcohol) intake
    - Symptoms during waking hours
    - Concurrent physical illness
    - Recent life events
    - Current emotional and mental status

19. a. Respiratory disease—may require additional pillows; breathing rhythm may be altered; nasal congestion and sore throat impair breathing and ability to relax
    b. Hyperthyroidism—increases the time needed to fall asleep
    c. Coronary heart disease—frequently awakened during the night; changes in stages of sleep

d.   Gastric reflux/hiatal hernia—discomfort in lower esophagus that is increased when lying flat; need for additional pillows to sit up or blocks to elevate the head of the bed

20.   Some common sleep disorders and anticipated treatments are:
   • Insomnia—chronic difficulty falling asleep, frequent awakenings from sleep, and/or short sleep or nonrestorative sleep. Treatment may include use of improved sleep hygiene measures, biofeedback, relaxation techniques, and treatment of underlying emotional or medical problems.
   • Sleep apnea—cannot breathe and sleep at the same time as a result of lack of airflow through the nose and mouth. Treatment may include use of therapy for underlying cardiac or respiratory complications and emotional problems, use of a continuous positive airway pressure device, improved sleep hygiene measures, involvement in a weight loss program, or correction of structural abnormalities.
   • Narcolepsy—central nervous system dysfunction of mechanisms that regulate sleep and wake states, results in a sudden wave of sleepiness and falling asleep during the day. Treatment may include the use of stimulants and medications that suppress cataplexy.
   • Sleep deprivation—decrease in the quality and quantity of sleep. Treatment may involve eliminating or correcting factors that disrupt the sleep pattern.

21.   3

22.   4

23.   1

24.   2

25.   2

26.   3

27.   3

28.   2

29.   3

30.   3

31.   1

32.   4

33.   1

CHAPTER 29—Promoting Comfort

CASE STUDY

a.   To successfully use a PCA pump, the client must understand the purpose and use of the medication and pump, as well as be able to locate and push the button on the pump that controls the administration of the medication.

b.   Teaching for this client should include:
   • Use of the equipment
   • Purpose of PCA, action(s) of the medication, expected pain relief, precautions, and potential side effects of the medication (CNS depression)
   • General precautions for an IV infusion
   • Caution against family members/visitors operating the device for the client

CHAPTER REVIEW

1.   a.   Pain—a complex series of sensations; an unpleasant, subjective sensory and emotional experience associated with actual or potential tissue damage
   b.   Analgesic—classification of a medication used for pain relief
   c.   Local anesthesia—injection or application of a solution/substance that creates a loss of sensation to a particular body part or area
   d.   Exacerbation—increase in the severity of symptoms
   e.   Remission—partial or complete disappearance of symptoms

2. a. Acute pain follows an injury, disease, or types of surgery. It has a rapid onset, varies in intensity (mild to severe), and lasts briefly. Chronic pain is prolonged, also varies in intensity, and usually lasts more than 6 months.

    b. Superficial pain results from stimulation of the skin. It is localized, of short duration, and usually a sharp sensation. Visceral pain results from stimulation of internal organs. It is diffuse, may radiate, usually lasts longer than superficial pain, and varies in sensation from dull to sharp.

    c. Referred pain is felt in a part of the body that is separate from the source of the pain. Radiating pain extends from the point of injury to another body part.

3. Physiological responses to pain:
    - Dilation of bronchial tubes, increased respiratory rate
    - Increased heart rate
    - Peripheral vasoconstriction
    - Increased blood glucose level
    - Diaphoresis
    - Increased muscle tension
    - Dilated pupils
    - Decreased GI motility
    - Pallor
    - Nausea and vomiting
    - Weakness and exhaustion
    - Decreased heart rate and blood pressure (parasympathetic stimulation)

    Behavioral responses to pain:
    - Vocalizations—moaning, crying, screaming, gasping
    - Facial expressions—grimace, clenched teeth, wrinkled forehead, lip biting, tightly closed or open eyes or mouth
    - Body movement—restlessness, immobilization, muscle tension, increased hand and finger movements, pacing, rhythmic or rubbing motions
    - Social interaction—avoidance of conversation or social contacts, focus on activities for pain relief, reduced attention span

4. Influence of pain on activities of daily living include change of sleep patterns, inability to perform hygienic care, sexual dysfunction, alteration in home or work management, and interruption of social activities.

5. a. Toddler—use of words that the child can understand ("boo-boo"), pictures, dolls to act out with, pointing at areas of discomfort

    b. Speaker of a different language—use of an interpreter, pictures, gestures and pointing to areas of discomfort

6. Information to be obtained on the characteristics of pain includes the onset and duration of the pain, location, severity, quality, pattern, relief measures, associated signs and symptoms, physical signs and symptoms, behaviors, affect on activities of daily living, and expectations of treatment.

7. a. Attention level—distraction techniques
    b. Anxiety—relaxation techniques, imagery
    c. Fatigue—promotion of sleep and rest
    d. Coping style—PCA

8. Nonpharmacologic interventions for pain relief include reduction/removal of painful stimuli, cutaneous stimulation, distraction, relaxation, guided imagery, anticipatory guidance, biofeedback, and hypnosis.

9. Adjuvant medications that may be used in conjunction with analgesics to manage pain are sedatives, anticonvulsants, steroids, antidepressants, antianxiety agents, and muscle relaxants.

10. Epidural anesthesia produces effective, longer-lasting pain relief with minimal sedation, eliminates the need for repeated injections, allows for earlier ambulation, has little effect on sensation or cardiovascular function, and produces fewer respiratory complications.

11. Individualizing a client's pain management may include:
    - Using different types of pain-relief measures
    - Providing pain-relief measures before the pain becomes severe
    - Using measures that the client believes are effective
    - Using the client's ideas for pain relief and scheduling
    - Suggesting measures that are within the client's capability
    - Choosing pain-relief measures on the basis of the client's responses
    - Encouraging the client to try measures more than once to see if they may work
    - Keeping an open mind about nontraditional measures
    - Protecting the client from more pain
    - Educating the client about the pain

12. The nurse may adapt/alter the client's environment to increase comfort by:
    - Straightening wrinkled bed linen
    - Repositioning the client
    - Loosening tight clothing or bandages (unless contraindicated)
    - Changing wet dressings or bed linens
    - Checking the temperature of hot/cold applications and bath water
    - Lifting the client up in bed, not pulling
    - Positioning the client correctly on the bed pan
    - Avoiding exposure of the skin or mucous membranes to irritants (e.g., urine)
    - Preventing urinary retention by keeping the catheter patent
    - Preventing constipation with fluids, diet, and exercise
    - Reducing lighting that glares/shines directly on the client
    - Checking the temperature of the room and the sensation of the client
    - Reducing the level of noise and traffic

13. Three types of analgesics for mild to moderate pain are nonnarcotic and nonsteroidal antiinflammatory drugs, opioids, and adjuvants or coanalgesics.

14. PCA allows for less total medication to be used by the client, with smaller amounts given at shorter intervals, and a more stable serum concentration of the medication being achieved. The overall effect is greater pain relief for the client.

15. A continuous IV narcotic analgesic drip is used for clients with severe pain (unrelieved with PO or IM routes), severe nausea and vomiting, clotting disorders, inability to swallow, delirium, confusion, or change in mental status.

16. True

17. True

18. True

19. False

20. False

21. False

22. 3

23. 2

24. 4

25. 3

26. 2

27. 4

28. 3

29. 1

30. 1

CHAPTER 30—Nutrition

CASE STUDY

a. To assist this client and the family with dietary planning, it is important to find out the following information:
   - Who prepares the food in the home?
   - Who buys the food, and where is the food purchased?
   - What foods are regularly eaten? Are there special foods for holidays or family occasions?

- What are the client's food preferences? In addition, the client should keep a record of dietary intake (usually recorded over 3–7 days).
b. Teaching about foods that are high in sodium and saturated fat is an important part of the plan for this client. Reading labels and menus (if the client eats out) will help in the selection of appropriate foods. The client and family also may be informed about possible substitutions for foods, spices, and oils that are high in sodium and fat. Alternatives, such as polyunsaturated oils, lean meats, and egg substitutes, may be incorporated into meal preparation. A separate meal plan for the client is usually not necessary because flavorings, such as lemon, can make foods attractive (as well as healthy) for the entire family. The most difficult times are often at holidays and special occasions when food plays a central role in the family's activities. Low-salt and low-fat substitutions, wherever appropriate, should be used. Fresh or frozen fruits and vegetables, without sodium or fat-based sauces or additives, may be more flavorful than low-sodium canned foods. The client also may be able to eat traditional foods, in moderation, on these occasions. Realistic expectations may work best for the client rather than offering harsh, uncompromising restrictions.

CHAPTER REVIEW

1. i

2. c

3. a

4. h

5. j

6. g

7. f

8. e

9. b

10. d

11. The factors that influence dietary patterns include developmental stage, culture and religion, socioeconomic status, personal preference, psychological factors, alcohol and drugs, and misinformation about food fads.

12. The goals are for individuals to increase their daily intake of fruits, vegetables, and grain products and decrease their intake of sodium and fat.

13. The Food Guide Pyramid is a basic guide for buying food and preparing meals. The pyramid identifies six different groups:
Fats, Oils, and Sugars (use sparingly)
Milk, Yogurt, and Cheese (2–3 servings/day)
Meat, Poultry, Fish, Beans, and Eggs (2–3 servings/day)
Vegetables (3–5 servings/day) and Fruits, (2–4 servings/day)
Bread, Cereal, Rice, and Pasta (6–11 servings/day)

14. General nutritional guidelines:
- Eat a variety of foods from the food pyramid—have plenty of grains, fruits, and vegetables.
- Balance the intake of food with the amount of physical activity.
- Reduce the intake of sugar, sodium, fat/saturated fat, and cholesterol.
- Moderate the intake of alcoholic beverages.

15. Examples of alternative dietary patterns include vegetarians, ovolactovegtarians, and lactovegetarians. In addition, clients from diverse sociocultural backgrounds may have dietary patterns that are unique.

16. Laboratory studies include CBC, albumin, transferrin, prealbumin, electrolytes, BUN, creatinine, glucose, and triglycerides.

17. A client's nutritional intake may be influenced in the acute care setting by diagnostic testing (NPO, fatigue), stress, medications (taste, actions), food presentation ("hospital

food" appearance), and health status (not feeling well or not able to eat).

18. Nasogastric, jejunal, and gastrostomy routes are used for enteral feeding. Problems that may be encountered with enteral feedings include aspiration, delayed gastric emptying, cramping, and diarrhea.

19. a. PN is used because the client is unable to ingest or digest enteral feedings.
   b. The nursing goals for PN are to prevent infection, maintain the PN system, prevent complications, and promote the client's well-being.
   c. Nursing interventions to prevent complications of PN therapy include weighing the client daily, monitoring I&O and caloric intake, testing urine or blood for glucose, obtaining blood samples for nutritional assessment, observing for fluid and electrolyte balance, and maintaining the correct infusion rate.
   d. The recommended infusion rates for acute care is PN infused over 24 hours. For home care, the recommendation is PN infused over 12–16 hours.
   e. The recommended infusion rate for lipids is 1 ml/min. Solutions should not be used if there is a separation of contents (oil/creamy layer on top) or it is more than 12 hours old.

20. For clients without teeth or with ill-fitting dentures, a soft diet may be ordered. Client preferences for foods should be taken into account, as well as consistencies, flavors, and colors.

21. The nursing history focuses on the client's usual dietary intake of food and fluid, food preferences, allergies, and any particular problems that the client may have with ingestion, digestion, or elimination.

22. For the client who is underweight, a nursing diagnosis of *Nutrition, imbalanced: less than body requirements* is indicated. An outcome for this client is that he/she will achieve

optimum weight for age and size, gaining $1/2$–1 pound per week.

23. 1
24. 1
25. 2
26. 2
27. 4
28. 1
29. 2
30. 2
31. 2
32. 4
33. 1
34. 4
35. 4
36. 2

CHAPTER 31—Urinary Elimination

CASE STUDIES

I. a. Before the IVP, the client should be assessed for:
   - Allergies to shellfish, iodine, or contrast dyes
   - Fluid status (avoid dehydration from bowel preparation that may increase the potential toxicity of the contrast dye)
   - Medical conditions that increase risk (e.g., renal insufficiency)
   - Recent barium studies (tests within 2–3 days of the IVP will obscure findings)
   The client should be instructed to:
   - Take the cathartic the evening before

- Remain NPO after midnight
- Expect an IV infusion to be started for the injection of the dye
- Expect a flushing sensation and a feeling of warmth, dizziness, or nausea when the dye is injected
- Expect that a number of x-rays will be taken during the test and that voiding will be done near the end of the test

    b. Following the IVP, the nurse will monitor I&O and report decreased or absent urination. The client will be informed that a normal diet may be resumed, fluid intake is encouraged, and any signs of an allergic reaction (itching, hives, etc.) should be reported.

II. The nurse may safely delegate the following urinary care measures: assisting the client with the use of the bedpan/urinal, monitoring I&O, maintaining aseptic technique, and promoting client privacy and dignity. In some institutions, the established policy may allow for additional measures to be delegated, such as routine catheter care and specimen collection. Delegation to unlicensed assistive personnel requires that the nurse evaluate their ability to safely and accurately perform the specified measures.

III. The action proposed by the primary nurse is unsafe to use because it could result in serious damage to the client's urethra. The correct procedure requires that you prepare a clean disposable towel, gloves, and a sterile syringe (same volume as the fluid in the catheter balloon). The client is positioned in the same way as for catheter insertion, the syringe is attached to the balloon port, and the entire amount of fluid is aspirated. The catheter then is pulled out slowly and smoothly. If resistance is encountered, an additional attempt is made to remove fluid from the balloon. The catheter then is wrapped in a waterproof pad and disposed of in an appropriate container, along with the drainage tubing and bag (after emptying and measuring the remaining amount of urine). Perineal care then is provided to the client, and the nurse will monitor the urinary output carefully.

IV. The client is provided with a sterile specimen cup, sterile disinfectant wipes, and clean gloves. He is instructed to apply the gloves and wipe the urinary meatus in a circular motion, moving up from the meatus to the glans penis. He also is cautioned against using the contaminated wipe repeatedly. After cleansing, the client should discard the initial urination and begin collection in the sterile cup at the midstream portion of voiding. The cover of the specimen cup then is replaced, and the specimen is sent to the lab within 1 hour of the collection. If necessary to promote client understanding, the use of more understandable terms, other than meatus and voiding, may be more effective.

CHAPTER REVIEW

1. d

2. g

3. i

4. h

5. a

6. j

7. e

8. b

9. f

10. c

11. Noninvasive procedures for examination of urinary function include abdominal roentgenogram (KUB), intravenous pyelogram (IVP), renal scan, and computerized axial tomography (CAT).

12. Nursing implications include:
- Monitoring vital signs frequently

- Promoting bed rest for 8–12 hours
- Assessing peripheral pulses
- Observing for bleeding
- Maintaining a pressure dressing over the site for 24 hours
- Observing the client for a reaction to the dye
- Monitoring the client's I&O

13. Intermittent catheterization is used for immediate relief of bladder distention, long-term management of clients with incompetent bladders, sterile urine specimen collection, assessment of residual urine, and instillation of medication. Indwelling catheters are used for urinary outflow obstructions, clients having surgery of the urinary tract or surrounding structures, prevention of obstruction from blood clots, accurate monitoring of I&O and prevention of skin breakdown in critically ill or comatose clients, and provision of bladder irrigations.

14. A female client may be placed in the lithotomy or Sims' position for catheterization.

15. 2000–2500 ml/day is the recommended fluid intake. Minimum output is 30 ml/hour.

16. a. Sociocultural—privacy needs for urination and expectations (e.g., intermissions/recesses)
    b. Fluid intake—increased intake will increase output (if fluid/electrolyte balance exists); alcohol, caffeine, and foods with high fluid content promote urination
    c. Pathological conditions—diabetes mellitus and multiple sclerosis cause neuropathies that alter bladder function, arthritis and joint diseases interfere with activity, renal disease influences amount and characteristics of urine, fevers reduce urinary output, and spinal cord injuries disrupt voluntary bladder emptying

    d. Medications—diuretics promote excretion of fluid and selected electrolytes, some drugs change the color of the urine, and some medications influence the ability of the bladder to relax and empty

17. Stress incontinence

18. a. pH 10 = unexpected
    b. Protein 4 mg = expected
    c. Glucose = unexpected
    d. Specific gravity 1.2 = unexpected

19. The condom catheter should be changed every day, with the skin checked for signs of irritation and breakdown. Perineal care is provided with each catheter change. The tubing must be checked frequently to ensure that there are no kinks or other obstructions.

20. To promote a client's urinary function in the health care environment, the nurse should:
    - Provide adequate hydration—2000–2500 ml of fluid, unless contraindicated
    - Provide comfort, privacy, time, access, and appropriate positioning
    - Provide or assist with personal hygiene
    - Teach exercises to strengthen pelvic muscles or use Credé's method
    - Prevent infection
    - Maintain skin integrity

21. To prevent infection in the catheterized client, the nurse should:
    - Follow good hand-washing techniques
    - Maintain integrity and asepsis of the urinary drainage system
    - Keep drainage bag below bladder level
    - Drain urine from bag regularly
    - Tape the catheter to secure it in place
    - Perform routine hygienic care every shift and prn

22. Skin integrity should be protected by providing a protective pad, removing urine from the skin as soon as possible, changing wet garments, washing the perineal area with mild soap and warm water, and applying skin moisturizer.

23. 1

24. 3

25. 4

26. 3

27. 3

28. 1

29. 4

30. 4

31. 2

32. 3

33. 4

34. 2

CHAPTER 32—Bowel Elimination

CASE STUDIES

I. Nursing Diagnosis: Constipation related to overuse of laxatives/enemas and inadequate dietary fiber (as manifested by client's statement that she is having difficulty with bowel elimination)

Goal: Client will establish a regular defecation pattern within 1–2 months.

Outcomes:
- Client will have a regular bowel movement within 3 days.
- Client's abdomen will be nondistended and nontender.
- Client will pass soft, formed stools at least every 2–3 days.

Goal: Client will maintain a diet that incorporates an adequate amount of fiber and fluids.

Outcomes:
- Client will identify and eat foods that are high in fiber and drink an adequate amount of fluid on a daily basis.

Nursing interventions:
- Instruct on foods high in fiber

- Instruct on the importance of an adequate fluid intake
- Encourage allowing ample/regular time for defecation
- Instruct on the adverse effects of reliance on laxatives/enemas
- Investigate family and social contacts for stimulation of appetite
- Identify that daily bowel movements are not absolutely necessary

II. Before the colonoscopy, the client should be instructed to:
- Drink clear liquids the day before
- Take some form of bowel cleanser (GoLytely)
- Take enemas until clear, if ordered

CHAPTER REVIEW

1. d

2. e

3. a

4. b

5. c

6. Dietary recommendations for constipation include:
- Increased intake of fiber (vegetables, fruits, cereals) and fluids
- Eating chopped foods, rather than pureed (for poor dentition)
- Eating mashed foods with fruit juices and hot tea (for difficulty swallowing)

7. Dietary recommendations for diarrhea include:
- Avoidance of spicy or high-fiber foods
- Avoidance of milk or milk products (for lactose-intolerant)
- Increased intake of low-fiber foods (chicken, beef, pasta)
- Fluid and electrolyte replacement

8. a. Diet—regular food intake, high-fiber foods, and gas-producing foods promote peristalsis; low-fiber foods slow

peristalsis; and lactose/selected food intolerance can lead to diarrhea and cramping

b. Positioning—squatting or sitting allows for intraabdominal pressure to be exerted and thigh muscles to be contracted to aid in defecation

c. Pregnancy—constipation commonly occurs because of pressure of the fetus on the rectum

d. Diagnostic tests—some tests require NPO or enemas in advance, and barium can harden and cause constipation if not eliminated after the test

e. Activity—immobilization decreases peristalsis, whereas regular exercise increases peristalsis

f. Psychological status—stress, anxiety, or fear can increase nervous stimulation and lead to diarrhea, whereas depression can decrease peristalsis; excessive pressure placed on children to become toilet trained may lead to chronic constipation

9. The nurse may provide local application of heat, sitz baths, or topical medications (as prescribed) to promote comfort for the client with hemorrhoids.

10. Increased total bilirubin–biliary tract obstruction

11. Clients should be cautioned against straining (Valsalva's maneuver) on defecation if they have cardiovascular disease, glaucoma, or increased intracranial pressure.

12. Risk factors for colon cancer include:
- Age older than 50 years
- Family history of colorectal cancer
- Ethnocultural background
- Personal history of inflammatory bowel disease
- Urban residence
- High dietary intake of fats, with low fiber intake

13. Adults are assisted to a left-lying Sims' position.

14. Kayexalate enema

15. a. A hypertonic enema works by exerting osmotic pressure, pulling fluid from the interstitial spaces, and filling the colon with fluid. The distention in the colon promotes defecation.

b. Hypertonic enemas are indicated for clients who are not able to tolerate a large volume fluid enema. They are contraindicated for infants and individuals who are dehydrated.

c. Fleet enema

16. a. Emotional stress—increases intestinal motility

b. Medications—irritate the intestinal mucosa (iron), increase intestinal motility (laxatives), or allow an overgrowth of normal intestinal flora that inflames and irritates the mucosa (antibiotics)

c. Tube feedings—hyperosmolarity of enteral solutions draws fluid into the intestine and promotes defecation

17. A focused assessment of a client's bowel function should include:
- Chewing—check the condition of teeth, gums, and mouth and ability to eat
- Mobility—observe the gait, ability to assist with transfer, positioning, activity, and use of toilet facilities
- Anal sphincter function—check for abdominal distention, impaction
- Abdominal muscle contractility—observe muscle contraction (bearing down) while palpating lower abdomen

18. General measures for a bowel retraining plan include:
- Establishing a daily routine
- Allowing adequate time and privacy
- Integrating nutritional/fluid needs

19. a. Colorectal cancer—end colostomy

b. Diverticulitis—temporary end colostomy with Hartmann's pouch

20. a. Skin care—keeping the skin clean and dry, changing wet or soiled clothing

quickly, using recommended or prescribed skin barrier

    b. Irrigation—using the proper amount
and type of solution and equipment

    c. Pouching—carefully measuring, cutting
(as indicated), and applying the appliance according to specified guidelines

21. a. expected
    b. unexpected
    c. unexpected
    d. unexpected
    e. expected

22. 3

23. 4

24. 4

25. 2

26. 3

27. 4

28. 3

29. 3

CHAPTER 33—Immobility

CASE STUDY

Mrs. B. may benefit the most from discussing her
feelings, needs, and concerns with the nurse, and
being involved, as much as possible, in the
decision-making process for her plan of care. In
addition, Mrs. B. may benefit from the following
interventions:

- Orienting her to the environment,
routine/schedule, and staff members
- Placing her with mobile clients who can interact with her
- Encouraging frequent visits from family
members and friends
- Providing her with materials she enjoys, such
as books and magazines
- Providing stimulating diversional activity
for her, such as music and games

- Engaging in conversation with her during
meals and implementation of nursing
actions
- Encouraging her to use any necessary assistive
aids, such as glasses
- Encouraging and assisting her (as necessary)
to attend to daily grooming
- Providing a stimulating physical environment
by changing her view, setting up personal
objects, etc.

CHAPTER REVIEW

1. Nervous, muscular, and skeletal systems.

2. The objectives of bed rest are to decrease
physical activity and oxygen needs, allow the
ill/debilitated client to rest, and prevent further injury.

3. Bed rest may be required for clients with cardiovascular conditions (e.g., myocardial
infarction, congestive heart failure), neurological conditions (e.g., head injuries, spinal
cord trauma), musculoskeletal conditions
(e.g., fractures), pulmonary conditions
(e.g., chronic lung disease), and other conditions where the client is severely weakened
(e.g., terminal phase of cancer).

4. Fluid and electrolyte imbalances that occur
with immobility include hypercalcemia and
hypovolemia (initial phases).

5. An immobilized client may react to the experience by exhibiting hostility, belligerence,
inappropriate moods, withdrawal, confusion, anxiety, and depression.

6. Anthropometric measurement allows for the
evaluation of muscle atrophy and determination of decreased protein (negative nitrogen
balance).

7. Cardiovascular system changes include:
- Orthostatic hypotension—move the
client slowly from one position to
another
- Increased cardiac workload—place the
client in an upright position (if possible),

provide regular exercise and adequate fluid intake

- Thrombus formation—provide regular exercise, adequate fluid intake, and antiembolitic stockings

8. Respiratory system changes include pneumonia and atelectasis. Nursing interventions may include encouraging coughing and deep breathing, adequate fluid intake, and exercise; turning; upright positioning; and chest physiotherapy.

9. Exercise for hospitalized clients may include, depending on their abilities, light walking, stretching, and range of motion.

10. The nurse assesses for deep venous thrombosis (DVT) by removing TED/elastic stockings, socks, or other clothing and checking for redness, warmth, tenderness, or pain in the calf area. Homan's sign may be noted if the client experiences calf pain on dorsiflexion of the foot. In addition, calf and thigh circumferences may be measured to check for edema.

11. General teaching for a client with limited mobility should include:
    - Explanation of the need for position changes
    - Explanation of the importance of, and demonstration and performance of, range-of-motion exercises
    - Description of the effects of immobility and risk for pressure ulcers
    - Discussion of stimulating diversional activities
    - Explanation of fluid and nutritional intake needs
    - Encouragement of participation in the plan of care

12. Dietary needs of the immobilized client are influenced by the presence of infection, need for wound healing, food intolerance, gastrointestinal functioning, and daily caloric requirements.

13. a. Integumentary—Pressure is exerted, with decreased circulation to the tissues leading to pressure ulcers. Nursing interventions include assessment of the skin, use of supportive devices, provision of adequate nutrition and hydration, change of position q 1–2 hours, and provision of meticulous skin care.

    b. Gastrointestinal—Reduced appetite (anorexia), nutritional imbalance, decreased peristalsis leading to constipation and possible impaction. Nursing interventions include provision of adequate nutrition (fruits, vegetables, fiber) and hydration, measurement of I&O, administration of prescribed cathartics, promotion of activity or movement, and institution of bowel program.

    c. Urinary—urinary stasis resulting in greater risk for infection and calculi. Nursing interventions include provision of adequate hydration and promotion of activity or movement.

    d. Musculoskeletal—loss of strength and endurance, reduced muscle mass, decreased stability and balance, with possible contractures and disuse osteoporosis. Nursing interventions include provision or encouragement of range-of-motion exercises, turning q1–2 hours, position changes, and referral to physical therapy.

14. 2

15. 3

16. 2

17. 3

18. 2

19. 4

20. 3

21. 4

CHAPTER 34—Skin Integrity and Wound Care

CASE STUDY

Nursing Diagnosis: Risk for impaired skin integrity related to prolonged pressure on bony prominences (as manifested by reddened areas [reactive hyperemia] to sacrum, elbows, and heels)

Goal: Integrity of skin and underlying tissues will be maintained.

Outcomes:
- Reactive hyperemia will subside and client's normal skin coloration will return within 2 days.
- Client will assist, as possible, with q1–2h turning and positioning.

Nursing interventions:
- Reposition or assist with repositioning q1–2h
- Encourage the client to shift weight when out of bed in a chair
- Assess skin and underlying tissues with each position change
- Use supportive devices—padding for mattress and bony prominences
- Keep sacral area clean and dry
- Measure, document and report reddened areas

CHAPTER REVIEW

1. g

2. h

3. b

4. c

5. j

6. a

7. i

8. d

9. e

10. f

11. Sites marked should include occipital bone, scapula, spine, elbow, iliac crest, sacrum, ischium, Achilles' tendon, and heel.

12. a. Stage I
    b. Stage II
    c. Stage III
    d. Stage IV

13. The following increase a client's risk for pressure ulcer development: shearing force, friction, moisture on the skin, poor nutrition, cachexia, infection, impaired peripheral circulation, obesity, and advanced age.

14. The older adult's skin is usually less tolerant to pressure, friction, and shearing forces. It is also drier and thinner, with a reduced rate of epidermal cell renewal. Circulation to the extremities also may be reduced.

15. The three major areas of nursing interventions include hygienic and topical care, positioning (30°), and application and maintenance of supportive surfaces and mattresses.

16. Documentation should include notation of:
    - Hyperemia—location, size, color, and hourly reassessment
    - Any blisters, pimples, or scabs
    - Client mobility
    - Nutritional status

17. a. Age—Infants and older adults may have decreased circulation, oxygen delivery, clotting, and inflammatory responses, with an increased risk of infection. Older adults have slower cell growth and differentiation, and scar tissue is less pliable.
    b. Obesity—Individuals have a decreased supply of blood vessels in fatty tissue (impaired delivery of nutrients to the site), and suturing of adipose tissue is more difficult.
    c. Diabetes—Individuals have small blood vessel disease (reduced oxygen delivery), and elevated glucose levels impair macrophage function.

d. Immunosuppression—A reduced immune response leads to poor healing. Steroids also mask signs of inflammation/infection, and chemotherapeutic agents interfere with leukocyte production.

18. Possible complications are hemorrhage, infection, dehiscence, evisceration, and fistulas.

19. a. Serous—clear, watery plasma
    b. Sanguineous—fresh bleeding
    c. Serosanguineous—pale, more watery, with plasma and red cells
    d. Purulent—thick, yellow, green, or brown, with dead/live organisms and white blood cells

20. To obtain an aerobic wound culture, the nurse should:
    - Cleanse the wound.
    - Place the tip of a sterile swab into fresh wound drainage.
    - Return the swab to the culturette tube.
    - Cap the tube.
    - Crush the inner ampule so that the medium coats the tip of the swab.
    - Send the culturette tube to the lab as soon as possible.

21. The steps for caring for a traumatic wound are:
    - Stabilize the client's cardiopulmonary function.
    - Promote hemostasis (stop any bleeding).
    - Cleanse the wound.
    - Protect the site from further injury.

22. The types of dressings available are:
    - Gauze—wet or dry
    - Transparent film
    - Hydrocolloid—gelling agents
    - Alginate—highly absorbent
    - Wound Vacuum-Assisted Closure (VAC)

23. The nurse may increase the client's comfort level by carefully removing any tape, gently cleansing the wound and manipulating the dressings and drains, positioning the client, and providing prescribed analgesic medication before the procedure.

24. The principles for wound cleansing are:
    - Cleanse in a direction from least to most contaminated.
    - Use friction when applying local antiseptics.
    - Allow irrigating solution to flow from the least to the most contaminated area.

25. The technique taught to the client/family at home is clean, rather than sterile. A "no touch" method may be used, where only the edges of the dressings are contacted.

26. a. Heat—used for arthritis or degenerative joint disease; localized joint pain or muscle strains; low back pain; menstrual cramping; hemorrhoidal, perianal, or vaginal inflammation; and local abscesses. The use of heat is contraindicated in an area of active bleeding or an acute, localized inflammation or for an individual with cardiovascular problems.
    b. Cold—used immediately after direct trauma (sprains, fractures, etc.), and for superficial lacerations, puncture wounds, minor burns, arthritis or joint trauma, and after injections. The use of cold is contraindicated for edematous injuries, for areas of diminished circulation, and for a client who is shivering. Safety measures include checking the skin frequently, observing circulation and sensation to the area, informing the client to report pain or a change in sensation, and monitoring the response to the therapy.

27. Basic principles for applying bandages and binders include:
    - Inspecting the skin and circulation
    - Maintaining asepsis
    - Providing protection and support without interfering with circulation or respiration

- Positioning the client correctly for application
- Applying bandages from the distal site and moving toward the torso.
- Applying securely
- Applying firmly, with equal tension over each turn
- Positioning pins, knots, or ties away from wound or sensitive skin areas
- Preventing friction between and against skin surfaces with padding

Bandaging techniques include:
- Small body part—circular bandage turn
- Joints—figure eight turn
- Head—recurrent turn
- Wrist/upper arm—spiral turn

28. Total score = 13 points
    Client risk = "at risk" status

29. 1

30. 3

31. 3

32. 4

33. 2

34. 4

35. 3

36. 3

37. 2

38. 2

39. 1

40. 4

41. 1

42. 3

CHAPTER 35—Sensory Alterations

CASE STUDIES

I. For this client, you may implement the following interventions:
   - Assist in arranging the environment so that the client knows where everything is and that clutter is out of the way.
   - Recommend/assist in obtaining books with larger print, audiotaped books, and music.
   - Allow time for discussion of feelings, needs, and concerns.
   - Refer the client to community agencies (e.g., Foundation for the Blind).
   - Instruct/assist in improvement of lighting in halls and stairways and use of color-coding (edges of stairs, medication bottles, appliance dials, etc.).
   - Instruct in importance of follow-up visits to the ophthalmologist.
   - Investigate family and social contacts.

II. A client in an intensive care unit (ICU) may experience sensory overload from the intensity of sounds and activity and/or sensory deprivation from restricted visits of family and friends. The nurse should try to organize care so that the client is allowed opportunity for uninterrupted rest, whenever possible. Monitors at client's bedside may have volume controls so that they can be turned down to a lower level. The nurse also should take time to sit with the client, either quietly or for verbal stimulation. Visits from family members and friends should be encouraged but not to the point of client fatigue. The environment may be arranged so that the client has a different or more pleasant view, and personal items (e.g., photos) may be placed within the client's field of vision. It may be a challenge for the nurse in this setting to adapt the client's sensory input, so creativity, within realistic limits, is recommended.

CHAPTER REVIEW

1. a. Visual
   b. Auditory

    c. Gustatory
    d. Olfactory
    e. Tactile
    f. Kinesthetic

2. Sensory deprivation is an inadequate quantity or quality of stimulation that impairs perception. Sensory overload occurs when the individual receives multiple stimuli and the brain is not able to disregard or selectively ignore some of the stimuli.

3. Clients at risk for sensory alterations include older adults, immobilized clients, and clients with known sensory deficits.

4.   a. Cerumen accumulation
    b. Presbycusis
    c. Cataract
    d. Xerostomia

5.   a. Age: Older adulthood
    • Decreased hearing acuity, speech intelligibility, and pitch discrimination
    • Increased dryness of cerumen, with obstruction of the auditory canal
    • Reduced visual fields; increased glare sensitivity; impaired night vision; and reduced accommodation, depth perception, and color discrimination
    • Reduced sensitivity to odors and diminished taste discrimination
    • Difficulty with balance, spatial orientation, and coordination
    • Diminished sensitivity to pain, pressure, and temperature
    b. Medications—may cause ototoxicity or optic nerve irritation (Chloramphenicol) or may reduce sensory perception (analgesics, sedatives, antidepressants)
    c. Smoking—may cause atrophy of taste buds and interference with olfactory function

6. Assessment of vision:
    • Ask the client to read

• Use the Snellen chart to check visual acuity
• Assess visual fields and depth perception
• Assess pupils
• Ask the client to identify colors

Assessment of hearing:
• Use ticking watch, whispering, tuning fork
• Observe client's conversation/interaction with others
• Compare ability to distinguish consonants and vowels
• Inspect external ear canal

Assessment of touch:
• Check for sensitivity to light touch and temperature
• Assess client's ability to distinguish sharp and dull stimuli
• Assess client's ability to distinguish objects in the palm of the hand
• Ask if client feels unusual sensations
• Ask the client to tie shoelaces or a bow

7. Sensory deprivation may lead to the following:
• Cognitive function—decreased learning capacity, poor problem-solving and task performance, disorientation, strange thinking, and regression
• Affective function—boredom, restlessness, increased anxiety, emotional lability, increased need for socialization
• Perceptual function—decreased attention span, disorganized visual and motor coordination, temporary loss of color discrimination, disorientation, confusion

8. Child eyesight safety includes avoiding toys with long, pointed handles or sharp edges; keeping the child from running with a pointed object; and keeping pointed objects and tools out of reach.

9. Sensory stimulation may be modified in the acute care environment by:
• Increasing the client's view outside and within the room

- Arranging decorations, plants, photos, greeting cards, and the client's personal items
- Providing audio books and large-print reading material
- Spending time with the client listening to and conversing with the client
- Playing pleasant music or putting on television shows that the client enjoys
- Providing attractive meals at the correct temperature
- Providing a variety of textures and aromas to enhance the client's appetite

10. The nurse may communicate with a hearing impaired client by:
    - Making sure that a hearing aid, if needed, is in place and in working order
    - Approaching the client from the front to get his/her attention
    - Facing the client on the same level, with adequate lighting
    - Making sure that glasses, if needed, are worn and are clean
    - Speaking slowly and articulating clearly, using a normal tone of voice
    - Rephrasing, rather than repeating information that is not heard
    - Using visible expressions and gestures
    - Talking toward the client's better ear
    - Using written information to reinforce spoken words
    - Not restricting the hands of deaf clients
    - Avoiding eating, chewing, or smoking while speaking with the client
    - Avoiding speaking while walking away, in another room, or from behind the client

11. Ototoxicity may be caused by:
    - Antibiotics—aminoglycosides, vancomycin, minocycline, polymixin B/C, erythromycin
    - Diuretics—ethacrynic acid, furosemide, torsemide, bumetanide
    - Analgesics—indomethacin, aspirin, ibuprofen, naproxen
    - Cardiac drugs—class Ia antidysrhythmics, quinidine, procainamide, disopyramide

- Antineoplastic agents—bleomycin, displatin, dactinomycin, mechlorethamine

12. a. Hearing deficit—amplify low-pitch sounds, use lamps with sound activation, use assistive devices for telephones, and obtain closed captioning for the television
    b. Diminished sense of smell—use smoke and carbon monoxide detectors, take special care with disposal of matches and cigarettes, and check the expiration dates on foods
    c. Diminished sense of touch—lower the temperature of the water heater, and use caution when checking the bath or shower water

13. Nursing diagnoses for a client with a sensory deficit include:
    - Body image, disturbed
    - Fear
    - Hopelessness
    - Risk for injury
    - Powerlessness
    - Self-care deficit, bathing/hygiene
    - Self-care deficit, dressing/grooming
    - Self-esteem, risk for situational low
    - Sensory perception disturbed
    - Social interaction, impaired
    - Social isolation
    - Thought processes, disturbed

14. General screenings include examinations for congenital blindness and visual impairment in infants and young children, routine vision and hearing tests of school-age and adolescent children, regular medical eye/ear exams every 2–4 years for individuals older than age 40 and every 1–2 years for those older than age 65.

15. 2

16. 2

17. 3

18. 1

19. 3

20. 4

21. 2

22. 1

CHAPTER 36—Surgical Client

CASE STUDIES

I.   Explain and demonstrate coughing and deep-breathing exercises with splinting of the abdominal incision. Assist in and encourage turning and positioning every 2 hours. Reinforce the use of the incentive spirometer. Explain and demonstrate range-of-motion exercises. Provide prescribed analgesia before activities, keeping in mind the action and dosage of the medication and its possible effect on the client.

II. Preoperative teaching for the client who is having ambulatory surgery may be done when the client comes for preoperative tests and physical assessment. There also may be telephone contact with the client on the evening before the surgery, as well as a 24-hour resource line for the client to use for questions. Additional teaching may be conducted immediately before the procedure and before the client's discharge. Information provided to the client usually includes instructions specific to the surgery and anesthesia (e.g., dressings, activity and dietary restrictions), signs and symptoms of complications, and time frame for follow-up visits.

III. Any significant change in the client's status should be reported to the surgeon and/or anesthesiologist immediately. Because of the effects of general anesthesia, temperature alterations are especially critical before surgical procedures. Surgery may be postponed until the client's temperature has returned to normal.

IV. The client should be informed that, under usual circumstances, all loose items are removed before surgery. If the client will be adversely affected by the removal of his "lucky" medallion, it may be pinned inside of the client's gown or surgical cap, depending on the type of surgery. It is very important, however, that the operating room personnel be informed that the client has the medallion in place before the surgery. It may be the policy of the agency that the client will have to sign a form stating that he has kept the medallion (or other jewelry) on his person in case of a loss.

CHAPTER REVIEW

1.   a. Elective surgery
     b. Major surgery
     c. Diagnostic surgery
     d. Emergency surgery
     e. Palliative surgery
     f. Transplant surgery

2.   The following medical conditions may increase a client's surgical risk: bleeding disorders, diabetes mellitus, heart disease, upper respiratory infection, cancer, liver disease, fever, chronic respiratory disease, immunological disorders, and abuse of street drugs.

3.   a. Cardiovascular—changes in structure and function reduce cardiac reserve and predispose the client to postoperative hemorrhage, increased blood pressure, and clot formation
     b. Pulmonary—changes in structure and function reduce vital capacity, increase the volume of residual air left in the lungs, and reduce blood oxygenation
     c. Renal—changes in structure and function increase the possibility of shock with blood loss, limit the ability to metabolize drugs/toxic substances, increase the frequency of urination and the amount of residual urine, and reduce the sensation of the need to void

   d. Neurological—changes in function reduce the ability to respond to warning signs of complications and may lead to confusion after anesthesia

4. a. Heparin—alters normal clotting factors, increasing the risk of hemorrhage. Should be discontinued at least 48 hours preoperatively. Further alters clotting factors if used with other medications, such as aspirin and ibuprofen.

   b. Insulin—diabetic client's need for insulin is reduced preoperatively because of NPO. Dose requirements may increase postoperatively because of stress response and IV administration of glucose solutions.

5. General information in preoperative teaching includes:
   - Preoperative and postoperative routines
   - Expected sensations
   - Pain-relief measures available (e.g., PCA)
   - Postoperative exercises
   - Activity and dietary restrictions

6. An ambulatory surgery PACU usually has two phases. The first phase is similar to the inpatient PACU, where the client is monitored closely and stabilized. The second phase of the ambulatory surgery PACU differs in that it prepares the client for discharge and self-care. Clients receiving local anesthesia may move directly to the second phase of recovery. Clients in the ambulatory surgery setting gradually will be progressed to sitting up, taking fluids, eating light snacks, and ambulating to the bathroom. When the client's condition becomes stable, he/she will be discharged home.

7. On the day of surgery in an acute care setting, the nurse will:
   - Complete the preoperative checklist documentation
   - Monitor vital signs
   - Provide or assist with hygienic care
   - Remove prostheses and cosmetics, and provide client with gown and surgical cap

   - Complete preparation of the bladder and bowel (e.g., enemas, catheterization)
   - Apply antiembolitic stockings
   - Complete any special procedures
   - Safeguard the client's valuables
   - Provide emotional support and promote dignity
   - Administer preoperative medications

8. Routine screening tests include complete blood count, serum electrolyte analysis, coagulation studies, serum creatinine test, urinalysis, 12-lead electrocardiogram, and a chest x-ray.

9.
   - Sedatives—used for relaxation and decrease in nausea
   - Tranquilizers—used to decrease anxiety and relax skeletal muscles
   - Narcotic analgesics—used to sedate, decrease pain and anxiety, and reduce the amount of anesthesia needed
   - Anticholinergics—used to decrease mucous secretions in the oral and respiratory passages and prevent laryngospasm

10. The circulating nurse cares for the client in the operating room by completing other preoperative assessments, establishing and implementing the intraoperative plan of care, evaluating the care, and providing for the continuity of care postoperatively. The circulating nurse assists with the operation of nonsterile equipment, provision of additional instruments and supplies, calculation of blood loss and urinary output, and documentation of the procedure. The scrub nurse is primarily responsible for maintaining the sterile field during the procedure and adhering to strict medical asepsis. This nurse applies sterile drapes, provides sterile equipment to the surgeon, and keeps count of supplies used during the operation.

11. The uses and side effects of anesthetics are:
    a. General anesthesia—used for major procedures that require extensive tissue manipulation. Side effects include

cardiovascular depression or irritability, respiratory depression, and liver and kidney damage.

b. Regional anesthesia—used when operating on a specific body area. Side effects include a sudden fall in blood pressure and respiratory paralysis.

c. Local anesthesia—used for minor procedures, especially in ambulatory surgery, and after general anesthesia for postoperative pain relief. Side effects include local irritation and inflammation.

d. Conscious sedation—used for procedures that do not require complete anesthesia. Respiration is maintained and the client can respond to stimuli. Side effects include respiratory depression and decreased level of consciousness.

12. Injury to the client may be prevented during the operation by ensuring that the equipment count is accurate, the client is monitored carefully, special equipment is properly managed (e.g., lasers, cautery), and emergency equipment is available.

13. Typical postoperative orders include:
   - Frequency of specific assessments
   - Types of intravenous fluids and infusion rates
   - Postoperative medications
   - Oxygen therapy or incentive spirometry
   - Dietary and activity restrictions
   - Positioning in bed
   - Intake and output
   - Laboratory tests and x-ray studies
   - Additional special instructions

14. a. Respiratory—atelectasis, pneumonia, hypoxia, pulmonary embolism
   b. Circulatory—hemorrhage, hypovolemic shock, thrombophlebitis, thrombus/embolus formation

c. Gastrointestinal—abdominal distention, constipation, nausea/vomiting

d. Integumentary—wound infection, dehiscence, evisceration, skin breakdown

15. The postoperative exercises are diaphragmatic breathing, incentive spirometry, controlled coughing, turning, and leg exercises (ROM).

16. 3

17. 1

18. 3

19. 1

20. 2

21. 2

22. 2

23. 4

24. 3

25. 3

26. 2

27. 1

28. 3

29. 2

30. 2

31. 4

32. 2

Performance
Checklists